Skid Row to Buckingham Palace

The Inspirational Story of Canada's
Most Colourful Bomber Pilot

Skid Row to Buckingham Palace

The Inspirational Story of Canada's Most Colourful Bomber Pilot

The autobiography of

Flight Lieutenant Louis Greenburgh, DFC and Bar,

as told to and recorded by his son

Ed Greenburgh

**Bomber Command Books
from
Mention the War**

First published in 1993 by Ed Greenburgh. This edition first published in the United Kingdom 2016 by Mention the War Ltd., Leeds, LS28 5HA, England.

Cover design: Topics - The Creative Partnership www.topicsdesign.co.uk
Cover image: Des Knock www.desknock.co.uk
Ditched airman re-enacted by Mick Lowis

A CIP catalogue reference for this book is available from the British Library.

ISBN-13: 978-0993336065

ISBN-10: 099333606X

Other Bomber Command books from Mention the War

Striking Through Clouds – The War Diary of 514 Squadron RAF
(Simon Hepworth and Andrew Porrelli)

Nothing Can Stop Us – The Definitive History of 514 Squadron RAF
(Simon Hepworth, Andrew Porrelli and Harry Dison)

A Short War – The History of 623 Squadron RAF
(Steve Smith)

RAF Bomber Command Profiles:
617 Squadron
103 Squadron
(Chris Ward)

Beach Boys and Bombers – The Aircrew of 514 Squadron (June 2016)
(Simon Hepworth, Andrew Porrelli and Roger Guernon)

A Special Duty – A Crew's Secret War with 148 (SD) Squadron
(Jennifer Elkin)

Lancasters at Waterbeach – Some of the Story of 514 Squadron
(Harry Dison)

The above books are available through Amazon in print, Kindle and, eventually, audio book format. For further details or to purchase a signed and dedicated copy, please contact *bombercommandbooks@gmail.com* or visit www.bombercommandbooks.com

Dedication.

This book is dedicated to Monsieur Reant, Gordon 'Strommy' Stromberg and all of the other men and women who gave their lives helping my father; and to my father himself, who has lived a life worth writing about.

Flight Lieutenant Louis Greenburgh, DFC & Bar

Contents

Introduction to the First Edition

Introduction by Flt/Lt. L. Greenburgh (Retired), D.F.C. & Bar:

The Story of Two Eagles

I was five years old during the summer of 1921. While wandering along a dirt road in the small town of Rosthern Saskatchewan, I spotted a crude wooden cage holding a beautiful live eagle.

Its wing spread was about 6 feet and it kept trying to flap its wings in the cramped space. It was obviously suffering and two of its claws were ripped. I begged the owner to let it fly away.

He said, "No, son, it's a real beauty. It's going to be stuffed and mounted."

I burst into tears. "Please let it fly away!"

"No, son, it's worth a lot of money, and it's a valuable exhibit."

I remember running home and crying all the way. I never forgot the tragic expression of the eagle's glassy eyes, and its struggle in that tight cage.

Sixty years later, I saw another eagle. What happened between the two eagles is described in a story by my son, Edwin.

He received little cooperation from me. In spite of his family, work, school and volunteer commitments, he still found the time to investigate, research, to probe, pursue, and spent years to get the factual story. He has my greatest admiration.

To those who gave their lives on my behalf, and to those who risked and suffered everything to make this a better world, my undying gratitude is not enough; the story must be told.

Lou Greenburgh

Reflections

I typed the words 'The Canadian Pacific Transcontinental Seaboard Special roared through the night' then sat back and reflected on the task I had undertaken.

I had begun a journey into the past, a journey on which I would relive amazing adventures, meet remarkable people, and learn about my father and myself. That journey would take place, for the most part, right at the desk where I sat.

I have been intrigued by my father's past for as long as I can remember. My first attempt to record these events was the writing of a short story as a university assignment. When I read that feeble script now I realize how little I knew and understood back then.

I was twenty-seven years old when I began a serious attempt to record the events of my father's life. I wrote a few pages from what I could remember of the stories I had heard as a child. I read Les Allison's account in <u>Canadians in the Royal Air Force</u> and the story in Macleans magazine. I typed out a brief account of a few incidents and showed it to my father for verification.

Dad told me that I was wasting my time. It was not a very promising start.

I kept plugging away at it. Dad was not encouraging me. As a matter of fact, he was worried that this activity might take me away from 'more important things' and made a point of trying to discourage me. He did, however, show me a hand written notebook in which he had once begun an autobiography. The opening passages of this book were quoted from it. My writing became more detailed and sophisticated. Dad could see that I was serious and began to cooperate.

The title I originally chose was "*D.F.C. & Bar: The story of Flight Lieutenant Louis Greenburgh as told to his son.*" The more I learned, however, the more I wanted to know and I began to seek outside sources of information. As I read about Bomber Command, I began to realize just how exceptional my father's exploits were. This book has become a tribute and so I renamed it accordingly. My father and I self-published it in 1993 with the title "*D.F.C. & Bar: A son's tribute to his father*".

Writing this story brought me much closer to my father. It has truly been a labour of love.

As the original book neared completion, my father told me that he had just come from a medical examination. I asked him how it went. "Well," he replied, "I asked the doctor how much longer I could expect to live. He checked his chart and then told me that I should have been dead four years ago!" My father lived another twenty-three years, passing away at home shortly after his ninetieth birthday.

My father was out-going and cheerful in public but those closest to him observed a deep bitterness. I sensed that he had felt forgotten and unappreciated.

With the publication of the original book, my father's disposition began to change. Although only 350 original books were ever printed, they were well received. Copies of the book were passed from hand to hand and soon my father was receiving letters and telephone calls from around the world. My mother told me that my father would read a bit of the book every day.

The years passed and I began a career with the social services branch of the local government. I told Lorne Hagel, the program manager responsible for foster homes, that my father used to find foster homes for kids. "No!" He exclaimed, "Not Lou!"

"Yeah," I replied, "Lou Greenburgh." I asked if he knew him. Lorne replied that he had never met him personally but that my father was a legend.

I appreciate this opportunity to continue spreading the legend of my father.

Ed Greenburgh

Sir Winston S. Churchill's Message to RAF Bomber Command at the Immediate Conclusion of the War In Europe in 1945

Now that NAZI Germany is defeated, I wish to express to you on behalf of His Majesty's Government the deep sense of gratitude which is felt by all the nation for the glorious part which has been played by Bomber Command in forging the victory.

For over two years, Bomber Command alone carried the war to heart of Germany, bringing hope to the peoples of occupied Europe, and to the enemy a foretaste of the mighty power was rising against them.

As the Command expanded, in partnership with the Air Forces of our American Ally, the weight of the attacks was increased, dealing destruction on an unparalleled scale to the German military, industrial and economic system. Your Command also gave powerful support to the Allied Armies in Europe and made vital contribution to the war at sea. You destroyed or damaged many of the enemy's ships of war and much of his U Boat organization. By a prolonged series of mining operations sank or damaged large quantities of his merchant shipping.

All your operations were planned with great care and skill. They were executed in the face of desperate opposition and appalling hazards. They made a decisive contribution to Germany's final defeat. The conduct of the operations demonstrated the fiery gallant spirit which animated your aircrews, and the high sense of duty of all ranks under your command.

I believe that the massive achievements of Bomber Command will long be remembered as an example of duty nobly done.

Signed

Winston S. Churchill

"We of Bomber Command rest content with that judgement...To you who survive I have this to suggest - that you have that message from that great man embossed and enframed. That you treasure it above your hearths for your children and your grandchildren to read and note. That they may know and well mark what their forebears achieved and what they forefended...'

Excerpt from a statement by Sir Arthur T. Harris, Marshal of the Royal Air Force.

Marshal of the Royal Air Force Sir Arthur Harris at his desk.

Acknowledgements

Many people contributed to the creation of this book. The first person I would like to thank is my father, who provided me most of my information and whose exact words I have quoted as much as possible. I would like to thank my mother for proof reading the text. I also apologize to my wife and son for the hours that Daddy spent with this book instead of with them. In addition I would like to thank:

- The people who replied to my letters. They were: Mr. Richard Roberts, Mr. Sam Dunseith, Mr. Gordon H. Ghent, Mr. Ray Worrall, Mr. Gordon Hand, Mr. Ronald Fox, Mr. Cliff Hallet, and Mrs. Aissa-Jeanne Rippingale, who (among others) are mentioned in these pages. Mrs. Elisabeth Lucas Harrison, the Secretary of the R.A.F. Escaping Society, gave me the addresses of people and organizations who have since provided me with information. Mr. Charles F. Weir, of Gloucester, provided me with a booklet entitled 'The Extra-ordinary Adventure of the Forest of Freteval' and a map of that part of France. Mr. Dudley Ibbotson, of West Australia, provided the names of his crew who hid in Freteval. R.C.M. King, of the Air Historical Branch (RAF)5, British Ministry of Defence, sent me many important historical documents including official reports describing the losses of my father's two Lancasters which did not return from operations. I would like to thank the Personnel Records Centre, National Archives of Canada, for sending me my father's service records.
- Mr. Les Weddle for providing the photographs of the North Sea rescue.
- Mr. Hal Wishart, the organizer of the Commonwealth Training Plan Reunions, for giving me Mr.Ghent's address.
- Mme Jacqueline Grange, several letters from whom are quoted in this book and with whom I have been corresponding. Her photographs of the forest camp are especially appreciated.
- Mr. F.H. Watt for providing me with a recording of the speech my father gave to the Commonwealth Air Training Plan Museum in

1980 or 81, and Mrs. Pat Davis, also of the C.A.T.P.M., for her encouragement.

- Mr. Lyle Gawletz for providing me with some photographs and technical advice.
- Mr. E.S. Lavender, who interviewed my father for his own book about the 'Helpers' who rescued evaders during the war, and who provided me with some encouragement and information.
- Mr. Bernie Pollock, who gave me some information during an informal reunion he had with my father.
- Mr. Jack Dixon, who is mentioned in these pages and who encouraged my father to cooperate with me.
- A special thank you to Mr. John (Johnny) Sandulak, who told me about the experiences which he and my father shared in the Forest of Freteval and who trusted me with his signed one hundred franc note.
- Mr. Les Alison, who wrote the book *Canadians in the Royal Air Force*, and to Mr. Murray Peden who wrote *A Thousand Shall Fall.* Both books provided me with a wealth of background information and without Mr. Peden's book I would not have known about the friendship between my father and Flying Officer Tommy Penkuri. I also appreciate the kind letters of encouragement I received from Mr. Peden.
- Mr. Vince Leah, of the Winnipeg Free Press, for permission to include the article which is found in Appendix 1.
- M. and Mme Omar Jubault for permission to include the booklet on Freteval which is included in Appendix 3 and for providing additional information.
- His Honour Harold Gyles for permission to include the speech he gave at my father's retirement dinner.
- Philippe and Virginia d'Albert-Lake for their assistance and for permission to quote passages from Virginia's unpublished autobiography. With M. and Mme Jubault they have my appreciation for rescuing Allied evaders.
- Gerard Renault for sending me a deal of information about the Forest of Freteval.

- Mr. Joseph O. Peloquin for sending me the article 'The Forest of Hidden Men'.
- Anna, Joan and Adelene Greenburgh for providing some information and historical documents.
- I would like to acknowledge the fine job the people of Kellett Copy did in printing this book's first editions and to express my confidence that this edition, published by Mention the War Ltd., will be of equal quality.
- Mr. Andrew Porrelli, of Mention the War Ltd., for transcribing my father's combat reports from the original microfiche records in The National Archives.

My final acknowledgement may come as something of a surprise to its recipient. On the wall above my desk is a yellowed copy of an article written by Mr. Gordon Sinclair Jr., a columnist with the "Winnipeg Free Press." Written during an aircrew reunion, the article is entitled, "*Memories that took wing: Some sons never learned daddy did in the war*." I have derived much encouragement from reading and rereading that article and it was in its spirit that this written.

Chapter 1: The Formative Years

The Canadian Pacific Transcontinental Seaboard Special roared through the night, its shrill whistle echoing through the Canadian Rockies. It was two o'clock in the morning on July 3, 1933[1]. A hundred derelict souls clung to the icy boxcar tops with throbbing fingers and prayed that they would not be hurled into the abyss below.

I hung on to an iron rung. Lying face-down on the roof of a lead car, I dared not lift my head for fear of losing my grip. A slight jar could dislodge me from my precarious perch near the chugging engine. I pictured myself tumbling through space to the bottom of the Yoho Valley and cursed the film of ice which coated the entire roof.

Tiny icicles formed on my brow, making it painful to open my eyes. I held one eyelid closed with my thumb and gradually opened the other. In spite of my discomfort and anxiety, I was awed by the panoramic beauty of Mount Stephen, whose majestic snow covered peak towered in the darkness above me like something supernatural.

But what use was scenery? I had not eaten in thirty-six hours, I had not washed for three days, and my clothes hadn't left my fatigued body for a week.

The whistle shrieked once more. The vibration and oscillation of the speeding train increased as it prepared to enter the famous 'spiral' tunnels. I could see sparks flying from the axle hot box as the clicking wheels increased their tempo; "Clickety-click, clickety-click, clickety-click." They seemed to be saying; "Beware of the cops, beware of the cops, beware of the cops."

Good old Jack Mandrick! There he was on my right, huddled under a thin blanket and shivering in the cold. In front of us lay Johnny McKee. They were both seasoned travelers of the road who knew most of the angles and ways of the professional hobo. The three of us had left Winnipeg together two weeks previously and were bound for Vancouver where - so it was said - a square meal could be had in a soup kitchen. I 'knew the ropes' as a hobo quite well for a boy of seventeen.

"Watch out!" someone shouted. I felt a tugging on my sleeve and looked to see Jack pointing at the tunnel entrance.

The engine's smoke stack missed the tunnel roof by a matter of inches. I hugged the freight car as close as I could and imagined the jagged rocks striking

---

1 *Most of the information in this chapter came from an unpublished account of his life which the author's father began in the early 1950's and never completed.*

my back, grinding me into a pulp. With my face pressed close against the wooden slats, I closed my eyes and braced myself.

A hollow explosion engulfed the train as the multitude of sounds were amplified in the claustrophobic space. My eyes opened to pitch blackness and stinging smoke. I coughed and gasped for breath as my lungs rejected the sooty air. I heard the thunder of cascading water in the darkness ahead and wondered what could cause a sound like that in the middle of a tunnel.

I soon found out. The sound of water grew louder and louder and I began to feel a fine mist. The icy droplets got larger and larger until they were coming down in torrents and we were deluged by an underground stream of glacier runoff.

The shower was over as quickly as it had begun. I shivered violently in my saturated clothes. Minutes crept slowly by until we finally emerged from the tunnel.

Some of my fellow travelers tried to make themselves comfortable on the barren roof. The curses and epithets being muttered all around me showed how futile their attempts were.

The train slowed down as we neared the border town of 'Field', where the Railroad and Provincial police were on the prowl for the like of me and my companions. Many a hobo riding the rods had met his end while trying to dodge the Dominion, Provincial, or Railroad police.

I was startled by a commotion at the front of the train and I heard someone yell "The bulls are here!" I leaped to my feet in a fit of panic. Policemen were swarming aboard the cars ahead. I dashed towards the opposite end of the moving train.

Glancing over my shoulder, I glimpsed the uniform of a Railroad policeman and ran like hell. I sailed across the gap between my car and the next behind without missing a step. Then the next gap and the next.

Objects appeared out of the darkness, forcing me to constantly shift my balance across the slippery surface in an effort to avoid them.

I tripped over a packsack and was pitched onto my stomach. I frantically grasped for a hand hold as I saw the edge of the roof slide toward me. I fell.

As I slipped over the edge, I spotted an iron ladder secured to the car's broadside and grabbed for a rung. My fingers closed around the solid bar and I hung for a moment with my feet dangling in the air. I managed a toehold and quickly climbed down the side of the car. With no time for caution, I jumped. I narrowly missed a signal post and landed head over heels in a ditch.

Where could I hide? I took off for the shelter of a nearby coal shed while John and Jack disappeared into the foliage.

I reached the shadows of the weathered, dirty structure and looked for an opening. I pulled the door latch in the dark and was relieved to find it unlocked. Ignoring the squeak of rusty hinges, I slipped inside.

My body crumpled on the bed of soft coal dust. I lay on my back like a child making snow angels and let my anxiety drift away. The police were not likely to find me here.

And yet I could not sleep. My mind wandered in and out of memories best forgotten but unforgettable. Why was I here, in a drafty old coal shed, when I should have been in a cozy bed somewhere dreaming about the girl I would take to a high school prom?

My father, Joseph Greenburg, was an immigrant from Russia and Mother, whose maiden name was Fleichman, was a refugee of some sort probably from Poland. Anyway, they met and married. I was born to them in Winnipeg on March 14, 1916.

I know they didn't want me. I was just there, a victim of circumstances, and there was nothing my parents could do about it. My father left my mother three months later and their marriage was later annulled.

Mother was in an awful fix. In a strange country, unable to speak the language, she had no job and no money. And she was stuck with useless little me.

It was not long before my mother's brother, Jack, arrived from Europe. Unfortunately, he had no money either. The three of us toured Canada in search of a living. None of us could speak English and I was the only Canadian citizen.

We travelled for two years. Mother did housework, scrubbed floors and did her best to keep things going.

By the time I was three years old, we had settled in an isolated little Northern Saskatchewan town called Rosthern, which was located on a branch line of the Canadian National Railway between Saskatoon and Prince Albert. At the time we moved there, Rosthern had a total population of about six hundred. There were two or three wooden houses and a small grocery shop.

Uncle Jack tried his hand at the cattle business and Mother paid the rent of a flimsy cottage by taking in boarders. The 'boarding house' had bunk beds in a few small rooms and everyone shared the washroom facilities, which were located in a little shed in the back yard.

Even as a baby, I was unpopular. I resembled my 'old man', so they say, and everyone disapproved. According to them, Dad must have been pretty stupid, lazy, and not a little bit off the beam. Mother made it very clear that I was a detriment to her boarding house. My father, she would say to the tenants by way of apology, had gone to New York to play with other women and left me without the guiding hand of a father.

I once asked her why Dad had left. "He couldn't stand the sight of you," was her curt reply.

My father did visit me once. I was only three years old but I still have a vague recollection. I remember how he sat me on his knee and kissed me. He had brought me a set of roller-skates from New York, along with a few other presents. Mother told him that he could only visit me in the future if he sent her a lot of money. It must have broken his heart because he was as penniless as anyone else and had no money to send. After a brief quarrel, he left the house dejected and I never saw him again.

When I was five years old, I fell in love with little Edythe Childs, my playmate next door. To prove my devotion, I tossed her a lucky horseshoe, which struck her in the forehead and put her away for three weeks. What a beating her dad gave me!

With the end of World War I came a great influx of immigrants from all over the globe. Not a few of these displaced souls found themselves tilling the fresh soil of Northern habituated Saskatchewan.

Rosthern grew by leaps and bounds. More and more trains arrived, bringing hundreds of settlers from the British Isles, Russia, Poland, Bohemia, Germany, France and China. Settlements were soon organized and the people adjusted themselves to their new homes. Each nationality formed itself into a separate group and tried to carry on the customs and traditions of its mother or fatherland.

One day a man who appeared to be an immigrant slinked up our front steps. Mother rushed to welcome him in the hope that he would be a new border but I chose to stay back and observe him from a distance. He cast me a sour apple look and I decided right then that I did not like him.

Ignoring me for the moment, the stranger inquired about a room. Mother's friendly smile dissolved into a frown when she saw that I was glaring at him. She berated me for my impudence. Her smile reappeared as she turned back to the visitor and apologized for my poor manners. As usual, she explained that fate had burdened her with my presence and she regretted any inconvenience it may cause to her tenants.

Day after day, I leered and gawked at him. Mother would apologize for my sake, but he would not accept apologies. Announcing that I needed discipline, he would drag me across his lap and demonstrate his authority across my beam end.

My dislike for him turned into a burning hatred. I lived only for the day when he would leave our house and let me live in peace. Alas, the day never came. Mother married him, making him my 'papa' when I was six years old.

Mother, my stepfather and Uncle Jack invited their European relatives to come and live in Canada. Our ramshackle little boardinghouse soon became an overflowing, international affair and would have been prosperous except that nobody paid for his or her lodgings.

The house was as peaceful as the League of Nations. One scene around the dinner table was typical: Cousin Sarah stated that Canada should be run on the lines of her native Poland. "I don't think so," replied Auntie Merle, "I think the Russian system would be more suitable." Cousin Jake stated his own views, accentuating each of his arguments by banging on the table with a hammer.

Mother thought I might miss my golden seat in Heaven because I was receiving little religious education. Some of our lodgers tried to teach me to pray from books written in Hebrew or Russian but they might as well have been written in Chinese for all the sense I could gather out of them. The household eventually found a tutor for me. A sixteen year old boy direct from Russia, his name was Reznitskowietzic but everybody called him 'Rez'.

Rez had an enormous nose and a tiny cleft chin. He wore a small peaked cap, a very loud checkered sports jacket, and oversized 'plus fours' which left three or four inches of his socks showing. Lines and protrusions above his ankles established that he wore long underwear.

Rez was of a nervous disposition and found that he could not teach me to become a true son of Abraham while the rest of the family looked on and interfered. After an especially frustrating session, he gave the family a hearty speech. "Leave all the tutoring to me." he said. "I have my heart and soul in this job and I will make 'Lable' (the Hebrew version of 'Louis') a true descendant of Moses if it takes me ten years to do it!"

Three days later, Rez went into town for the weekend and never returned. The last I heard, he was doing very well in the furniture business.

The years rolled on and life in the quiet town became pleasant enough. I would play ice hockey in winter and truant in summer.

Hank Beareworth, Freddy Eagle and I spent some of our summer afternoons in the old swimming hole at Dirkson's farm, where mixed 'skinny-dipping' was usually in progress. Or we would catch gophers, kill them, and sell their tails for a nickel apiece. There was a bounty on gopher tails.

I regret doing that and wouldn't hurt an animal now. Some people enjoy hunting but I think of the poor animals and could never get pleasure from harming one.

I saw one of my uncles slaughter a calf once, when I was about eight years old. It sickened me and I've never forgotten the sight of it.

Even insects want to live. The other day I was revolted by the sight of a large beetle lying upside down. I almost stepped on it. But then I looked closer and observed the spindly legs working themselves into a frenzy as the helpless creature tried to right itself. I turned it over and let it scurry off to safety.

A pleasant childhood memory was of the time Freddie and I built a boat with a few boards and nails. With great pride, we launched it on the local creek and invited our eight year old girl friends to step aboard. The boat sank to the bottom and left our screaming ladies up to their waists in chilly water. We handled this situation in a very rational manner. As the girls cried out for assistance, Freddie and I went off to look for new girlfriends.

My work at school was not very promising and every member of the household took a special interest in my progress as a dunce. Even Mother called me "Looney Louis" or "Machiga', which meant 'crazy one'. Arnold Love, the next door neighbor's lad, was as bright as Venus and the family continually chided me over his accomplishments. Didn't he come top of the class? And didn't I come bottom? I thought it was unfair that my rations of brains, personality, initiative and character were so meager.

I had to be very careful whenever I did my homework. Try as I might, I could not write with my right hand. I remember when my stepfather caught me writing with my left hand. He flew into a rage and struck me with a wooden ruler. "This is for your own good," he growled as he gave me another wallop. Then he tied my left hand behind my back and forced me to write with my right hand. He took one look at the illegible scrawl which resulted and beat me some more. "If I ever catch you writing with that hand again," he threatened, "it'll be the end of you!"

From then on, I was constantly on the lookout, ready to pass the pencil into my right hand at any moment so that I could pretend I was right handed.

When he was not beating me, my stepfather paid me as little attention as possible. He and my mother soon had their own son, little Harry. I wasn't even allowed to sit with the rest of the family at meal times. They would all sit together at the kitchen table and I would sit by myself at a little card table. My stepfather would frown at me from the head of his table and point a menacing finger in my direction. "That is my food you're eating," he would scold as I munched on some table scrap, "You are eating my food." I often laid awake at night, listening to my parents fight. He would shout, "He's not my kid, why should I pay for his food?!"

Lou Greenburgh (front). Auntie Meryle; Uncle Jack; Louis' mother; Uncle Maurice.

I began to look upon Uncle Jack as my father. Three months after Harry was born, however, Jack got married and moved to Esterhazy, a little town in the south. I missed him very much and just didn't understand how he could leave me for something as unimportant as marriage.

About this time, Auntie Meryle returned from a trip she had taken to New York and told me a very interesting story. She had met a man who was also from Winnipeg and they had talked a bit about their backgrounds. Auntie Meryle had told him about her family and had mentioned me. The man had looked at her for a moment and sadly stated, "I'm his father."

Auntie Meryle then reached into her purse and pulled out an expensive looking watch. "He asked me to give this to you," she said. She also handed me a letter he had written.

I was excited to know that my father had thought about me and wanted to contact me. Mother sat down with me and together we drafted a reply. Or, rather, Mother dictated a reply. The letter stated that my father should never contact me again unless he was prepared to send a lot of money. I wish that he had known that I didn't want to write that letter.

While cleaning out a barn near the boarding house, one day, I was thrilled to discover a coin under some sacking. I bought myself a new neckerchief.

My mother, my stepfather, and my stepfather's cousin (who was boarding with us) were sitting in the kitchen. They saw the new neckerchief I was proudly wearing.

I glanced from Mother to the border and back. My elation gave way to puzzlement and then to concern as their expressions hardened into scowls.

"Thief!" growled the cousin as he grabbed me by the arm. "Only eight years old and already he is a thief!"

"No, no!" I cried, "I didn't steal it, I found the money for it!"

The tenant beat me incessantly. I screamed for mercy but still he beat me. As the blows fell on me I could hear my mother's voice in the background. "Hit him good!" she called," Look what his father did to me!"

My tormentor tied my hands behind my back, dragged me upstairs, threw me onto a bed, and continued to beat me. When he felt that I had been sufficiently beaten (or when he had grown too tired to beat me further) he and one of my uncles dragged me out of the house and down the street to the local jail. Rosthern was small enough to require only a volunteer policeman and the jail was unattended except on the rare occasions when the cell was occupied. My stepfather's cousin and my uncle tossed me onto the cold, hard floor of the cell. I heard the steel door clang shut.

I was let out the following morning. My bruises eventually healed but the incident had its effect on me through the years that followed.

I left home for the first time a few days later. A search party found me in a cabbage patch, half starved, frozen, and in a filthy condition.

I separated from all my playmates and spent my spare time in the woods with Sheila, my only friend.

Months passed. Sheila and I became inseparable companions. She would meet me after school every day and we would go for long walks in the country.

One sunny Saturday afternoon, as I relaxed under a tree beside a little babbling brook, Sheila came over and lay beside me. She was getting fatter, and I realized that my suspicions were correct. Sheila was going to have puppies.

She looked at me with knowing eyes and softly licked my hand. "So that's what you've been doing while I was in school," I muttered.

Miss Bjarnason, my school teacher, was very annoyed with me. Not only was I backward and at the bottom of the class, but I usually made myself a nuisance in other ways. To hide my feelings of inferiority, I tried to act clever during the classes by bursting out with some wisecrack or corny joke.

One day, after being sent out of the class, I went outside and found a stick. I then came back and hammered on the classroom door. Miss Bjarnason gripped me firmly by the earlobe and dragged me upstairs to Mr. Goble, the principal, who belted my palms with a leather strap.

I think Mr. Goble regretted the severe punishment he had meted out to me. Two days later, he offered to let me take part in the school play, which was to be shown in the town theatre.

My part was small, but my ego rose to terrific heights; I was somebody, now. I had the part of a child who accidentally finds himself dancing a jig on the stage and has to be dragged off by a fishing hook.

Nothing could hold me back. I was an actor now! Arnold Love, the bright scholar, just sneered at me but I figured he was secretly jealous.

By the time I finished telling our household about my forthcoming performance, the family had begun to look at me with a new respect. Uncle Maurice said "One day Louis will be like Charlie Chap, eh?"

The evening of our school play finally arrived. The tiny theatre was packed with proud parents eagerly awaiting their young offspring's display of talent. I was concerned, though, because I could not see anyone from my family.

Just before the curtain was to be raised, there was a disturbance in the rear. Our whole boarding house had arrived to see me in action. All of the seats had been taken but the family refused to leave the theatre. They caused quite a commotion, shouting in Russian, Polish, and Yiddish. Someone eventually placed some extra chairs at the rear, the family were seated, and the play began.

Cousin Jake could not understand the play and did not seem very interested. He began to read a large Russian newspaper, which blocked the view of an Englishman sitting behind him. An argument ensued, although Auntie Merle tried to intervene. A nearby German patron tried to settle the dispute but epithets started to flow in several languages and it looked like punches would soon be flying. Cousin Jake eventually mumbled some Russian words and left the theatre. The place calmed down a bit and the show went on.

Everyone was disappointed at the insignificant little part I played in the show. The family's hopes of my becoming another Jackie Coogan were dashed and my stepfather ordered me to bed in disgrace.

Before retiring, I went into the barn where my little Sheila lay on an old blanket. I sat down beside her and stroked the back of her neck. Sheila was a one man dog, my only friend, and always turned up when I needed someone.

Arnold Love paid me a visit the next morning. I knew he had only come to laugh at me. Although Arnold had been blessed with more active cerebral regions, I was much stronger than him. He ran all over the house in an attempt to escape my wrath.

I found myself chasing him along the roof. Arnold opened a bedroom window and jumped through it. The window slammed shut and I was locked out. I gripped the wooden sash and struggled to force it open. To my dismay, the glass shattered into pieces.

My stepfather wouldn't listen to my explanation and my beam end once more became the target of his fury. When the beating was over, I took Sheila for a walk and dreamed of retribution.

I stood on the steps of Rosthern School one day and was surprised to see an 'Oakland' car pull up in front. Three men got out of the car and came up the steps towards me.

A short and stubby man handed me a quarter. You can imagine my surprise; it was like fifty bucks in those days. Then he pinched my cheek and told me that I was a good boy. I followed the men into the school.

It turned out that the strange man was William Lyon Mackenzie King, the Prime Minister of Canada. The kids were all herded into the hallway to hear him speak. His topic was the proposed Free Trade Bill, which would remove trading tariffs between Canada and the United States and which was being promoted by his 'Liberal' government.

My brother, Harry, was there too. A lot of Rosthern's citizens came to the school. It wasn't every day that they would get a chance to see the Prime Minister.

Things were not going well at the boarding house. It was decided that the non-paying members would have to vacate. That meant that all of the members would have to vacate. Auntie Meryle decided to go to Winnipeg to get married or to work, providing she could get a husband or a job. Cousin Sarah decided to do the same thing. Cousin Jake went up north to look for work. Uncle Maurice went into the pig breeding business and bought himself a small car, which made him quite popular with the ladies. Sammy Badeker and the two other boarders decided to stay in Rosthern and start in business as general merchants.

My stepfather and Mother decided to leave Rosthern. I thought of poor little Sheila, whose puppies were almost due, and begged my stepfather to let us stay until the puppies were born. My pleading was of no avail. Three days later we left for a little town called Lemberg.

I will never forget the moist, sorrowful look in Sheila's eyes as she gazed at me before we parted. She needed me and I knew there was sadness in her heart. She seemed to understand. I often worried, and wondered.

We soon found ourselves living at the rear end of a general merchandise retail store, where my stepfather worked as a junior partner.

I decided to start life anew and soon found many young acquaintances. Every Saturday evening we'd gather in the back alleys to play run sheep run, tag, follow the leader, and many other childhood games while the grownups were enjoying themselves in the pool rooms, beer parlors, or community meetings of this cheerful little town.

Life was grand until I heard that school was about to start. The very thought of attending classes made me miserable. But the powers that be thought it was a good thing for ten year olds like myself to go to school and so I had to go.

After the first four weeks, my studies began to drop below 'average'. My teacher kept me in afterhours one day and warned me that I would be put back a grade if my work didn't improve. I was terribly worried.

Alex Lutz, the German lad who sat at the next desk, annoyed me day after day with defamatory remarks about my heritage, breed and religion. To make things worse, we were both in love with the same young lady.

One dark night, I accidentally bumped in to Alex as he came out of a back alley. We had both intended to meet little nine-year old Eva Burton.

Alex struck me across the face. That was it! We went hammer and tong against each other and fists flew in all directions. Blood dribbled from my nose and spurted from a severe cut in Alex's upper lip. We wrestled and fought in the darkness until exhaustion overtook us. Alex could hardly stand and I was on my knees, when little Eva Burton appeared.

She just walked by, arm in arm with Kellet Cole, and paid no attention to the two bruised and battered bodies which had been waiting for her.

Alex feebly raised his arm and we shook hands. We then embraced and wept on each other's shoulder. I don't understand why we had fought over that frivolous little female. Years later, I heard that she had become a woman of questionable virtue who could be had for the price of a nights' lodging.

Weeks passed. My personal troubles continued to interfere with my school work. I could not concentrate on anything and was finally put back a grade. I was put in a new class, where I sat next to Kellet Cole. I thought the bottom had fallen out of my life. I consoled myself with the thought that Kellet was also backward and he and I soon became good friends.

Perhaps my friendship with Kellet was too good. He was very popular with the young ladies but very unpopular with our school teacher. We both hated school and played truant on the odd occasion.

The odd occasion became more frequent and we found ourselves hopelessly behind in our studies. Kellet and I didn't care. We started petty little rackets to make a few pennies while the other kids wasted their time in school.

It was a simple matter for me to telephone a beer parlor. While the attendant was busy on the 'phone, Kellet would quietly slip in the back way. He would eventually emerge with enough empty beer bottles for us to cash in to keep us in chocolate bars for a month.

People soon became suspicious of our little schemes. The lid blew off when Kellet was caught stealing chickens from a nearby farm in the early hours of the morning.

Kellet was about to leave with a hen under each arm when Farmer Hess apprehended him. The door of the coop was left open and many of the birds escaped as Hess gave him the thrashing of his life. From my hiding place, I could hear Kellet's screams above the cackling of the hens and the crowing of the cocks.

My stepfather warned me never to be seen in Kellet's company again and Kellet's dad forbade him from going with me again. We continued to see each other on the sly. We would meet after dark and sneak into the grain elevators.

I enjoyed operating the lifts. We would ascend to the top of the lofty building on a little one man platform held by only a thin rope. On one occasion, the rope parted. Down we went!

Our fall was broken by about two feet of muddy water in an unused grain bin. We were in an awful state and blamed one another for our troubles. Our friendship came to an end.

Years later, we were assigned to adjoining cells in a Regina jail. Although I tried to make conversation, he refused to reminisce or be sociable in any way.

A blanket of snow soon covered our little town. Sleigh bells tinkled as horses drawing runner-fitted sledges trotted through the sparkling streets. People wearing heavy clothing, overshoes and furs hustled about in the crisp weather.

We all had season tickets for the new skating rink. Thursday nights were reserved for the hockey team but the rink was the center of our social life on every other evening. We had skating parties, ice dances, speed skating, and figure

The first house at Redwood Avenue (left) and 451 Aberdeen Avenue Winnipeg (right) from which Lou Greenburgh ran away in 1933. The photos were taken in 1992.

skating contests. The town band supplied the music as we danced and glided on the ice.

Christmas was celebrated with a dance on the crystal clear ice. The whole town turned out and everyone had a good time. New Year's Eve was received with a festive ice carnival and the night sparkled with fun. It all seems like an enchanting dream as I recount those days that are lost forever.

How well I remember chasing attractive little Marian Roberts. She wore a brightly colored Indian-painted flannel windbreaker, a short brown skating skirt, and white ankle socks. Her golden hair waved and her flashing silvery skates dazzled with every movement of her well-shaped limbs. We were playing tag and I was in hot pursuit of my quarry. Poor little Marian tripped on a loose shoelace and was badly hurt.

Five weeks later, Mother went to Winnipeg. Another baby was on its way, so my stepfather put me on a train to the little town of Esterhazy. I arrived at my destination, all by myself, and had to enquire as to where my Uncle Jack lived. He came to the door and asked, "What are you doing here?!" I told him that I had been sent to live with him. I stayed with Uncle Jack for five months. At night I could hear his wife complain about the way I had been dumped on them. My anxiety led to constant bed wetting, which caused me greater feelings of shame and did nothing to increase my welcome.

I remember how puzzled I was at the fact that Harry was allowed to stay at home but I had to leave. Perhaps it was my youthful naivety or my longing to be accepted, but I honestly did not realize the truth until years later. They did not want me.

I was quite popular with the children in Esterhazy. St. Valentine's Day brought me many precious greetings. Even the school teacher was quite pleasant and attributed my failures to the change of country schools. I developed new friends, mingled with the crowd, and learned all the local gossip.

There was Mr. Camplin, a very well-to-do retired businessman who bored me rigid with his exploits in Hollywood. He was often seen in the company of the two young Hoffman sisters and the rumour was established that they cost him a pretty penny.

Uncle Jack did not like the companions I had chosen, so I made friends with Ernie Flook, the postmaster's son. Ernie was a clean-cut boy and never got into mischief. With Uncle Jack's approval, Ernie and I became close friends. We went to school together and were hardly ever apart.

Years later Ernie was wanted by the police for grand larceny and murder. He committed suicide by blowing his brains out with a .45 caliber revolver.

With the birth of my half-brother, Willie, the family moved to Winnipeg. We rented a small house on Redwood Avenue, in the 'North End' district. The North End at that time was a hodge-podge of ethnic communities. Located near the CPR rail yards, it had actually been built as a low rent district to house the immigrants who labored for the railroad. There had been very little planning done and social services were inadequate, partially because of the pace by which Winnipeg was growing and partially because the people of the North End had very little political influence[2]. We were literally on the 'wrong side of the tracks', separated from the wealthier districts by the almost impenetrable railroad yards. Except for the ungainly Arlington Bridge, most of the bridges and underpasses which now span the yards had not yet been built.

My stepfather was unable to pay the rent, so we soon left our cramped little house on Redwood and moved into another cramped little house just down the street. We couldn't afford the rent there either, so we moved into an even less attractive residence on Aberdeen Avenue.

---

[2] *Pask, Jim. "Where it all began; The history of the Lord Selkirk- West Kildonan Community, Published by the City of Winnipeg, Lord Selkirk- West Kildonan Community Parks and Recreation Branch, 1982, page 18.*

I came downstairs one winter morning and found that the front door had blown open. The living room floor was buried under two feet of snow and it took forever for the little wood-burning stove to make the house warm again.

I began to pay my own way at an early age. When I was about twelve years old, my mother and my stepfather let me get a paper route on the condition that I gave them half of everything I earned. I used the money I had left to buy clothing and other necessities.

My money was hard earned. Winnipeg winters are notorious for their severity and long duration. Inadequately dressed, I would trudge for hours through snow drifts up to my waist and with the ever present risk of frost bite from the penetrating wind, which knifed through my clothing. I could not afford street car fare, so I was forced to walk from our house in the North End to Point Douglas, where I picked up my papers.

While delivering papers, I made friends with a boy named Charles Soloway. Charles, who I always called 'Chuck', was hardworking and conscientious. I am sure he was a good influence on me. Our friendship was to last indefinitely.

Chuck introduced me to a friend of his who made model airplanes out of balsa wood. I thought that was an interesting hobby and was soon building my own airplane models out of scrap materials or balsa wood. Actually, I had been making models of sorts since I was about eight years old. I would take a piece of shingle and shape it into an airplane. I would then tie a piece of string onto the end of a stick, loop it on the 'airplane' and swing the stick so that the toy airplane flew into the air.

As my thirteenth birthday approached, I began to look forward to my upcoming bar mitzvah. According to the Jewish religion, a boy becomes a man on his thirteenth birthday. A bar mitzvah is the Hebrew ceremony which signifies that event.

I smiled to myself as I ignored the bitter cold and warmed myself with anticipation. My family could not afford to pay for any religious training for me, but Chuck and I had been studying the Torah on our own (with the help of a kind rabbi who let me sit in his class) and I was now able to recite the benedictions. Mine would not be an elaborate bar mitzvah, but I pictured myself in front of my family and a few friends as together we would celebrate my entry into manhood. How proud they would be!

About a week before the great day arrived, I hurried downstairs to the kitchen, where my stepfather and my mother were about to have breakfast. "Ma, Pa," I exclaimed with pride, "I have a surprise for you. I've been studying the Torah and I'm ready for my bar mitzvah!"

My stepfather glanced up from his morning paper just long enough to cast me a disapproving frown. "Humph," he grunted, and pointed his finger at me. "That bastard wants a bar mitzvah? I'll give him a bar mitzvah!"

Uncle Jack had joined the family in Winnipeg and was running a second hand store. The boots I wore were the cast-offs from one of his customers. I had lined them with cardboard to keep the snow out of the holes and appreciated having them. In fact, Uncle Jack had always been good to me. I decided to drop in on him to see if he could cheer me up.

Uncle Jack listened as I told him my story and I watched his face grow taut. He reached into his pocket, pulled out his wallet, and handed me a dollar bill. As he replaced his wallet he spoke sadly but seriously. "Louis," he said, "you are all alone. You have nobody. Remember that. The best advice I can give you is to get a piece of good, strong rope and hang yourself."

I was at a loss for words, but I thanked him for the dollar and left.

I felt the pain again, some years later, when Harry and Willie each had an expensive bar mitzvah.

I think it was that summer that Johnny Reed and I rode a bus to the city limits, then walked a mile or so out to a little airstrip called Stevenson field to watch the airplanes take off and land. There was only a field and a couple of hangers; they didn't even have a proper runway. I was mesmerized by a Gypsy Moth biplane which was doing loops and rolls and I was awed by the thought that a man could fly like that.

Eventually, the little biplane circled the field and came in for a landing. The engine sputtered a few times, then quit as the plane rolled to a stop.

The pilot looked like a movie hero. I watched as he pushed back his goggles and unstrapped his leather helmet. A white scarf fluttered in the breeze as he swung himself out of the cockpit. With his head held high he strutted over to the waiting mechanic. I thought to myself that such a man must be very important.

It was an impossible dream, but I turned to my friend and said, "Someday, I want to be a pilot."

I began to spend all of my free time at the airstrip, watching the Gypsy Moths buzz around in the sky. I was thrilled one day when I was allowed to actually sit in a cockpit. I read everything I could about flying and the old 'Great War' aces became my heroes.

A three-engine Junkers 57 with corrugated sheet metal fabric landed at Stevenson Field. The airplane wasn't much by modern standards but its arrival was a big event for those days and was mentioned in the newspapers. After delivering my newspapers, I made my way out to the field so I could gaze at that enormous aircraft. I saw the pilot step out of the plane and was overcome with hero worship. At school the next day, that JU 57 was all I could talk about.

'Rosen's' was a little store down on the corner. We used to sit on the steps there and discuss politics and all of the current situations. We discussed the graft that was going on.

I remember sitting on those steps and talking to Johnny Reed. We were talking about flying. I said, "You know what I'd like to be? I'd like to be a pilot. But there's no hope of that, ever."

My school work continued to be below standard. I knew I had not passed my grade nine exams so a friend of mine broke into the school board office and stole all of the exam papers. I paid him about a nickel for each paper. We were eventually found out and my academic career came to an end.

I realized that there was nothing to keep me with my family. I left home when I was sixteen and worked at a relief camp for a few months, but I returned shortly after.

When I had just turned seventeen, I looked my stepfather in the eye and said, "I can't stay here and eat your food."

"Go." was all he said.

Deep inside, I had hoped that he would stop me, that someone in that household would want me to stay. The rickety wooden stairs creaked as I crept upstairs to gather my meager belongings. At the top of the stairs was the cubby hole in which I slept. I pulled some clothing out of a drawer, fetched my toothbrush, and packed everything up into a knapsack. I was ready to leave.

What about Mother? Surely, I thought, she would want me to stay! I picked up my bundle, hopped down the stairs, and wandered into the kitchen. Mother was working hard, as usual. I think she was scrubbing the floor. She always seemed to be working. When I think of her, I picture her cleaning chicken coops and things like that. I told her that I was leaving.

"We don't want you to leave," she told me, "but you will keep in touch?" She then suggested that I visit my uncle, Dr. Abby Greenberg, in Edmonton.

Edmonton was a long way from Winnipeg, especially to a penniless seventeen year old boy, but I had nowhere else to go. I slipped on my worn jacket, shouldered my bundle, and began the long and perilous trek to anywhere.

I called on a good friend of mine, John Mckee, and told him of my plans. "Wait a minute," he said, "I'll get my things and come with you."

John and I called on Jack Mandrick, who also decided to come along. The three of us would ride the freight trains together.

Chapter 2: Tramping

The 'Great Depression'. Those words conjure up images of dire poverty, of soup kitchens and hobos. Bums and beggars panhandled main drags during the day and gathered on the outskirts of the city at night. They lived in makeshift tents, shacks, caves and even ditches. These gathering places, known as the 'hobo jungles', were the Mecca of the bum.

Some of the inhabitants of these dens of degradation were professional bums. Others had been forced to leave their homes and had eventually intermingled with the jungle community. Many were young lads who had left poor families in search of employment or adventure. They found themselves easy prey to hardened bums and rubby-dubs, who drank rubbing and wood alcohol until they were temporarily blinded by the effects. The jungles were also places of escape for thieves, dope fiends, sex offenders, and other criminals.

As the depression lingered on, more and more 'stiffs' flocked to the hobo jungles. The local police forces responded to these ramshackle villages by enforcing vagrancy laws, causing the jungle hobos to drift from one part of the country to another. Their only means of transportation was the freight train.

John McKee, Jack Mandrick, and I 'rode the rails' for about three years. We started out by walking to the 'jungles' on McPhillips St., which was on the outskirts of town, and there we met an old bum who told us some of the ins and outs. "Be very, very careful." he said. "Grab the rungs. Because if you don't, you'll kill yourself. You'll fall under the wheels."

We saw a freight train in the distance. As it got closer, we could see that it was covered with hundreds of little black dots, like bugs. As it grew closer still, we could see that those little black dots were hobos.

As the train was passing by, all of the hobos from the jungle ran like hell, swarming like flies around your lunch on a hot day. I jumped, and just managed to catch the rung. The train was shaking from side to side like a dog shaking off a rat. I climbed up to the top and held on for dear life. It was pretty cold up there.

On our very first ride, we got as far west as Portage La Prairie before we were stopped. The police had searched the train and my colleagues had escaped. I was caught by a Mountie whose stern expression must have hidden a kind heart. "What am I going to do?" I asked. "I have nowhere to go," I told him, trying hard to keep from sobbing, "and my friends are on that train."

He rocked back and forth on his heels, hummed and hawed for a moment then, to my delight, exclaimed, "Well, what are you waiting for? Get back on the train!"

The Mountie was doing me a favor but it almost cost me my life. Oh, it was no trouble getting back on the train that time because it wasn't even moving. Shortly afterwards, though, I jumped for the rung of a moving train and grabbed it with both hands. The rung came off in my hands and down I went, seconds away from a gruesome death or dismemberment under the train wheels.

I threw away the rung which had come loose and managed to grab a lower rung on the way down. The wheels were about six inches below me and their "Clickity-click, clickity-click!" still echoes in my mind as I think about it. That may have been the first time that my quick reflexes ever saved my life. It would not be the last.

Before long, I would get to know just about every soup kitchen in Western Canada. Those soup kitchens were like little restaurants, where a guy who was down on his luck could go and get a decent meal. At the time we cursed R.B. Bennet, and I remember the socialists criticizing his government because there were soup kitchens and work camps. Looking back now, I realize that we were lucky Bennet had enough vision to establish the soup kitchens and commission huge public works, such as the Trans-Canada Highway.

I lost Jack and John in Field. Another freight train lousy with hobos came along and I hopped aboard.

As the train approached Kamloops, a fellow travelled along its length talking with the other tramps. "Listen," he said, "I've heard that the cops are pretty tough in Kamloops and they'll try to kick us off the train. But there won't be more than four or five of them and there are dozens of us. So we're not going to let them. We'll hang on tight no matter what they do, so we can stay on this train."

We all agreed. As the train neared the city, I could feel the tense excitement among our group. We were ready, we were united. We'd show those policemen they weren't going to shove us around.

The train rolled to a stop and I knew that the confrontation was imminent.

A policeman walked over to the train. One single, solitary, policeman. Not a big fellow either, and armed only with a billy stick. It looked more like a walking stick as it hung lazily in his grasp.

"Okay, guys." he said, almost conversationally, "Get off the train."

The first person to jump off was the guy who had organized our planned resistance! The rest of us tamely followed and were escorted into the little police kiosk. He sat down at the desk, still the only policeman in sight, and did whatever administration related to this sort of thing, then he let us go.

I met up with a French speaking fellow who couldn't speak much English and walked with him from Spence's bridge to Lidden. We walked there in the middle of the night. I was a bit apprehensive, and kept checking the shadows for cougars and grizzly bears. I could hear the river rushing below me in the darkness and nothing I could do would put my fears to the back of my mind. I was a thousand miles from home; no, not from home. From Winnipeg. I had no home.

After a very lonely and unpleasant journey, I arrived in Vancouver penniless and without having eaten in nearly two days. I stood opposite the old Vancouver Hotel, on Grenville Street, in the pouring rain. I just stood there, destitute, soaking wet, and cold.

I watched well-dressed men and ladies arrive at the hotel in their fancy automobiles and taxi cabs. They were attending a charity ball to raise money for the poor people. I longed to go inside but, of course, I couldn't afford a ticket.

A distinguished gentleman wearing a trench coat over what looked like a new suit came down the front steps of the hotel and approached a waiting taxi. He hesitated and stared in my direction. He said something to the taxi driver, then closed the car door. With his head down to avoid the rain, this 'sport' ran across the street to where I had taken shelter beside a little coffee shop.

"What's the matter with you, son?" he asked with genuine concern. "You look as though you lost a dollar and found a nickel. You look in a bad way, son."

"I just came into town a couple of days ago," I told him, "I'm broke, I haven't eaten, and I don't know who to turn to."

"Well," he said, "at least I can get you something to eat. Come on."

He led me into the coffee shop. The smell of bacon and eggs had been driving me crazy and I was so glad to get out of the cold and rain. A platter was put in front of me and I gulped down a cup of hot coffee. It took some of the chill out of my bones. The fellow paid for my meal and handed me a five dollar bill. It was more money than I had seen in a long time. Then he buzzed off.

Now that I was warm and had a full stomach, my spirits rose a bit. I was able to find a bed for the night at a place called the Men's Institute. It was a Salvation Army type of hostel which was run by the city and had rows of beds in a large dormitory. It was full of vagabonds like myself. I was very pleased to find that John and Jack were also staying there.

Once I had settled in, I told some of my new companions about the 'sport' who had given me five dollars. One guy said "Yeah, he's probably some rich bastard. Five dollars is probably nothing to him. Probably doesn't know what a day's work is."

"Oh, I don't know." I replied, "I really appreciate it." Deep inside, though, I felt that my benefactor couldn't possible know what it was like to be poor.

I registered for a job at a work camp the next day. I worked on the Trans-Canada Highway for about a month. I was then transferred to a camp near Revelstoke, where a crew was building the Big Bend Highway.

The camp site was situated way up on the side of a mountain. At the base of the sheer cliff were the foaming rapids of the Columbia River. I looked over the edge and shivered.

Like tiny spiders against the awesome backdrop, a team of men were building a rope bridge across the chasm. Cables had been passed and the bridge seemed secure enough to support the weight of several men.

The bridge began to sway slightly as about four of our fellows put it to the test. They were halfway across when I decided to follow them and set foot on the wooden planks which had been secured to the rope cables. The ropes creaked as they took up my weight and I placed my hand on the rope handrail. The fibers were prickly to the touch and a few prickles went up my spine as I thought of the drop below. I looked at the vast span in front of me, swaying ominously with the weight of the men who were crossing ahead, and I felt like a tight-rope walker working without a net.

A loud "Crack!" sounded from the far side. The bridge gave a lurch and I had just time to grab the hand rope with both hands before there was a second "crack!" and the bridge gave way beneath me. I heard the screams of my coworkers as I swung against the cliff face, dislodging some loose dirt and pebbles which dropped into the emptiness below.

There was a commotion up above. I wanted to call for help, but couldn't find my voice. Finally, someone looked over the edge. "Hey, give me a hand!" he shouted over his shoulder, "Somebody's hanging on down there!" A dozen leathery palms, well used to heavy labor, buckled on to the rope from which I was dangling and hauled me up to the edge. A pair of strong arms gripped my shoulders and lifted me to safety.

I was shaken but unhurt, except for some rope-burn. The foreman told me to take the rest of the day off. I wandered back to camp.

When I arrived at the collection of makeshift huts, I saw a bearded fellow who looked familiar. I couldn't quite place him, but I was sure I knew him from somewhere and I needed something to take my mind off the horrible event I had just witnessed. I walked over to him and said "Hello."

He looked at me with a frown of concentration and said "You look a little familiar to me."

"Yeah," I replied, "I've seen you before."

"Oh, yeah!" he exclaimed, "You were the kid who hadn't eaten for a couple of days and I gave you five bucks."

I asked him what he was doing there. "I gave you my last five bucks," he replied, "I had to register for a place to work."

That near miss on the bridge convinced me that I had to find something better than what I had. I wanted to make something of myself. I didn't know where to go, but I decided that I would try my luck in Victoria.

I made my way back to Vancouver and got a room at a shelter. I was back to bumming around and living with bums. A guy was murdered in front of my room with all kinds of blood marking the place where it happened. I started looking for another residence.

About two days later, I found a room at the Y.M.C.A. Someone told me that there was a good hearted fellow there who helped people out. I went over to him, introduced myself, and asked him if he would please finance my trip to Victoria so that I could perhaps find a job and make something of myself.

"I'll do that for you." he said, "You look sincere." We went to the ferry terminal and he bought me a ticket to Victoria. It cost a dollar and a quarter.

I booked into the Salvation Army hostel. While I was staying there I did odd jobs for them as a casual laborer. They had a little restaurant of sorts on Pandora Street called 'Captain's Vanity'. A person could go in there for a meal. If you could afford a meal, you paid. If you couldn't afford to pay, you didn't.

I was still frustrated and desperate for a decent job so I went to a rabbi. I told him that I was a Jew, that I didn't have a job, and that I was getting away from the Jewish culture. I asked him if he knew of any prominent Jews who could give me a job.

"Well," he replied, "there's the head of the Kinsmen Club, Mr. Rubin[3]. He's an eye doctor but he's a jeweler, too."

The rabbi got me in touch with Mr. Rubin. Mr. Salmon, who was a multimillionaire, was a friend of Mr. Rubin. Mr. Rubin got me a job working as an assistant gardener on Mr. Salmon's massive estate in Saanichton.

I lived with the head gardener in his little cottage. It was a beautiful part of the country, right at the top of the Saanich Peninsula. To the North were the scenic Gulf Islands with the distinctive summit of Saltspring Island. To the East, across the Strait of Georgia, were the mountain peaks of the mainland. There was a picturesque escarpment to the west and south of us was the City of Victoria, a bit of England transplanted.

---

[3] *Not his real name.*

Mr. Salmon lived in a big house where he kept a mistress. She was supposed to be just his servant but I found that hard to believe.

I enjoyed working on the estate. Every evening I would see Mr. Salmon. He would entertain me and I would tell him jokes. I met a pretty girl named Dorothy Warren, whose father also had a big estate, and before long we were going steady. While I was working his estate, Mr. Salmon organized a lottery. The prize was about $60,000. Mr. Rubin won.

About a month after I had started working, Mr. Salmon told me that Mr. Rubin had a good job for me and took me to Mr. Rubin's house in Victoria. Mr. Rubin invited me to work in his jewelry store. I told him that I really appreciated the offer. He replied, "Oh, that's all right. We've got a place for you."

Mr. Rubin took a personal interest in me, and even found me a decent boarding house to stay in. I was a little concerned about the cost, but then Mr. Rubin knew my salary (after all, he gave it to me) and I was sure I could trust his judgement. Naturally, I had to buy new clothes as well. Mr. Rubin assured me that I would make enough to pay off the debts I was incurring. "You won't make much to start with," he told me, "but you'll get promotions and pay raises. You have a real future with this company." I made friends with a fellow named Roy Wellove. He was a Baptist, I think, and he kept trying to convert me into being a Christian. I made some other friends, too, and started going to the gym. My future was looking bright.

Mr. Rubin used to take me with him all the time. When there was a big party or a big do, I would come along. At first, he used to take me to exhibitions at the stately Empress Hotel. Jewelers from all over the world came there exhibit their stock. After about a month, though, I got the feeling that Mr. Rubin was getting a bit fed up with me. I guess I wasn't as shrewd a business man as he had expected.

One day, an American lady entered the shop. She asked me for the diamond bracelet she had pawned a short time before and presented her receipt. I remembered her from her previous visit and knew that her bracelet was worth about $5,000.

I couldn't find the bracelet. She was very concerned. "You have to find it!" she exclaimed, "I'm going back to the 'States today. My boat leaves in 45 minutes."

I told her I would do what I could. I decided to contact Mr. Rubin and ask him where the bracelet was. I picked up the 'phone and called his house. He wasn't home. I called everyone I could think of, but nobody knew where he was.

I asked the lady to wait and ran out of the store. I went to all of the places Mr. Rubin might have gone for lunch or amusement. They all drew a blank.

Discouraged, I headed back towards the store. As I walked past the library, I decided to look inside just in the off chance that Mr. Rubin might be there.

In the darkest corner of the library, with his back to the door, sat Mr. Rubin. I breathed a sigh of relief and ran over to him.

"Mr. Rubin," I said with urgency, "the lady is here for her bracelet. Her boat leaves in half an hour. You'd better come right away!"

He turned towards me with a disgusted look on his face. "You fool!" he snarled, "Don't you know anything about business? I don't want to give it back."

At that moment, I lost what was left of my boyish innocence and saw the man I had looked up to as he really was. I turned and walked away.

I left the library and wandered about the street in a daze. I could not believe that my idol could be so corrupt, or that I could have been so mistaken about anyone. I was terrified by the thought that this man might have control of my future.

I was brought back to reality by Mr. Harrison, one of our watchmakers, who saw me on the street. "What's up Lou?" he asked, "You look like you've got something on your mind."

I told him what had happened. His expression grew deadly serious and he looked me right in the eye. "You're in debt, aren't you?"

I nodded. He pulled some money out of his pocket, handed it to me, and said, "Mr. Rubin has got his hooks into you, the same as he's got his hooks into the rest of us. You'd be his slave for life. There's a boat leaving for Vancouver in ten minutes. Get on it."

I protested, saying that I had to get my things.

He shook his head emphatically. "No, no, no! Mr. Rubin is very influential in this city. Leave your things; it will be worth it in the long run. You must get out of Victoria now!"

Frightened by what was happening, I took Harrison's advice and ran to the ferry terminal. I boarded the ship in the nick of time and found myself a seat. I had left all of my luggage behind: all of my clothes, my souvenirs, and the few photographs I had taken of my travels. I had also left my girlfriend. I rested my head on my arms and cried.

I arrived in Vancouver and walked the streets, begging for a meal. I told people that I hadn't eaten all day and asked them if they could spare me fifty cents. I managed to collect a dollar and a half.

I looked at the dollar and a half in my hand and thought of my family back home. My little brother, Harry, could use that dollar, I thought, so I got a stamped envelope and mailed him the dollar bill. I then used the money I had left to buy a fried egg with bread and butter. When I had finished, I found a bed at the local men's institute and signed up for another work camp.

I worked hard at that camp and during the summer I helped fight forest fires. The only firefighting equipment we had were shovels, with which we would pile dirt on the fires in hopes of establishing barriers. There were no such things as water bombers in those days.

From Revelstoke, I rode the rails to Edmonton. I had decided to take my mother's advice and visit my Uncle Abby, who was a doctor. I wanted to make a good impression, so before I went to see him I worked on a nearby farm to earn enough money to buy some new clothes. I wasn't sure what to expect, but I thought Uncle Abby might be able to help me get established.

Clean and well dressed, I entered Uncle Abby's office. I told the receptionist that I was her employer's nephew. She gave me a quizzical look and stated, "He has no nephew."

Uncle Abby walked into the room just then. He remembered me, and my hopes went up when he said, "I held you when you were just a baby." He then invited me downstairs for a hamburger.

We sat down together in the cafeteria. I was starving, as usual, and the hamburger was very welcome. I nearly chocked on it, though, and tried hard to hide my disappointment when he looked at his watch, excused himself, and said, "If you are ever back in Edmonton, drop in again."

After I had been away about a year, I decided to go back home. I walked up the familiar wooden steps and knocked on the front door.

My stepfather opened the door. His face was half covered in shaving cream. He did not say a word, but his eyes gloated with obvious satisfaction. I followed him into the house as far as the bathroom, where he finished his ablutions. He handed me the dirty razor, which I rinsed under the tap and wiped clean.

"So," he smirked, breaking the silence. "You came back, did you? Came back to eat, didn't you?"

I realized that I was no more welcome than I had been before. I hopped on an east-bound train the next day and rode it out to Ursula, Ontario, which was located just before Lake Superior. When I arrived, I signed on with a work camp which was building the Trans-Canada Highway. The work was hard, but I earned a dollar a day with free room and board.

I very badly wanted to join the Canadian Air Force. If I worked hard, I thought, I might be able to join as an aircraft mechanic. I knew it was a small air force, though, and people I spoke to about it told me that it was something of a 'closed shop'. Besides, I was told, they would never accept someone with my lack of credentials.

Tramp, tramp, tramp. That's what I was and that's what I did. I sometimes sang a little song to myself; "Tramp, tramp, tramp, keep on a tramping - nothing for you here. If I catch you 'round again, you will wear a ball and chain... Tramping is the best thing you can do."

I had to knock on doors and beg for a hand out. It's strange, looking back, but in those days most people didn't lock their doors and they were pretty quick to give food to a guy who was down on his luck. Nowadays, people would be scared to answer their door. And yet, there was more unemployment then so it isn't because of the economy.

I like to tell the story of a fellow who asked a lady if he could cut her grass for a meal. "Oh, you don't have to do that," she replied. "You can eat it off the ground the way it is."

I have trouble remembering the order in which some of these things happened, it was so long ago. Even when I was in Winnipeg, I usually didn't go home. I used to take showers at the Salvation Army hostel and would eat at soup kitchens. I expected nothing from my family and that's exactly what I got.

I was with Johnny McGee and Jack Mandrake for most of my tramping days. On one trip, we were accompanied by Bernie Poluck[4], a boy who lived across the street from the house we had rented on Redwood Avenue. Bernie was a year or two older than me and I had always envied him because he had a real family. His father worked for the Canadian Pacific Railroad (CPR) and actually owned a car, which was rare in my neighborhood. Bernie was always good at school and I remember him being in leadership positions. In fact this particular excursion was his idea. We had heard that some relief camps were hiring and Bernie thought, "Why not? Let's get in on it."

Bernie hadn't run away to join us, he was on summer holidays. In fact, although I didn't know it then, his father had given him a railroad pass and told him to use it if he needed it. But Bernie had come along for adventure and chose to ride the top of the freights with us. Besides, none of us had passes.

The four of us rode the rods to Calgary. We signed up for a work camp at Agassiz, beyond Banff, where we would be working on the Jasper Road. It

---

4 *Information in this and succeeding paragraphs was gained during a coffee meeting with the author's father and Mr. Poluck in August of 1990. It was the first time they had seen each other since the Depression.*

was pretty cold when we got there. I asked one guy, "Is the weather like this all the time?"

"No, no." he replied, "It's kinda' warm today."

Work wasn't scheduled until the following day, so Bernie and I decided to go mountain climbing. We climbed Mount Hector, which was pretty steep. It wasn't so bad climbing up but we had a heck of a time getting back down. We didn't have ropes or any special equipment so we couldn't rappel. We just worked our way down as best we could.

A little while later, my friends and I had a falling out about something. Our quarrel made me depressed, and I flopped down on my cot to mope. The whole mattress, with me on it, dropped to the floor. One of those pranksters had replaced the springs with twine.

Our quarrel soon ended but we got involved in a bigger dispute. This one was with the camp administration and might have been over food, I'm not sure. There were about a dozen of us involved. Anyway, we found ourselves dumped back in Calgary.

Bernie went his own way, working as a harvester before returning to school. The next time I saw him we talked about maybe going off to Australia. Before we could make any firm plans, however, Bernie was accepted as a mechanic in the Royal Canadian Air Force and began a career working on airplanes. Was I envious!

I also did some harvesting after that Agassiz camp, travelling around Alberta and Saskatchewan, wherever I could get jobs. I got a dollar a day and slept in the hay loft.

We worked from sunrise to sunset. I was a 'field pitcher', which meant I was out in the field pitching hay. I was also 'stooping', gathering the sheaves. I hated that.

But I did enjoy field pitching. My partner and I would start at one end of the field and another team would start at the other end, working towards us. I started pitching with enthusiasm but my partner asked me to slow down. "Go slow" he told me, "then they'll have to do the whole lot of work. They'll do it all and we'll get the credit for it." So we'd go slowly and they'd work like hell and come up to us.

We took turns at the bailing machine. We had to stand in line, and use it one at a time, loading straw. Off the rack and into the machine. We had to load it with horses, not with a tractor, with horses.

I was standing at the docks of Vancouver in March of 1935 when a German cruiser, the KARLSRUHE, arrived on a 'goodwill' visit. I was very interested in the huge ship, which majestically glided to its berth. When all of the lines had been secured, I watched the officers come ashore in their immaculate white uniforms.

A couple of sailor-boys left the ship and I followed them down the street. I could speak German because a lot of people in Rostern were from Germany and used to speak German to me. I introduced myself to them and we became quite good friends. They told me all about ships and I showed them around Vancouver. Their ship was in port for about a week and I saw them every day.

I told them that I was a little bit concerned about the way Hitler was treating the Jews. One of them replied, "Oh, you wouldn't have to worry. Hitler's not against the Jews. Except that he has to make a few laws, now. You couldn't join the armed services, but you could still visit Germany."

"Visit Germany?! I couldn't even visit another city in Canada! I'm absolutely broke. I have no money, no home, no friends. I have nobody. Strangely enough, you two guys are the best friends I've got!"

Before they sailed, one of them gave me a white and blue duffel bag as a keepsake. I still have it.

It seemed that I would spend my life as a nobody: no job, no money, no family, nothing. I began to listen to the agitators who decried our form of government and our economic system. I began to think of myself as a socialist.

I was working in a logging camp near Pender Harbour, a beautiful little fjord on the West Coast, when I heard a speech by a man named Arthur H. Evans. Standing on a wooden box, he shook his fist and whipped up a furor as he decried our government and blamed 'the system' for our plight. He extorted us to march 'on to Ottawa' to demand political and economic reforms.

I stood up and said that Evans and his like were communists out for their own political gain. That brought a chorus of boos. The speakers criticized me and made similar accusations. One of my friends got up and told them that I was sincere, that I was "all for the boys".

Under Evans' leadership, a large group of desperate and determined men decided to leave their British Columbia work camps and head east to demand action from the Prime Minister. In spite of my criticisms, I was desperate enough to join them. Hundreds of us boarded freight cars and began an historic trek to the East.

We stayed in Vancouver flop houses. The organizers wanted to make sure we would have money, so they gave us each a little card. With this card, we were entitled to beg!

There was a little park just opposite 'The Province' newspaper. We would gather there to listen to Arthur H. Evans' speeches. He openly admitted that he was a communist and devoted much of his content to praising Russia, telling us how wonderful it was over there. I began to admire Evans and became one of the officers of this thing, one of Evans' helpers.

After a few weeks in Vancouver, I found myself a girlfriend. She took me home and introduced me to her father. I began to think about looking for a job and maybe settling down.

My thoughts of a domestic life ended amidst a riot in downtown Vancouver. We marched through the streets, causing mayhem, and stood on street corners, screaming. To my horror, someone picked up a rock and threw it at one of the Hudson's Bay Company store's large display windows. The rampage continued throughout the store, with display cases being smashed and merchandise destroyed. After my initial shock, I got into the 'spirit of things' and did my share of damage. We had makeshift clubs and we used them to smash everything. Evens thought that what we were doing was just great and commended me for my part in it.

Mayor Taylor held an emergency rally in a stadium. An elderly man, he wore a very distinct red tie. "Listen," he said, "if you will leave Vancouver peacefully, I promise you that you will have safe escort out and I will provide you with some meals."

Evans got up on the podium and pushed the mayor aside. "Don't believe him." Evans shouted, "He's just trying to get us out of town so he'll look good during the election."

The rally turned into a general forum, with many of us, including myself, standing up on the podium to express our views. When it was over, we left the stadium but stayed as a group.

I saw Mr. Taylor in the Vancouver Hotel on Granville Street a couple of days later. He recognized me from the rally. "There's nothing more I can do for you." he said, "I've just lost the election and now I'm out of a job, too."

Thousands of us gathered around the CPR station, boarded freight cars again, and continued on our trek to Ottawa. My girlfriend came to the station with me and took pictures of us boarding the trains. "Don't worry." I told her, "I'll be back before long, and we can get married." I never saw her again.

Anyway, we all piled on the freight trains and travelled for a couple of days. We sang songs on the way. When we got to Revelstoke (and then Glacier National Park) we all got off the trains, built big fires, and set up camps. We managed to scrounge hot dogs and potatoes and anything else we needed to keep going.

We got off the trains in Regina, where the authorities let us stay in a big arena. There were thousands of us in there, sleeping on the floor at night. During the day, we went out begging for food.

All kinds of people got up on the podium to lecture to us. The local pastors, parsons, and priests all gave us lectures. They said we were in such a bad way because we didn't believe in Christ. Communist leaders got up and told us their point of view.

Arthur H. Evans and another guy went on ahead of us to talk to the Prime Minister, R.B. Bennett. From what I heard, Bennett offered Evans and some others a job, but nothing came of it.

I met another girl in Regina and started to enjoy life a little, even if I did have to live in that arena. I slept on straw, like an animal in a stall, and I kept everything I owned in my packsack.

There was a big meeting in the market square upon Evans' return. It was Dominion Day; July 1, 1935. Evans was up there, in front of the mob, practically telling us to commit more violence. Another communist leader got up. "We're going to raise hell when we get to Ottawa!" he roared.

A large but unobtrusive-looking van was parked behind the meeting. I heard a shout and was startled by a loud explosion. The doors of the van opened and dozens of mounted police poured out with their clubs waving and God knows what. It seemed like there were hundreds of them.

Tear gas bombs were flying and exploding all over the place. Everyone was running for shelter, but there was no shelter. My eyes were wet and I could hardly breathe, with tear gas burning through my lungs. I couldn't see a thing.

Something grabbed hold of me. I tried to break loose but I couldn't. I got knocked over the head.

Prime Minister R.B. Bennett had been warned of our intentions, saw them as incipient revolution, and ordered the authorities to stop our trek in Regina. The police attacked the public meeting I was attending and the Regina Riot began. The fighting lasted for hours. One police officer was killed.

I was hit with a baton, but I don't think it was done deliberately. A policeman was just waving it back and forth to clear the area.

When the dust had settled, I found myself locked up in a Regina jail. Still, I had been in worse places and I made myself as comfortable as I could.

I spent about two months in jail awaiting the decision of the courts. My charges were eventually dropped.

Evens was in the cell next to mine. He had a typewriter with him and always seemed to be typing. I now believe that he was probably being paid by Russia, because he was always telling me how good things were over there. He told me that Russian Jews were treated very well. In fact, he said, they even had a separate place just for them, called the Gulag. I later found out that the Gulag was a concentration camp.

It seemed to me that Evens was being treated like a lord and was running the whole show. He even seemed to be running the guards.

As I hinted at earlier, Kellet Cole was in the jail there as well. I wanted to talk to him and maybe rekindle our old friendship but he stayed a bit aloof. He wasn't rude or anything like that but I could see that he really wasn't interested in seeing me.

When my stepfather heard that I was in jail, so I'm told, he remarked, "Wherever there's trouble, he'll be in the middle of it." Those words, spoken in 1935, were prophetic.

One of the guards, an Irishman, was friendly enough and his conversation helped me pass the time. Among other things, I told him that I was very interested in airplanes and dreamed that one day I might even fly in one.

"You know what you ought to do," he said, "hop on a cattle boat and sail over to England. I bet you could get into their Air Force."

Chapter 3: A Meal Ticket

I arrived in England with high hopes and great aspirations. It had been an uncomfortable passage in the 'steerage' class of an old freighter that doubled as a cattle boat. Those of us in steerage got a reduced fare because we were supposed to help with the livestock but we didn't really and no one seemed to care.

I shared the cramped accommodations with the family of an English fellow who had been living in Toronto. He had given up a good job as the Toronto harbor master because he wanted to return to England. They sort of adopted me and said that I could stay with them in England. They were going to settle in a rural area, though, and I wanted to be near a Royal Air Force recruiting center.

When we were near the middle of the Atlantic, I looked at the expensive watch on my wrist and thought of all that it represented. Everything my mother had told me about my father was bad. I was going to England to begin a new life, or so I hoped, and needed no reminders of my past. I tore that watch off my wrist and threw it through an open porthole. Now I'm sorry that I did.

I was fortunate to find a job with the 'Church Army' addressing envelopes. The pay was very poor but at least I had enough for a place to stay. With that modest success to build on, I headed for the nearest Royal Air Force recruiting station and offered them my services.

They turned me down. It was the same old story; I had no education, no references. I was just a bum off the street.

Actually, I did have one reference. I wrote to the prison guard who had suggested I try my luck in England and he sent me a very nice letter of reference. You'd think the R.A.F. would have jumped at the chance to hire a man who'd been a model prisoner.

My token job with the Church Army did not last long and I soon found myself back in my old lifestyle. I slept in parks, corridors, and I nearly starved.

With lots of time on my hands, and little money to spend, I often wandered about London. I enjoyed seeing the historic sights and it didn't cost anything to look.

So it was that I was in Trafalgar Square when I noticed a prominent building called 'Canada House'. I wandered over to it and was pleased to discover that a party was being hosted there for visiting Canadians. The Governor General of Canada and the Mayor of Winnipeg were both going to be attending.

I returned to the Salvation Army hostel where I was staying at the time. I had no suitable clothes to dress in, but one of my 'mates' had a jacket which fit me and another one lent me a pair of pants. My shoes were old but a bit of polishing made them presentable. Feeling like a poor man's Cinderella, I headed off to the ball.

I wasn't sure if there would be a charge at the door. I didn't want to take any chances so I waited until the door attendants were busy and slipped past them.

My chest puffed out a bit as I tried to fit in with all of the dignitaries who were in attendance. Judging by the clothes they were wearing, most of the guests were quite 'well to do'. The orchestra struck up a waltz and couples flowed onto the dance floor. I spotted a pretty girl and decided to make her acquaintance.

I said "Hello" to her and she smiled at me. She told me that she didn't know many people in England, having just arrived from Winnipeg, and she was thrilled when I told her that I was also from Winnipeg. She said her name was "Donna".

She asked me my name. "It's, uh, Austin," I replied, and glanced at the floor.

"That's a nice name," she said. "So tell me, what are you doing in England, Austin?"

"Well," I began, looking at the ceiling, "I'm on a diplomatic mission. I'm here to investigate the possible introduction of Canadian sports in England. You know, to see if the English would be interested in forming hockey teams, that sort of thing."

We spent a wonderful evening, dancing and talking about 'home'. As the evening drew to a close, she gave me her phone number at the Seymour Hotel and seemed very enthusiastic about seeing me again. We made tentative plans to tour London together.

As I walked down the steps of Canada House, I looked at the telephone number in my hand and knew that I would never dial it. I later found out that she was Donna Warren, the Mayor of Winnipeg's daughter, but she would never find out who I was.

I moved into a Jewish shelter for refugees from Europe. Hitler's racial policies were already causing alarm and many Jews who could were fleeing the mainland. I made friends with a guy named Paul, who came from Abyssinia.

A confidence man from what was then known as Palestine was going around collecting money, supposedly for Jews in Palestine. He asked Paul where he could find some rich people.

Paul was very helpful. He told him to go to the Houndsdich and ask for the head manager - Lou Greenburgh.

I was working at the Houndsdich as a floor sweeper. This guy finally found me sweeping the floor. His disappointment was obvious. "Are you Lou Greenburgh?" he moaned.

I got fired from my job at the Houndsdich for not being a good floor sweeper. I found another job working at a laundromat.

I must have been a strange sight to the Commanding Officer of the Kingsway Recruiting Office. What he saw was an unshaven, uneducated, ragged bum who presented himself over and over again and pleaded that he had come all the way from Canada to join the Royal Air Force. No matter how often he told him "no" and no matter how hard he tried to get rid of him, the Commanding Officer was constantly pestered by this poor excuse of a recruit who violated all of his recruiting guidelines.

He must have felt sorry for me, because one day he looked at me with sympathetic eyes and said, "You've had it pretty hard, son. I'll try to get you in. You'll never go very far in the Air Force, I'm afraid, but at least you'll have a meal ticket."

It took some time, but he eventually fiddled me into the R.A.F. On July 21, 1937, I was given the lowly rank of AC II (General Duties). On July 23 I arrived at Henlow, where I set to work cleaning toilets and scrubbing floors for the princely sum of two shillings a day. I felt like I was a somebody.

The recruits at the induction center were a real cosmopolitan group with guys from all over the Commonwealth. The lady filling out information forms would ask each recruit his country of origin. Most of them were Australians or New Zealanders, with even a few Americans thrown in for good measure. When asked his nationality, one fellow replied, "I hope it's all right... I'm English."

I became buddies with a "Kiwi" fellow named McIntrick, who was signing up the same time as me. He told me that he planned to become a "fitter" and suggested that someday I might become a mechanic. He already had some civilian qualifications and it seemed like he was destined to become something important, maybe a sergeant. I figured that I was destined to clean toilets.

I heard a story about another induction center recruit. It probably isn't true but I'll tell it to you anyway. This fellow wasn't very bright, but he acted rather self-important. He was sitting on a chair in the barracks, casually reading a newspaper which rested in his lap. The corporal in charge of the recruits came into the room looking a bit agitated. He asked the fellow in the chair if the C.O. was around. Without looking up, the new AC II shook his head. The corporal left the room but returned again within a few minutes. He again asked if anybody had seen the C.O. They told him that they hadn't and he left the room again.

Not long after that, a senior-looking officer accompanied by some of his staff members entered the barracks. The AC II put down his paper, got out of his chair and walked over to the senior officer. "Are you the C.O.?" he demanded.

The officer looked a bit indignant at this show of insubordination, but answered that he was, in fact, the commanding officer.

"Well, you're in s..t!," the AC II smirked, poking his finger at the officer's chest. "The corporal's been looking for you!"

Actually, we thought that the corporal was God. And if the corporal was God, then the lance corporal was the Pope. He put us through our paces, really throwing his weight around. I remember the corporal asking an AC II how long he had been in the service. With obvious pride, the AC II replied, "I've been here for a whole week!" He was a seasoned serviceman.

ACII Greenburgh (centre) as a new recruit.

I recently heard the song "September in the Rain". It reminded me of my time as a raw recruit because it had been popular back then. I remember looking at the other guys in the barracks and feeling that I now belonged in something bigger than myself, that I was not alone anymore.

I had only been in the Air Force for about a week when Paul was arrested for smuggling. He needed a character reference so he told the authorities that he had a really close friend who was in the Air Force - me.

Next thing I knew, I was locked in a cell and suspected of smuggling. I was never officially arrested, mind you, but I was cleaning a cell that day when it clanged shut behind me. I was told that nobody on base had a key and I would have to wait until the next day to be let out. I was told that the guy with the key had gone home. The Air Force just didn't want me going anywhere until they had checked out those smuggling allegations. With a friend like Paul, I didn't need enemies.

I was briefly posted to Cardington, where the hangers had been built for the big dirigibles R100 and R101. I started my training for 'General Duties'.

It was a beautiful summer evening. I sat outside the barracks and gazed at the gentle twilight which bathed those enormous hangers just a short distance from my quarters. From an open window came the soothing strains of 'Goodbye Hawaii' which flowed from a radio. Over in the canteen, a group of guys were cheerfully drinking beer and singing a rousing chorus of "Old Faithful, we'll ride the range together... ", which blended into the song on the radio and added to my mellow feeling.

"Sure," I thought to myself, "I'm just an AC II. But I've got three square meals a day and thirty shillings to boot."

I don't remember if I was sitting on a stone or just on the grass but I do remember that there was another fellow with me. "You know," he said to me, "I think I'm going to quit the Air Force. I don't have a trade and I don't want to clean toilets all my life. I want to make something of myself."

I was saddened to hear him talk like that. In a way, though, it made me feel even more appreciative of my new surroundings. "Look," I said to him, "we may just be AC II's, but at least we're involved with flying and with history. Look over there, those hangers are part of history and so is that grave yard over there where the crews of the R100 and R101 are buried. Sure, you and I will probably never fly but at least we can talk with flyers and be involved with them."

"Yeah," he said, "but most of the guys they're promoting are coming in with trades. We'll never make corporal."

"Okay," I replied, "so we probably won't make corporal. But we've got three meals a day and a place to live. What more could we really want? Besides, we could probably get on some kind of course someday. Maybe we could become mechanics or something."

We talked like this for quite a while. "Wouldn't it be great to fly?" he sighed, "I mean, as a real pilot?"

"Boy," I replied, "If I could get my pilots' wings, I'd be willing to work for free for the rest of my life, just to have those wings!"

I think I talked him out of quitting. We went into Balmoral the next evening to try and pick up some girls. Instead we wound up sitting on a riverbank dreaming to each other about our futures, limited though they seemed.

From there I went to Manston, an airbase near the coast. I arrived on October 10, 1937. My primary duties were to wash the dishes, squeegee the floors, and perform other mundane tasks as the service required. I was on the fire crew when a report came in that two Avro Ansons had collided. One of them had lost its hydraulics and couldn't lower the undercarriage. So we got into the fire truck.

The airplane crash landed on its belly. We ran up there in our old fire truck with the bell clanging away. It was a real primitive thing and our firefighting equipment was just a bit of water and soda in a tank. On the way to the crash site, the fire truck caught fire. We had to use an extinguisher from the crashed airplane to put out the fire in the fire truck!

A girl came to the gate one time and asked for "Squadron Leader Forester." We scratched our heads and replied that there was no squadron leader named 'Forester' on the base. "We have an 'AC II' Forester," we told her.

The buildings at Manston were in pretty bad repair. Our mess hall was an old barn with holes in the roof. Birds would actually fly among the rafters above the tables where we ate.

Cameron Aitken, another Canadian, was sitting across from me. An innocent looking little bird was poised high above his plate and released a globular excretion. I watched it land with a plop right in the middle of Aitken's dinner.

"Yuck!" I grimaced, "Some bird droppings landed in your mashed potatoes."

"Doesn't bother me," he replied with an unconcerned look on his face. He scooped up a big fork full of the white mush and shoved it into his mouth. I nearly retched. He finished his meal with an exaggerated relish. I lost my appetite.

"Couldn't fool me!" he laughed when he was done.

The corners of my mouth turned downward as I looked from his face to his plate and back again. "I wasn't kidding," I insisted, "a bird really did crap in your potatoes!"

His eyes grew wide and a look of horror spread across his face as the truth gradually sank in. "Come to think of it," he choked, "they did taste kinda' strange." He backed away from the table with his hands covering his mouth and ran to the nearest washroom.

Like any military unit, we occasionally went 'camping'. One time, a fellow kicked a young lady out of his tent and reported her to the military police. The flight sergeant commended him to his face and said he had done the right thing. As soon as the young man had left, however, he remarked, "The damn fool. I would have given her twenty-four hours to get out!"

I was scrubbing out the barracks when I noticed a sergeant pilot sitting on his bunk. I felt self-conscious talking to someone as high ranking as a sergeant, especially one who was also a pilot, but he was quite friendly and before long I began enjoying his esteemed company the way some people enjoy the presence of royalty.

The sergeant gave me a lot of encouragement and said I should try for aircrew. He agreed that I had no hope of ever being a pilot but figured that I could at least become an air gunner.

An auxiliary squadron of 'weekend fliers' operated out of Manston. They flew Hawker Hinds, open cockpit biplanes. The sight of those aircraft buzzing around conjured up pleasant childhood memories of afternoons spent watching the airplanes fly from Stevenson Field. I wanted to go up for a flight.

Flying Officer Stranton agreed to take me up. Bursting with enthusiasm at the prospect of my first airplane ride, I quickly drew a parachute from stores. I slipped it onto my shoulders and fumbled with the clumsy straps. Looking like a turtle in its shell, I waddled off to get permission from the flight sergeant.

The flight sergeant examined me with his eyes. "Have you had parachute training?" he demanded. I told him that I hadn't. "You can't go up until you've had your parachute training. Go see the sergeant about it."

I grumbled to myself as I went off in search of the sergeant. "Oh my God," I thought, "don't tell me I'll have to take a course before I can have a flight." I found the sergeant and told him I had been sent for parachute training. "Hmm," he said, "you'd better see the corporal about that. He'll give you your parachute training."

It was awkward trying to walk in the bulky parachute. It had been designed to be sat in and the straps were binding in my crotch. I finally found the corporal and told him I needed parachute training. "Yeah," he replied. Pointing to my D ring, he said, "Pull this. Now off you go!"

Having completed my parachute training, I donned the mandatory white scarf and headed out to the Hawker I would be flying in. I climbed into the seat behind the pilot beaming from ear to ear as the corporal helped me get settled in.

The engine coughed into life and we bounced along the grassy strip. The wind blew in my face and my scarf began to wave in the slipstream, making me feel like Baron von Richthofen. Then the ground dropped away below. I was flying!

The pilot flashed me a smile over his shoulder and eased back on the stick. We soared up to four thousand feet and another aircraft formated on us. I marveled at this bird's-eye view of the world.

We dived to gain speed, then the pilot pulled hard back on the stick and we zoomed upwards. The climb became steeper and steeper until we were approaching inverted flight. I floated away from my seat and a wave of horror

Lou Greenburgh beside the Hawker Hind in which he had his first flight.

swept over me as I realized that I wasn't strapped in! There was nothing for me to hang on to, either.

I felt a reassuring tug, like a hand grabbing me from underneath. I then realized that the corporal had secured me to the airplane by a chord stretching between my legs and attached to a ring under my parachute harness. Thus standing upside down, hanging by a chord, I saw the world upside down for the first time in my life.

The pilot flipped us back into normal flight, completing an Immelmann. I was thoroughly enjoying this introduction to flight and was sorry when it came to an end. I quickly volunteered to be an air gunner so that I could fly again.

Becoming an air gunner in 1938 was no big deal. There was nothing to shoot at and no one shooting at you. I was given an old badge, the 'winged bullet', and 'poof', I was an instant gunner. This was just a temporary duty to do in addition to my usual chores. When I was posted to Feltwell, on July 17, 1939, I again donned my winged bullet and fired imaginary bullets from the rear turret of a bomber.

RAF bases at Manston and Feltwell

I eventually did become a flight mechanic. A friend told me that we would soon be short of pilots, but to imagine myself as a pilot was a dream that bordered on fantasy.

As a matter of fact, a lot of people told me that we would soon be short of pilots. They all said, "We'll soon be short of pilots, with you as a flight mechanic!"

In September of 1938, Neville Chamberlain (who I often referred to as 'Chambermaid') was meeting with a Chaplinesque little former corporal to decide the fate of Europe. On September 30 he signed the Munich Agreement which gave in to Hitler's demands on Czechoslovakia. I watched a newsreel in which Chamberlain was disembarking from an aircraft after returning from Munich. In an historic gesture, Chamberlain waved a piece of paper and proclaimed 'peace in our time'. I shook my head in disgust and wondered how a politician astute enough to be elected Prime Minister could have been so naive.

On October 10, 1938, I arrived at the RAF's technical school at St. Athan, in Wales, for my mechanics course. (I'd already had some training at the technical school at Manston.) St. Athan was the largest RAF technical school in Great Britain.

As we often did on Friday evenings, some friends and I decided to head into Cardiff, the 'big town' about forty miles away. We went to a familiar dance hall and soon made the acquaintance of some young ladies who were more than willing to be our dancing partners.

The evening was drawing to a close and I was just about to escort my companion home when a scuffle broke out. As best I could tell, a great big guy who had been throwing his weight around all evening was trying to cut in on a smaller guy. It was an 'excuse me' dance, but the smaller fellow objected to being cut in on and the big guy wanted to bully him. "Let's go outside, if you've got the guts." he snorted.

The smaller guy didn't say a word, but just headed for the door. The bully had a smug look on his face as he turned to follow him. A man put his hand on the bully's shoulder. "I think you ought to know," he confided to him, "that the guy you challenged to a fight is Peter Kane!"

The bully's face went white. Peter Kane was the Flyweight boxing champion of the World.

The dance hall was emptied as we all poured outside to watch Peter Kane knock the hell out of this bully. We gathered around Kane and waited for the slaughter to begin.

"Kanie!" exclaimed the bully as he appeared outside. "I was only joking. I wouldn't fight you; I'm your friend. I've been following your career for a long time."

Peter Kane looked at him in disgust. "You act tough, but you're not tough," he told him. Then he added, "You only smell strong."

I remember another, less pleasant incident which happened at Cardiff. One of the civic officials there happened to be Jewish and wanted to make a show of all the Jews who were serving in the armed services. He therefore invited all of the serving Jews in the area to a dinner in their honor.

Another Jewish serviceman and I were rambling along in the tediously slow and unreliable train which was the main transportation link between the school at St. Athan and the town of Cardiff. My previous experiences had taught me never to turn down a free dinner but I didn't have any enthusiasm for the event. My companion, on the other hand, was quite enthusiastic and looked forward to the festivities. "We'll be making speeches and stuff." he said.

"No," I muttered, "he just wants to show us off. He doesn't care about us. He's just using us."

We finally arrived at the banquet, tired and hungry. The official who was hosting the dinner walked up to us with a stern expression on his face. "Why didn't you come earlier?" he demanded.

We explained that we had come as quickly as we could but he was not satisfied with that. Turning his back to us, he called to the waitress, "If there's any food left, give it to these two."

I waved a finger at the official's departing back and told him where he could put his food. Then the two of us left.

I was resting on my bunk in a crowded barracks. It was the eve of World War II and my air force companions and I were listening to one of Goebbels'

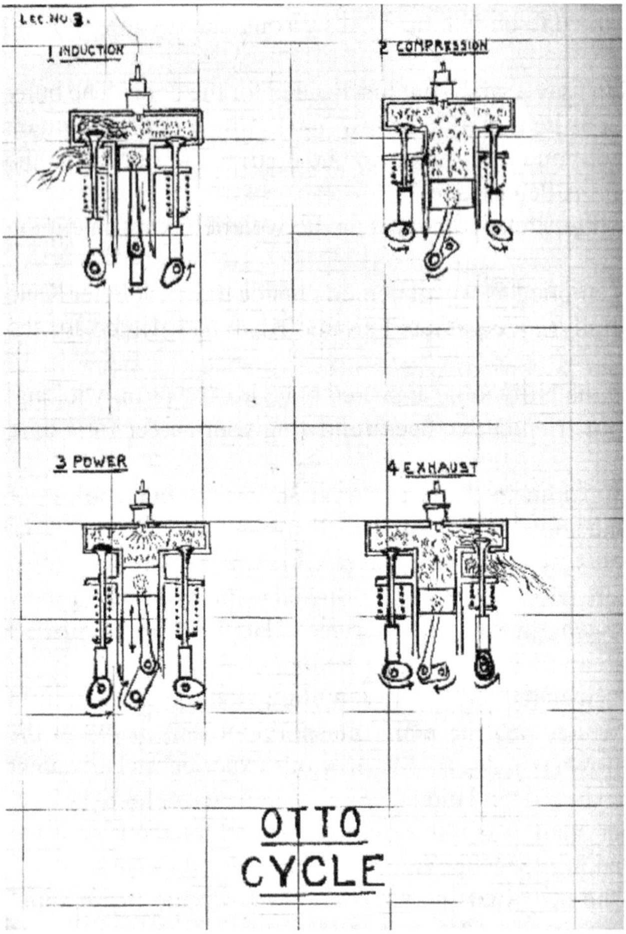

Even the absence of a formal education did not stop Lou making meticulous notes during his mechanic's course.

speeches on the radio. With my limited German, I could understand parts of what Goebbels was saying.

"You know," one of my companions said, "I think Hitler's got something there, about the Jews."

I got up off my bunk and walked over to where he was standing. "Do you really mean that?" I asked.

He told me that he did. Smack! His feet flew up from under him and he landed flat on his back, his face a bloody mess.

"Oh, Lou," he whimpered as he gingerly touched his bleeding nose, "I didn't mean you. We're friends."

"Well," I retorted, I meant you!" I stepped up on a cot and rolled up my sleeves. "Alright," I said as I surveyed the bewildered crowd, my fists ready, "who's next?"

There were no takers. The fellow I had just thumped continued to protest that he hadn't meant to offend me. I cooled off a bit and sat down on the bunk.

We became good friends after that. I have often found that a punch in the nose can form the basis of a friendship.

Actually, I've always been pretty good with my fists. We used to have boxing matches every two months and I was usually able to hold my own.

I remember one time when the guys in my barracks asked me to fight a fellow named Forbes. "I could handle him with one arm tied behind my back." I bragged.

Anyway, the fight was arranged and I was looking forward to an easy victory. I climbed into the ring first and did a bit of shadow boxing, dancing around and showing off while I waited for my victim to enter the ring.

A few minutes later, my ego fell to the floor. The smile disappeared from my face and I stopped dancing. Instead of Forbes, the station champ had stepped into the ring. He knocked the hell out of me. I was being so badly beaten that the referee had to stop the fight.

I was at a dance the next week. A girl asked me about my black eye.

"You should see the other guy." I replied with a worldly smile.

I enjoyed my mechanics course. I remember one class we had where the instructor asked us some rather perplexing questions. "Greenburgh," he said to me, "what would you do if an aircraft carrier landed on the field?"

"Get some water for its boilers." I replied.

The next question was what one should do if he accidentally put his foot through an airplane's fabric. The answer was "Pull it out."

The final question was a real stumper. We were to imagine that we were flying an open cockpit aircraft with the King of England in the passenger seat. We had just done an aerobatic maneuver and the King had fallen out. "Now," the instructor asked, "what is the very first thing you should do?"

Nobody could think of an appropriate answer, so the instructor told us what to do. "Adjust the trim to allow for the lost weight."

The commanding officer at St. Athan was a real bastard. Among other things, he insisted that we all have our washing done at a certain laundry. I later found out that he was a part owner of that laundry.

The discipline was as strict at St. Athan as at the next RAF base, but we paid for our own laundry and we felt we had the right to choose which laundry service we wanted to use. We held a meeting, which I attended, and told our views to the C.O.

The C.O. didn't push the matter, probably because he didn't want his superiors to find out about his little enterprise.

The mess where we ate was short of cutlery. Those who arrived too late to get a knife or fork had to go into the NAAFY canteen and get one. Technically, I guess we were taking equipment without authority. But we needed it to eat in the mess and we always returned it when we were finished. What were we supposed to do? Eat with our hands?

Short Stirling (courtesy of Steve Smith).

I mention this because a new 'gung-ho' military policeman who had just started working in his trade caught me and a couple of other guys borrowing cutlery. There I was, caught red handed with a fork and table knife.

I was brought up before the commanding officer, that same commanding officer who had seen me at the meeting a few weeks before. He found me guilty of theft and sentenced me to fourteen days of 'jankers', which was real punishment.

After working and studying all day, I had to march about the parade square with a rifle and a full pack until late in the evening. I couldn't leave the base. It was like being in jail.

I completed my mechanics course on July 17, 1939, and was posted to Feltwell, in Norfolk. It was there that I saw the prototype of the Stirling bomber. Built by the Short Brothers Company, it was coming in from a cross country flight. I admired it as it circled the field and wondered if it was really as big as it looked. I was just awed by its enormous size. The huge wheels swung from their casings behind the engines and it touched down. When it finally taxied in to the parking area, it loomed above the other airplanes like a Tyrannosaurus Rex. The Royal Air Force's first four engine bomber, the Stirling was to be the heaviest bomber of World War II.

My love affair with the Stirling had begun.

Chapter 4: The Battle of Britain

On February 22, 1940, I was posted to Church Fenton, with the newly formed 'Canadian' 242 Squadron. The original idea was to form an R.A.F. squadron out of serving Canadians so that it would be a homogenous Canadian unit and could eventually be taken over by the R.C.A.F. Distinct R.C.A.F. squadrons soon began serving in England, however, and many non-Canadian reinforcements began to dilute the Canadian-ness of 242. So 242 Squadron remained 'British'.[5]

While I was there, so I heard, a new chaplain joined the base. The guard challenged him at the gate and he didn't have his identification card with him. "But I'm the base chaplain!" protested the unfortunate cleric.

The guard was unmoved by his protest. "I don't care if you're 'Charlie' Chaplin," he replied, "you're still not getting in without I.D."

I was standing outside when my attention was drawn upward by the scream of a diving airplane. Way above me was a Spitfire spinning towards the earth. Around and around it spun and I realized with alarm that it was not going to pull out. It spun right down to the ground and exploded. A ten foot crater marked its point of impact. I thought to myself, "Oh my God! There's a man down there!" To my relief, I then saw the welcome sight of a parachute floating from above. The station loud speakers later blared out the announcement that anyone who witnessed the crash was to report what they had seen but I couldn't be bothered.

The flight commander, a Canadian Flight Lieutenant named Donald Miller, didn't like me. I was a bit of a nuisance to him but it wasn't really my fault. I was trying to act like a 'big guy'. I wasn't going to take orders from any Canadian who came overseas the same time as I did just because he happened to be an officer.

I saw him in a pub one time when I was out with my buddies. I walked up to the little group of officers he was sitting with and began acting real 'buddy-buddy'.

---

[5] *"Against All Odds", The Battle of Britain 50th Anniversary Appeal, published on behalf of the Royal Air Force Association by the Rococo Group, 1990, article 'Units of Strength' by Lieutenant General F.R. Sutherland R.C.A.F., page 179.*

"Where are you guys from?" I asked. I deliberately omitted the mandatory 'sir' at the end of the question (and every other sign of respect, for that matter). I was being a real 'smart-aleck'.

It wasn't Miller, really, who objected to my behavior. It was his executive officer, Flying Officer Standsfeld, who took offence. Standsfeld had us formed up the next day and delivered a strong lecture. "We are officers and you are enlisted men." he stated. "Whether we're in a pub or whether we're on duty you have to give us some respect."

He quoted a recent incident where one AC II had been very snotty to an officer in front of a lot of people. "We're not having any more of that!" He seemed to be looking at me as he spoke.

On Standsfeld's recommendation, Miller had me posted a few weeks later (March 13, 1940), shortly before Sir Douglas Bader, the famous 'legless pilot', took over command of the squadron. He had me posted just to get rid of me. It's just as well. 242 Squadron was posted to France in May. Because of my impudence, I missed my chance to huddle on the beaches of Dunkirk.

I was transferred to 215 Squadron, at Honnington. I did better there, lasting until April 21, 1940, (over a month!) before being posted again. This time, I was posted to the 11th Operational Training Unit at Bassingbourn, Cambridgeshire, and worked on the tubby twin engine bombers called Wellingtons.

They were affectionately known as 'Wimps'. Wellingtons didn't look very impressive, with their fabric skin and blimp-like fuselage, but at that time they were one of our main front line aircraft and one of the few bombers capable of carrying a respectable bomb load right to the heart of Germany. Mind you, the aircraft I would be working on were no longer fit for operations and had been reassigned to a training role.

I recently came across a poem by an unknown author which pretty well expresses the Wellington's place in history. It was entitled 'Wimpy'[6] and went like this:

---

[6] *The poem 'Wimpy' appeared in a newsletter published by the Stirling Aircraft Association of Canada - Abbotsford B.C., Volume 2, No. 1, Winter 89/90.*

I've heard so many stories,
Of aircraft swift and strong,
Their virtues have been portrayed,
In picture, word and song.

The Hurricanes and Spitfires,
The Hallies and the Lancs,
To hear some people tell it,
They warrant all the thanks.

But there were other aircraft,
And one above them all,
The men that flew in this kite,
Should stand up proud and tall.

We bombed the Ruhr when moon was full,
The German coast, we mined it,
We joined the search for a battleship,
Thank God we didn't find it.

We joined a thousand other planes,
And bombed Cologne one night,
Stuff going up and coming down,
It really was a sight.

One day we flew a daylight raid,
We thought we'd gone to glory,
Port motor gone, we ditched in the sea,
But that's another story.

And now she's in a watery grave,
That valiant old work horse,
You must have guessed what plane it was,
'Twas a WELLINGTON of course.

Lou Greenburgh in the cockpit of a Wellington.

I got along very well with Flying Officer Fred Lanbart, the pilot of an aircraft I serviced. Also from Canada, Lanbart had joined the R.A.F. in 1936, flying Harrows with 115 Squadron. He had transferred to 99 Squadron in September of 1939 and had flown on the December 14 raid on Heligoland when five out of the twelve aircraft had been shot down. After several more raids on Heligoland and Norway in April of 1940, he had been posted with 214[7]. I had a great deal of respect for him and figured that he was destined to reach high levels.

Lanbart would sometimes walk over to me as I adjusted this or that and we would shoot the breeze for a while.

"You know, Sir," I said to him one day, as I struggled with a wrench on some particularly irritating job, "I'm tired of being a 'grease monkey'. I'd like to get into aircrew so at least I'd be a Sergeant and could feel like I was somebody. I want to get into some action."

He listened to me patiently, although he had heard me talk on that subject many times.

"Yeah," I continued, "I bet I could make it as an air gunner, at least."

---

[7] *"Canadians in the Royal Air Force", op. cit., page 159.*

"Well Lou," he said, "I don't know if I can do anything about that, but I'll keep it in mind."

The mess sergeant was a WAF named Patty Violet Hamling. We started dating. The next thing I knew, we were married.

Royston was a little town outside of Bassingbourn and it was one of the nicest little towns I've come to know. A lot of the airmen from Bassingbourn used to go there. I used to take Pat dancing in Royston.

My favorite place in Royston was a little open air café with a swimming pool. People would swim while you were eating and music would play. I went there by myself one day and who should I see but Johnny Talbot, an old friend of mine from my mechanics course. He had been assigned to my station and we worked together.

Johnny was at the restaurant with his girlfriend but he invited me to come join them. He was a very nice person, who wouldn't swear or anything, and his girlfriend was very nice. We met quite often in that little restaurant, sometimes going for a walk after dinner and then returning for a cup of coffee. On Sunday mornings we would sometimes go there for a swim. I used to meet Johnny in the canteen when we were on the station.

An enemy aircraft was approaching our field flying very low. The twin radial engines and large 'greenhouse' at the nose marked it as a Junkers 88, Germany's most versatile fighter-bomber. I would say that he was only about one hundred feet above the level of our base. A sight like that would normally inspire me to imitate Roger Bannister, but there was something unusual about that particular JU 88. It had its undercarriage lowered and was ready to land.

Now, when an enemy airplane has his wheels down you don't shoot at him because he is coming in for a landing and may be trying to defect.

The aircraft circled the field several times. Everybody came out to watch it circle and marvel at the novelty of inspecting an enemy fighter-bomber in flight. The JU 88 continued to circle, then touched down and landed at our auxiliary field.

Guys piled into a truck and headed off to the auxiliary airfield to get a good look at the R.A.F.'s newest prize. I stayed in the barracks but Jimmy Henderson, my roommate, did go out there and he described it to me. He said that the pilot and crew came out, surrendered, and were taken to the guardhouse.

They were all very happy to surrender and seemed quite friendly.
Once set up in the guardhouse they were guarded by only two guards. Jimmy had actually spoken to the pilot of the aircraft, who knew some English.

I met a flying officer in Bassingbourn who was the son of the math teacher I had had before my expulsion from school at the beginning of grade ten. We were pretty good friends. One day he asked me to lend him thirty shillings.

I was only making about four shillings a week, and his flying pay was probably more than that. But I scraped together twenty-five shillings and borrowed another five to make up the thirty shillings which my friend wanted to borrow. He was posted before he had paid me back.

"What are we going to do?" I asked my wife one day, "We can't afford to replace all of that lost kit on what I'm making."

I had lost much of my issued kit. I had left it lying about and what had not been stolen was misplaced. A kit muster was scheduled for the near future and I would have to pay for such things as the pack sack which I would never see again.

She was worried but tried to reassure me. "Let's just hope that something happens," she sighed.

I was resting on my cot that night, unable to sleep. How could I pay for my lost kit? Worrying about my dismal financial situation, as usual, I tossed and turned. Exhaustion finally overcame my worry and I drifted into a restless sleep.

It must have been about one o'clock in the morning that I was stirred by a distant buzzing sound. As I shook off the cobwebs I recognized the horrible whine of a German JU88 fighter-bomber. It made a couple of low passes while I listened anxiously, expecting the worst. To my relief, the sound grew fainter and finally disappeared.

I was trying to settle back into sleep when the noise returned suddenly, at increased volume. The noise grew louder and louder until it reach a screaming crescendo. The ceiling boards gave way and a bomb fell right into the room. A flash of light inundated the room and my eardrums nearly burst from the concussion of hundreds of pounds of exploding cordite. My cot was tossed into the air like a whiplashed toy. I landed with a thump and a curse, surrounded by flying lead and shrapnel. The room was full of smoke and the man who had been sleeping in the next cot was dead.

The blast had shattered my window. I sprang through it and landed in a large bomb crater. I covered my head with my arms. The stench of burned gunpowder offended my senses.

Three other men had also taken refuge in the crater. They told me that I had guts, but I don't really know why they would have said that. I guess because I had dived out the window.

I lay there in my pajamas. I could hear the roar coming around again and when I peeked above the rim of the crater I saw the black form of a twin-engine fighter, straight ahead and coming from the north. Flames spat from the nose of this black airplane and flashes like little bomb bursts erupted on all sides of me as the machine guns chewed up the ground. There were rows and rows of puffs on the ground where the machine gun bullets were hitting.

I was afraid. I cautiously looked up from my refuge then quickly pressed my face back against the cool soil. After the fighter had made a few circles, I could hear the machine gun fire coming from the other side of the field. The German pilot was intent on strafing the entire field, firing at any target which might present itself. The noise became quieter and the intruder, his orgy satisfied, flew back whence he had come.

Gradually, I realized that the attack was over. I stood up and tried to stop trembling. The wailing sound of an air raid siren was crying in the night and searchlights were piercing the darkness of the night sky. Those of us who had dived into the bomb crater checked each other to make sure they were unhurt.

People were creeping out from everywhere. It was funny, watching them crawl out of their hiding places like bugs coming out after dark. After about five minutes there was life and activity in a place that had seemed empty. People had appeared out of nowhere.

The front of the barracks was badly damaged and all of the windows were broken, possibly blown out from the inside. The place was just full of smoke and my bed was destroyed. When I checked the room later I found a large bomb crater in the floor.

I think his name was Reggie, the fellow who was killed in my room. I hadn't known that he was dead, I found out after the attack.

Across the road from us was another barracks, also mauled by the fighter. A body was hanging across a window terrace. Someone had put a coat over him, but I knew that he was dead. One of my companions told me that the dead man was Johnny Talbot.

"Are you okay, Lou?" somebody asked. People were flocking in from all over the place and everyone seemed to care about me.

I was thankful to be alive, but I was horrified at the sight of poor Johnny. I could see the body sticking out there. I could see his head. "I'm kind of shook up," I said to no one in particular.

I was so upset. I had been looking forward to going to the Royston swimming pool with Johnny and his girlfriend, looking forward to being friends together. Now this.

I never saw Johnny's girlfriend afterwards. I don't know what happened to her.

I saw my wife the next morning. "Well," she said, "now you won't have to pay for your lost equipment."

A few days later, on May 27, 1940[8], I pulled guard duty beside the ammunition dump. I was standing around, feeling bored, when I heard the oncoming sound of a twin engine aircraft. Nerves were still on edge from the recent air raid and some of my companions started heading for the air raid shelter.

"It's alright," I called to them. Although the sky was heavy overcast and visibility was low, preventing a clear visual identification, I recognized the drone of a British Whitley bomber and saw its faint outline. "It's only a Whitley!"

My colleagues hesitated for a moment. Then the bombs began to fall. They obviously missed the ammunition dump or I wouldn't be telling this story.

"Sure, it's a Whitley," my friends chorused when I joined them in the shelter.

"I tell you, that was a Whitley," I insisted, but they remained unconvinced.

About forty years later, I was at an Air Force reunion with Jack Dixon, an old friend of mine. Jack introduced me to his companion who, he said, had been a radio operator on a Whitley crew during the war.

"Don't tell me about Whitleys," I laughed, "I was bombed by a Whitley at Bassingbourn!"

Jack's friend smiled sheepishly. "I know about that." He replied, "That was my airplane. We thought we were over Cologne."

The Whitley[9] was from 10 Squadron and the pilot's name was Warren. As they headed east, they ran into a severe electrical storm and lost their bearings. They searched through cloud cover until they saw what they thought was the Rhine river and dropped their bombs on the nearby airfield.

Warren must have felt sick when he eventually realized that they had spotted the Thames estuary and had dropped their bombs on the runway at Bassingbourn. He was demoted and known thereafter as 'Baron Von Warren'. Two Spitfires flew over the Whitley's base at Dishforth and dropped Iron Crosses.

I just wish I could tell that to those guys who laughed at me fifty years ago!

---

8 *The date was provided by Mr. Emmerson Lavender in an excerpt to a book "The Evaders" he was in the process of writing for publication by McGraw Hill and in which he features the author's father. His source of information was a book by Max Hastings entitled "Bomber Command".*

9 *Ibid.*

Actually, I have always been very proud of my skill at aircraft recognition. I consistently scored 100% on all of my aircraft recognition tests. I remember one sunny afternoon, I was waxing the broad wing of a Wellington. To help pass the time, I showed off my recognition skills to my co-workers. The visibility was good and I had no shortage of subjects.

"See that one over there," I pointed with my polishing rag, "that one's a Spitfire." I looked around and saw a Hurricane, which I pointed out, then a Wellington.

Directly overhead was an unusual aircraft. "Now, you see that one right above us," I lectured, "That's a Dornier. You can tell by the twin engines and the long, narrow fuselage... A Dornier!!" I took to my heels after my friends, who had already gone, as the bombs began to fall.

On August 13, 1940[10], I was preparing F/O Lanbart's aircraft for a training flight. With a bit of a smile on his face, he strode up to where I was waxing the plane and said, "Greenburgh, there's something I want to talk to you about as soon as I get back from my next flight. I have some news for you."

"Yes Sir!" I replied. My heart began to race as I thought of the possible types of news he might have. Maybe I was being recommended for aircrew! In fact, the more I thought about it, the more certain I was that F/O Lanbart would be recommending me for aircrew. What else could it be?

The port engine ignited with the rough pop-popping which characterized piston engines, then the starboard propeller also began to spin. Turning off the magneto switch under each cowling, I remembered how Lanbart had once told me, "It's very gratifying for me to have you as my mechanic because you always turn off the magnetos. A lot of mechanics don't do that."

I pulled away the wheel chocks and stepped back from the aircraft.
I waved as the plane began to move forward and through the glass canopy I could see the head of the student who would actually do the flying.

As I watched the Wellington move down the runway, I imagined myself as an air gunner and wondered if that was really what Lanbart wanted to tell me about. I felt thankful that Lanbart was my pilot and could visualize those sergeant stripes on my sleeve.

The plane was taking its time lifting off, but slowly it began to rise. Too slowly. The left wing lifted slightly and the right wing dropped. The plane veered to the right and disappeared in a fireball as it collided with a parked aircraft.

I froze in horror as the ambulance and fire trucks raced towards the inferno. I couldn't bear to watch them poking through those blazing metal

[10] *"Canadians in the Royal Air Force", op. cit., page 159.*

skeletons as they extinguished the flames and searched for bodies. With my head turned so I couldn't see the carnage, I ran into the nearby canteen and stayed there as long as I could. I didn't want to come out.

I still wonder what Lanbart wanted to tell me.

Like anyone else in those days, I took the occasional trip into London when I had some leave. The blitz was on and the city was scarred by enemy bombs.

I watched many air battles. One took place on September 7, 1940. A Spitfire was chasing a Dornier D 17 and I watched as pieces flew off of the enemy aircraft and the crew bailed out. Trailing clouds of smoke, it plummeted right into the Victoria Train Station.

The sergeant I was with made a sympathetic comment about the crew of the destroyed aircraft and said, "It's about time they stopped this war."

"I don't feel sorry for them!" I growled as the parachutes drifted down, "What were they doing over London?! I only feel sorry for the people that they bombed."

I was in a movie theatre a few days later and saw that air battle replayed in the news reels.

I didn't know it then, but the target that Dornier had bombed was Buckingham Palace[11]. The bombs had missed, however, and no damage was done. The Spitfire's pilot was a Canadian named Keith 'Skeets' Ogilvie. He was later shot down, captured by the Germans, and sent to Stalag Luft III. He participated in the famous 'great escape' but was recaptured. Of the 76 airmen who made it through that tunnel, 73 were recaptured. Fifty of those were then murdered by the Gestapo on orders from Hitler[12].

Speaking of attacks on London, everyone was issued with a gas mask to wear in the event of a chemical warfare attack. I noticed that one of my buddies was out with a young lady who had neglected to bring hers.

When I saw him later, I asked, "Tell me; if there had been a gas attack, would you have given her your mask?"

He looked at me as though I were out of my mind, and blurted out, "After carrying the damn thing around for months, you expect me to give it away? Do you think I'm crazy?"

---

[11] *Ward, Stephen. "Battle of Britain air veterans gather to fete 50th anniversary," Winnipeg Free Press, Saturday, Sept. 15, 1990.*

[12] *The details of the 'Great Escape' were also published in the above mentioned Stirling Association newsletter.*

The big threat back then was that Hitler might launch an invasion across the channel. Whether or not he could have or would have has been much debated since. I think he would have found England a hard nut to crack.

Churchill wasn't bluffing when he said, "We shall fight on the beaches, we shall fight on the landing grounds, we shall fight in the fields and streets and in the hills... We shall never surrender." I remember discussing it with one lady who was indignant at the thought of Britain being over-run. "In my barn," she said, "I've got a big bucket of pepper. If one of those Germans tries to come inside, I'll let him have it right in his face!"

In spite of all the crashes I had seen, stories I had heard, and comrades I had lost, I kept trying to get assigned to aircrew. I didn't want to be a floor scrubber, a cleaner-upper, all my life, but I wasn't getting anywhere. The first time I applied for the air gunners' course, I was turned down because of that knife I had 'stolen' from stores. The base commander didn't want a sergeant who had a record like that.

I had passed my interview and everything else so I was really disappointed when I got a letter saying that I was being held back because of that trivial incident. Just think, if I hadn't borrowed a knife and fork I might have spent the war as an air gunner (if I survived). I consoled myself that at least I was safer in my present job and I didn't really want to risk my life. But I very badly wanted to be a sergeant.

I was talking with my corporal one day as I scrubbed an engine cowling, and I told him how frustrated I was that I couldn't get onto aircrew.

He laughed at me. "Well, why don't you try a pilot's course?" he asked me sarcastically, "You tried everything else."

The funny part of it was, a selection board for pilot were on the base and were interviewing all of the potential candidates (most of whom were men with high education, university degrees and all that) so I said to my corporal, "You know, maybe I should try for pilot."

He burst out laughing. "Go ahead!"

I saw the commanding officer, who recommended me for the selection board. No one would believe that I was actually going before the selection board.

The same corporal said, "Don't be ridiculous! This must be some kind of a joke. Clean that other cowling over there. Here's the brush."

The board was being held in Cardington. On the day of the board, I walked past the R101's huge hanger and remembered those early days when I had dreamed of becoming a mechanic. I entered a classroom with dozens of other pilot candidates. We were each handed a written examination to complete before our interviews.

My heart sank. I looked at the exam questions, many of which required knowledge of higher mathematics, and knew that my situation was hopeless. I didn't even try to answer the questions.

Finally, the allotted time was up. I handed in a blank sheet.

One by one, each candidate was called out of the room. It was eventually my turn. I went down the hall to an office in which was seated a panel of Air Force Officers.

The senior officer, an air commodore, read the paper in front of him with a quizzical expression on his face. He looked up and asked, "It says here that you didn't complete the entrance exam and handed in a blank paper. Why was that?"

"I couldn't do it, sir." I replied. "I don't know anything about math. Most of those guys have university degrees. I've only got a grade nine education."

The officer lowered his eyes and said, "That's all, Greenburgh."

"Sir," I said, "I guess I won't be selected, will I?"

The officer looked at me again. His face was impassive, but sympathy was showing in his eyes. "I said that is all."

"I know I wasn't selected because I couldn't pass that test. I don't have much education and I don't know much about math and stuff but I'm willing to make up for that with hard work and enthusiasm. You know, I came all the way from Canada in the hope that I might be a pilot."

The officer studied me thoughtfully and rubbed his chin.
"Why do you want to be a pilot?"

"Well, sir," I began, "you're a pilot. You know what it's like. All my life I've been a nobody. People have pushed me around and stepped on me. This would be a chance to really make something of myself."

The smirks on the faces of some board members told me that I had made a fool of myself. I expected them to start laughing as soon as I left the room.

The senior officer exchanged glances with the other board members. Their expressions ranged from guarded sympathy to open amusement. He studied me again with an amused twinkle in his eye. "Come back in two minutes, Greenburgh."

When I reentered the room, a flight lieutenant who had been amused before was now scowling. The air commodore was sitting upright with a smile on his face. "I can't tell you the board's decision officially," he stated, "but you are being slated for a medical examination."

Chapter 5: The Pilots' Course

The destroyer escorts maneuvered in a graceful ballet as white clouds of mist danced across their bows. From the deck of a rusty freighter, I watched them leave their patrol sectors to rendezvous astern of our convoy. Now they were in line abreast formation and fountains of white foam were erupting astern of each ship.

I looked at the fellow leaning on the rail beside me and commented, "If I saw a torpedo coming, I'd jump overboard so fast..."

"I'd laugh like hell if it missed!"

There had been a submarine alert and those of us who wanted to survive the voyage were waiting on deck for either the 'all clear' or a violent explosion. The escort ships broke off their attack and I heard someone yell, "They got the bugger!"

We were enroute to Moncton, New Brunswick, from where we would travel to Ponca City, Oklahoma, for pilot training with the U.S. Army Air Corps. After we had been at sea about a week, a fellow I didn't know asked me to direct him to the men's room.

My accommodations were pretty cramped. I shared a 'cabin' with several other passengers. We each had enough room to sling a hammock, and that was it. I had one chair I could sit on when the hammock had been rolled up for the day. That hammock space was my bedroom, dining room, and living room. I spent my spare time scrubbing decks and throwing snowballs. And yet, we had a lot of fun on that freighter, my friends and I. It was one of the biggest adventures I'd had.

The waves were mountainous, buffeting the ship from all directions. I watched the bow plunge downward to be obliterated in a white, foamy spray. The ship would wallow for a moment, then the bow would struggle to the surface as if the ship were gasping for breath. This was the North Atlantic in January, 1942. I watched another freighter disappear behind the waves. Was it still there, I wondered for a moment, or had its passengers and crew begun the cold and final voyage to the bottom? Were they the victim of a torpedo, of heavy icing, or had the sheer force of the wind and waves proved too much for the vessel's weary seams. Then I watched it reappear as if by magic to continue its struggle against the elements with one minor victory won and an infinity more needed.

There were some recreational activities onboard. I remember one boxing match where the loser was getting the hell beaten out of him. There was blood pouring from his battered nose and he could hardly stand. He wanted to quit.

One fellow from the same town called out to him, "Don't quit now, we're enjoying this. Keep it up!" He said he should keep fighting for the honor of their home town. "Keep it up," he repeated, "we're really enjoying this." There was also a fellow who would dress in ladies' clothing.

Most of my pilot training to date had taken place on the sea. We had just come from a course in marine navigation, where we had to navigate small training ships (minesweepers, maybe). We had to identify headlands, plot fixes, calculate speeds made good, that sort of thing. There was always an instructor onboard to make sure we didn't run aground or collide with anyone, but we were basically running the ships ourselves. We were learning skills we would have to apply a heck of a lot faster once we were flying.

That course had been held at a summer resort on the southwest coast of England, where we were billeted in the Grand Hotel. That was one of the most posh hotels in England, where all the millionaires would stay.

The ground school part of that introductory course was pretty stiff. It was like studying a university degree. We had to learn airmanship, meteorology, and Air Traffic Control. We took turns in the tower so that we would understand what was going on when we were being controlled.

I was sitting in the mess taking a break from my studies when I heard President Roosevelt’s cultured voice on the radio. "Yesterday, December 7, 1941," he began, and continued on to announce that the Japanese had launched an unprovoked attack on the United States naval base at Pearl Harbor. The Americans had come into World War II.

A fellow next to me remarked, "That's it. The 'States is finished, now."

I thought about America's huge industrial complex, modern technology, and natural resources. "No." I replied, "We've just won the war."

Going back even further, there were certain tests I had to pass before I could even get on the course. They tested you upside down, right side up, your reflexes... You had to be absolutely physically fit.

After passing those tests, I was sent to ACRC in London where I lived in a posh hotel which had been requisitioned for aircrew trainees. While I was awaiting passage to Canada, I stayed with some people in Eaton Park, Manchester. It was about that time that my wife told me she was pregnant.

The ship finally arrived at New Brunswick. We then went on to Oklahoma, where I joined number 6 British Flying Training School and was assigned an instructor. I nearly had a fit! He was a German fellow named Mr. Hans Myer. I needn't have worried, though. He proved to be a heck of a nice guy and we got along fine.

'No more freights'. En route to Ponca City, Oklahoma.

Our flying training began with Early Flight Training School on Stearmans. Mr. Myers took me for my first familiarization flight in one on March 14, 1942. He rolled the aircraft into inverted flight and crossed the controls into an inverted sideslip. With the aircraft in that unwieldy attitude, he let go of the controls and said, "Okay, you take it now!"

I loved those old biplanes and was thrilled to put one through its paces. My favorite maneuver was the Immelmann, in which I would begin a loop but switch to a snap roll at the top. The instructors didn't make things easy for us. As a matter of fact, they took pains to make things difficult and the airplane's designers had helped them. For example, the under carriage wheels were pretty close together for an aircraft of that type. If you didn't come in just right, if one wing drooped slightly, the narrow undercarriage would cause the plane to ground loop. I really believe that was done on purpose so they could tell if a guy's judgement was less than perfect.

Although I excelled in flying, I had a horrible time with the ground school part of my training. Jimmy Smith, one of the guys on my course, was already a private pilot. I respected his opinion on flying matters and was very concerned one day when he said to me, "Lou, you'd better prepare yourself in case you don't pass the course. I'm just telling you this as a friend, but I don't think you're going to make it."

I couldn't sleep for weeks. Guys were washing out right and left. The fellow in the bunk next to mine was washed out. I had a wife and kids. If I washed out, what would I do? Spend the rest of my life as a private?

A few weeks into the course, Jimmy Smith came to me almost in tears. He had been washed out.

It was a sad thing. So many people who had their hopes of getting pilots' wings and never did.

One of the guys on my course, named 'Haley,' fell in love with a young American girl and decided not to go back to England. He said that he planned to desert from the Air Force and marry her, and that his parents were very upset about it. He used to come to me to discuss his problems with his girlfriend.

Lou Greenburgh in front of a Stearman.

Starting the engine.

We had a visit from a wing commander who would give the odd fellow a test to see how his training was. He gave us a lecture. "Now a lot of you fellows are going around telling the American people here how much you suffered in England and how much you're deprived." he said. "And when they invite you over to their place, I've heard that people sit in the corner like a dog begging for food and having people feel sorry for them. Well, that's a lot of nonsense."

We also had a visit from Wing Commander Johnny Kent, D.F.C. & Bar, A.F.C., V.C. (Polish), who was inspecting the training centres. I'd heard of him because he was famous as a Battle of Britain fighter ace.

It just so happened that Johnny Kent was also from Winnipeg. Like me and about two thousand other Canadians, he had made his own way over to England and joined the R.A.F. before the war. Johnny had gone over in 1935, two years before I did. I don't suppose he saw that many guys from Winnipeg down in Oklahoma, so he sat with me in the mess a few times and we had some drinks together.

Johnny had grown up in the suburb of East Kildonan[13], which was just across the Red River from where I had been living. He told me about his flying career and I was really impressed. Only two years older than me and already he was a Wing Commander! He had flown experimental aircraft, reconnaissance Spitfires, and had commanded fighter squadrons during the Battle of Britain. He was the only Canadian in the R.A.F., or the R.C.A.F., to win the Polish V.C. (Virtuti Militari)[14].

My meeting with Wing Commander Kent inspired me to try and become the sort of pilot that he was.

---

[13] *Allison, Les, "Canadians in the Royal Air Force•, op. cit., page 51.*

[14] *Ibid., page 50.*

Student pilots. Note the worried expression on Lou's face.

Old Hans Myer hadn't spoken to me for a couple of days. He just went "Hmm... hmmm," as he scribbled notes about me on his clip board. "What the heck is he writing about me?" I wondered. "Is my flying bad? Why doesn't he say so. If my flying's good, why doesn't he say so?"

A lot of fellows had gone solo by April 1, 1942, and I was a little worried because I hadn't soloed yet. Mr. Myer climbed into the plane with me and told me to fly to the auxiliary field. When we arrived, he said "Now, I want you to make a good landing."

It occurred to me that the auxiliary airfield was where all of the students made their first solos. They didn't let us do it from the ordinary airfield. I guess that was in case we might crash into another airplane, cause some damage or something like that.

I did my best to make a good landing but I was really nervous because I thought he was going to fail me. Just before we came in he said, "Now let's see you, for a change, make a good landing."

It was to be a glider type approach. I was so excited that I over controlled and my front wheels hit first. They bounced up and the nose went down and the wheels hit again and bounced up once more. I almost ground-looped.

I could hear the instructor's voice through the tube. "I've had enough! This finishes you! That's it." He undid his safety belt, got up, and stepped out of the airplane.

I didn't know what to say or do. "I'm sorry, Mr. Myer." I said as I unhooked my safety belt. I started to get out of the airplane.

"Get back in that airplane again!" he shouted. "Come on, get out of my sight! Take off, away you go!"

Boy! I don't think I even fastened my belt. I just opened the throttle. The slipstream knocked my instructor down, but he didn't mind. I was so glad to be in the air by myself that I could hardly believe it.

That was one of the greatest moments of my life.

I circled around twice and made a very good landing, a perfect landing. Myers signaled to me and shouted, "Go on again, go around again!"

I went around again. Myers was still waving his arm.

I did some steep turns then circled around, throttled back, and made the most perfect three point landing you've ever seen on a Stearman.

Mr. Myers climbed back in. "I'm proud of you, boy." He said.

When we were airborne again, he said, "Well, it's all in your hands from now on. You'll be flying the thing. But just because you made a good landing, don't be cocky about it."

My training continued with more advanced subjects. The flying became more difficult and more exhilarating. We went into complex maneuvers such as loops, slow rolls, stall turns, and Immelmanns, then coordination exercises with S & 8 turns, cross country flying, chandelles, lazy 8s and night flying.

We started doing 'forced landings'. You know what that was? You're just taking off and the instructor cuts the throttle.

I had a little trouble with night flying and was worried because the time came when I was the only one left in my class who had not yet done a night solo. I was very disturbed one evening when Mr. Myer said, "Greenburgh, we'll have to delay your going solo. The weather is closing in."

I thought that he was just making excuses, that he didn't think I was ready to fly solo at night. Was I going to be washed out as a pilot?

"Well, I'm a little worried, sir." I said, "But I know I can do it."

Mr. Myer thought a moment, then pointed to the small Stearman and said, "Hop in there! Make one quick circuit and land."

Boy, did I hop in there! I almost forgot to tighten my seat belt in my excitement. I opened the throttle way up and eased back on the stick.

There were no advanced instruments, just turn and bank indicators, an airspeed indicator, that sort of thing. I didn't even have a radio.

I got up to three hundred feet and entered my landing circuit. Raindrops began to splatter against the windshield of my open cockpit machine.

The rain got worse and worse. I couldn't see the ground. I was flying blind on my first night flying solo.

I decided that the only thing to do was climb up to three or four thousand feet and bail out. "Oh my God!" I thought, "If I do that, I'll be washed out for sure."

Could I do a circuit blind? I didn't know if I was right side up or upside down. A pencil was dangling by a string, one end of which was secured to the instrument panel. The pencil was hanging horizontally and I didn't know which way to turn the airplane.

I tried to 'feel for the ground'. Was I worried! I flew around for about three or four minutes then thought, "To heck with it, I'll bail out, and to heck with the pilots' course. Alright, so I failed, so I won't be a pilot."

Just as I decided to bail out, I saw a light shining from below through a hole in the cloud. I circled around, watching the light. I didn't want to lose it. I didn't want to lose the ground.

I fell so fast... The nose was being dragged down and the wing wires were vibrating like violin strings. I glanced at the airspeed indicator and was shocked to see that my little Stearman was doing over a hundred and eighty. I lost the light.

I tried to steer back again, but it was too late. The plane began to spin. I gave opposite rudder but we had no altitude. Somehow, I leveled out. The wheels struck the ground hard, then the engine hit. The aircraft pitched forward and flipped onto its back in a foreword roll. I was left hanging upside down in my harness.

I could hear the distant roar of engines as aircraft were taxied to shelter. The storm got bigger and the rain was falling heavily.

An ambulance appeared. I heard a shout, "There it is!" followed by footsteps squishing on the soggy ground and rustling in the high grass.

Mr. Myer reached me first. "Oh my God!" he exclaimed, "Are you all right, Lou?"

"Yeah, I'm alright." I replied. The harness was digging into my shoulders and blood was rushing to my head. I felt like a monkey hanging by its tail.

"I guess this finishes me as a pilot." I sighed, dejectedly. "Will I be washed out, now?"

He was incredulous. "You still want to fly?"

"Do I ever!"

He shook his head. "After this, I'd think you'd want to be washed out. You must be the world's greatest masochist."

The Liberator had just come out during this phase of my training. It wasn't really a bomber yet; the weapons systems weren't finished. One landed at our field. I looked at it and it seemed to be a massive thing, especially since I was just flying little Stearmans.

One guy said, "That's something, flying one of those, eh?"

I added, "Boy, I bet that guy must feel pretty good!" I thought that I would never arise to anything like that.

Stearman B227 after Lou's first night solo.

Another view of B227 after the crash. The aircraft did fly again and, surprisingly, was later destroyed in a similar accident during which the pilot received a dislocated hip.

Lou Greenburgh relaxing with friends from his course.

I finally got the required fifty hours on Stearmans. I had my last flight with Mr. Myers on June 10, 1942. I was sorry to hear, from pilots taking a later course, that Mr. Myers was killed in a plane crash.

An assessing officer took me up for a flight. My log book was stamped with a box containing the words 'ASSESSMENT OF FLYING ABILITY' beside which the inspecting officer wrote 'Average'. Underneath, where it said 'the following points in Flying or Airmanship should be watched,' the officer stated that I lacked confidence and was tense under pressure.

The native community in that area was very hospitable. They invited us to several 'pow wows' where they would put on their ceremonial dress and beat the drums and stuff. Some of the Indians invited me back to their homes but I didn't take them up on their offer.

I was ready to take some leave before starting my more advanced training. I decided to visit my family back in Winnipeg.

A lot of the British boys wanted to see some of the 'States and they were hitchhiking all over the place. It wasn't hard to get a ride because the Americans had just come into the war and were very interested in people wearing uniforms. I would just step out in the street, wave, and people would pick me up. "What kind of uniform is that?" they would ask.

(Above) BT13As lined up beside the runway. (Below) The cockpit of a BT13A.

I would proudly reply that I was a British cadet with the Royal Air Force. Most of the people were pretty upset over the Japanese attack, which had happened only three or four months before, and were glad to help out anyone who had actually taken part in the war.

When I arrived in Minneapolis I found a bunk and a meal at a Gospel mission. It reminded me of my hobo days. The next morning, I hitchhiked the rest of the way to Winnipeg.

I knocked on the door and my little brother answered. He hadn't seen me for years but he knew who I was. "Hey, Ma," he called out, "Lou's here!"

I heard my mother reply, "Lou who?" She came to the door and remarked, "Oh, for God's sake!"

She asked me how I was, then mentioned a boy down the street who had joined the Air Force. "You know," she said, "he always has part of his paycheck sent home to his parents."

"Ma," I said, "he's in the Canadian Air Force. The R.A.F. don't get paid anywhere nearly as well as the Canadians."

I stayed about a week, visited some old friends, then hitch-hiked back to the 'States.

I thoroughly enjoyed the later stages of my training. After EFTS I did Senior Flight Training School on Vultee BT-13A's, which looked something like a dive bomber, and then on Yales, which were an advanced version of the Harvard trainer.

The first time I looked in the cockpit of a Vultee, I was intimidated by all of the instruments. There were instruments for the hydraulics, instruments for the engine, all kinds of instruments. My instructor took me up for a familiarization flight and before long I was able to keep track of which dial was for what and I was able to relax a bit. I did a few maneuvers, came around the circuit and made a good landing. The whole conversion took about three hours. As we rolled to a stop after the fifth flight, the instructor got out of the plane. "Okay," he said, "off you go by yourself. Away you go."

I started to realize that there was one thing I could do well. I could fly.

I remember how my instructors used to say "When you go on ops, you'll have to know this and you'll have to know that." The instructors had never been on any operations. I wish I'd known then what I know now. Ops was nothing like they said it would be. I thought they knew about ops, but they didn't.

A fellow named Mugarage was coming in for a landing in a Yale. He had forgotten to lower his landing gear and the tower was trying to warn him. They were calling him on the radio, telling him that his wheels were up. There was also a warning horn in the aircraft which always went off if you throttled back with your landing gear up.

"I can't hear you with this horn going off." was his reply. He did eventually lower his wheels.

I could book an aircraft for a training flight and fly all over the southern states.

Wing Commander Ball came to the unit to inspect us. He wanted to check my precautionary landings, which was basically to test my ability to land in a short space. On July 15, 1942, we took off in our AT 6. We had not been airborne long when he said, "I want you to make a precautionary landing." He pointed to the small field we used for precautionary landings and said, "Land there."

There was a fence across the field. The idea was to land on the far side of the fence, as close to it as possible. I began the landing circuit and monitored our descent in relation to that fence.

There was a point in our 'downwind leg' when the fence would be behind me and to the right, out of my field of vision. As we turned onto our crosswind leg, the fence came back into view and I judged us to be at the correct altitude in relation to the circuit. When the fence was almost at right angles to our track I turned onto the final approach and lined up our glide path to cross the fence. Then I reduced power to steepen our descent.

When an aircraft is going to fly above an object on the ground, that object will appear to creep 'down' the canopy and gradually disappear under the nose. When an aircraft is going to land ahead of an object, that object will appear to creep 'up' the canopy, until it finally meets the horizon. That fence was staying in one spot.

I watched that fence get closer and closer and I hoped that Wing Commander Ball wouldn't notice how nervous I was. I wanted to open the throttle to give us some more clearance, but then Ball would know that I had misjudged my descent.

We were almost on top of the fence when I pulled back on the stick to reduce our glide angle. The fence passed slowly beneath us, missing us by a matter of inches. Then I pushed the stick forward to prevent us from stalling and made my landing.

The plane rolled to a stop. "You came pretty close to that fence." commented my evaluator.

"Yeah," I replied, trying to sound natural, "I planned it pretty good, didn't I?"

"Boy," he continued, "you could land anywhere in an emergency!" We then took off again and flew back to the base. When we had landed, Wing Commander Ball stepped out of the aircraft without saying a word.

I also logged training on the Link Trainer, which was used to simulate emergency situations and give practice in procedures which would be dangerous or difficult to teach in real aircraft. Nowadays, I suppose, there are kids' video games more sophisticated than the Link Trainer, which was mainly mechanical, but at the time it was the best thing we had to simulate flying. It wasn't very big and looked a lot like some of the kiddie rides one can see in shopping malls, where you put in a coin for each ride. Near the end of my initial training, I received word from my wife that I was the father of a baby girl. We named her Paulina, after my friend Paul, but we always called her 'Anna'.

I had my last flight of British Flying Training School on September 18, 1942. My final assessment read: 'Average', followed by ‘Tense in night flying’.

I graduated on Wednesday, September 23, 1942. There were hundreds of us formed up on the parade square. One by one we were called to the dais so the Mayor of Ponca City could pin our wings on.

During the course, I'd had second thoughts. I had thought that to be a pilot you just had to be able to fly and to do a little bit of book work. You'd be surprised at the books we had to learn and the stuff we had to go through. Holy smoke! The flying part was the easiest part of all. But it all paid for itself when I was in the lineup.

I marched up to the dais. The Mayor congratulated me and pinned the silver wings of the United States Army Air Corps onto my chest. It was the proudest moment of my life.

The Mayor also presented me with a solid silver ring. On the front of the ring, outlined in black onyx, was the emblem of the United States Army Air Corps. The emblem was also embossed on the sides of the ring. I was to wear that ring throughout all of my subsequent adventures.

Our graduation dinner was held at the Jens-Marie Hotel. I still have my invitation. Tim Wroe, a buddy of mine, wrote his home address on the back of it and we said we would write to each other. We had intended to at the time, but we never did.

Pilot Cadet Lou Greenburgh flying BT 13As number B258 (above) and B262.

Nor did Haley ever desert. He graduated along with the rest of us. Years later, when I was flying on operations, I saw a picture of him and his girlfriend in the Sunday 'News of the World'. There was quite a story about him coming back to England. He was blind. The picture showed him wearing his pilots' wings. I think he started having trouble with his eyes just after he graduated. Who knows? It might even have been self-inflicted.

We were given a questionnaire about what type of aircraft we would prefer to fly, fighters, bombers or whatever. I didn't care what I flew as long as I flew. I figured they'd put me where they wanted to anyway and I don't think I even sent back my reply. I suppose bombers or transport would have been the most to my liking because I would be able to fly a lot of different airplanes, big ones with a crew. If I got fighters, it would likely be Hurricanes or Spitfires, not much else. Flying an AT-6 was like flying a small fighter.

I went to Chicago for three weeks, where part of the Steven's Hotel, the largest in the world at that time, was given over to the American troops. I had a wonderful time in Chicago, showing off my brand new sergeant stripes and strutting down Michigan Avenue like I owned the place. I think I walked down the street with my arm first, so everyone could see my stripes.

From there we went to Toronto. I received a 'phone call in the sergeants' mess and was stunned when the voice on the other end of the line said, "Mr.

Greenburgh, you're going to be turning in your kit. Go get all of your sergeant uniforms."

My heart sank. Someone must have discovered that I'd cribbed on the exams, I thought, and my precious wings were being taken away as a result. Under my watch band I had hidden thin strips of paper with some of the answers written on them. I had also paid the guy beside me twenty dollars to feed me answers. Mind you, such misdemeanors were condoned by my ground school instructor, who turned a blind eye. He once said to us, "Because of our high success rate, it has been insinuated that we are half encouraging cribbing. That's not true. We encourage it whole-heartedly!"

I was given the address of the supply building to report at. I bundled up all of my sergeant uniforms and reported to an address on Young Street.

I was a bit confused because all of the signs indicated an officers' supply depot. I guessed that they would be fitting me for civilian clothes.

I introduced myself to the desk clerk. He checked his list of names and said, "Oh yes, Pilot Officer Greenburgh."

"Yeasss..." I replied, puffing out my chest and trying to contain my surprise. I was an officer!

Why they chose me for a commission I'll never know. Out of the thirty five graduates in my class, there were only four of us picked and the others all had university degrees. I think that it must have been on Wing Commander Ball's recommendation because of that landing I'd made with him.

Dressed in my new uniform, it wasn't long before I experienced my first salute. On the other side of the street was a grizzled old soldier with lots of ribbons on his chest. I crossed over to his side and marched close to him with the muscles in my right arm a bit tense, ready to return the salute which I expected to be forthcoming.

The soldier raised his arm as if he were about to salute, then scratched his nose instead. My hand was already moving before I realized that I wasn't getting a salute. The old timer then pretended that he hadn't noticed me before. Coming to attention, he assumed the air of a general receiving a march past and acknowledged my salute with a curt nod of his head.

Some of us who had been commissioned were posted to Maxwell Field, in Montgomery, Alabama, where we took an instructors' course. With the United States' entry into the war, there was a great demand for flying instructors.

I was taking care of some urgent business in the men's room on my second day at Maxwell Field. As I was so engaged, another fellow in the uniform of a newly commissioned R.A.F. pilot entered the room and began using the facilities next to me.

"You know," he said to me, "there is a little old lady in my village who asked me to keep a look out for her grandson while I'm in the 'States. She wants him to contact her. I've been searching everywhere for him. His name is Bobby Stuart. Have you seen him?"

"Oh come on!" I guffawed. "You'll never find him. How are you going to find a 'Bobby Stuart' in a place as big as the United States?"

There was a rustling noise in one of the stalls and the toilet flushed. A fellow opened the door and stepped out. "I'm Bobby Stuart." he said. "You say my grandmother asked you to look for me?"

After I had completed the instructors' course, I was sent to Turner's Field in Georgia where I began instructing on Yales and Vultees.

A brief came through from Air Force Headquarters requesting that volunteers return to England and go on operations. One of the fellows I was with, a guy named Woodward, asked me if I was going to volunteer. I had it pretty good as an instructor so I told him "no".

Woodward told me that the rest of the guys were all going to volunteer. Priestly, another instructor, also encouraged me to apply. I thought about it, then decided that if the others were going on ops, I would go too. I filled out a form and waited for an operational posting.

They'd pulled a fast one on me! When my posting came through, I was the only one going back. Everyone else had backed out. One guy laughed like heck that I was going into combat while the rest of them were living 'the life of Riley' as American flying instructors. He was killed in a mid-air collision the next week.

The next thing I knew, I was travelling through Moncton on my way to England. I boarded the converted luxury liner RMS *Queen Elizabeth* and was impressed by the contrast between my new accommodations and the living conditions I had endured on my earlier passages. I shared a stateroom with one other officer and had stewards to take care of the domestic chores. Distaining the slow moving convoys, liners depended on their speed for safety and so we were across the Atlantic in no time.

Chapter 6: Apprenticeship

I went to Harrogate, where I was initiated back into the R.A.F. From there I was sent on a commando course at Bucklind Camp, where I threw live hand grenades, went camping, and learned how to hide. This course was to make my life easier, and longer, in days to come. Mind you, life wasn't easy during the course and at times it seemed like the course was designed to shorten my life, not prolong it. It was the same course the real commandoes took before commencing activities on the enemy's shore, so you can imagine what was involved in it. The ammunition being fired over our heads as we crawled through dirt and wire was live. So were the hand grenades I had to throw. We'd pull out the pins and launch the 'pineapple'. The ground would shake and a brief roar of flame reminded us that we were not playing with toys. I bet I lobbed those grenades further than I've ever thrown a baseball. The first time I threw one of those grenades I didn't throw it far enough, a fact which caused some concern among the training staff around me.

The training was pretty rigorous, too. We had to climb walls and jump off from the top, climb ropes and crawl under barbed wire (with the aforementioned bullets whizzing over our heads). We did our share of running, too, with a full pack.

We were taught a bit of German, which I already knew, and some French phrases. I remember them telling us to be very careful who we made contact with. If you need help, I was told, never go right up to a house or a village. Lay in hiding for a while, the instructor said, and see who comes and goes.

I took a brief trip to the summer resort at Bournemouth, where I met a very pretty young lady and took her home in a taxi. As the taxi rolled to a stop I told her that I liked her and would meet her again, that sort of thing. She said, "I bet you're married."

I said, "I am." Without saying another word, she opened the car door and ran. I guess it was something I said.

After the commando course, I went to Little Rissington and began training on twin engine aircraft. My instructor on the Air Speed Oxford was Alex Strell, who was also from Winnipeg. I had a bit of trouble with Oxfords, but after a few flights Alex and I were talking to each other again. I then went on to the Operational Training Unit at Chipping Warden for training on Wellingtons.

My course was not due to start for about two weeks. The commanding officer announced that we were in luck. Some Good Samaritan had invited us to attend a luxury resort while we were awaiting our course.

We piled into a 'lorry' and were driven out to this resort. We passed a number of farms and figured this resort must have been some sort of country estate.

We drove up to this 'estate' and I realized that we'd been hoodwinked. It wasn't an estate, it was a farm! We spent the next two weeks toiling in the fields.

The town of Banbury was located near Chipping Warden and it was there that we would go for recreation. I was in a Banbury pub one time when I decided to us the washroom. I was secured in the little stall when two other guys game in and one of them began banging on the door. "Hurry up," he badgered, "I've got to take a crap."

I was embarrassed. I wished they would go away and leave me alone. Through the space under the door I could see their shoes and pant legs and knew that they were soldiers.

The one who was bothering me remarked that he was going to see who was taking so long. His fingers grabbed onto the top of the stall and were soon followed by his face as he chinned himself up. If he had been drunk, as I suspect, he sobered up immediately.

"It's a f--king officer!" he exclaimed, and jumped back to the floor. They both scooted out of the washroom.

I was soon in command of my own Wellington bomber. The Wellington was an awkward thing that resembled a beached whale with wings. But I was the 'skipper' of my own aircraft with my own crew and I thought it was great.

It was quite a jump going from a light aircraft like an Oxford to something as heavy as a Wellington. It wasn't anywhere near as heavy as a Stirling, of course, but it was much heavier than a DC 3. It had heavy turrets and gun equipment and it had powerful Hercules engines. The landing approach speeds were also much higher than on the lighter aircraft I had flown before. There were bound to be accidents.

At least the condition of our equipment had improved. Before 1943, the Operational Training Unit was equipped with worn out, unreliable aircraft deemed unsuitable for operations. Since Wellingtons had been removed from the front lines, OTU was now supplied with aircraft which would otherwise have been retained by operational squadrons. For all I know, a newer aircraft might have prevented the accident which killed my friend Lanbart.

One of our aircraft was lost, I don't know if it was from an accident or from enemy action, and the crew bailed out. Everyone was accounted for except a gunner, who went missing. He turned up three weeks later, tired but with a smile on his face. He had parachuted right onto the grounds of a home for girls!

That reminds me of a lecture we had from M.I. 9 (Military Information 9) which was a branch of the 'secret service' set up to assist aviators who had been shot down over enemy territory. The following story was told to emphasize that part of our training:

'A sergeant pilot in the R.A.F. was shot down close to a French convent. Before the Germans could catch him, a number of nuns appeared and spirited him inside. Walking in the convent garden, the sergeant, dressed in the habit of the Order, found himself beside a beautiful nun. After he had made shy advances, she turned and replied in masculine English, "Don't be a bloody fool. I've been here since Dunkirk[15]."

Wing Commander Bray gave us a lecture on ditching. He had ditched a Wellington in the North Sea and described it now in detail. A chill went through me as he mentioned the temperature of the water and how a man could die of exposure in a matter of minutes. I dreaded the thought of that ever happening to me.

My crew mutinied. It's a rather embarrassing way to begin the story of my operational career, but I'll tell you what happened.

My bomb aimer was the only other Canadian on my crew. He had been a big shot in civilian life, a financial expert or something, and thought he should be the captain of the airplane. I thought that was ridiculous and had no intention of turning my authority over to him. He was really a thorn in my side. We were cruising along one day, with a clear sky and not another aircraft in sight. I decided to have a bit of fun and get even with my insubordinate bomb aimer, who had just stepped inside the tiny cubicle which held the chemical latrine. There was a regulation that the pilot was supposed to notify his crew well in advance of any aerobatics, but I just called out, "Hold on boys, here we go!," and threw the plane into a power dive.

Although it was muffled by the roar of the engines, I can imagine the shriek which must have come from the rear of the aircraft. My victim was thrown out of the latrine and the oozing muck which flowed after him turned the bomber

---

[15] *The story was related by the author's father. It can also be found in: Neave, Airey, Saturday at M.I. 9, Hodder and Stoughton Limited, St. Paul's House, Warwick Lane, London, E.C.$, by Ebenezer Baylis and Son Limited, The Trinity Pres, Worchester and London 1969, pages 66-67.*

F/O Greenburgh (front row, centre) with his original operational crew. Rear row left to right: Wireless Operator Sgt Gordon 'Strommy' Stromberg; Flight Engineer Sgt Les 'Geordie' Weddle; MU Gunner Sgt Fred Carey; Navigator Sgt Pat Butler. Front row left to right: Rear Gunner F/Sgt Colin Drake; Lou; Bomb Aimer Sgt Don Bament.

into a flying cesspool. That wasn't part of my plan. Gagging and retching, we all tended to our business as best we could. The cursing bomb aimer wiped excrement from his face while I made an emergency descent and returned to base as quickly as I could.

I don't think that bomber was ever clean again, and I bet who ever flew it after me must have wrinkled his nose once or twice. My crew refused to fly with me after that. They were all transferred to a different pilot and I was assigned a new crew.

My new wireless operator was a likable fellow named Stromberg. For the life of me I can't remember his real first name because I always called him 'Strommy'. He and I hit it off right from the start and soon became good friends. He said to me, "I'm so happy that you're our skipper." I didn't know it then but I later heard that he'd had some problems with his former skipper and was glad to be off his crew.

My other crew members were Pat Butler (navigator), Don Bament (bomb aimer), Fred Carey (mid upper gunner), and Colin Drake (rear gunner). The flight engineer's name was Les Weddle, but we all called him 'Geordie' because he was

Sgt Les Weddle's photo and medals have been kept by his family (Laura Eggeling).

from Northern England, around Newcastle, and that was a slang name for people from that area.

Except for Fred Carey, they were a bunch of kids who should have been in school.

One thing about Wellingtons; the engines were placed very close to the cockpit. I suffered a slight hearing problem in my left ear which I'm sure was the result of engine noise. I didn't tell anyone because I didn't want to risk being grounded.

Among other things, we did 'synthetic bombing', which was the bombing of dummy targets on our own territory. Some of these targets were near the enemy and we lost some planes due to enemy action. We also did fighter affiliation, where we maneuvered with our own fighters and fired at them with cameras instead of guns.

My last flight with OTU was on August 24, a pamphlet raid on the coast of France. It had been on just such a raid that Bray had ditched. My heart was in my mouth during the whole trip and I was glad when we finally returned to base.

After our brief time on twins, my crew and I were sent to 1651 Heavy Conversion Unit at Waterbeach for conversion to four engine bombers. It was September 2, 1943. We soon heard the news that Italy had surrendered. My biggest concern was that the war would be over before I had the chance to go on operations.

I will never forget the first Stirling which arrived at the base. I was standing on the tarmac watching the huge aircraft circle the field, just as I had when I was a mechanic watching the very first Stirling. I knew that it was brand-spanking new, fresh from the factory. As it circled I admired the four Hercules engines and the long, chunky fuselage. That airplane seemed bigger than the landing field!

I studied the landing approach. The pilot did a beautiful three point landing but the nose of that tail-dragger still looked like it was fifty feet in the air. The undercarriage wheels were as tall as I was!

As I stood there, gaping at the huge bomber in front of me, I spoke to one of my instructors. He was Flying Officer Blair, who had the honor of being Lord Louis Mountbatten's personal pilot.

"My God!" I exclaimed, "I guess you'd have to be a superman to fly one of those!"

"Well," he replied, "it's a tough airplane to fly. It's a very heavy aircraft and it's got a very high wing loading."

"But look at the size of it!" I marveled. "Don't you think the man would need extra skills? I guess guys like me would never be able to fly a machine like that."

"As a matter of fact, Greenburgh," he replied with a hint of mischief in his voice, "that's your airplane. You're going to fly it tomorrow. You're going up with me for a familiarization. We'll do a cross country, do a few landings, then let's see if you can take it over. That's your airplane. As a matter of fact, we're even putting your initials on it."

I was stunned. "What?! Me flying one of those things?!"

The next day, I met Blair and we went out to my airplane. I sat down in the copilot's seat and was just mesmerized by all of the instruments. There were dials everywhere: dials for the gun turrets, for the hydraulics, for the engines. Although I had done well in my ground school, I didn't think I could ever really get to know them.

Blair could see that I was a bit intimidated by all of the gadgetry. "There are no wizards here," he laughed.

Imagine coming off a Wellington and getting into this great-big thing! The runway was so far below that I almost thought we were airborne. I soon learned that the high canopy made it very difficult to judge altitude for landings. In fact, I've heard it said that if you could fly a Stirling you could fly anything and I think that's probably true.

Blair went over all of the cockpit procedures with me and we made a short flight during which I merely sat back and watched. Blair took us up again for about half an hour. He directed me to take over control and I put the aircraft through a few maneuvers, then landed. We switched seats and it was my turn to do the takeoff.

Each of the four engines had two thousand horsepower, and I could feel those eight thousand horses in the palm of my hand as I pushed forward on the throttle and the Stirling rose majestically into the air. I had to use a lot of left rudder and juggle the throttles to counteract the bomber's tendency to swing to starboard.

After a few basic maneuvers, Blair instructed me to cut two engines on one side. We continued the flight with the two dead engines and I made the landing in that disabled condition. Blair unstrapped himself and said. "Okay, take it up yourself. You'll need a flight engineer to lift the undercarriage and stuff." I shifted over to the left seat and Blair climbed out of the aircraft.

Geordie gave a mock groan, "Oh, no!"

I puffed out my chest and said, "Oh, yes!"

Geordie shook his head in feigned dismay. "And he's dragging us with him."

Despite his pretended chagrin, Geordie took his place in the copilot's seat and Strommy settled into the wireless operator's position. I looked towards the rear of the enormous fuselage and couldn't believe that I was in command of such a huge ship. I thought it looked as big as a football field. It had not been so long before that I was cleaning toilets.

To my great surprise I topped the course in both flying and ground school and finally began to feel like somebody.

After I had left Wellingtons and gone on to Stirlings, who should come along behind me but Alex Strell. My old instructor was just starting to train on Wellingtons. I was now ahead of him. It just goes to show you; one minute you're looking up to your instructor as an 'expert', and the next moment you're the big guy.

My crew and I were posted to 622 Squadron at Chedburgh, where I was assigned a Stirling designated 'C Charlie'.

On October 2, 1943, the first page of my log book was endorsed with the notation that I was 'qualified as first pilot, Day and night, on Stirling Mk.I. land planes, w.e.f. 1.10.43'. I was slated for my first operational flight the next day. I was scared to go on ops. but I was more afraid to back out.

I climbed into the right hand seat of a Stirling. It was R.A.F. policy to send a pilot on his first op. as a co-pilot. One would rarely have the opportunity to learn from one's mistakes.

Our target was Kassel, an industrial complex deep in the heart of Germany. It was a production centre for a variety of equipment including rolling stock, heavy machinery, and assorted types of precision instruments[16]. No sooner had we crossed to the enemy coast than we were under attack.

The entire airplane shook as the gunners let go at an FW190. I held my breath and braced myself for a cascade of cannon shells but it never came. The

---

[16] *Peden, Murray, "A Thousand Shall Fall", op. cit., page 263.*

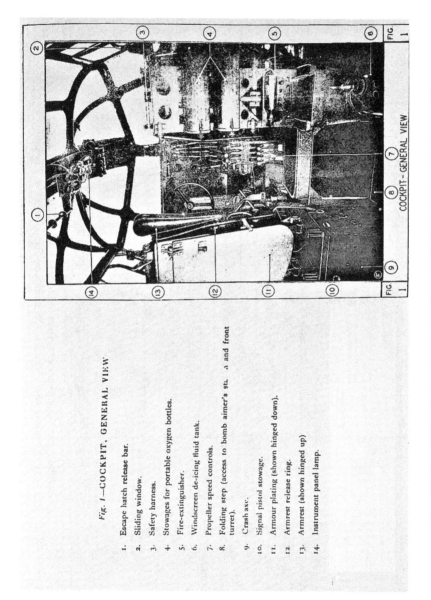

Fig. 1—COCKPIT, GENERAL VIEW

1. Escape hatch release bar.
2. Sliding window.
3. Safety harness.
4. Stowages for portable oxygen bottles.
5. Fire-extinguisher.
6. Windscreen de-icing fluid tank.
7. Propeller speed controls.
8. Folding step (access to bomb aimer's st[illegible]n and front turret).
9. Crash axe.
10. Signal pistol stowage.
11. Armour plating (shown hinged down).
12. Armrest release ring.
13. Armrest (shown hinged up)
14. Instrument panel lamp.

From Pilot's and Flight Engineer's Notes for Stirling I, III, IV. Her Majesty's Stationery Office and Air Publications, St. Anne's-on-Sea, Lancashire, England.

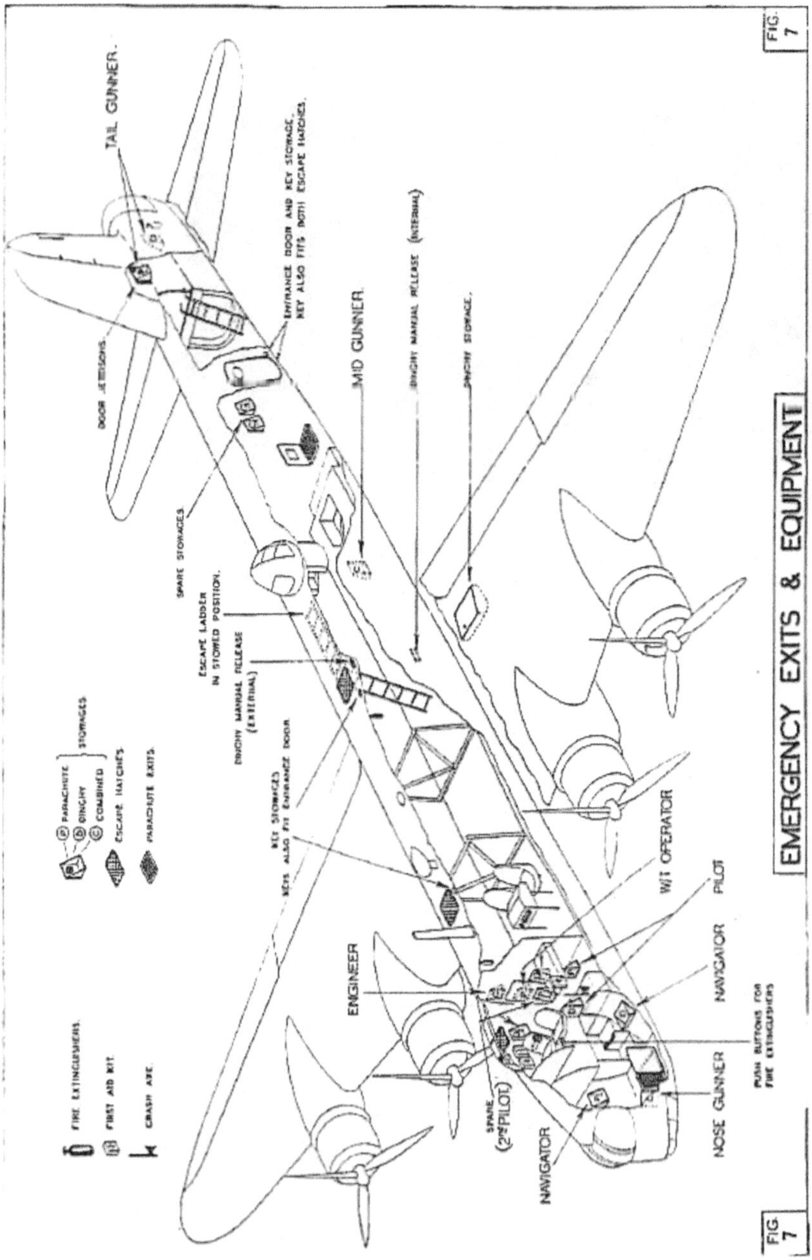

From Pilot's and Flight Engineer's Notes for Stirling I, III, IV. Her Majesty's Stationery Office and Air Publications, St. Anne's-on-Sea, Lancashire, England.

enemy fighter seemed to be out of control and disappeared into the darkness. "I think I got him." reported one of the gunners.

The night was lit by a dozen searchlights which probed the sky. They all converged on a single aircraft, which I took to be a Stirling. Big flashes surrounded the bomber, which immediately threw itself into spasmodic maneuvers in a futile effort to evade the condemning beams. Flashes were bursting all around it as it went down.

"Oh my God!" I thought, "Do I have to do this every night for the rest of the war?"

The city of Kassel was covered by a thick haze which reduced visibility[17]. I saw the mist drifting by the aircraft and in my anxiety at being over enemy territory I worried that it might be some sort of gas attack! In spite of the haze, the darkness was pierced by intense fires burning throughout the general area. To the northeast of the city was a particularly bright flame. Although I did not know it, that blaze was caused by bombs hitting a large ammunition dump.

It was almost impossible for us to get a good fix on our target. We flew over the general target area, let go our bombs, and headed home.

There was the customary debriefing when I got back to Chedburgh. "Boy did you ever get a hot one for your first target!" someone remarked. The guys told me that Kassel was one of the hottest targets. I was pleased to hear that they weren't all that bad.

The losses on the Kassel raid were later computed at 4.4%. We had lost twenty-four aircraft: 14 Halifaxes, 6 Stirlings, and 4 Lancasters[18]. I hate statistics and maybe such quotes are one of the reasons why. The numbers don't tell of the horror and suffering which they represent. How could such things be measured?

On the other side of the coin, 118 people were killed by our bombs, at least 68 of whom were civilians[19]. The poor visibility had caused most of the bombs to be released over residential areas and among the buildings hit was the city's main hospital. The raid did, however, cause major fires at two aircraft factories.

---

[17] *Middlebrook, Martin & Everitt, Chris, "The Bomber Command War Diaries: an operational reference book, 1939-1945", Penguin Books Canada Ltd., 2801 John Street, Markham Ontario, Canada, 1985, page 436. This reference includes other descriptions in this paragraph.*

[18] *Ibid.*

[19] *Ibid.*

After the raid on Kassel, we did some air/sea rescue work. I never actually rescued anyone during my time with air/sea rescue. We would report ships at different locations, that was about all.

I enjoyed flying C Charlie. We were off on a training flight one day when I decided to 'shoot up' a nearby American base. I pushed the throttle wide open and zoomed down to ground level, roaring between two buildings and climbing skywards.

"Skipper," I heard Strommy say over the intercom, "I think we're in trouble. The Yanks are calling us."

I turned on my headset. "C Charlie, C Charlie, come in C Charlie."

"This is C Charlie."

"We are having a party here on Saturday night. How'd you like to come?"

"Roger."

"Is this Lou Greenburgh?"

"Roger."

"Thought so. By the way, d'you call that a shoot up?!"

I got to know some Americans quite well. Fortresses were flying from Chedburgh and we would often see them struggle back after a raid, with crewmen dead or wounded and the aircraft badly mauled.

I met a Thunderbolt pilot who wanted to fly my Stirling. I took him up for a 'flip' and let him take the controls. He then showed his appreciation by letting me take his Thunderbolt for a spin. It was a heavy thing! I cut the throttle when coming in to land and it just fell from the sky. I quickly opened the taps again to slow my descent. I didn't log either flight.

We were ordered to lay mines in the Kattegat and the Skagerrak. I enjoyed going out there because it gave me the chance to do some low flying. We would skim just 50 feet above the water. It was very interesting because we would see the coasts of Norway and Sweden, the odd Allied destroyer, and German flak ships. I gave ships a wide berth. We saw the odd aircraft flying overhead, but we were so low they wouldn't even notice us.

One time we were laying mines between Norway and Sweden. The weather was bad back at base so we landed at a base in Scotland and operated out of there for a couple of weeks.

I will never forget one mine laying op. We reached the target areas and 'planted our crop'. We were returning to base around sunset. Just as we crossed the British coast, we could see tracer flashing in the darkness ahead of us and I knew there were enemy aircraft in the vicinity. Even so, I decided to have some fun with the young W.A.F.s in the control tower.

I called them up and said, "This is 'C Contraceptive', 'C Contraceptive'. Request clearance to land."

A female voice replied, "We have you C Charlie and you are cleared to land. But be careful, C Charlie. This is Air Traffic Control, not Birth Control."

One of my flights was memorable because of what happened after our landing. I'm not sure which aircraft we were in but it was probably G Golf.

All of the runway lights were out. We were low on fuel, as usual, so I had to get down quickly. How the hell I did it, I don't know, but I managed to set us down in a little satellite. There was no runway, just a grass field. As we rolled to a stop, I contacted the tower and told them we were down. "I can't see a thing." I informed the controllers, "I don't even know where I am."

"That's all right, G Golf. We have you on our screen." The controller proceeded to give me taxying directions.

If you can't trust an ATC, who can you trust? I opened the throttles gently and G Golf began to move forward. Without warning, I felt myself falling and heard the words "Oh my God! Oh my God!" come from the air traffic controller. I think I'd rather hear a dentist say "Oops."

There was a loud splash and I realized that I had just ditched a valuable Stirling immediately after a perfectly safe landing. It was a bit of a surprise, since we had been on dry land just seconds before, so we didn't have time to send out an SOS or to grab anything. As the huge bomber began to sink, the life raft was automatically released and we all prepared to pile into it.

I opened the large viewing panel on one side of the canopy and climbed out of the cockpit. I contemplated jumping into the water and making a swim for the raft when I realized that the plane had stopped sinking. That stork-like undercarriage had reached the bottom of whichever body of water we had landed in and prevented us from sinking further. I climbed onto the top of the fuselage to assess the situation and saw that my crew had all climbed up through the upper escape hatch.

It was like being huddled on the back of a hundred and twenty foot crocodile. All that was visible in the darkness was a narrow strip along the aircraft's spine. The rest was submerged, and little waves rippled against the sides. As my eyes grew accustomed to the dark, I peered down into the liquid blackness and could just make out the shape of the wing root. Out there, about forty feet out, could that be a wingtip? I guess so, since there was a matching one on the other side.

Bombing up a Short Stirling (Steve Smith).

The rear turret was hanging above dry land. We made our way towards the towering dorsal fin and climbed across the tail section to reach the shore.

As my feet landed on the beach, I turned around and surveyed my command. "Oh my God!" I thought, as the realization hit me that the aircraft would be a total loss. G Golf must have cost about a million dollars, which was a lot of money in those days.

We had taxied over the edge of a shallow cliff and landed in a flooded gravel pit. The incident wouldn't be held against me since I had been obeying the directions of Air Traffic Control.

Upon our return to Chedburgh, we were assigned another Stirling. A month later, I flew over the satellite field and saw that a forlorn looking fin was still protruding above the muddy water of the gravel pit.

In spite of its huge size, the Stirling had relatively short wings and couldn't carry a very large bomb load. Those stubby wings also limited its altitude to about 16,000 feet. But I'll tell you; of all the aircraft I've flown, I'm proudest to have flown the Stirling.

Chapter 7: The Battle of Berlin

NIGHT BOMBER

Eastward they climb,
Black shapes against grey of falling dusk,
Gone with the nodding day of English fields.
Not theirs, the sudden glow of
Triumph that their fighter brothers know, only
To fly through storm, through night, and to
Keep their purpose bright, nor turn, until
Their dreadful duty done, westwards they climb
To race the walking sun.

Anonymous

I joined Conversion Unit 1678 at Waterbeach in December of 1943 for conversion onto Lancasters. I had training flights on December 4, 10, 11, and then I was ready to go. The Lancaster was a smaller aircraft than the Stirling and I found it much easier to fly.

While I was converting onto Lancasters, I happened to take a communications flight as a passenger in an Anson. The pilot was circling so the passengers could see some interesting spectacle on the ground below. I wondered what everyone was looking at.

The passenger beside me commented, "Look, some asshole tried to land in a gravel pit!"

I winced but said nothing at the sight of poor old 'G Golf' still sitting in her gravel pit. I later told the pilot that I was the 'perfect asshole' who had landed in the pit.

My crew and I became part of 514 Squadron, also based at Waterbeach, and I was assigned a very special aircraft. It was a new Lancaster Mark II, serial number DS821, with four Bristol Hercules 2,000 h.p. radial engines instead of the usual in-line Merlins. The Mark II was developed, apparently, because the powers that be were worried about having too much reliance on the Merlin engine and they wanted to have a ready alternative in case Merlin production was ever

Avro Lancaster MkII LL734, JI-O of 514 Squadron. This particular aircraft served with 115 Squadron before joining 514 Sqn at Waterbeach. The aircraft's Bristol Hercules radial engines differentiated the MkII from the vast majority of Lancasters, which were powered by Rolls-Royce Merlins (514 Squadron Society).

interrupted[20]. Only 300 Lanc IIs were ever built, most of them going to the Royal Canadian Air Force. There were only two British squadrons flying Lanc II's.

Those radial engines gave incredible power. During my first take off in a Lanc II, I didn't believe my instruments. "Somethings wrong," I said to my flight engineer, "we're climbing and accelerating."

That particular flight was just for a practice bombing over the English city of Rushford. When we had landed, my crew approached me in an informal meeting. "Skipper," one of my crewmen said, "We'd like you to promise us that you won't volunteer for any missions."[21]

I could understand their concern and I didn't want to get shot down any more than they did. My ambition was always to die of old age. "Okay, guys," I replied, "I won't volunteer for any missions."

On December 29, I met with the commanding officer, Wing Commander Sampson. He welcomed me to 514 Squadron and offered me a cigarette. As I put it to my mouth and took the ritualistic first puffs, he mentioned that he needed one more crew for a raid that night. "It's an undefended target," he quickly added, "just across the channel."

---

[20] *Ebbs, Heather, and Vincent, Carl, "LANCASTER II - the RCAF service of a little known bomber," "High Flight, bi-monthly, volume 1, number 3, published by Canada's Wings Inc., Box 393, Stittsville, Ontario, page 99.*

[21] *The basic outline and some of the details of this chapter were based on an article written by the author's father. It was entitled "An eerie postscript to the bombing of Berlin," and was published by "Maclean's" magazine (Montreal, September 8, 1962).*

A line up of 514 Squadron Lancaster MkIIs at Waterbeach between successive night raids against Berlin, 2nd January 1944. Few of these aircraft survived the war; DS813, JI-H (foreground) was shot down on 28th July 1944 on a raid against Stuttgart whilst LL624, JI-B crashed whilst taking off with a full bomb load on 25th August 1944 for an attack on Vincly. Her crew, fearing an explosion, abandoned the aircraft even before it came to a full stop! (514 Squadron Society).

I remembered my promise not to volunteer. But it sounded like such a breeze... a short, safe way to get the combat experience we so badly needed.

"Alright, Sir, we'll do it."

My crew hit the roof! Five of them blew up when I told them how brave I had been on their behalf.

Fred Carey, said, "Skipper, my wife's just had a baby. I've got a son I've never seen. I don't want to go into action yet!"

"I understand," I told him, "but it's an undefended target. We'll be alright. It's just across the channel."

"Like hell it is!" exclaimed Geordie. "They're going to Hanover or Leipzig or some place. They're loading up those aircraft to full capacity!"

We rushed out to find Wing Commander Sampson and discovered that he was in the briefing room. "He doesn't want to see Greenburgh." we were told.

I had to say something to my crew to ease the tension we all felt. "Remember, guys," I said, "if we go on an operation, we get a free chocolate bar."

"Free chocolate bar!" Strommy snorted, "That's all our skin is worth, is a free chocolate bar?!"

Colin Blake, my Australian rear gunner, seemed jumpy and morose.

It wasn't too long before all of us felt as miserable as Colin looked. When the map was uncovered in the briefing room that afternoon and I saw the

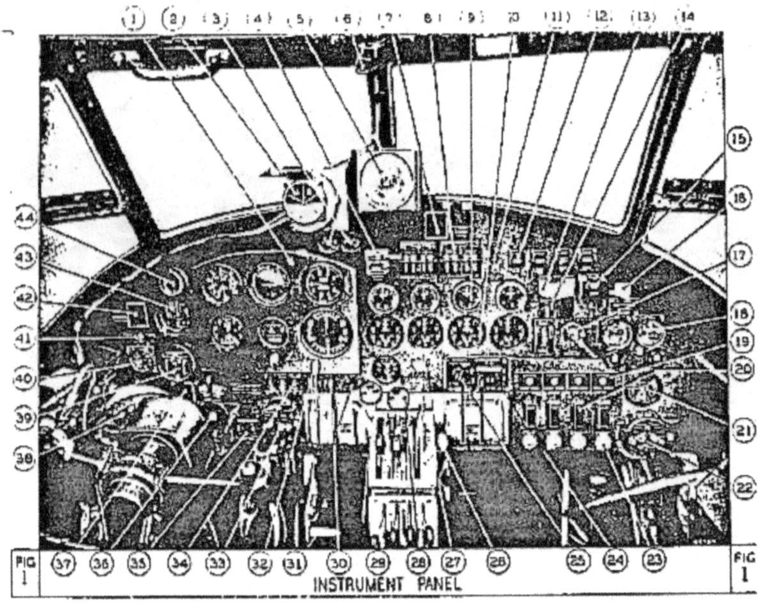

PART V—ILLUSTRATIONS

Fig.—1 INSTRUMENT PANEL.

1. Instrument flying panel.
2. D.F. indicator.
3. Landing lamps switches.
4. Undercarriage indicator switch.
5. D.R. repeater compass.
6. T.R.9 remote controller.
7. D.R. compass deviation card holder.
8. Ignition switches [illegible].
9. Boost gauges (four).
10. Engine-speed indicators (four).
11. [illegible] switch.
12. Engine starting pushbuttons (four).
13. I.F.F. emergency switches.
14. I.F.F. master switch.
15. Bomb containers [illegible] switch.
16. Bomb [illegible] control.
17. Suction pump changeover cock.
18. Oxygen regulator.
19. Propeller selector switches (four).
20. Propeller feathering switches (four).
21. Brakes triple pressure gauge.
22. Signalling switch box (identification lamps).
23. Fire extinguisher push buttons (four).
24. Two-speed superchargers control.
25. [illegible] master engine cocks (two).
26. Mixture control (if fitted).
27. Friction adjusters.
28. Throttle levers (four).
29. Propeller speed controls (four).
30. [illegible] master engine cocks (two).
31. Rudder pedal.
32. [illegible] cut-out.
33. Signalling switch box (recognition lamps).
34. [illegible] identification lamp selector switches.
35. D.R. compass switches.
36. Auto controls—steering lever.
37. P.4 compass deviation card holder.
38. P.4 compass.
39. Undercarriage indicator.
40. Flaps indicator.
41. Flaps indicator switch.
42. A.S.I. correction card holder.
43. Beam approach visual indicator.
44. Watch holder.

Above and following page: from 'Pilot's Notes for Lancaster II', Her Majesty's Stationery Office and Air Data Publications, St. Annes-on-Sea, Lancashire, England.

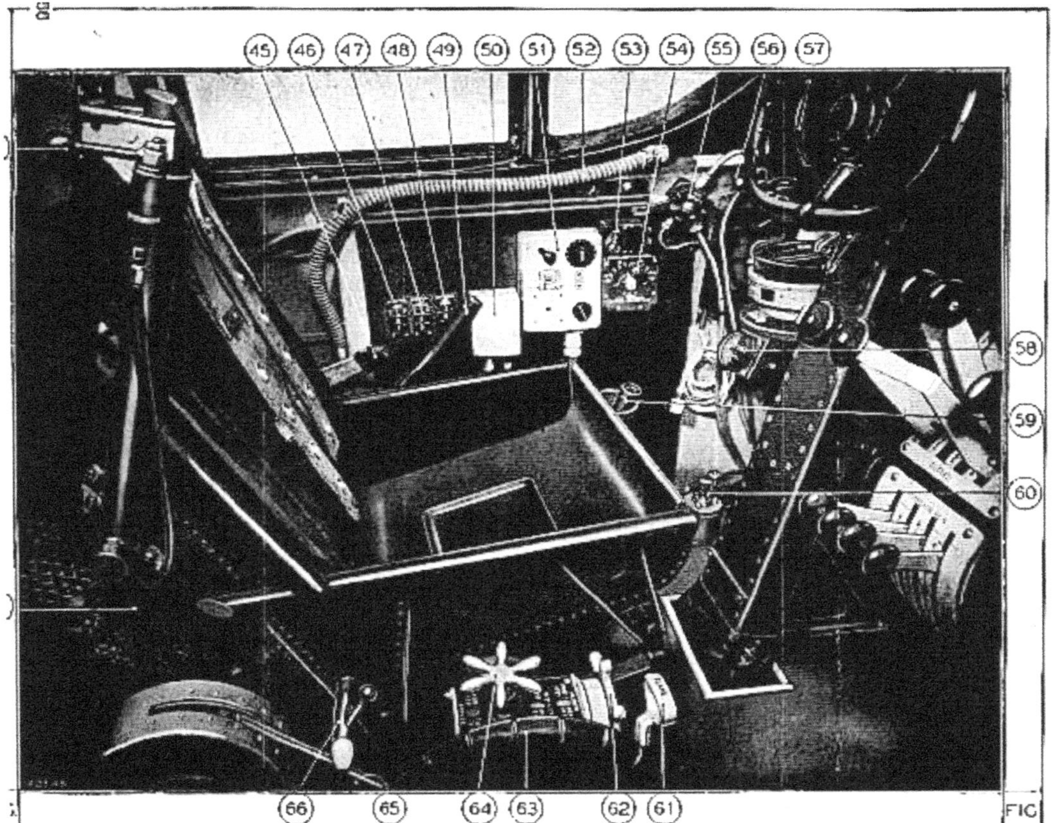

PORT SIDE OF COCKPIT

FIG 2

Fig. 2

COCKPIT—PORT SIDE

45. Bomb doors control.
46. Navigation lamps switch.
47. T.R.9 switch.
48. Auto-controls main switch.
49. Seat operating lever.
50. Mixer box.
51. Beam approach control unit.
52. Oxygen connection.
53. Pilot's call light.
54. Automatic controls—attitude control.
55. Automatic controls—cock control.
56. Automatic controls—clutch control.
57. Brakes lever
58. Automatic controls—pressure gauge.
59. Pilots mic./tel. socket.
60. Windscreen de-icing pump.
61. Flaps control.
62. Aileron trimming tab control.
63. Elevator trimming tab control.
64. Rudder trimming tab control.
65. Undercarriage control lever.
66. Undercarriage control safety bolt.
67. Portable oxygen container stowage.
68. Pilot's harness release lever on folding arm rest.

red circle around our target, I felt sick. There had been a last minute switch. Fred Carey's face was ashen and he gestured to me in desperation, but there was nothing I could do. By now it was too late to switch crews and the 'undefended target just across the channel' was Berlin! I smiled meekly at my men but couldn't blame them for not smiling back. After all, I had promised not to volunteer and we still hadn't finished our training.

The horror we felt was expressed by this quote from Flying Officer R.E. Luke, a bomb aimer of 426 Squadron:

'The murmur which swept through the briefing room when the target map of Berlin was revealed paid tribute to the severity of the defenses which, particularly on a cloudless night, struck fear into the hearts of those crews ordered to attack it. It seemed to us that only the best German personnel were posted to defend the city. An enormous cone of searchlights ringed the city, which could be seen a long way off, and it did not seem possible to breach them. In all our thirty-three operations we encountered no target more heavily defended than Berlin'.[22]

We were to be one of 457 Lancasters on this raid[23]. There would also be 252 Halifaxes and 3 Mosquitoes. The red tapes marked out a long approach route. We would pass south of the Ruhr and then within twenty miles of Leipzig.

As the briefing continued, I felt worse and worse. The target would be surrounded by anti-aircraft batteries. We were informed that the Germans had rockets. There would be heavy fighter opposition.

The briefing officer pointed out the locations of the spoof targets - Dusseldorf, Leipzig, and Magdeburg[24] - which would be attacked by Mosquitos as a decoy.

At the conclusion of the briefing, I was handed my escape kit and went to the mess for some bacon and eggs. The fellow opposite me looked me in the eye with a serious expression on his face and said, "Yesterday, there was another fellow sitting in your seat. He got the chop." The guy had been balancing a knife with the handle on the table and the blade in the air. He let the blade slide to the table with a thump, to emphasize the word 'chop'. I lost what was left of my appetite.

---

[22] *Middlebrook, Martin, The Berlin Raids: R.A.F. Bomber Command Winter 1943-44, published by the Penguin Group, 27 Wrights Lane, London W8 5TZ, England, 1988, pages 25-26*

[23] *The Bomber Command War Diaries, op. cit., page 462. The information in this paragraph and part of the briefing which follows is from an abstract of this raid.*

[24] *Ibid.*

At dusk that night, a station bus dumped us beside the big metal flank of our Lancaster, "S for Sugar", a plane I felt less and less able to fly.

We entered Sugar's long, dark fuselage, closed the hatches and adjusted our harnesses. I checked over the instruments and did the hundred and one things a pilot had to do before takeoff. As I reached the end of my checklist, I knew that Sugar was ready; but was I?

"We'll be alright, boys." I said, "Don't panic."

"Yeah," they mimicked with sarcasm, "Be alright, boys, don't panic!"

I looked out through the glass panels of the canopy. In the fading twilight I could see the dark outlines of a row of bombers, stretching out into the darkness on either side of us. A lone figure stood beneath my cockpit and flashed me a victory sign. I couldn't see his face in the shadows but I knew it was the commanding officer, come out to wish us luck. A green aldis lamp flickered from the runway control tower. One by one, each bomber would flash up her engines. I watched sparks fly from the glowing exhaust vents as they each taxied down the runway in preparation for takeoff and lined up in single file as if they were paratroopers waiting to jump. Like a distant earthquake, the low grumble of their engines died away to silence as they taxied out of earshot. Dead silence turned to a roar as one by one they rose into the sky. As soon as one plane lifted off, the next one would go, so it was a constant stream.

"Skipper." Strommy spoke quietly from the wireless operator's station behind me. "It's our turn now."

I eased the throttles forward a bit and the engines roared to life. When we reached the take off point I saw the green light flash our signal to take off. I opened the taps and set my jaw as Sugar rumbled down the runway. I pulled back on the wheel, adjusted the trim control (a small wheel under the instrument panel) and we were airborne. The time was 1701 hrs.

The plane was vibrating like hell from the weight of our bomb load. Just as we left the ground, I checked with Geordie and throttled back to four pounds boost. "Constant speed on props." I ordered, "Revs 2,500."

"Constant speed on props." the engineer repeated, "Revs 2,500".

We began our routine checks. "Temperature?" I asked.

"Temperature okay."

"Trim?"

"Trim okay."

"Oil pressure?"

"Oil pressure okay." I set the trim for a steady climb to our assigned altitude, about 21,000 feet, and told each of the gunners to check his hydraulics. The turrets all rotated and the guns were elevated and depressed to make sure they were functioning. They would have been test fired, but in this darkness there was too much danger of hitting another Lancaster.

"Rear gunner, hydraulics okay."

"Mid upper gunner, hydraulics okay."

"Front gunner, hydraulics okay."

The altimeter needle gradually rotated clockwise. At 10,000 feet I ordered the crew to don their oxygen masks and the engineer checked the oxygen system to make sure it was functioning.

I looked down below and saw the coast of England slipping past. In the distance I could see the odd burst of flak from the German flak ships in the North Sea, but we didn't pay them much attention. I set course for the Frisian Islands, which was our focus point. From there we would head for Berlin. Sugar was one of 400 bombers above the North Sea.

Hundreds of bombers all around me and yet I could see none of them in the darkness. My entire world consisted of the dim glow of the instruments and a few shadowy companions. Sparks here and there reminded me that we were not alone and I cringed at the thought of propeller blades ripping through the cockpit.

Colin was singing 'Lillie Marlene' as we approached the enemy coast. I began to see flashes, like fireworks. The odd flash here, the odd flash there. I looked over the side of my Lanc just as I reached the coast and saw a little ball of fire slowly coming up. It seemed to be almost standing still, hardly moving. It gradually came up and then it whizzed past me and exploded with a blinding flash. Colin stopped singing 'Lillie Marlene'.

The flak had begun whacking away at us as soon as we hit enemy territory. The flashes got more and more intense as I flew along. Shrapnel rattled off our fuselage. A string of burning globes was coming right at us. I veered sharply to port and watched the stuff bursting - Boof! Boof! Boof! – right where I would have been if I'd kept my course.

That near miss woke me up to the real danger posed by anti-aircraft fire. After that, I used to do a gentle corkscrew here and there just in case some unseen gunner was trying to draw a bead on me. "Keep your eyes open, fellas," I said to my gunners, "There's probably no fighters around but there's lots of anti-aircraft." Our course was 090 degrees; due East. We had an indicated airspeed of 155 knots.

About an hour after crossing the coast, I saw flashes off to the south. It was the spoof attack over Leipzig. As we droned on in the dark, I began to feel pretty good and smiled to myself at the thought of German fighters tricked into attacking Mosquitoes. I thought of the shock the German fighter pilots would have when the fat and clumsy bombers they were intercepting turned out to be lean, twin engine fighters. I was sure more than a few would be surprised. I even began to hum.

"JU 88 on our tail!" shouted Colin, "Corkscrew port!"

I yanked the wheel over to port and saw a fighter behind us. Then it disappeared. I was just leveling out when somebody yelled, "He's under us!" and a rocket projectile caught our port wing. There was an explosion followed by a massive vibration. I thought the wings had been blown off. I saw an orange glow under the port wing.

"What the hell happened?!" I exclaimed.

"I think they got a tank, Skipper." reported Geordie, "Port outer tank. We're losing fuel fast."

"Keep your eyes open, for God's sake, fellas!" I ordered, "I think we've been hit!"

We evaded the German, but Sugar began to skid and seemed to be losing her grip on things.

I felt more vulnerable than ever. Geordie told me that we had lost so much fuel he didn't think we could make it home. We must have had one hell of a big hole in our starboard outer tank because I looked at the gage and could actually see the needle move as the rest of the fuel drained out.

I turned to Geordie and said, "Close off the pipes to prevent any more fuel leaking out." There was a complex system of fuel transfer pipes and valves to use in cases like this. I was glad to have an engineer to take care of that while I concentrated on flying.

"To hell with this nonsense." I grumbled, "I'm going to turn back." That was my initial response. But as I thought about it, I realized that there was no easy solution to my dilemma.

What was I to do? There was some safety amidst the huge armada bound for Berlin, but a lone aircraft enroute back to England would be a sitting duck for enemy fighters. And besides, this was my first real combat mission. How could I turn back?

"Of all the airplanes in the world," I heard Colin moan, "why did I have to end up in this one?!"

Miles from Berlin, we could see a wall of searchlights. They encircled the German capital like the battlements of a medieval walled city. I didn't know how we would ever get past them. They didn't look like searchlights at all. They looked like a wall, like a shining wall. And we had to fly right into it.

The Lancaster was skittering along between two layers of orange and red clouds which seemed to be on fire and bursting with sparks. I'll be honest with you, I was pretty nervous.

We had no lighting in the aircraft when we were over enemy territory but the instruments glowed in the dark. I checked the fluorescent glow of all the instruments, establishing what was to be a standard procedure for me whenever I approached a target. I studied the engine instruments first, checking that the revolutions were correct and the engines were intact. I didn't want to lose an engine this close to Berlin because I knew I would need all the power I could get for evasive action. Then I scanned the flying instruments, which I did periodically anyway. I glanced from side to side, scanning the entire instrument panel. The whole check took just a moment, because the place which required my immediate attention was outside the airplane. I looked left, right, up, down, all over and I kept on scanning. I kept in touch with my gunners. "Keep your eyes open, fellas." I repeated, just to remind them that I was depending on them. They didn't need much persuasion to keep a good lookout. Especially over Berlin.

We could see aerial combats in the distance. We saw bursts of tracer fired from the powerful guns of fighters and cannon fire and we saw the smaller answering fire coming from our fellow Lancasters.

Sugar was developing a will of her own and I found her tougher and tougher to control. I guess the port aileron must have been damaged when we were hit and who knows what else. The sight which greeted us as we passed through the searchlight belt was such as the world will never see again. Talk about fireworks! Ack ack, fighters zipping in and out, burning aircraft. The sky was full of explosions and I wondered how the Germans could possibly miss us. Our wings seemed to stretch across the whole flaming city.

High above us, enemy bombers were dropping parachutes with brilliantly burning payloads. It was terrifying to see this fire creeping down from above and at first I didn't know if the things were flares or missiles. I soon realized that they were illumination flares, intended to light up our bombers to aid the fighters in making contact. It worked.

Ahead of us I could see the glittering tentacles of a weapon we called 'scarecrows', or 'Christmas trees'. These were strands of barbed wire suspended from parachutes and laced with fragmentation bombs. Those deadly webs were hung all around the city. You'd see them right in front of you and wonder how you would ever get through. You couldn't judge the distance to them so you couldn't take action to avoid them. I held my breath as some glided past my wing tips.

We had maintained radio silence all the way to the target. Immediately before the bombing run, however, we got last minute directions from the Master

Bomber. The target was cloud covered, so we would be making our target run on a burning 'sky-marker'[25].

I saw the target marking flare and got the go ahead to begin my run. Four hundred other bombers would be starting their runs at the same time.

This was the most dangerous part of the whole attack. We were all converging on the same point in space and the danger from collision was very real. I braced myself against the imagined impact and also considered the possibility that a five hundred pound bomb, or an incendiary, could drop on us from above. A bomber unfortunate enough to be below us when we released our bombs could suffer the same fate. And the pilot had to maintain a steady altitude and attitude during the run in to the target. Even a slight movement at the point of release could be translated into a miss of hundreds of yards by the time the bombs reached the ground. A large bomber flying straight and level for several minutes or even seconds made a beautiful target for flak and fighters.

I pointed our nose in the direction of the flare and we began our bombing run. "Okay, Skipper," came the voice of the bomb aimer. Don had left the forward turret and was lying stomach down on his padded 'biscuit' over the forward escape hatch. Looking through the Perspex bubble on the nose, he had calibrated his bomb sight to our present altitude and speed. His viewing panel was circular but flat to avoid distortion. I would follow his directions for the rest of the bombing run.

"Steady, steady," he instructed with a calm, professional cadence. "Left, left, right. We're coming onto the target. Go easy, we're going there. Left, left, left. Open the bomb doors, Skipper."

I reached down beside my seat with my left hand and pulled the lever which opened the bomb doors. We had been flying straight and level for several seconds. Was a hail of hot lead even now reaching up for us?

"Bomb doors open!" I announced.

"Steady, steady," Don continued, "steady, steady, steady, steadeee... Bombs gone!"

I pulled the bomb doors closed and threw the airplane into a dive. I pulled up and saw that a Lancaster right beside me was on fire. The whole airplane was on fire. It could have been us.

We had survived our first bombing run on a major target. I caught my breath and turned the airplane onto a westerly course. We had an indicated airspeed of 175 knots at 21,000 feet. Now we had to fight our way home.

---

[25] *Ibid.*

It was 2200 hours. We were back over the area in which we had encountered the fighter that had damaged our fuel tank. I saw a bright yellow flare about half a mile to starboard.

"Starboard!" yelled the mid upper gunner. I kicked right rudder and turned the wheel but I could hardly control the aircraft. She just skidded all over the sky.

Fred opened fire with three short bursts. Colin blasted the Junkers 88 with multiple short bursts of fire which ripped into the enemy aircraft. It broke away upwards and to starboard, then began to wobble as if seriously damaged. A red glow erupted from the centre of the fuselage and we saw no more of it.[26]

Things looked pretty bad. The plane was damaged and we had lost tons of fuel. I didn't know for sure if we would get home.

I throttled back in an effort to save fuel and told Geordie to set the propeller pitch on 'high'. I told the crew I thought we might make it to England. The airplane was vibrating badly. With our speed reduced, we started lagging behind the other bombers.

Dirty weather hit us. I tried to get below the storm but I couldn't. We were being iced up. Propeller ice flew back against the fuselage with a 'rat-tat-tat', rain pelted against the windscreen, and we were tossed about by the severe turbulence. I didn't know the full extent of our damage and was worried that something might give under all of this stress. The ship was shuddering and sliding horribly.

Cursing the weather, I pushed the throttle forward and let those powerful engines fill with precious fuel. We began to climb.

"Skipper!" Geordie exclaimed, "You're using more fuel! For God's sake, we won't even make the coast!"

"We've got to do something." I shrugged. "We've got to get above this stuff."

We were about twenty minutes from the coast. Geordie said, "I doubt if we'll make it to the coast, Skipper. We're going to wind up behind enemy lines."

"Okay." I acknowledged. "Are you sure? Give us a true picture of what's happening."

---

[26] *The 1st Jagdkorps reported that three twin-engined night fighters were lost out of 66 sorties despatched during this raid on Berlin. All nine Luftwaffe crewmen perished. There are no details of individual losses but if the Ju 88 was in fact destroyed by Colin, it was probably one of these. Source – Nachtjagd War Diaries, Dr. Theo Boiten.*

Geordie gave me his professional assessment. "We'll never make England again," he stated, "because we've lost all of the fuel from the port outer tank and we're using too much fuel to get above the overcast."

We were just passing over Holland. "Well, guys," I said over the intercom, "Get ready to bail out."

"What about you, Skipper?" someone asked.

Strommy answered for me. "With a name like Greenburgh?! Would you bail out?"

Colin snorted, "They'd cut his balls off!"

I told them that I would try to make it back. Geordie said, "We'll never make it. But if you're going to try, we're with you, Skipper."

They all decided to stay with the aircraft. "Skipper, we've got to get back to England!" exclaimed the bomb aimer, "I've got a date with Susie tonight. If I don't get back, that damned sailor will go after her!"

I set course for the East Frisian Islands off the German coast. It was taking nearly all the strength I owned just to keep the wheel straight. Slowly, slowly, we gained altitude. We were over the North Sea. Then the canopy cleared and the turbulence stopped. We were above the storm at 17,000 feet. The time was 2215.

An orange flare burst a mile away to starboard, followed by two more of the same. "Corkscrew starboard, Skipper!" I threw the aircraft into a spiral to starboard as Colin reported a Ju 88 on the starboard quarter at 400 yards, closing in and firing. Fred saw him a moment later and both he and Colin began shooting, Fred letting loose a series of short bursts and Colin one long burst. The fighter broke away upwards to the port quarter then swung back for another attack. It passed over to our starboard side then had another go at us as it passed to our port side. I kept corkscrewing and the gunners kept firing. So did the enemy.

We finally lost him. I don't think he actually hit us, but our fuel shortage was now critical. With more than a hundred miles to go, Geordie told me that we had only six minutes' fuel left. That's when Colin began to scream again.

"An airplane with a beard," he wailed. "It's an airplane with a beard. A Fortress with a beard, a Fortress! It's coming after us."

Another fuel gage needle moved to EMPTY. An engine went. Then a second engine, and a third. It was obvious that we were not going to make the coast. I forced myself to remain calm. "Strommy," I said, quietly, "You'd better get started with your "MAYDAY" routine." The altimeter showed 17,000 feet.

Pat checked his charts and told Strommy our position. Strommy sent off the following message: "Petrol low, crossing coast 5235 North, 0143 East." The time was 2310 hrs. It was the last message from Sugar which anyone would ever receive.

I ordered the crew into forward crash positions. Pat's latest position report had placed us within a few miles of the English coast so I decided to stay aloft as long as possible and get as close to England as I could. We would have no power left for a soft landing.

We flew on one sick motor for a while and then it failed, too. We started down.

I pushed the nose down to keep the wings from stalling. We were falling like a brick, a 50,000 pound brick with seven men aboard, and it seemed like we were going straight down. I knew that I would have to pull back at just the right moment; too soon and we would stall and crash, too late and we would explode on impact.

The wind shrieked against the metal fabric. I could picture Strommy tapping out SOS messages on the wireless. The mid upper gunner's intercom was

open; I could hear Fred praying for the son he would probably never see. All the way down, I heard Colin babbling about that bearded Fortress on our tail.

The wheel ripped itself from my hands and we began to spiral. The shrieks increased as I opened my side window panel. I regained control of the wheel and divided my attention between the open side window, the altimeter, and the air speed indicator, trying to check everything at once. I knew that I would never see the stormy ocean in that pitch blackness and was almost frantic for some clues about when to pull up. I struggled to remain in control of myself, fighting the urge to pull back on the wheel.

A flash of light radiated through the clouds, spoiling my night vision, and we were buffeted by an explosion. As if I didn't have enough problems, a damn flak ship was firing at us!

The altimeter was unwinding. "10,000 feet, 9,000 feet, 8,000 feet, 7,000 feet..." Another shell burst nearby.

Lancaster MkII 'S for Sugar' (DS821, JI-S) ditching on December 29th 1943. This illustration originally appeared in the Macleans Magazine article 'An eerie postscript to the bombing of Berlin'.

"For God's sake!" I hollered, "Can't somebody do anything?!" I was completely helpless. But I managed to stay in control of myself. As totally absorbed as I was in trying to save the aircraft, I accepted the fact that I was about to die. I even did a little praying.

Salt water burst through the open window panel and the altimeter showed zero. I hauled back on the wheel for all I was worth, forcing the tail down. The aircraft skipped through the top of one wave and bounced onto another one. Colin jumped onto the main fuselage when the tail section dragged through a wave top, slowing the aircraft, then broke off. The canopy shattered as Sugar rammed into a vertical wall of water.

I woke up coughing. As my consciousness returned, I found myself up to my chin in heart-stopping cold water. I had no strength to struggle against the waves which pushed me around the sinking cockpit. My head dropped below the surface again and I was helpless.

The cockpit began to rise and most of the water drained out. Someone stepped on my head as he scrambled through the escape hatch above me. Hands unclipped my harness. I was dragged out of my seat and through the upper escape hatch. I lost my balance and fell into the sea, taking Geordie with me. Somehow, we made it to the half inflated and leaky raft and were helped aboard.

Shivering with cold, I grasped the rubber fabric to keep from being tossed out of the tiny craft. Water eight inches deep sloshed back and forth, keeping us sopping wet. Bailing was impossible. Sleet pelted against my face and stung my squinting eyes, but I could see that everyone had made it to the raft.

Don Bament groped towards me. Hair was plastered across his forehead and water dribbled down his cheeks but he clasped my hand and gave it a firm shake. "I've got to hand it to you, Skipper," he said, "Nobody else could have done it." The rest of those castaways each congratulated me and shook my hand in turn.

Looming above us was a ferocious sea monster[27]. We were connected to Sugar's broken fuselage by an umbilical cord and as the waves tossed and battered her hulk it was obvious that we could be crushed beneath her thrashing wings. They were as dangerous as Moby Dick's flukes. The wind swung the aircraft around and at times those wings were above our heads.

The airplane reared right up like a broaching whale and we held our breath. The nose began to fall. I thought it was going to come down right on top

---

[27] *The details of the life raft situation were recorded in an impromptu speech which the author's father gave at the Brandon Aviation Museum in 1980. A tape recording of that speech was provided by Mr. F. H. Watt of the Brandon Aviation Museum.*

of us. A pressure wave built up and pushed us clear of the colossus as it crashed down into the sea.

I realized with horror that we were still attached to Sugar and had no knife to cut the cord. I thought we would be dragged down with her. To my relief, the rope parted and we floated free.

Sugar reappeared a moment later. We had drifted downwind from her and were no longer in danger of being rammed but we were still in peril from the massive waves, which were later confirmed at being over forty feet in height. They were higher than a three story building.

Our immediate problem was to keep the dinghy from capsizing. We had to shift our bodies as ballast, jumping to one side or other as the raft threatened to tip. It's a miracle we didn't go off our rockers. Water cascaded aboard and the raft almost broached. I heard Strommy yelp and I grabbed his foot as he was washed over the side. His boot came off in my hand and I thought he was a goner. He had a grip on the safety line which encircled the raft and we were able to pull him back in.

"We can't stand this." Geordie gasped, "Another half hour and we'll all be drowned!"

That night was sheer hell. I tried to keep the men's spirits up by telling jokes. We laughed about the dates which had been planned for that night. It sure looked like we would be going 'stag' that New Year's Eve. "Poor Suzie!" groaned the bomb aimer. "You mean lucky sailor!" laughed Strommy. Pat said that he planned to join the Navy to see the world. Strommy kidded him, "So you joined Lou's crew and you'll see the next world." But we could only keep it going for so long.

Fred wanted desperately to see his son. "Let's try." he said, and began to paddle with his arms. That was futile.

By morning we could barely move and had pretty well given up hope. We did not know it then, but Air-Sea Rescue had been called off because of the weather. Sugar was still afloat and would remain so for at least twelve hours after the crash. About a mile in the distance, looking like the flukes of a large whale, was the dismembered tail section. In that part of the aircraft was our emergency radio and most of our supplies. At least the waves had settled down a bit and we were in less danger of capsizing.

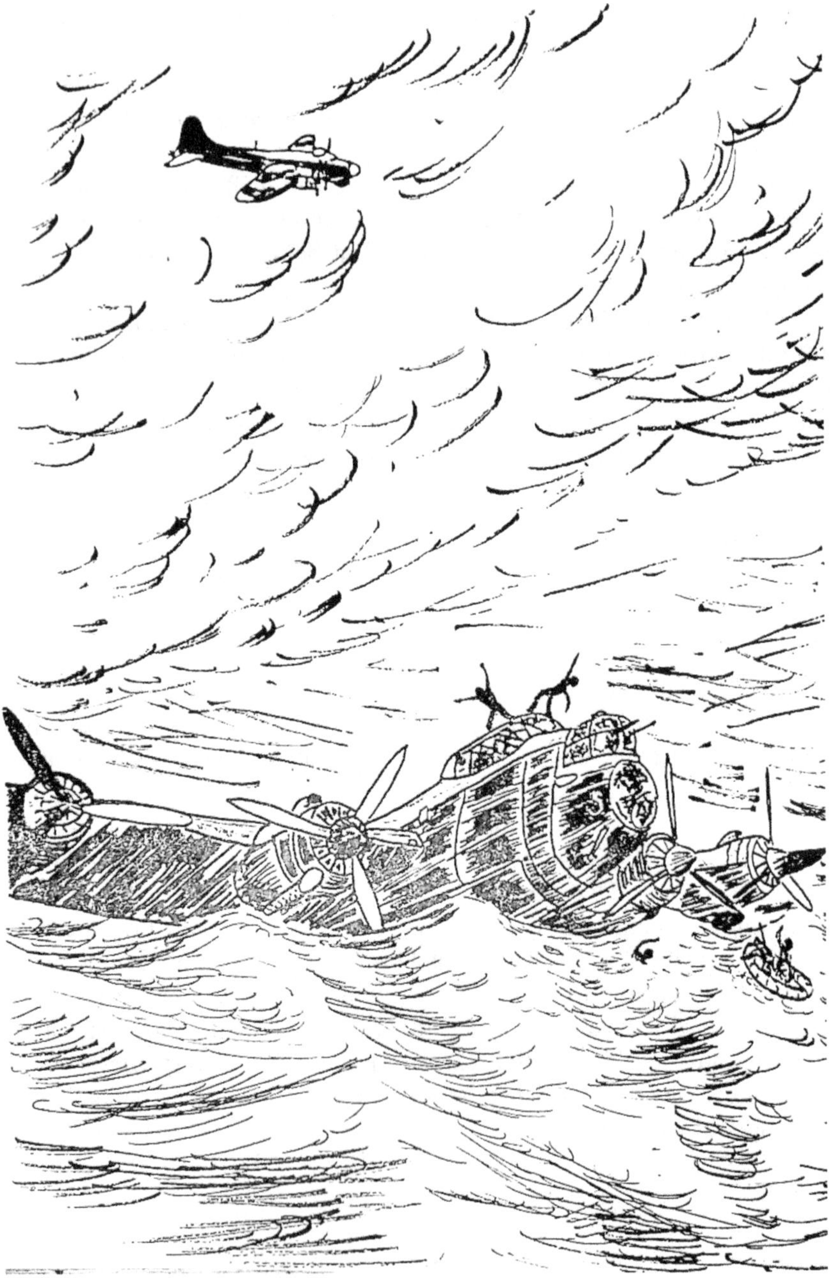

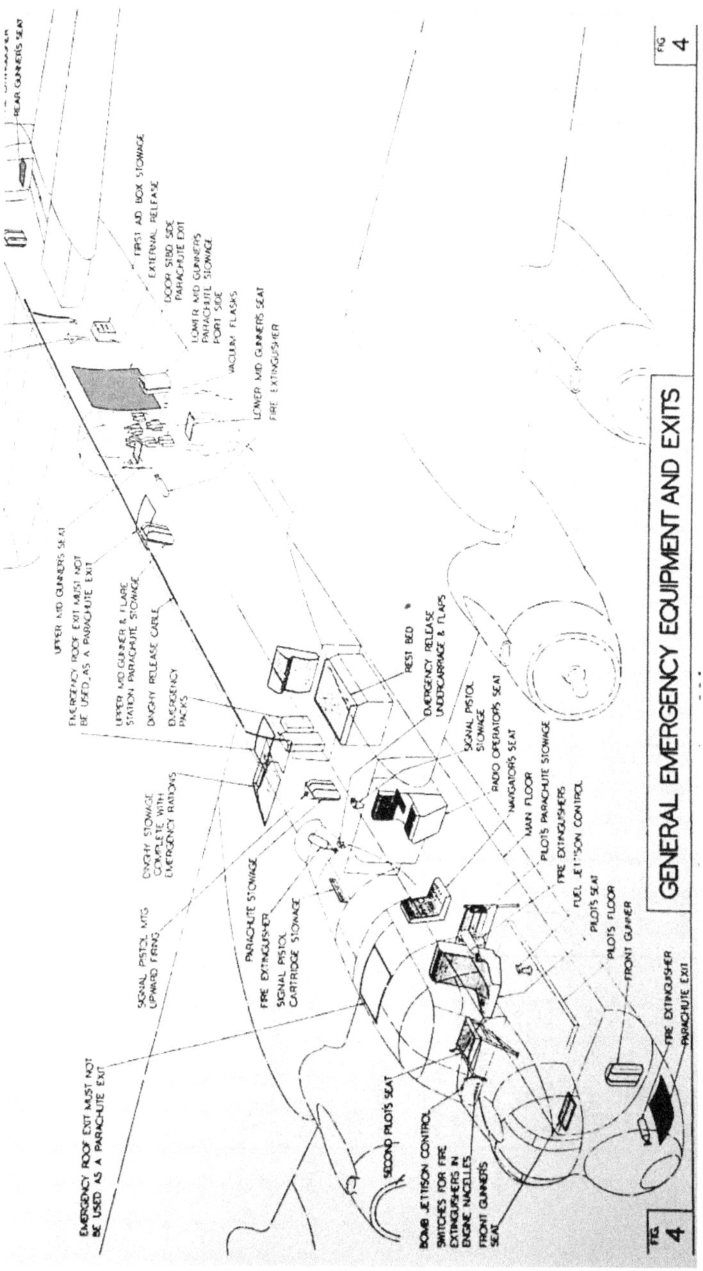

From 'Pilot's Notes for Lancaster II', Her Majesty's Stationery Office and Air Data Publications, St. Annes-on-Sea, Lancashire, England.

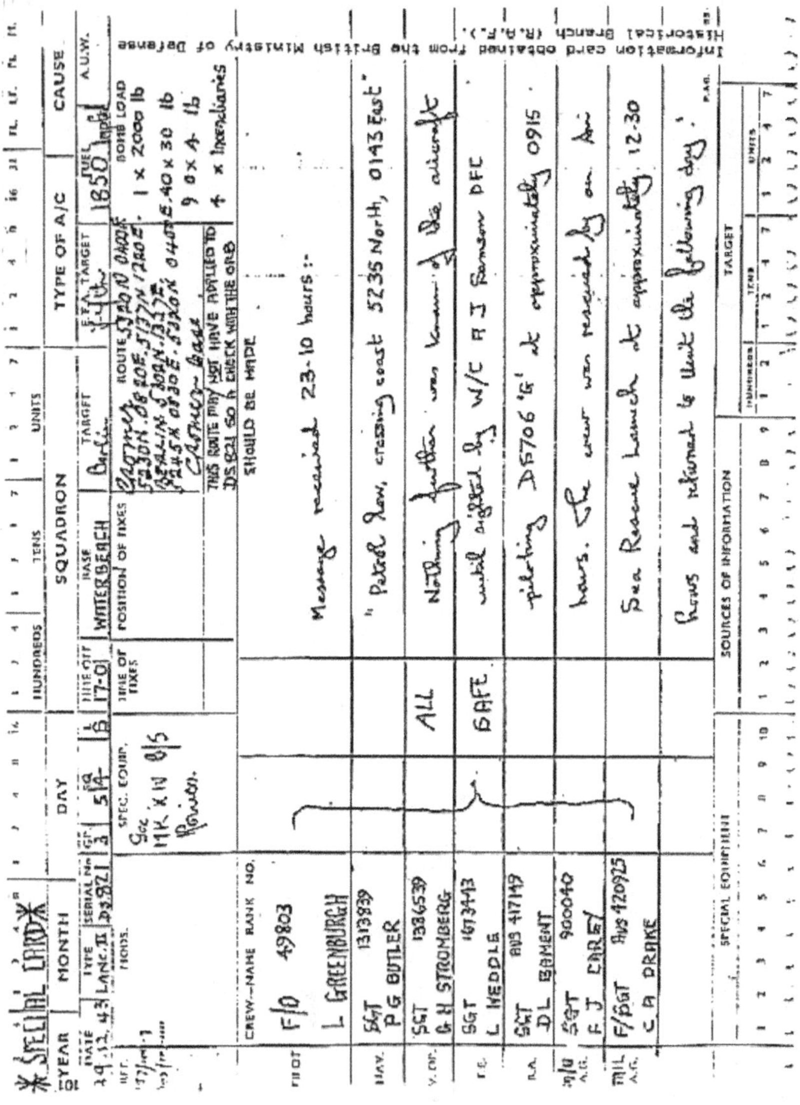

Air Ministry Loss Card giving recorded details of the ditching of DS821 and her crew.

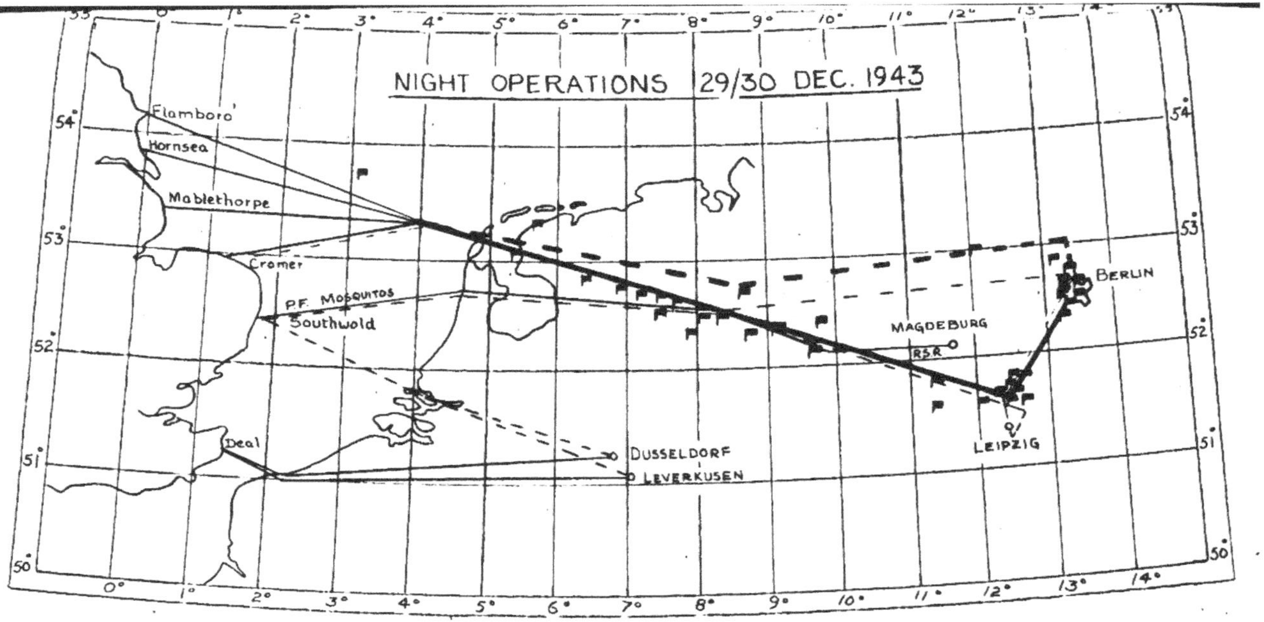

Night Operations map for 29/30th December 1943. The 'l' in Southwold shows the approximate position of ditching. Black flags denote the location of lost bombers, white flags denote other combats. Source: Bomber Command Night Raid Reports via The National Archives.

Oberfeldwebel Karl-Heinz Scherfling is believed to be the pilot responsible for finally shooting down Lou Greenburgh's Lancaster DS821 on the night of 29/30th December 1943. Scherfling himself was shot down and killed on 21st July 1944.

The dinghy had been leaking all night and we were up to our knees in water. The thought of the dinghy sinking from under us was not very appealing. "I think I can save the dinghy." Geordie announced after searching the raft. "There's a pump in one of those patches there!" Geordie had also found some meager but vital emergency rations.

For the next two hours we took turns pumping up parts of the dinghy. It was difficult for we were working under conditions of extreme cold. Don't forget, it was late December in latitudes approaching the subarctic and the icy wind bit like a Winnipeg blizzard. The only thing which kept us from freezing to death was the fact that our flight suits had captured water like a diver's wet suit. That water had warmed to body temperature and gave us some extra insulation. But that would only prolong the inevitable and we were still in immediate danger of frostbite.

Speaking of frostbite, it was dangerous even to go to the washroom. If somebody had to go, we all stood up and linked together to keep the raft from tipping. We did away with such niceties as personal privacy. Our only concern was survival.

I told the guys that everything would be alright, but I don't think my words were very convincing. Not even to myself.

Only Colin stayed active. His eyes were glazed and brine dribbled from his mouth but he kept screaming and pointing to imaginary ships and planes.

"They're just the funny Fortresses you saw last night," Strommy told him.

"Dammit, I did see one," Colin croaked, "and it chased us. Why didn't anybody else see it?"

I knew why. Even without beards, American Fortresses in Europe were only flying on daylight operations.

"Right," I snorted, "We were shot down by a Fortress!"

At about 0915 hrs, Colin began to scream again. He pointed at the horizon and yelled, "It's a Lanc, it's a Lanc!"

"You're crazy." I said. "It's like that damned Fortress you saw that was chasing us down."

"I know I saw that damned Fortress," he retorted, "And I know I saw that damned Lancaster!"

Then I saw it, too. I grabbed the Very gun, pointed it at the sky, and fired off our last flare. The Lanc turned in our direction and began to circle us. We released a package of marker dye, which turned the water around us fluorescent green.

The pilot of that Lanc was Wing Commander Samson, the commanding officer of 514 Squadron. His rear gunner had seen the very light. Sampson was to spend the next three hours circling us, giving direction to the rescue operation.

"I had told you it was an easy target," he later confided to me, "and talked you into volunteering. I wanted to make damn sure you were rescued." At first light, he had rounded up a scratch crew. He then climbed aboard his Lancaster and flew into the storm.

After several suspenseful hours, two Air-Sea Rescue Ansons arrived. In spite of our weakened state, we raised a cheer at the sight of supply boxes, shaped like bombs, which were dropping by parachute. We knew that those boxes would

The crew survived due to Greenburgh's piloting skills and the leadership of 514 Squadron's commander, W/Cdr Arthur Samson DFC. Samson assembled a scratch crew, flew to the last reported position of Greenburgh's aircraft and located the crew in their dinghy (514 Squadron Society).

Greenburgh's Lancaster DS821, JI-S, still afloat in the North Sea the morning after his successful ditching. The aircraft is missing her starboard wingtip and the tail section.

contain enough food, water, and extra clothing to keep us alive until we could be rescued.

The supplies splashed into the sea not more than ten feet from where we clung to our bobbing cork of a raft. The mountainous waves swept them beyond our reach as we cursed and gnashed our teeth in frustration. I thought it was the end of everything.

Pat summed up our feelings. "If they don't come soon, they might as well not come at all."

Another dinghy was also on its way down. We managed to reach it and climbed aboard.

What was left of my strength seeped out of my body. I could only lay in the bottom of the raft and wait for the numbing cold to drain my life away.

At about 1230 hrs, a rescue launch arrived. The rescue operation was very difficult because of the heavy seas and my crew showed great courage. I was too exhausted to move, but somehow I was lifted aboard. We spent about a week at the Yarmouth Naval Hospital, just for observation. We had a room to

29.12.43.	LANCASTER 'S'	F/O. L. Greenburgh	Captain.	1701		Bomb load 1 x 2000, 40 x 30, 900 x 4, 90 x 4 incendiaries.
	DS 821	Sgt. F.G. Butler.	Navigator.			Primary target BERLIN. Aircraft "Ditched" owing to petrol
		Sgt. D.L. Bament.	Air Bomber.			shortage due to combat with enemy aircraft. Crew rescued
		Sgt. G.H. Stromberg.	WOP/A.G.			unhurt.
		Sgt. F.J. Carey.	M.U. Gunner.			
		F/S. C.A. Drake.	R/Gunner.			
		Sgt. L. Weddle.	F/Engineer.			

The 514 Squadron Operational Record Book notes the ultimately successful outcome to the sortie.

ourselves and were treated like heroes. "Hey, guys," Fred laughed, "Remember the skipper shouting 'S.O.S., S.O.S!' Same Old S--t!"

We then got sixteen day leaves.

About three weeks after our ordeal, I was called to the station headquarters. I searched my conscience, as usual, and wondered what the CO wanted to talk about. He stood up as I entered his office. "Congratulations." he said, as he shook my hand, "You have been awarded the Distinguished Flying Cross."

The rest of the boys mobbed me good naturedly as I left the headquarters building. Strommy pounded me on the back and yelled, "Didn't I tell you guys it's a pilots' air force?"

For all the fuss that was made, and in spite of all the people around me, I was still a loner. I spent time by myself, constantly reliving that horrible crash. I was confused and the strain of my ordeal kept playing on my mind.

I sat by myself in the mess, playing a solitaire game of 'shove ha' penny'. I looked up to see a tall, dark haired fellow with a quiet manner standing on the other side of the little table. "You look kind'a glum," he said.

"Wouldn't you be?" He shrugged a bit to acknowledge my question. "Mind if I join you in a game?"

I was glad to have the company and invited him to play. He knew who I was, and maybe even what I was thinking, because as he sat down he said to me, "I really have a lot of admiration for you. Not many could have come out of it." I talked to him about the crash and he seemed to understand what I was going through. We became very close friends. His name was Tommy Penkuri[28].

I spent the next three weeks on a lecture tour, telling other pilots how to ditch a Lanc II. Apparently, I was the first person who had ever done that. (Until my ditching it was uncertain if the radial engines would allow a Lanc II to be successfully ditched.) It reminded me of the time I had listened, awestruck, to

---

28 *Murray Peden relates the details of his own close friendship with Tommy Penkuri in his book 'A Thousand Shall Fall'.*

Wing Commander Bray's lecture. Incidentally, one other bomber had ditched after that same raid. Only the rear gunner survived.

Years later, when I was flying on the Berlin Airlift, I met a buddy of mine named Taff Richards who had trained with me at Chipping Warden. I told him that he was the last person I had ever expected to see again.

We had a few drinks together. He looked at me with an amused twinkle in his eye and said, "You sure got wet on the night of 29th December, '43."

"Yeah," I agreed.

He smiled. "I saw you go down."

"You son of a gun, you!" I exclaimed. "What were you doing over the North Sea at the time?" He told me that he had been flying a 'Radar Fortress'. It was a hush-hush job, Top Secret, an electronic countermeasure aircraft used to jam the German radar. He had followed us down a ways and radioed our position to Air-Sea Rescue.

His Fortress had a huge radar dome, called a 'chin dome', mounted under the nose. It looked just like a beard.

A 214 Squadron Flying Fortress. Note the beard-like 'chin dome'. (Crown Copyright)

The crew of Lancaster 'S for Sugar' huddle together in their dinghy. They survived a sixteen-hour ordeal in the North Sea.

At 1230hrs the following day an Air Sea Rescue launch reached the crew, conveying them to safety.

Lou's first operational flight to Berlin was nearly his last. Over 10,000 people were bombed out in what Bomber Command considered to be a concentrated attack.

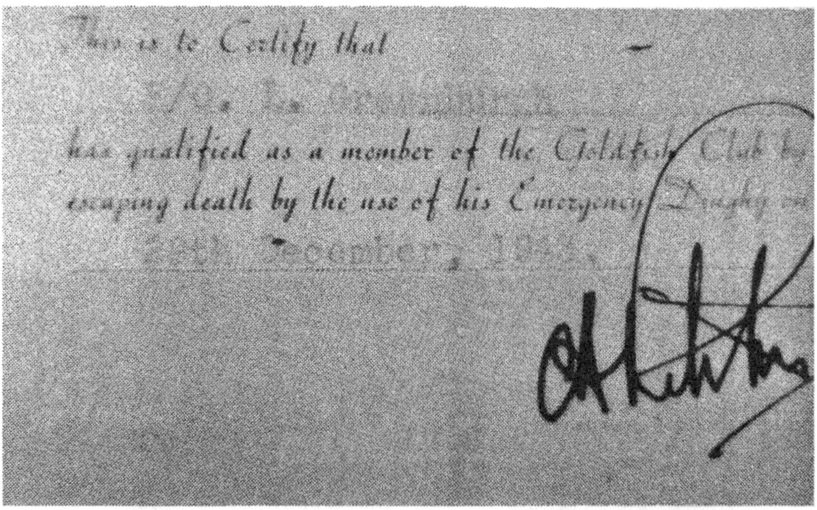

This is to Certify that

has qualified as a member of the Goldfish Club by
escaping death by the use of his Emergency Dinghy on
December, 194

For his efforts, Lou Greenburgh received a membership card (above) for the 'Goldfish Club', reserved for aircrew who survived the experience of ditching. He was also awarded his first DFC.

Chapter 8: The Battle of Berlin Continues

When my lecture tour was completed, I returned to 514 Squadron and was assigned a new Lancaster Mark II, serial number LL727, designated 'C2'[29]. It had a caricature of Charlie Chaplin painted on the nose.

A story about that caricature was related in a letter from Richard Roberts, who was part of my ground crew at that time:

'The painting was done by an airman named Robinson (nicknamed 'Robby'). He wasn't part of the ground crew but he must have been a painter on civvy street. It was a fine painting.

'One night Robby went on a night flight as a passenger on a bull's eye, which was a flight which tested the crew if they were caught in the search lights. The story was that the aircraft was over the U.K., went off course, and was shot down by ack ack fire. All were killed. And because my nickname was also Robby, some friends thought I'd bought it that night.'

There was something about Tommy Penkuri's personality which seemed to click with mine. He was a really nice guy, quiet, but with a sense of humor. He used to laugh at my jokes and could cheer me up with some dry comment which would be hilarious in the context he'd put it. After that first incident where he helped me deal with the trauma of my crash, we used to hang around together all of the time. We would go to the bar together, have lunch together. We played many games of shove ha'penny. In spite of the intense pressure we were under, Tommy as much as anyone else, he always seemed to be relaxed and that helped me to cope with my own fear. I hope I may have done the same for him.

I was able to talk to Tommy about things I normally would have kept to myself. I told him how afraid I was, and that the main reason I kept on flying was just that I was more afraid of what people would think of me if I quit. I had an inferiority complex, probably caused by the way my family had treated me.

Tommy helped me to develop more confidence in myself. "You know Lou," he once told me, "I've seen the way you handle an airplane. It's like it's a part of you." He also filled me in on what Strommy was saying about me. He

---

[29] *514 Squadron aircraft in 'A' and 'B' Flights bore the squadron code JI- followed by an individual letter (JI-A, JI-B etc). Those in 'C' Flight were coded A2- (A2-B, A2-C etc). The aircraft were referred to by the final letter, those in 'C' Flight carrying the suffix 2. Therefore Lancaster 'C2' was A2-C of 'C' Flight.*

Canadian pilot F/O Tommy Penkuri was a popular figure in 514 Squadron. As was so often the case, his time on operations was all too short. (514 Squadron Society)

said that Strommy had bragged that his skipper had more guts than anyone else's. That little bit of information did nothing to lower the camaraderie I was developing with Strommy.

We took a couple of training flights on January 22 and 26. Our next operation was for January 27; Berlin again.

This operation was to be performed without the Halifaxes; there would be just 515 Lancasters and 15 Mosquitoes. Some Halifaxes with H2S would be used, however, along with Stirlings and Wellingtons in an elaborate diversion into the Heligoland Bight[30].

With its usual ominousness, target Berlin approached. The whole place was lit up. There were rockets, tracer. I had never seen such fireworks. Enemy fighters, Mosquitoes, Lancs, all wove in and out, lit up by exploding shells and burning aircraft.

Fred was startled by a near miss and ducked. A good thing too; moments later his turret was shattered by a direct hit.

The target was cloud covered. We aimed our bombs on a sky-marker and headed back. The diversionary raids off the Dutch coast had drawn off much of the fighter defense but when the final count was taken we still had lost 33 Lancasters, 6.4%[31].

We made it safely back to base. The damage our aircraft had sustained was a blessing because we were able to miss a maximum effort raid planned for

[30] *Middlebrook, Martin, The Berlin Raids, op. cit., page 233.*

[31] *Information in this paragraph was from The Bomber Command War Diaries, op. cit., pages 467 & 468.*

the next night. You can imagine the disgust of crews ordered to hit Berlin for the second time in two nights.

We were continually being informed of new gadgets which the 'wizards' had developed to make our lives a bit easier – and longer. I attended a lecture on one of these devices shortly before leaving on this run to Berlin.

According to the officer conducting the lecture, our aircraft were being equipped with a radio detection device called '*Monica*'[32] which would inform us if an aircraft were close on our tail. A light at the bottom of the instrument panel would indicate that we were under attack.

The aircraft was repaired in time for our next operation on January 30. The target was Berlin.

We had good flying conditions for takeoff and were able to gain altitude before reaching cloud, which was now below and would hamper the fighters as they rose to intercept us. We were, however, cursed with moonlight so bright that some of the bombers actually formatted on each other[33].

We crossed the German coast just south of the Danish border, crossed that narrow peninsula, then turned towards the target. The last few attacks had also come from the north, so the Germans were expecting us to come over Holland this time. Their confusion allowed us to get within seventy miles of Berlin before meeting serious fighter opposition[34].

The full moon lit up enemy fighters such that we could see them plain as day. And I knew they could see us.

Tracer was all over the sky. It was so thick I didn't think we could fly through it. It was a real mishmash of constant attacks.

I heard the rear gunner's excited voice as he claimed credit for a 'kill'. Enemy fighters usually just disappeared into the night, and we were happy to see them go. With such a bright moon, however, he saw that one go down.

My gunners claimed a total of two enemy fighters, which they had seen go out of control and crash, but they probably shot down more than that. One of them said to me, "You know, Skipper, if I shoot down another fighter... you'll be a real hero!"

Colin reported a fighter on our tail. As I began to corkscrew, I saw a light shining at me from the bottom of the instrument panel. I screamed to the tail gunner that the fighter had broken our beam, that he was still close on our tail.

---

[32] *A description similar to that given by the author's father can be found in A Thousand Shall Fall, op. cit.*

[33] *The Berlin Raids, op. cit., page 250.*

[34] *Ibid., page 251.*

"I can't see him, I can't see him!" yelled Colin, over his rear gunner's intercom.

"He's there," I yelled back, "I know he's there. He's breaking our beam! I know he's there!"

I corkscrewed like I'd never corkscrewed before. Beads of sweat were running down my forehead. The warning light shone steadily, damningly. Never had a fighter hung on so closely.

"Oh God!" one of the men groaned, and then began to vomit spasmodically as he was overcome by motion sickness. I could tell that the rest of the crew would soon follow his example, but still I corkscrewed.

Were my crew blind, that they could not see him?! The phantom clung to our tail, ready to blast us into oblivion the moment his guns would bear. I cursed that steady white light!

All the way back, I corkscrewed. I corkscrewed over Germany, I corkscrewed across France, I corkscrewed above Holland, and I corkscrewed above the North Sea. For four solid hours, I corkscrewed, while the sweat ran down my face and my crew retched and vomited. "Are you crazy?!" someone cursed.

Around and around, climbing and diving, this way and that. So close to base and yet so far from safety. But do what I might, I couldn't shake our tenacious assailant. I corkscrewed for all I was worth. I had heard of bombers being shot down while landing back at base; knew crews who had been killed within minutes of safety.

Soon another danger appeared, one as fatal and inevitable as death itself. We were running out of fuel.

I no longer had a choice. To keep evading the fighter would only prolong our lives for the few minutes before our fuel ran out. At least if we came in to land, the gunners might give us a chance.

I eased back on the wheel and gave some opposite rudder to slow our turn, then entered the crosswind leg of our landing circuit. I braced myself for the hail of cannon shells which I expected would follow.

Why didn't he fire? The white light continued to shine, and it seemed like the enemy was following us into the circuit.

I was committed now. Evasive action was impossible as I eased back the throttle and the plane settled gently into her final approach. The light was still on as the wheels touched down. Either the fighter had landed with us or something was wrong.

I discussed it with the mechanics as soon as I had a chance. The little white light which I had been so afraid of had been telling me that our undercarriage was not completely up. It was just a minor electrical fault.

There were 33 aircraft lost that night[35], presumably some shot down on the journey home.

I was getting tired of all these Berlin raids. We had a reprieve during the month of February, which we spent conducting training exercises in bombing and fighter affiliation. The daytime fighter affiliation exercises were called 'ERICs'.

I used to go into the briefing room to see the battle order, the list of crews who were flying on ops that night. Was I ever relieved if my name wasn't on it!

They wouldn't tell you what the target was until you were in the briefing room, ready to go. Then they'd start handing out the escape kits and all the other stuff. I'd think "Oh my God!"

Our next target, on March 1, was Stuttgart (another heavily defended target). Heavy cloud on the routes to and from Stuttgart hid us from fighters and

---

[35] *The Bomber Command War Diaries, op. cit., page 469.*

our losses were relatively light, if you can call the loss of 4 aircraft and their crews 'light'[36].

It may have been on returning from Stuttgart that Fred Carey remarked, "Look at 'Joe' down there. The asshole's got his lights on!"

I looked down. Far beneath us was an FW 190, his lights glowing as if he were on a peacetime excursion. He probably hadn't seen us, because our lights weren't on.

"Keep a watch on him, guys." I instructed. The lights bobbed just out of range, coming closer then dropping away. All of the machine guns which would bear were trained on those lights, moving as they moved.

We wondered why he would be flying with his lights on. It might have been a ruse of some sort, or maybe he had turned them on by mistake. I don't know.

"Don't kid yourselves, guys." somebody commented, "He's a darn sight more scared than we are." To our relief, the lights soon faded off into the night.

Tommy and I used to wave at each other from our cockpits. When we could, we liked to line our aircraft up near each other before takeoff. Our friendship was making the war a little less unbearable.

On March 7 we did a low level attack on Le Mans. I had a copilot on this one, Sgt. Johnson.

We attacked at dusk, flying very, very low. The squadron's targets were the munitions factories which produced arms for Germany. It was pretty light out so I could see what I was doing. After dropping my bombs, I saw some truck convoys and stuff which I figured was worth our attention. Pretending that I was flying a fighter instead of a four engine Lancaster, I peeled off, swerved around, and put her into a dive.

The enemy had some flak guns but no air cover. We were unopposed as we swept down upon the enemy formations with our forward guns blazing. "Let them have it, boys!" I shouted. The whole airplane shook from the stuttering recoil of the front turret.

We flew over some railway freight cars and the front gunner fired into them as we passed. I pulled back on the wheel and said to my co-pilot, "I wish we had another couple of bombs. We could bomb those sheds."

I heard the rear gunner say, "There's another Lanc behind us, Skipper, doing the same thing. As I swerved around, I could see that I had two or three other planes following in line astern formation. The whole lot had seen us and

---

[36] *Ibid. page 477.*

were all pealing down. I could see sparks flying from their noses as they followed us on our strafing run.

We were really enjoying ourselves because there wasn't much opposition. If there were any fighters around, they sure kept clear of us. They couldn't have done anything anyway because we were so low.

There was an explosion under the airplane as we were hit by some light flak. It must have lifted us about thirty feet in the air. We shook. We could hear the shrapnel bouncing off of us. But there was no damage.

It was a great night for us. A target badly hit and not a single aircraft lost![37] Unfortunately, some bombs missed the target and 31 French people were killed, with another 45 injured. Such casualties did nothing to endear us to the French.

We hit Stuttgart again on March 15. We flew over France almost to the Swiss border before turning north-east. The fighters arrived just before we reached the target[38]. There were the usual fierce air battles, and a total of 37 aircraft out of 863 would be lost, but for once we escaped relatively unscathed.

The aircraft shuddered as we received a blast of flak. "Alright," I growled over the intercom, "who hiccoughed?"

Every night, except for that recent Le Mans raid, there were always at least a couple of crews who had not returned by the scheduled debriefing interrogation. Sometimes we would wait up for them. "Where's so and so?" someone would ask. Then we might hear an aircraft coming in, and somebody would point excitedly through the window and say, "There he is!" Other times we would drag ourselves off to bed and next day ask our mates, "Who's gone missing?"

On the morning following our March 15 raid on Stuttgart, Tommy Penkuri and his crew didn't come back.

I waited at the interrogation meeting, hoping against hope that some minor problem had delayed them. Maybe they had lost an engine and were limping home at a reduced speed. Maybe they had been diverted to Woodbridge, where an extra wide and specially equipped runway had been built to accommodate damaged aircraft. I waited without any sign of a last minute arrival or communique and eventually had to assume the worst.

Reluctantly, I headed off to the mess for my bacon and eggs. I sat down with the plate in front of me and my knife and fork in their respective hands. I

---

[37] *Ibid. page 479.*

[38] *Ibid. page 481.*

was about to cut into my meal but found that I had no appetite. I just sat there, staring at my food.

My vision began to blur. "Please, God...," I pleaded, in a quiet voice choked with tears. "Please let Tommy be alright. Please let him not be killed. Let me see Tommy Penkuri again."

This official record is quoted from the memorial register at the Commonwealth Air Training Plan Museum in Brandon, Manitoba:

'PENKURI, KAIHO THOMAS F/O (P) J20187. From Port Arthur, Ontario. Killed in Action Mar. 16/44 age 21. #514 Squadron (Nil Obstare Potest). Target – Stuttgart, Germany. ... Flying Officer Pilot Penkuri is buried at Villars-le-Pautel, Haute-Saone, France.

Tommy lies with members of his crew on each side of him.

On March 18, we were enroute to Frankfurt at an altitude of 18,000 feet. At 2350 hours, Colin reported a twin engined aircraft on our starboard quarter at 800 yards. It didn't fire and neither did Colin or Richard Woosnam, who was filling in for Fred Carey. They watched the fighter as it followed us. Colin and Ricard eventually grew tired of this waiting game and each fired a few short bursts. Colin then called for a corkscrew to starboard. We lost the fighter in the corkscrew and I resumed our course to the target.

I dropped my bombs over Frankfurt. I thought about my friends from the KARLSRUHE and remembered that one of them had family in that city. When the KARLSRUHE was sunk, I had worried about my friends.

March 22 found us over Frankfurt again. We dropped our bombs and headed for home at 19,000 feet. I was dismayed to see our Monica indicator light up and this time I knew it was no malfunction. Colin reported a JU 88 on the port quarter, level, at a range of eight or nine hundred yards. The enemy aircraft followed us in that position, just out of range of our guns, and began dropping flares. Two bursts of machine gun fire erupted from the nose of the aircraft and Colin ordered a corkscrew to port as the tracer passed close to the tailplane. I put the plane into a corkscrew to the left and Colin told me that the enemy was still firing at us.

I threw the Lanc into violent maneuvers. After what seemed an eternity, but wasn't more than two or three minutes, the enemy aircraft was lost to view. I steadied up (both the aircraft and myself) and resumed our course for home.

A woman once commented to me, "You must really hate the Germans to keep on going back like that."

"No," I replied, "I don't hate the Germans. No German ever tied me to a bed and beat me."

Chapter 9: The Night of the Big Winds

On March 24, 1944, we were preparing for our thirteenth operation. It was to be our fourth raid on Berlin. The C.O. kidded me, "Now Lou, try to bring this Lanc home in one piece. These babies are scarce.[39]"

I replied that at least he knew I pressed on with my attacks. Other crews had been known to drop their bombs in the sea or bomb the fringes of a target. Reconnaissance often showed that the bombs had 'creeped back' as bombers dropped their loads further and further from the center of the target.

Air Marshal Harris had stated "You must not think that the size of Berlin makes accurate bombing unimportant. There is no point in dropping bombs on the devastated areas in the west and southwest.[40]"

Most of the bombing of Berlin had been done blind, with the Pathfinders dropping their flares based on H2S radar navigation and the Main Force aiming at inaccurate sky markers. Berlin's distance from England had prevented the use of Oboe, a more accurate form of radio navigation. Eighteen previous raids on the German capital had done significant damage, seriously affected German war production and the deployment of their forces. They had not provided the knock-out blow that Bomber Harris had hoped would end the war. This raid was intended to be that knock-out blow.

The weather had held a prominent place in our briefing. Frontal cloud was moving eastward and might obscure the target, we were told, so Brunswick was identified as an alternate target. The plan was to fly over the middle of Denmark and approach Berlin from the northeast. A moderate north wind had been forecast.

Once again, we boarded the station bus. Somebody pulled out a harmonica and we sang Air Force songs accompanied by its homey chords. "Coming in on a wing and a prayer," we sang, "We've got one engine gone, but we'll still carry on, coming in on a wing and a prayer!" One by one, each crew

---

[39] *Some details of the navigator incident were based on the chapter "Berlin Again?," in 'Canadians in the Royal Air Force', by Les Allison, published by Les Allison, Roland, Manitoba, 1978. Printed by Friesen Printers, Altona, Manitoba. Some details of the event were also taken from Pat Butler's memoirs. They can be found using the link: http://www.butlersweb.com/Dad's%20Memoirs.htm. Pat's account differs from the author's account in some details.*

[40] *All references to the weather and many technical details were found in 'The Berlin Raids' by Martin Middlebrook, op.cit., pages 277 to 281. Harris' appeal was quoted from page 276 and footnoted from Alan W. Cooper, 'Bombers over Berlin'.*

was dropped off beside a gloomy black hulk. Berlin was confirmed as our target shortly before takeoff[41].

We didn't feel very heroic. I had a sick feeling in the pit of my stomach which grew worse as we took off and headed into enemy territory.

The winds were far stronger than had been forecast. In fact, they were so strong that experienced navigators would not believe their own calculations. 'Windfind', a procedure where selected navigators transmitted their wind calculations back to base so that they could be averaged and relayed back, was actually making things worse. Most navigators were scaling down their estimates before sending them to headquarters and headquarters was doing the same thing, compounding the problem. The winds were over a hundred miles per hour and the force was being scattered. This would later remembered as 'the night of the big winds'[42].

"Where the hell are we, Pat?" I asked after a while. "We seem to be off course. It doesn't look familiar down there."

"Just been doing some checking," Pat replied. "The met people told us there was supposed to be a moderate north wind. Hell, it's a strong southwest wind, and we're nearly a couple of hundred miles north of our course. Those searchlights must be Flensburg- almost on the Danish border."

There were searchlights all over the place and we were dodging the flak like crazy. The sky was lit up like daylight by the constant flashes of anti-aircraft fire. Then the firing stopped. "Skipper," Colin said from his rear gunner position, "the ack-ack seems to have died down."

There were no more flashes. I felt a cold sweat break out on my brow and it was an effort to maintain normal breathing through my oxygen mask. When there were no flashes, I knew, there were fighters.

The searchlights were trying to get us into 'cones'. When a bomber was caught in a searchlight, other searchlights would move onto it, providing a brilliant target for night fighters. The story was that once you were caught in a cone, you were finished.

"Keep your eyes open and steer me clear of searchlights," I ordered.

Just as I said it, I was blinded by a dazzling white light. I looked down beneath the instrument panel to keep the spotlight out of my eyes. It was like looking directly into a powerful flashlight.

"Hold on!" I shouted as I twisted the wheel, "I'm going to put this thing into a spiral dive!"

---

[41] *Ibid. page 277.*

[42] *Ibid. page 281.*

The whole airplane was lit up like a torch. The wings stretching out on either side of me were bright silver and the glare from the instruments was so bright that I could barely read them. We were a sitting target.

I tried every evasive trick in the book, but it was hopeless. The Lancaster was trapped in the searchlights like a moth wriggling in a spider's web. I couldn't get rid of the searchlights.

I pulled the nose right up. As our airspeed bled off the left wing fell and I pushed the nose right down into a power dive. We still had a full bombload and with those radial engines booming the airspeed indicator was off the clock. We were doing nearly five hundred m.p.h.

I heard a scream from the bomb aimer and was horrified to see a black shape directly ahead of us. I banked hard to port and so missed a fiery death by the skin of my teeth.

We had almost hit another Lanc. When I pulled out of the dive, we were clear but the other Lanc was trapped in the searchlights. Within seconds it was going down in flames.

Someone said, "Thank Christ for that."

We were down to about 13,000 feet so I set the aircraft to climb and we were back at 21,000 feet by the time we approached the outskirts of Berlin. The city's defenses started about fifty miles from the center.

There wasn't much activity because the Pathfinders hadn't dropped their flares yet. We started to circle the city in preparation for our bombing run.

Dozens of searchlights began sweeping the sky, lighting up hundreds of bombers. I could see silhouettes all around me and I involuntarily braced myself for collision. The thought of collision was constantly on my mind during these raids, with so many aircraft doing complex maneuvers without lights, and it scared the hell out of me. The memory of our own near miss didn't help much either. I peered into the blackness ahead and all around.

Ahead of us dangled the deadly webs of Christmas trees.

"Skipper," the bomb aimer reported, "there's 'testicles' all over the place."

My stomach was tied in knots, as usual. Sitting there in the dark, not knowing what was ahead of me, was worse than being chewed out by an employer.

What was keeping those Pathfinders?! We were one of the few crews which compensated for the strength of the wind by circling Berlin. Some planes had been blown right past Berlin and bombed other towns or just got rid of their bombs. Others who had been blown past were fighting their way back against strong headwinds. A few stragglers were marking time by flying into the wind.

They would later zoom across the target in record time, bombing as they went[43]. We usually weren't over the target for more than a few minutes and here we were going around and around like ducks in a shooting gallery.

"Look guys," I said into the microphone, "if we don't see something soon, I'm going to drop the bombs and get out of here." The crew agreed with me.

"Starboard!" screamed Colin from his tail gunner position. I immediately spun the wheel hard right and kicked right rudder. A mass of brilliant lights zoomed past on our immediate left. Ducking down as low as I could inside the armor plating of the cockpit, I finished the corkscrew and did another circuit.

The perspiration prickled under my flight suit. "Let's drop the stuff and get to hell out of here!" I exclaimed. A red flare burst right below us so I changed my mind. "Forget that, get ready to bomb."

An urgent voice came over the radio. "Don't bomb that flare - that's a German spoof!"

A burst of light caught my attention for a second. It was a bomber going down in flames. Then another, and another.

A white flare appeared over to our right. The Master Bomber's voice came over the radio again. "That's your target, boys."

Wing Commander Lane, a Canadian, had arrived over the target on time and was trying in vain to organize a concentrated attack. He gave us encouragement as he orbited the target. "Those bastards wanted a war" he growled, "now show them what war is like.[44]"

I had never seen a target so brightly lit. The Germans were shining their searchlights into the clouds to create a diffused light and burned phosphorous torches on the ground. It was so bright that you could have read a newspaper[45].

We began the bombing run. Colin screamed again. "JU 88 up our ass, Skipper!"

Don Bament yelled, "I got it right on, don't move!"

I hesitated for a split second, then felt a jerk as the bombs were let go. The aircraft buoyed upwards.

I headed home at 20,000 feet, steadying up on course 217 degrees at 175 knots.

By 2235 hours we were approximately 15 miles south of the target. "Corkscrew starboard!" Fred called out, "JU 88 on our starboard quarter at 300 yards and closing in!"

---

[43] *Ibid., page 285.*

[44] *Ibid., page 286.*

[45] *Ibid., page 288.*

Fred and Colin opened fire as I threw the plane into a spiral. The enemy aircraft fired a few short bursts and disappeared to port

Two minutes later, Colin reported a JU 88 attacking from 400 yards on the port quarter. He gave it a two second burst and ordered a corkscrew to port. Fred Carey joined him with a four second burst as C Charlie swung over to the left. The enemy aircraft followed us into the turn, firing long bursts of machine gun fire as he went. Our gunners' bullets struck home on the centre section of the enemy and we parted company.

Sitting at his flight engineer's seat at my right, Les caught a glimpse of an aircraft coming at us from the front, and yelled "Starboard for Christ's sake!" so I cranked the wheel and kicked the rudders hard to the right. The starboard side canopy shattered into fragments and a hail of bullets riddled my instrument panel. The inner starboard engine burst into flame and the starboard outer engine also quit as the velocity of our turn sucked the fuel out of its carburetor.

The port wing came up and we barrel rolled onto our back. I knew we were upside down because the altimeter showed that we were losing altitude and the direction indicator showed that we were going 'up'. The direction indicator was upside down. Completely out of control, we accelerated into a spiral dive.

Dense smoke filled the cockpit and tracer bullets were still whamming into us from the fighter, which was following us down. We could explode any second.

"Bail out!" I yelled. Fred Carey, who had seen the shell explode as it hit the engine, left his turret and prepared to jump. I felt a blast of cold air about my knees as either Geordie or Don ripped open the forward escape hatch and they both dived through that tiny rectangular hole in our nose, one after the other.

We were going around and around in a circle over the center of Berlin. The air was full of flak. I tried to regain control of my stricken aircraft but within seconds we had fallen to 7,000 feet.

"I can't get out, Skipper!" screamed the tail gunner through the intercom. "I can't get out of this thing!"

Smoke was filling the cockpit. "You've got to get out!" I yelled. I knew we wouldn't be airborne much longer.

"How the hell am I going to get out of here!?"

"I don't know how, but you've got to!"

Strommy and Fred Carey headed aft to assist Colin, who was using his emergency axe to free himself, cutting an oxygen line in the process. I unclipped my harness and began moving to the front escape hatch, tearing open the buttoned flap which covered my rip cord handle and trying not to snag on the multitude of metal objects which stuck out of the forward turret and bomb aimer's position.

Pat was standing at his navigation berth and seemed frozen. His gaze was focused on the route to the escape hatch and a look of horror marked his features.

"Get the hell out of here!" I yelled. The din was incredible, with the sounds of the crashing bomber, all of us shouting, and the wind roaring through the hatch.

"I can't, Skipper," Pat replied, "I've lost my parachute!" The pack had slipped from its storage and disappeared out of the open escape hatch.

What could I do? "Take my goddamned parachute!" I ordered, without thinking, but navigators wore a type that clipped on in front and pilots wore the type that you sat on. As I reached back to unclip it I realized that even if I could get it off in time, Pat would be unable to use it. And I didn't want to die, either! It was one hell of a situation.

The plane rolled onto its back again and Pat practically fell on top of me. I bounced against the ceiling for a moment, then the plane righted itself.

"Don't worry, Pat, I won't leave you!" We were hundreds of feet closer to the ground with each rotation. Every split second counted.

I dragged myself back to the flight deck. I grabbed the throttles with one hand and the back of my seat with the other. What dials I had left were spinning like the hands of a stopwatch. "How the hell am I going to stop this?" I muttered to myself.

With no time to think, I had to respond instinctively. As I swung into my seat I cut power to the engines. With the imbalance corrected, the plane started to respond. My entire body ached as I strained at the controls. I glanced at the altimeter as we pulled out of the dive and was shocked to see that we were at 2,000 feet, then less than 2,000 feet. From eighteen thousand feet! I pulled back on the wheel to convert the speed from our dive into as much altitude as possible and then gave her some throttle, gently this time. We levelled out at about three or four thousand feet. It wasn't until then that I realized I had two dead engines. Good thing the Lancaster was a very stable aircraft with two big fins and counterbalanced rudders.

Pat joined me in the cockpit. Strommy, Colin, and Fred had decided to stay with us and were busy putting out fires with an extinguisher.

Everything was smashed. The gyro was a useless lump of metal and the rest of our navigation equipment was ruined. The Monica had caught fire during the spin.

I decided to fly west and hoped to recognize places as we passed them. "Well guys," I called out, "we're going home!"

Pat and Strommy grinned. I felt a wave of relief that we had pulled out of the dive but was worried about the ordeal ahead.

With both dead engines on the starboard wing, the drag on that side was crippling. It took all of my skill and all of my strength just to keep us on course, so evasive action was out of the question. We scanned the skies above us, dreading the sight of an enemy fighter.

I hadn't feathered the starboard props yet. I managed to get #3 engine restarted and I hoped that I could keep it going, but it soon quit again. I couldn't get either of the starboard engines to restart after that so I feathered the props, cut off their fuel, and resigned myself to a long and difficult trek.

As 'Fortress Berlin' drew astern of us, light flak began to fire on our left. We managed to dodge the predicted flak.

It was almost impossible to turn left with the tremendous drag to starboard but just relaxing the controls was enough for a turn to the right. Maneuverability was further impaired by the severe damage which had been done to our flaps and ailerons. I realized that with each maneuver we were losing altitude we could never hope to regain.

Our low altitude was a mixed blessing; at least we were too low to be tracked by radar and the fighters were concentrating on targets higher up.

"We should be going due west," shouted Pat above the roar of the port engines. The usual noises were amplified with the canopy all shot up. The bullets had come in over my right shoulder, shattering the starboard vision panels. Fortunately, the main windscreen was still intact. "Those big lights ahead to the left should be Brunswick or Hanover. Keep well to the right. If it's Hanover, the flak will be hellish."

The loss of our navigation equipment and charts was a grave matter. Many aircraft, even those fully operative and competently navigated, had been lost when they strayed just a few miles off their intended track and over a defended area. Strommy copied down hourly wind broadcasts received from the base. They referred to conditions high above us but we were able to get some use from them.

I wanted to estimate our fuel supply but all of the gages had been wrecked. I was sure that we had lost everything on the starboard side. We were fighting a strong headwind and I estimated that our speed over the ground wasn't more than 100 knots. With six hundred miles to go, that made for a long trip - if we had enough fuel. I tried not to think about the last time I had been forced to ditch.

While Strommy and the others were putting out fires and assessing the damage, Pat was sitting up front with me. He gave me encouragement and told me that he really appreciated what I was doing for him.

"Lou," he said, "I'll never forget you." He said I could be like part of his family and invited me to spend my leave with him. He offered to introduce me to his sister.

We spotted some more lights to the left and guessed that they were Osnabruck. My arms and legs were aching by now and I was scared of losing control and spinning to the ground. I could have taken some of the pressure off of the rudders by raising the starboard wing higher but that would have put us into a bit of a sideslip and made it even more difficult to maintain our altitude.

The starboard wing continued to burn. I prayed that it would hold together. Other aircraft had been lost when their wings actually fell off.

I was relieved to see the familiar landmarks of Holland. As we approached the coastline near the Walcheren Islands, we were attacked by coastal batteries and some flak ships. We avoided the flak, but at a significant cost in altitude. We were down to only 2,000 feet.

Pat went back to see how Strommy's damage check was going, then rejoined me in the cockpit. "Skipper," he reported, "we're just riddled with shell holes. It's a miracle that none of the cables were cut."

We finally had the open waters of the North Sea below us.
I could stop worrying about flak batteries but I was still very concerned about our fuel supply. We had been flying for over ten hours already and still had more than two hundred miles to go. Even with both feet on the port rudder pedal the effort was agonizing.

Way off in the distance, a bit to the south of our track, was a beacon of light. In blacked out England, that could only be the emergency landing field at Woodbridge. The 'drome was equipped with FIDO (Fog Intense Dispersal Of), a pipeline of sorts which ran on either side of the extra wide runway. All along each pipeline was a series of burning jets which were visible in almost any weather. That was of great assistance to aircraft landing in reduced visibility or with damaged navigational equipment. And that wide runway would give you a greater safety margin when landing a disabled aircraft.

But Goddammit! That burning light could attract fighters like a light bulb drew moths. I'd heard that they swarmed above Woodbridge, hoping to pick off an easy target or two. I was also worried about traffic congestion. Suppose I had to wait in line behind someone else, or found the field cluttered with damaged aircraft? We could arrive safely, only to die in a collision on the ground.

Another concern of mine was the altitude we would lose if I tried to bank to the left. Waterbeach was ahead of us and not much further than Woodbridge. Besides, Waterbeach was home. I didn't like the idea of landing a disabled aircraft at an unfamiliar field.

"What do you think," I asked my comrades, "should we try for the emergency 'drome at Woodbridge?"

Strommy piped up from the rear. "I've got a date tonight, so it would sure be nice to make it home to Waterbeach."

Pat and I exchanged grins. "OK, Strommy," I called over my shoulder, "we'll keep north and try for base."

Strommy's date was the last thing on my mind.

With the coming of daylight, we could see the English coast ahead and were soon navigating by familiar landmarks. I aimed the crippled aircraft a bit further north and was glad when Pat told me that Waterbeach was just a few miles ahead.

Our twelve hour odyssey had left me completely exhausted and I dreaded the landing to come. Our radio was useless, so I made a wide pass around the field to show that we were in a disabled condition. As we neared the tower, I ordered Pat to fire off some red flares, which started a hub-bub of activity down below. We were losing altitude fast, but I held us in the turn until we were facing the wind. Ordering the others into crash positions, I pointed the nose towards a grass strip to the west of the runway and throttled back to near stalling speed. The controls were sluggish at that low speed but the ground slowly rose up to meet us.

I felt a sudden loss of power and knew that one of our engines had quit, but I was too excited to notice which one. The one remaining engine began to sputter. Thank God we were on our final approach!

I cut the throttles just before we hit. We ploughed into the sod like a great ship grounding on a sandbar. There was a tremendous grating sound as our belly was ripped out and I thought the plane would be torn into a thousand pieces. The instant silence had an unreal quality about it and as my muscles relaxed I slumped into a state of shock.

The ambulance and crash wagon were on the scene in a matter of seconds. I was so numb that I could hardly get out of my seat. I gradually forced my tired body out of the cockpit and wandered over to the waiting ambulance. None of us were in the mood for dinner so the ambulance took us directly to our debriefing.

Wing Commander Sampson met us outside the debriefing room and shook my hand. "I don't know how that plane was able to fly, Lou," he said, "it's so full of holes. And half of the starboard wing's burned off." Engineers checking out the fuel tanks the next day would find them bone dry.

A pilot once said of the Lancaster, "If there was one quarter of one left by the German defenses, that quarter would fly home.[46]"

We entered the debriefing room where 'Tommy', the intelligence officer, was waiting to get our story. I told him how I had returned to the cockpit after Pat had lost his parachute.

"What the hell, Lou!" Pat interjected, "Are you trying to get the bloody VC?! If it hadn't been for me, we'd likely all be P.O.W.'s or dead by now!"

That was the end of our beautiful friendship. I guess the strain had been too much for the both of us.

As we left the debriefing, I heard Strommy tell Pat that he thought I did deserve a Victoria Cross. I couldn't have cared less. My nerves were shot.

I went to the mess after the debriefing to try and enjoy the treat of bacon and eggs which was always provided for returning aircrew. I forced down a few bites but could barely swallow. My stomach began to churn so I abandoned my dinner and ran outside and around behind the mess. I heaved my guts out.

To this day, I can't eat a decent meal without bringing up.

I was sick all night. I vomited again and again, until I thought my guts would tear. By three o'clock in the morning, it was obvious that my condition was serious and a doctor was called in to examine me.

He started off by doing all of the usual things a doctor would do when examining a patient, in the usual businesslike way. He collected a sample of my stomach acid - there was more of that around me than inside me - and disappeared into the next room to run some tests.

He returned a few minutes later. I put aside the pail I had been retching into and gathered my breath.

He sat down in a chair near me and said, quietly, "Your stomach acid is extremely strong. I've read the debriefing report. You must have gone through quite a bit."

I nodded and fought back the urge to vomit again. "It was hell." I croaked.

"I have a confession." he said in a quiet voice, "For years I have hated Jews. But after what you've been through, I will have to alter my thinking."

---

[46] *Tubbs, D.B., "Lancaster Bomber", op. cit., page 9.*

Chapter 10: The Invasion Approaches

After a brief leave period, I was flying again. I was assigned a new navigator as well as replacements for those crew members who had bailed out. Flight Sergeant Eric Rippingale was my new bomb aimer, F/Sgt Frank Collingwood was my new flight engineer, and Sgt Richard Woosnam was my new rear gunner.

My new navigator's name was Flight Sergeant Ronald Fox. He was a survivor from the disastrous Nuremberg raid of March 30/31, during which Bomber Command lost ninety-four aircraft out of a force of eight hundred. Bomber Command lost more aircrew that night than Fighter Command had lost during the entire Battle of Britain. Fox's aircraft had crashed at base on returning from that raid[47].

Strommy and I were becoming quite close because of the experiences we had shared and I remember that he was always following me around like a beloved puppy. If I went into the officers' mess, I could expect to come out and find Strommy waiting for me. He once confided in me, "You know Skipper, I think you should have got the Victoria Cross."

Amazingly, C2 LL727 was not a write off. The damage was extensive, of course, but the Lancaster was designed with the lives of a cat. Because of its modular construction, entire wings could be unbolted and replaced. Major parts such as wings, engines and tail planes were kept on hand so that damaged aircraft could be put back into service as soon as possible. There was a large trailer used to ship whole fuselages to a factory for repair. We called it 'The Queen Mary'. I don't know the exact details, but I guess that the starboard wing and the bomb bay doors were replaced, the fuselage was repaired and then the Air Force gave her back to me.

I used some spare aircraft while I was waiting for C2's repairs to be completed. We did some fighter affiliation maneuvers and other exercises. I was glad to have a short break from operations and the exercises gave me a chance to get to know my new crew members.

The speed of the Lanc II continued to impress me. When I opened the taps and put the nose down I could even outrun a Hurricane. I know that because during maneuvers the pilot of a Hurricane called me on the radio and asked me to slow down.

---

[47] *Mr. Ronald Fox informed the author of his Nuremburg experience in a letter dated October 13, 1991.*

I got C2 LL727 back on April 20. We bombed Cologne. In my log book, I noted that the German name for that city was Koln.

I took the airplane up for the usual pre-operation air test before our next op. Afterwards, Ronald came with me as I checked the bomb load and talked to the ground crew. I was usually pretty informal with the mechanics who looked after my plane. One new fellow kept calling me 'Sir'. I told him, "Don't call me 'Sir,' call me 'Skipper'.[48] "

We later met at the briefing room. I was handed my escape kit as I entered the room and took a seat in front of the veiled display board. When the curtain was pulled aside, I saw that the target was Dusseldorf. We were going back to 'Happy Valley', the Ruhr.

The lecturer pointed out technical aspects of the target and then turned the presentation over to the Meteorological Officer. He gave us a rundown of the weather conditions and told us to be especially careful of the wind, which was coming from the North at about a hundred miles per hour. The navigator and I discussed that briefly before we headed out to the plane.

We took off at dusk and joined the main formation as the sky got dark. Once darkness fell, each plane had to rely on its own navigation because you couldn't see well enough to formate on someone else. Although we were flying the same route from the same departure point to the same target, and usually wound up being together, each plane was making its own way.

We were heading on a course of 180. Ronald and I had an ongoing dialogue. "Checking the course." I said.

"One eight zero," he confirmed. "One eight zero."

"Okay," I acknowledged, "One eight zero."

We carried on for a while before the navigator said, "We're a little off." I said, "Okay," and waited for the navigator to compute a new course. After a moment he came back with "Skipper, make it 'eighty-seven'."

I made a minor course adjustment and steadied up on course 187.

After a while, we began to draw quite a bit of flak. I hadn't expected so much at this stage of our journey and I was concerned that nobody else seemed to be drawing any. If you're on your own, they can single you out.

"Are you sure we're on the right course," I asked, "We're getting quite a bit of flak."

"Yes, Skipper." he replied, "We're on the right course."

---

[48] *That insight into Lou Greenburgh's character was provided by a letter from Mr. R. Roberts, who was part of his ground crew.*

I wasn't so sure, so I questioned him again. "We've been flying a long time on this 'One eight seven'."

"One eight seven!" he exclaimed. "Skipper! Skipper! I meant course 'eighty-seven' not 'One eight seven!"

"Jesus Christ!" I cursed, "There's no way we can turn back!" We had been flying at right angles to our proper course with a hundred miles per hour tail wind.

"No'! No'!" he concurred, "We're a hundred and forty miles off course now!"

The antiaircraft flashes were all aimed at us. I wondered where the hell we were.

"Skipper..."

I interrupted him. "How far are we from Dusseldorf?"

"I don't know, Skipper, but we're outside of Paris."

"Jesus Christ! Well, what are we going to do? We've got our bombs. We can't waist them and we can't take them back."

There were still plenty of lights on in this area. I guess nobody was expecting the Allies to bomb France. Sitting about forty miles outside of Paris was the distinctive form of an aerodrome. I decided to head towards it.

The flak died down and then stopped. As I circled the aerodrome in preparation for my attack, I saw that it had its own airplanes flying around. They probably figured that we were one of theirs.

"Listen." I said to the navigator and the bomb aimer, "Get ready. We're going to bomb this enemy airport."

I pulled the lever to open the bomb doors and began an approach which would line us up with the runway. Then I saw some large, rectangular buildings by the side. "It's no use bombing the runway," I said to my bomb aimer, "because they can take off and land in the field beside it. Aim for those buildings."

I made another circuit to line up with the new target and began to take direction from the bomb aimer. "Left, left, left, we're coming on to the buildings." he said. Then I felt the aircraft heave and heard him say, "Bombs gone!"

An instant later we saw one or two explosions smack in the middle of the buildings. All of the lights went out for miles around and the sky was suddenly full of antiaircraft flashes.

I pushed the wheel forward and gunned the throttles, swooping down to 150 feet off the ground. I was afraid that I might hit a high mast or something but I was more afraid of fighters. They would be after me like nobody's business.

I stayed at a low level until we hit the coast, then began to climb a little bit. We still had to be careful because there was flak coming up at us from flak ships.

At last we saw the beacon from our own aerodrome. I came in and requested permission to land. We were all alone and way ahead of schedule. The air traffic controllers were surprised.

Since we were the only ones back, we had our own private debriefing. I told the officers what had happened and was a bit worried about possible repercussions. They didn't seem to mind, though. And the next day, Intelligence confirmed that a German training station had received a direct hit. We must have killed quite a few young pilots.

I made a note in my log book, "April 22, 1944. Ops Dusseldorf. Bombed Airfield NE (Paris)."

It was about this time that we had a visit from some Russian 'brass'. The Soviets were pushing for a second front to take the pressure off of their guys who, they felt, were fighting the war by themselves. Two generals were going to interview us to get some idea of what we were doing.

We all gathered in a classroom. The senior officer told us to hold nothing back but to give the Soviets an accurate picture of what we were going through. Our bosses wanted the Russians to know that our raids were not a 'piece of cake'.

It was strange, seeing those Soviet uniforms. The only Soviet uniforms I had ever seen before were in the movies. One of the generals was quite young and spoke English well. The other one was older and needed some translation. He probably learned what he needed to know by the sound of our voices and the look in our eyes.

"Hey," somebody said, "if you want to know about air battles, you should talk to Greenburgh!"

With that introduction, I told them about some of my experiences. I think they got the message.

We did an air test on April 24 before attacking Karlsruhe that night. We had bad weather on that raid. We looked forward to bad weather. When I got back, my skin still intact, I went into the mess as usual. I thought about my friends from the cruiser *Karlsruhe*, drank my drink, and then forgot about them. I had other things to worry about.

April 27, 1944, found us in the troubled skies above Friedrichshafen, on the Swiss-German border. Oh, you could see fighters all over the place, mainly FW 190's! There were fighters and searchlights and Lancasters, all mixing in, all trying to get a bead on one another. We could see scarecrows and Christmas trees dangling. We could see the fighters circling.

My rear gunner and mid upper gunner were both hammering away at the same enemy fighter. It disappeared into the night and I don't know if we drove him off or shot him down. We may have killed the pilot and left the plane flying. One of the fighters went under us. I told my gunners to keep a watch out. The rear gunner yelled, "Starboard!"

Soviet Air Attache Maj. Gen Andrei Sharapov presents a medal to a US serviceman. Sharapov and his assistant, Lt. Col. Rouday, were amongst the VIP visitors to Waterbeach. They had a conversation with F/O Lou Greenburgh which was, no doubt, interesting to both parties (514 Squadron Society).

I corkscrewed to starboard just as a whole hail of bullets went by. They just missed us. They would have blown us to pieces. I could see the shells, like sparks, going by ahead of us.

I kept corkscrewing. My rear gunner said, "He's gone under us, Skipper!" I took more evasive action.

Shells exploded right where we would have been had we not swerved aside. The rear gunner said there was another '190 on our tail.

"Well," I stated, "I know how we're going to get out of this!"

Underneath me were the two big sheds which had been used for the former 'Hindenburg' and other large zeppelins. I circled them. I could see the factory where the zeppelins had been manufactured. The whole place was lit up from all of the fires. I pushed the nose down and came screaming in.

We were heading for those two hangers, almost between them. I clicked on the intercom and said to the crew, "I wish we had another bomb!" We would have made short work of those hangers.

I didn't fly directly between the hangers because I was afraid of hitting some obstruction. But we were low enough to scrape off any fighters which might have been under us.

I thought we were clear of the enemy and started to climb. "He's still up our ass, Skipper!" called the rear gunner. We were attacked again. I tried veering left and circled the burning factories. The fighter followed us. I couldn't evade those guys.

Eric said, "Skipper, let's get the hell out of this! I've never seen so many searchlights in all my life! Or so many fighters!"

I put the nose down to gain speed and said, "We'll get out of this! I'm going over Lake Constance. That's neutral territory. They wouldn't dare follow us!"

Rockets were whizzing by, tracer was whizzing by. My gunners fired on the fighters as they made a pass and disappeared into the night.

"Wouldn't they?!" demanded the rear gunner, and the mid upper gunner added, "They're right behind us!"

The rear gunner yelled, "Those god-damned bastards are following us! They don't give a damn about Switzerland!"

Of course, neither did we. There were two large fighters on our tail, twin engine, and it was a hell of a situation.

I could see the mountains in the distance and knew that we would have a chance if we could reach them. I put her right down and practically skimmed across the surface of the lake.

There was a dark spot between the hills. I flew right into that and kept on flying over Switzerland.

We could see the fighters circling in the distance, looking for us. We flew off over Switzerland and then back home.

When I was filling out my log book that night, I wrote in the routine information then added the comment, 'Panic'.

I was lying in the barracks one time, listening to a speech by Herman Goering. After each statement in German came an English translation. "Twenty-seven Jews died behind enemy lines today." the translator said, "There are no Jews on the front lines."

"Hey Greenburgh!" somebody called out, "What are you doing here?"

I've never flown a Lancaster in peacetime, but I did lots of practice flights. I sometimes visited the old places where I used to work as a mechanic so I could 'lord it over' some of the guys who never got promotion: the ones who had laughed at me or given me a hard time.

I ran into that corporal whose sarcasm had convinced me to apply for the pilots' course. He couldn't believe it when he saw my wings and my rank. Couldn't believe it at all.

I went back to another station where my old flight sergeant, my boss, had once said to me, "If you work very, very hard, within six months I'll make you a corporal. But you've got to work hard and show me you can do the stuff, Greenburgh, because, you know, you're really not very bright." He wanted me to do his bidding.

Anyway, I took the station engineer and a few other guys up in a Lanc and went to see this guy. I'll tell you something, his face turned white when he saw me. I asked him if he remembered me.

"Yeah," was all he said.

"Did you know I went on a pilots' course?" I persisted.

"I didn't know what happened to you. I've got to go back to work." With that, he turned his back and walked off. I think he was a bit embarrassed. He didn't want to stay and talk to me.

By the beginning of May, 1944, the objectives of Bomber Command were beginning to shift. We stopped hitting targets with harsh German names and were being assigned targets with softer names, French names. Rather than destroying Hitler's industrial and military resources, our new operations were intended to prevent him from deploying those resources on the coast of France. We were hitting communications networks; railway lines, bridges, aqueducts.

Rows and rows of Lancasters were formated in the dusk sky, May 1, 1944, heading for the gun emplacements at Chambly. There was moderate ack ack and the tracer flashes in the dark were evidence of enemy fighters.

Three of the Lancs ahead of us went into dives with sparks shooting out from the front. I clicked on the crew intercom and instructed "Have your guns ready, front guns."

This raid was to be conducted at a low level, so I dived down to the attack altitude. I picked out a cement block with guns sticking out and headed straight for it.

"Bombs gone, Skipper." said Eric Rippingale.

Our machine guns sprayed the coast with a deadly rain as we strafed the gun emplacements at ground level. We veered to the right and I hauled back on the wheel, soaring up to 3,000 feet. I set course back for base.

As we crossed the French coast, Fred Carey shouted, "FW 190 on our port side, 9 o'clock!"

I looked to my left and there, in the hazy twilight, was a Focke Wulf flying a parallel course, as if we were in formation together. He was within two hundred feet. I could see the pilot's head in his cockpit and could clearly see the German markings. Even at that range, though, my gunners could not be sure of scoring a hit.

I ordered the gunners to keep their weapons trained on him. "The second he veers towards us," I said, "let him have it."

It was a Mexican standoff. The fighter had ten machine guns pointed at him, even if they were puny 303's. I decided to wait and see what would happen. If we missed, and he got underneath us, we were finished. As long as we didn't fire, he wouldn't know that he was out of our effective range. Feeling a bit melodramatic, I let the General Wolfe in me creep out and ordered, "Don't shoot until you see the whites of his eyes."

I didn't think his fuel would last much longer and hoped I could win a waiting game. After a few minutes, he waggled his wings at us, waved, and flew away.

I waved back.

We bombed Courtrai on May 10. On May 11, I had a copilot named F/Lt Norbury for an operation over Louvain, in Belgium. We had a bit of a reprieve from May 14 to May 16, just flying on exercises. We did an air test, fighter affiliation, and practiced flying in formation. F/O McFeteridge was my copilot for an attack on Le Mans on May 19. These were low level raids we were flying now and I was becoming very concerned about the light flak which was far more accurate than heavy flak. There was dense light flack during the Le Mans operation. On May 19, we bombed Duisburg.

We did a cross country flying exercise from Westcott to Chipping Warden on May 23.

It was May 24. I gunned the throttles on takeoff and, to my horror, the Lanc veered off the runway. I managed to get her into the air but we were just barely climbing. Sgt. Collingwood noticed that there was some trouble with the oil pressure in one of the engines. After a few minutes, in which he tried to remedy the situation, the engine spluttered and quit. "Starboard outer motor's gone, Skipper." He told me that there was nothing he could do.

I think the crew expected me to scrub the mission. But what the hell, in the past few months I had flown with less than four engines so much that it was almost routine. I told them that we would carry on to the target.

The rear gunner grumbled over the intercom, "That's just like the Skipper! He'd be a real hero... on the backs of all of us!"

I feathered the dead engine. We would never be able to climb up to the usual cruising altitude but I figured we'd at least reach about 16,000 feet. With our speed reduced we couldn't keep up with the main stream. I'd have to pick out an alternate target.

"He's crazy." somebody else added, "He never gets scared."

Lou Greenburgh with his daughter, Anna.

Much as I didn't like overhearing criticism, I had to smile a bit at that last remark. If only they knew! I was so scared I could hardly think and my stomach was in knots. Not just then but whenever we headed for a major operation. I could picture the bullets heading right for me, ripping through the fuselage of the aircraft and shredding my own fuselage. I remembered what a close thing it had been before, how many narrow squeaks I had had in the recent past. Even after an op., when I had been granted a few more hours of life, I would wonder when my luck was going to run out. And then I would start vomiting again.

If only they knew! But I couldn't let them know. I was their commander, the captain of the aircraft. I couldn't let them know how afraid I was.

We reached the gun batteries at Boulogne area, dropped our load, and headed back.

I saw a shadow close ahead of us. I cranked the wheel hard to the left and kicked left rudder. The shadow flashed past as we flipped to almost 90 degrees of bank. I don't know if it was one of ours or one of theirs. We headed back through the coastal flak batteries to the relative safety of the sea.

It had been a hell of an ordeal, as usual, but compared to some of our previous missions it was practically a walk in the roses. We had few bullet holes if any.

It was just about sunrise when we reached the British coast. "Well, guys," I said, "we're coming in."

"Yeah." Fred Carey remarked, "Coming in on a wing and a prayer!"

I looked at our wings in the morning light as the sun slipped above the horizon. There were shadows moving about the three good engines, with transparent blurs spinning in front. Marking the fourth engine was the distinct outline of the feathered prop. I started to feel pretty good, and began humming the tune of a popular song.

Somebody else added the words, and in a moment the entire crew was singing, "Coming in on a wing and a prayer! Coming in on a wing and a prayer! We've got one motor gone, but we'll still carry on. Coming in on a wing and a prayer!"

We sang it like a round, with guys joining in at different times so it sounded like "We've got one motor gone, one motor gone, one motor gone... Coming in on a wing and a prayer."

We bombed Angers on May 27.

Since the targets had shifted to France instead of Germany, our average casualty rate had fallen from over 4% per raid to about 2% per raid. But that two percent statistic was still measured in aircraft missing, bodies destroyed or mutilated, lives lost or ruined. The danger was still there and so was the fear.

I could see that Strommy was becoming more apprehensive after each raid. Well, why shouldn't he? I was too. Although I was less nervous than I had been on our earlier raids over Berlin, I desperately wanted to quit, to do anything but fly over enemy territory. I guess the reason I didn't was because I was more afraid of what people would think of me if I did than I was of the enemy. I didn't want to be branded 'L.M.F. (Lack of Moral Fiber)' busted down in rank and taken off flying.

I knew that Strommy was planning to get married and was starting to look forward to life with a future. The only future he could look forward to in this business was the time before the next raid, because there might not be any time left after that raid. I should have sat down with him and talked to him about how he felt, asked him about his future plans, tried to do what was best for him. But I didn't. I was afraid he would ask me to let him quit, and I would have. I was afraid of losing a good man.

Chapter 11: The Last Mission

On May 31, 1944, we performed a daylight raid on the large railroad center at Trappes. There was no German air cover, so once the bombs had been let go I whipped the aircraft into a tight turn and dived down to treetop level. Tiny figures on the ground were scurrying over debris, trying to escape from the deadly mechanical bats up above. They grew larger as we swooped down on them.

"Okay Charlie!" I called to the nose gunner, "Let them have it!"

I later had a survivor from Trappes as a batman. He told me how the Lancasters had machine gunned almost everyone. He was one of the nicest guys I've ever met, always asking me, "Would you like me to bring you a coffee, Sir? Is there anything I can do for you, Sir?" He also informed me that Jews didn't know how to fight, just how to make money. I found that rather amusing.

I'm sure we killed a lot of very nice people.

The Allies were making the final preparations for the greatest amphibious assault in history. We couldn't be sure exactly where or when it would happen, but I was sure it would be soon.

Bomber Command had suffered extremely heavy losses throughout the war and especially during the offensives of 1943 and 1944. By June of 1944 almost everyone who was on my squadron at the time I joined it was either dead, missing, or had quit.

Guys used to ask me the secret to surviving an air battle. I told them that survival in an air battle depended on the enemy fighter pilot's harness. "That's right," I would say. "The enemy is just about to shoot you down. But his harness is too tight. So he reaches down to loosen his crotch, and then you escape."

I was gaining seniority, having recently been promoted to the rank of flight lieutenant, and was next in line to be the flight commander. On June 2, I led 'C' Flight during an air test. If things continued to progress, it was likely that I would soon be promoted to the rank of squadron leader.

A new pilot named Warrant Officer Les Sutton came to the unit. The C.O. introduced him to me and asked me to show him the ropes. He was a young fellow (weren't we all?!) just out of training and he seemed a bit apprehensive. I took him under my wing, so to speak, and told him he could fly as my copilot.

The great invasion was launched on June 6, 1944, a day which is now referred to as 'D Day', the 'Invasion of Normandy'. Our part in the invasion was scheduled for the night of June 7, 1944.

The briefing was conducted with the usual thorough detail. Huge aerial mosaics of the Normandy coast were marked with the red ribbons which indicated our intended flight paths. We would be bombing railway targets in French cities to prevent the Germans from sending reinforcements to the Normandy battle front[49]. The cities of Acheres, Juvisy, Massy-Palaiseau and Versailles would be attacked by 195 Halifaxes, 122 Lancasters, and 20 Mosquitoes. My aircraft would be attacking Massy-Palaiseau, which was not far from Paris. These targets were all further inland than the battle front and the enemy fighters would have more time to intercept us than they'd had to intercept the earlier raids on Normandy. We had no way of knowing it then, but our losses would be a staggering 8.3 percent.

As we left the briefing room and were handed our escape kits, Strommy turned to me and said, "Skipper, I want to quit flying."

I could see that he was serious. "Why, Strommy?" I asked.

"Skipper," he said, "I've found a wonderful girl and we're going to get married. I've got too much to live for now. I want to go L.M.F."

"Why didn't you tell me sooner?" I winced, slightly irritated. We'd already had our briefing and were about to leave. It was no time to go looking for another WOP and it would go hard with Strommy when the Squadron Leader found out.

He told me that he had wanted to tell me sooner but he couldn't bring himself to do it. He was afraid that I'd be disappointed in him.

"Okay, Strommy, I understand." I told him, "But we've already had our briefing and we're ready to go. I'd like you to make one more trip, but I promise it will be your last one. And you won't go L.M.F. either. You've already been through too much. I'll find you a job and arrange a transfer."

"Thank you, Skipper," Strommy replied with sincere appreciation. "I'll make one last trip. But I wouldn't have done it for any other skipper."

Those words were to haunt me for the rest of my life.

I told my new 'second dickie' that he had nothing to worry about. "It's a target just across the channel," I reminded him. "As a matter of fact, you don't even have to bother with putting your flying suit on. But anyways, it's good experience for you." I didn't put my flying suit on either because I thought it was just a matter of flying over, bombing the gun positions, and flying back. It shouldn't have taken more than a couple of hours.

"You're Okay." I told Les as he smoked a cigarette. I think our little chat made him feel a bit more confident and he seemed less nervous.

---

[49] *Details and statistics are from The Bomber Command War Diaries, Op. Cit., page 524.*

"Thanks a lot, Sir." he replied.

"Lou Greenburgh is my name," I smiled, "not 'Sir'. I think you've met most of my crew." I added, indicating the guys who were now gathered around us.

"Oh yeah." he said.

Everybody was confident that there would be no problem on this trip and they helped to reassure the new copilot.

We took off about midnight with a load of eighteen five hundred pound bombs. Everything was straight forward. Visibility was excellent and we could soon see the flares and the bombs going off across the channel. We came upon the target at 10,000 feet. There was flak all over the place and we could see fighters silhouetted under the clouds. Down below us I could see fires burning. The invasion was in full swing. I circled the target once. As well as groups of green target indicators there were two groups of red ones, so one of those would be my target.

The defenses were heavier than I had expected. It surprised me and was making me nervous. The copilot was really nervous. "Did you say this is 'nothing', Sir?!" he asked, "Is this the normal flight?!"

"Keep a good lookout." I replied in acknowledgement to his question. I heard the bomb aimer's voice over the intercom. "We're just coming onto the target, Skipper." We were silhouetted against the moon. I prayed that no fighters would see us.

It was a terrible holocaust. Airplanes were going down right and left, the air was full of tracer and flak. Looking up or down you saw nothing but flashes in the sky. Every one of them seemed to be heading for me.

I told the gunners to keep a good watch out. "This isn't the easy target I expected to see." I stated.

"Well, we're just coming onto the target now, Skipper." Eric repeated. "Go easy, go easy..."

"For Christ's sake!" interrupted the mid upper gunner, "We've got a fighter on our tail! Corkscrew to port, go!"

"No! No!" yelled the bomb aimer, "We're just coming up to the target! We're coming right on target. Hold still!"

The rear and mid upper gunners were both screaming, "They're almost on top of us!!!"

The bombs dropped an instant later and I began a violent corkscrew to port but by then it was too late[50]. Tracer zoomed past my head, probably fired from the port quarter, level, and I heard strikes on the fuselage. A fire erupted in the starboard wing immediately behind the inner engine and spread rapidly in both directions. The duralumin fabric burned off like charred skin and I could see the bare ribs underneath. The wing seemed to flutter and I hoped it was just loose fabric flapping in the wind. I felt the heat of the flames and thought the fuel tanks would blow.

I steepened the dive to blow out the fire and avoid the tracer but was hit in the starboard outer engine, which cut. Although I did not then know it, we had also lost the hydraulic system for the mid upper turret, which was now unserviceable, and the mid upper gunner's intercom was damaged.

I pulled out of the dive at about six or seven thousand feet. We appeared to have shaken off the fighter but the fire was still burning brightly and I knew we could be seen for miles. Flames were licking back behind the cowling of the starboard inner engine but it seemed to be functioning satisfactorily.

The light flak was even worse than the heavy flak at this altitude because the guns could be trained over more quickly. I was dodging light flak right and left.

I began to climb. A fighter flare dropped straight ahead of us so I made a detour around it. Some of my crew members were already putting on their parachutes. The second pilot got out of his seat and stood beside me. "We'll have to get out of this, fellows." I remarked, then ordered "Jump, jump, jump!"

I've never seen anyone leap into action as fast as the second pilot. He bailed out. For his first op., it had been some experience.

The fire seemed to be dying down a bit so I yelled, "Hold it!" The bomb aimer, the flight engineer, and the navigator had already followed the second pilot out the escape hatch.

Strommy, Fred Carey, and the rear gunner were still with me. Well, I had brought this airplane home under even worse conditions. I steadied up on an approximate course to avoid defended areas as well as I could. The aircraft had a slight swing to starboard and it was necessary to apply full aileron control in order to maintain course.

Up until now I had been too busy to feather the dead engine's prop. I was just reaching for the right lever when a searchlight beam flooded the cockpit and I knew we had been coned. After my initial blink, I saw a wall of light flak

---

[50] *Lou Greenburgh's memories were augmented by the official Report of Loss of Aircraft on Operations.*

coming up towards us and heard one of the crewmen ask "Do we bail out or don't we?!"

"Hold on!" I replied. I turned 45% to port and dived straight at the searchlights. Flak was passing all around us but we weren't hit. "Good show, Skipper!" the rear gunner exclaimed, "Good show!"

We lost the searchlights by the time we reached 5,000 feet and the slipstream seemed to have blown out the flames. I leveled out and started to climb.

Ten seconds later we were coned again. Once again, I dived to port and into a wall of light flak. Fragments struck the fuselage, which now filled with smoke. I lost rudder control.

We pulled out at 3,000 feet. I applied full left rudder but found it wasn't enough to maintain our course and had to keep the control column hard over to port. The rear gunner later informed me that one of the rudders was half shot away.

The Lancaster was vibrating badly but at least the fire in the wing was burning itself out. I told the remaining members of the crew that I would bring them back to base.

"Strommy," I said over the intercom, "send out an emergency signal that we might have to ditch. And get a fix."

I adjusted the trim, got that dead engine feathered, and steered roughly north east. I ordered the rear gunner to cooperate as best he could with the mid upper, who I now knew was off his intercom. They got in touch somehow and arranged a means of keeping a lookout in all directions.

"Skipper," reported the rear gunner after a very short interval, "we're being followed by a JU 88 showing a red navigation light".

I pushed the nose down immediately. The fighter's guns struck home; cannon shells ripped through the navigator's compartment behind me and the fuselage filled with acrid smoke. I felt the plane swing to starboard and was horrified to see smoke belching from the starboard inner engine.

Strommy left the wireless and came forward. "I think it's time to get out, Skipper." He said.

Something seemed not quite right with Strommy and I think now that he might have been wounded in that last attack. I ordered him back to his post.

"The others have all gone, Skipper," he replied, "and I'm going too. So long, Skipper!"

"Okay," I replied, "Bye. Lots of luck!"

I tried to gain height but failed to hold the height I had. The plane kept swinging to starboard and I had to admit to myself that I could no longer control it. I ordered the gunners to bail out. The rear gunner acknowledged my order but said, "I can't get out, Skipper, while you're veering." He then wished me luck and jumped.

There was no reply from the mid upper gunner. "Get out!" I yelled again. "I can't hold it much longer!" I didn't know that Fred Carey had already gone.

I was too tired to corkscrew anymore. In spite of my difficulty keeping the aircraft under control I was trying to keep it airborne and hoped to make it back to England. I banked over as far to port as I could in a last effort to counter that swing to starboard. The flames had reached the fuselage and their heat was singeing me.

As I banked over, I saw the dark form of an enemy fighter coming straight for me. The single radial engine marked it as a Focke Wulf 190.

The fighter banked over with me. It was so close that I could see the pilot sitting in the cockpit. I waved at him and expected him to wave back. I thought he might show some chivalry and let me go.[51]

He knew that I was absolutely helpless. My whole crew was gone; he could see that the turrets were empty, the guns unmanned. I kept waving at him as he flew underneath me. I thought, maybe, that he was gone.

I felt an explosion under my port engines. Bullets whizzed by on either side of me. I saw rockets blasting a fiery trail past me and knew that it was only a matter of time before one hit.

The Lancaster rocked to the impact of a second explosion. I glanced over my shoulder and saw that fire had entered the cockpit. "My God!" I thought, "I'll be burned alive!"

I unclipped my Sutton harness and pushed myself away from my seat. The plane turned on its side and I knew it was about to crash.

Crawling under the instrument panel, I looked down the narrow and cluttered passage to the tiny rectangular escape hatch. Ignoring the ladder and the hundred and one things which might snag me on the way down, I dived head first toward the escape hatch like a dolphin passing through a hoop. I plummeted into the empty darkness. I heard a loud 'boom' and was buffeted by shockwaves as the airplane exploded.

[51] *Lou's Lancaster LL727, A2-C was claimed by Hauptman Herbert Lorenz and the credit is accordingly noted in 'Nachtjagd War Diaries' by Dr. Theo Boiten. However, Lorenz flew the twin engined Ju 88 rather than the single engined FW190. If the claim is correct, Lou's aircraft was the only victory credited to Hptm. Lorenz who was himself shot down and killed ten nights later.*

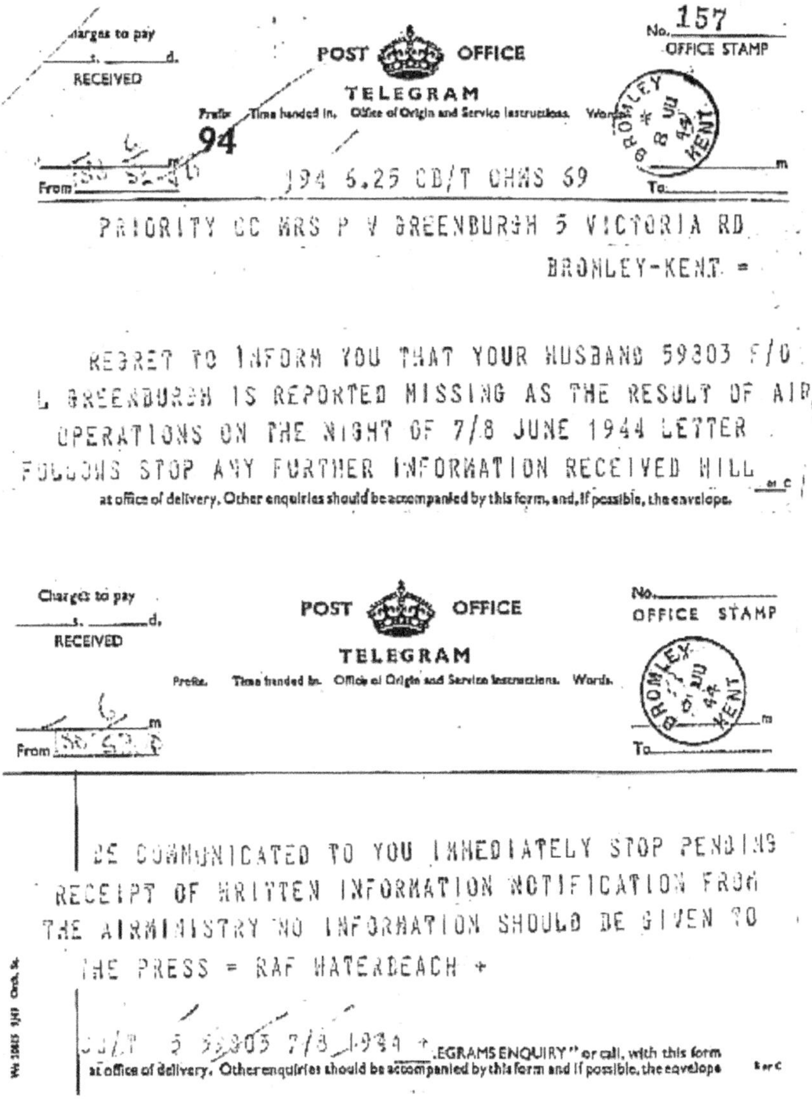

POST OFFICE TELEGRAM

No. 157

OFFICE STAMP

BROMLEY KENT 8 JU 44

94

194 6.25 CD/T OHMS 59

PRIORITY CC MRS P V GREENBURGH 5 VICTORIA RD BROMLEY-KENT =

REGRET TO INFORM YOU THAT YOUR HUSBAND 59303 F/O L GREENBURGH IS REPORTED MISSING AS THE RESULT OF AIR OPERATIONS ON THE NIGHT OF 7/8 JUNE 1944 LETTER FOLLOWS STOP ANY FURTHER INFORMATION RECEIVED WILL

at office of delivery. Other enquiries should be accompanied by this form, and, if possible, the envelope.

POST OFFICE TELEGRAM

BROMLEY KENT 8 JU 44

BE COMMUNICATED TO YOU IMMEDIATELY STOP PENDING RECEIPT OF WRITTEN INFORMATION NOTIFICATION FROM THE AIRMINISTRY NO INFORMATION SHOULD BE GIVEN TO THE PRESS = RAF WATERBEACH +

CD/T 5 59303 7/8 1944 + ...EGRAMS ENQUIRY" or call, with this form at office of delivery. Other enquiries should be accompanied by this form and if possible, the envelope

The telegram that families dreaded: Lou Greenburgh's wife is notified that he is 'missing as a result of air operations'. In all too many cases there was no happy ending.

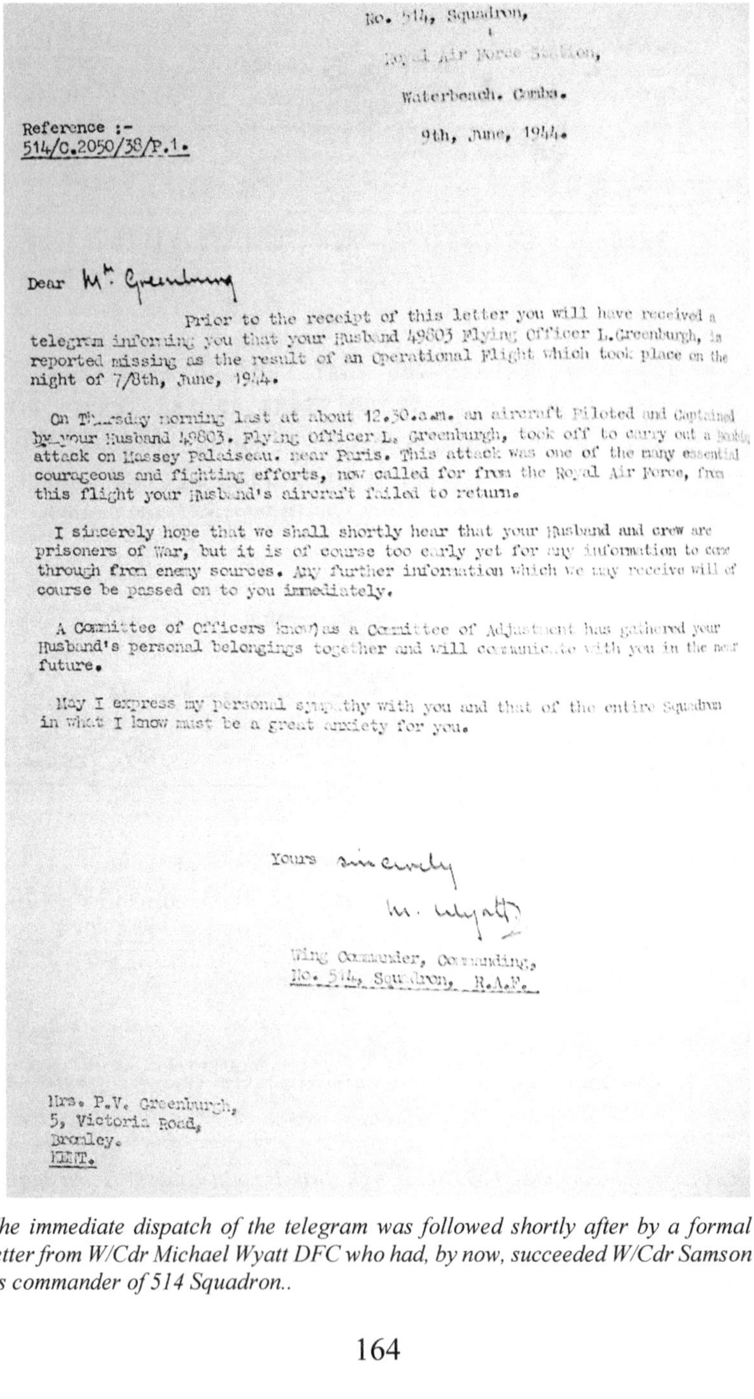

No. 514, Squadron,

Royal Air Force Station,

Waterbeach. Cambs.

Reference :-
514/C.2050/38/P.1.

9th, June, 1944.

Dear Mr. Greenburg

Prior to the receipt of this letter you will have received a telegram informing you that your Husband 49803 Flying Officer L.Greenburgh, is reported missing as the result of an Operational Flight which took place on the night of 7/8th, June, 1944.

On Thursday morning last at about 12.30.a.m. an aircraft Piloted and Captained by your Husband 49803. Flying Officer L. Greenburgh, took off to carry out a Bombing attack on Massey Palaiseau. near Paris. This attack was one of the many essential courageous and fighting efforts, now called for from the Royal Air Force, from this flight your Husband's aircraft failed to return.

I sincerely hope that we shall shortly hear that your Husband and crew are prisoners of War, but it is of course too early yet for any information to come through from enemy sources. Any further information which we may receive will of course be passed on to you immediately.

A Committee of Officers known as a Committee of Adjustment has gathered your Husband's personal belongings together and will communicate with you in the near future.

May I express my personal sympathy with you and that of the entire Squadron in what I know must be a great anxiety for you.

Yours sincerely

M. Wyatt

Wing Commander, Commanding,
No. 514, Squadron, R.A.F.

Mrs. P.V. Greenburgh,
5, Victoria Road,
Bromley.
KENT.

The immediate dispatch of the telegram was followed shortly after by a formal letter from W/Cdr Michael Wyatt DFC who had, by now, succeeded W/Cdr Samson as commander of 514 Squadron..

For Les Sutton the war went on after his return to England. He and his crew completed 38 operations with 514 Squadron, mostly in Lancaster NN773, JI-K, pictured here with the crew prior to setting out for Dortmund on 12th March 1945 (514 Squadron Society).

Lou's nemesis: Luftwaffe records credit the shooting down of Lou's Lancasters to pilots flying Junkers Ju 88 nightfighters on both occasions.

Chapter 12: Evasion

A powerful blast of air forced itself into my lungs. Groping madly, I found the D ring and pulled. To my disappointment, the rip cord came out in my hand and I was still falling. "Well, this is the end." I thought. I'm surprised by the calmness with which I accepted the inevitability of my immediate death. I held the handle in front of me and watched the rip cord whip behind like the tail of a crashing kite.

I felt a rustling against my back and was pulled upright with a shock. So taken by surprise was I that my boots were jerked right off my feet and my escape pack fell out of my shirt. With them plummeted my knife, rations, maps, compass; and my pistol.

Pieces of metal were raining down all around me. Rocking gently with my stocking feet dangling, I wondered how long it would take me to land. I couldn't see the ground, of course, because it was pitch black. Suddenly, my spine seemed to go right up into my head. I was overcome by paralyzing pain and collapsed on the spot.

Gradually the pain died down and I was able to move. I was extremely vulnerable because everything I needed for survival had been in my lost boots and survival kit. All I had left was an identity disc with the word 'Jew' prominently displayed.

The burning hulk of what had once been my bomber lay only a hundred yards from me. An enemy aircraft overhead dropped three flares and by their light I could see the parachutes of two crewmen, possibly my gunners.

Burning pieces of aircraft were lighting up the area and machine gun ammunition was exploding, scattering bullets at random. I wanted to get away quickly. I started gathering up my parachute and winced as a stab of pain shot up my back. I dragged my 'chute into a nearby wood. The effort of dragging my parachute had reignited the pain's intensity so I lay down among the shrubs and soft mosses, where I was reasonably comfortable. The cool moisture of the ground felt good against my injured back but I was temporarily immobilized. When I could move, I hid my parachute, harness, and Mae West in some tall nettles and started to walk south in the direction of the descending parachutes.

I spotted a truck coming towards me and hid by the side of the road.

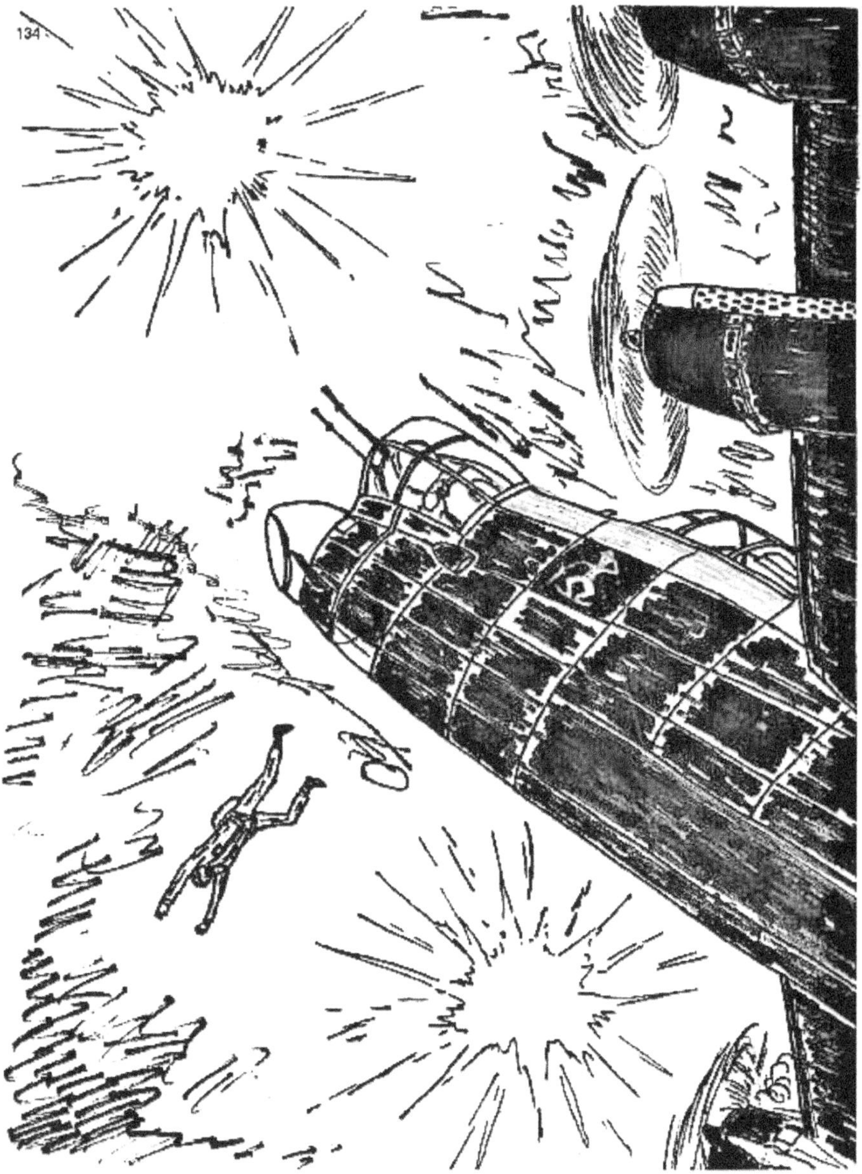
134

There were sounds coming from only a few yards away. I was distressed to hear a guttural voice ordering "Achtung! Achtung!" and saw the outline of a German helmet.

I could soon hear voices all over the place and I realized that I was in the midst of a German convoy. Among the sounds of heavy vehicles I heard the neighing of horses and the tramp-tramp of soldiers' boots. A sidecar-equipped motorcycle rattled by. I saw a scrawny, bespectacled soldier in a helmet and thought to myself, “So this is the ‘master race’”.

German voices were everywhere. I could see the columns of German transports on their way to the front lines. That was obviously not a very healthy place to stay, so I crawled back into the woods. The other side of the woods had to be better than the side I had just left so I crawled over to it. I lay there awhile, giving the pain a chance to die down again, and decided that I would have to find someone in a French village who would be willing to help me.

We had been informed that some Frenchmen were hiding Allied airmen. Unfortunately, it was difficult to tell who were working for the 'Resistance' and who were working for the Germans. Some would hide you, others would turn you in.

I headed down a lane and walked for about twenty minutes. It was about five o’clock in the morning, I guess, when I reached the outskirts of a small village. I rested for about half an hour.

I peeked over a low stone wall which encircled a little farm and saw that an old man with a young girl was leaning on the stone fence just a short distance from me. I decided to feel him out. Were he to appear hostile, I was going to knock the hell out of him.

I took off my tunic and approached the old man from out of the darkness. "Ami." I said with my hand extended, "Ami." I pointed to myself and to the sky. "J'ai tombee." I told him, meaning that I had been shot down.

He looked at me without saying a word. "I need help," I said, in desperation. "We are friends, ami, together. I can't be found by the Germans."

When he spoke, it was with a tremor that showed his fear. "I think you are a German agent."

"No," I told him. I told him how I had lost my flying boots and showed him my RAF wings and my identity disc. He considered the matter with a serious expression on his face, then said I should come with him.

Just before we got to the farm house, he turned around and told me to wait, then disappeared into the house. Two men came out and began to question me in French. I told them that I was an Allied flier.

"Yes," one of them nodded, "there has been quite a battle going on here tonight." The two men led me into a small summer kitchen. One of them lifted up a bread box, revealing the radio which was hidden underneath. "BBC." he stated, "We listen to the BBC. You are very lucky you came here, because had you gone to the other side... he is working for the Germans. There are lots of informers here. You are very, very fortunate that you came here. But," he added, "We have to get you out of here."

My benefactors gave me some food and civilian footwear. One can imagine the value of those shoes when you realize that all items of clothing were closely rationed and in very short supply. They then cut off my badges.

I had landed about ten miles north of Froissy (Oise), which was north of Paris. I informed my hosts that there were three others in the neighborhood. The son went off to tell other farmers to keep watch for them.

All of a sudden the strain of the last few hours, the pain in my back, and my physical exhaustion almost overcame me. "I'm very, very tired," I told them, "I have to relax."

They said that was alright. Someone produced a woman's dress for me to wear and I was directed to tie a 'babushka' around my head. So disguised, I was taken to another small farm house where I found a bed made up in a little room. I was soon fast asleep.

Next morning, I awoke to the sound of gunfire. I was so confused by the events of the previous day that it took me a while to realize where I was. Still in a daze, I went out into the yard, where I saw a formation of American P-47 Thunderbolts flying towards me. I stood out in the open and waved to them.

My wave was answered by staccato bursts of machine gun fire. The American fighters were shooting up the highway out front like nobody's business. "What's the matter with you guys?!" I yelled, and then I remembered that I was in enemy territory. The fighters were attacking German convoys and transportation networks. It felt strange to be watching that and I wondered, "How will I ever get out of this mess?"

The place was just crawling with German soldiers.

The girl I had seen the day before came in with my parachute, which she kept. "One of your crew," she told me, "The wireless operator, was caught up in the telegraph wires. He was injured and has been taken prisoner."

The next day, two of the people in the house informed me that I was to be transferred to a small chateau which was the district headquarters of the Underground. I was dressed like a farmer, with coveralls and a straw hat, and shown a picture of Fred Carey. I took a seat next to the driver of a horse drawn wagon. It was just a small wagon, more like a buggy. We reached the chateau after a day's travel.

I was greeted at the door by a man named Hendre, who was the chief of the Maquis in that area. As I stepped inside, I was greeted by a familiar voice. "Hi, Lou!"

My rear gunner was in the chateau. We shook hands and greeted each other, but it was a bitter reunion.

Every day, they told me, somebody was being arrested. After about two days, one of the Frenchmen entered the room looking very concerned. "The Germans are getting wise to us." he said, "You will have to be moved."

That night, the two of us were led out to a bomb crater at the edge of a German aerodrome. In the darkness we could hear the roar of an Me 109 as it took off on a deadly mission, and then another one took off, and another and we could make out their outlines in the moon light. In between takeoffs we could see fighters coming in to land.

We climbed into the crater. Our guide quickly removed some brush and I could see why we had been brought here. Behind the bushes was the opening of a large cave. Inside the cave, who should I find but Fred Carey. The three of us hid in the cave, which became our home for the next three days. Day and night, the drone of German fighter engines reminded us how close we were to imprisonment or worse.

As I listened to those engines, a daring plot began to form in my mind. I crawled out of the cave and lay on my stomach, in broad daylight, surveying the airstrip. I could see a row of Messerschmitt 109s lined up on the tarmac within a stone's throw of where I lay, concealed. I could see the pilots standing near the aircraft and I could hear them talk.

I was determined to steal a Messerschmitt. If I waited long enough, I reasoned, some pilot might leave his engine running while he attended to other business. That would be my chance.

I watched formations of Messerschmitts circle the field, fresh from sorties. I watched them land and I watched them while they were being serviced. I watched them as the pilots climbed in and started the engines. I watched them taxi to the edge of the runway. I watched them as they idled, warming up in readiness for takeoff.

I pursed my lips and clenched my fists as I watched them idle. They were so close! All I needed was for one of those pilots to leave his cockpit, just for a moment.

And then I would sigh and unclench my fists as the fighters rolled down the runway and out of my reach. Though I waited for hours on end, my chance never came.

An agent of the underground came into the cave. He pulled me aside and told me that he had some grave news. Strommy had died in hospital two days after his capture.

No! No! Not Strommy! I had lost comrades before, but not like this! Not after all we had been through! It couldn't be true. And it was all my fault!

"Are you sure?" I asked, hoping against hope. He nodded his head, and told me that his source was reliable. Strommy - cheerful, faithful, Strommy - was dead. He had trusted me, and I had let him down.

After three days, it was decided that we should travel separately. A man came to move me to a different area. I said goodbye to what was left of my crew and we agreed to meet back in England someday, "if everything was alright."

I climbed up into a horse and buggy with the fellow who was taking me away. We moved along a side road, where we were passed by several trucks carrying German troops. It took an effort for me to keep from bringing up.

We entered a small village and the driver pulled up in front of a pub. After securing the horse's reins to a hitching post, my companion motioned for me to follow him. I climbed out of my seat with something less than enthusiasm and followed my guide through the front door. Music was playing and the place was just packed with German soldiers. They were too intent on enjoying themselves to spare a glance for a couple of French peasants but I still felt like Daniel entering the lions' den.

We walked right by the German soldiers and into the kitchen. I was distracted for a moment, then realized to my horror that my guide had disappeared. With my heart racing, I tried to devise some sort of escape plan. A man by the door said, "You are coming along with us!" He was standing with a small group of German soldiers.

The man must have realized my apprehension, because his tone immediately softened and he added (in English), "Don't worry, you're alright. Never mind the German soldiers."

The soldiers in the pub laughed like heck at the sight of me being taken away. I was led outside and put into a van. My captors drove me out of town to a small castle. A man came out of the castle, greeted me, then turned to the soldiers and said that everything was alright. "I wish to interrogate this man, personally." he said. The soldiers and the man who had 'arrested' me drove away in the van.

I was led through the back entrance of the castle and up a flight of stairs. I thought about trying to escape but I didn't see how I could. And I was very confused.

The man led me to a large office on the third floor. He closed the solid door behind him and seated himself at a large wooden desk. He motioned for me to take a seat, which I did.

"I am the Prefecture of Police," he began. "I am in charge of the police in the Paris area. I am cooperating with the German government and the Wehrmacht. But...," he leaned forward for emphasis, "I am also a British agent."

I couldn't believe it. He said, "You're going to stay here for a couple of days until we find a place to hide you."

Two days later, he took me by horse and buggy to a deserted castle in the country. It was almost a ruin. There were large gaps where the walls had crumbled, leaving heaps of rubble scattered about the grounds. One or two rooms were still inhabitable and I would sleep on the stone floor with a couple of blankets wrapped around me.

My only companion was an old woman whom I saw once a day when she brought me food. I wanted to make conversation with her but soon understood that the less we communicated the better. A flock of sheep were grazing in a nearby field, however, and they would come up to me and let me pet them. Admittedly, petting sheep is not something I really miss doing but I like animals and it lessened my boredom.

The food I was brought was surprisingly good, considering the circumstances. There were fresh vegetables, including asparagus. I still love asparagus.

I was standing in what was once the 'great hall' on my second day at the old castle. I looked up and was shocked to see a young boy, not more than ten years old and with golden blond hair, looking down at me from the rafters with a mischievous smile on his face. "I know who you are!" he giggled.

I didn't know what to do. I figured that I had better have a good talk with this kid, let him know how important it was that he keep my presence a secret. "Come here," I said, "I want to talk to you."

"Oh, no you don't," he laughed, and then gloated, "I know who you are. You're the enemy!" Then he scampered away.

He was a nice little boy, but he was driving me crazy with worry. He often visited me to tell me that he knew who I was, always running away when I tried to get close to him or when the old lady arrived with my food. I was very impressed by the quality of the food she brought me and I once asked her where she got it from. "I can't talk." was all she would say. I tried to lure the boy closer to me by offering him some food, but he just laughed and said, "Oh, no. I know what you are trying to do. I know who you are!"

After I had been at the castle for about a week, I heard the pounding hoof beats of a hard-driven horse and the rattling of a buggy as it pulled up to the front of the castle. The driver beckoned to me with a gesture of urgency. "We've got to get out of here quick!" he called, "The Germans have surrounded the castle. They caught the British agent who was Prefecture of the Police. We've got to get out of here mighty quick!"

I said "Okay" and was about to leave when I heard the young voice from the rafters. "Monsieur, please don't leave me!"

I looked up to see my mysterious companion. "Please, please don't leave me here in this place. Take me with you!"

The little boy's eyes were filling with tears and his plaintive voice tugged at my heart strings as he begged me not to leave him alone. It broke my heart to tell him that we couldn't take him, then we made a hurried departure. As we rode away, I glanced over my shoulder at the receding castle and saw a pair of tear-streaked eyes watching me leave.

I tried to shake the boy from my mind and said, "Well, take me back to Hendre, the chief of the original place we went to, the District Headquarters of the Maquis."

He shook his head. "No, they got Hendre. We can't go back there. I know a place where we can go."

We rode alongside roads for a while, then left the roads completely and jostled across wheat fields, doing our best to avoid the masses of German troops who were rushing to the coast to repel the Allied invasion. The sky was full of air battles as both sides struggled to control the air space above the embattled troops.

We eventually reached a small farm house about fifteen miles from the castle. I was told to wait outside. Standing among the stalks of wheat, I could hear a heated argument going on in the house and with my broken French I could tell what they were arguing about. I heard a woman's voice cry, "No, no, we can't! We just can't! We'll be informed on. If the Germans catch us that will be the end of us."

My escort reappeared with a discouraged look on his face. He shrugged his shoulders and said, "They are afraid to take you in. Especially because you are Jewish. For harboring Jews and Allied fliers... That would be the end of them."

Another resistance man arrived with someone I presumed to be an Allied airman. He introduced himself with a slight Scottish bur. "My name's Bill Brown, but most people call me 'Jock'."

The door of the house opened. A gentleman who introduced himself as Monsieur Reant stepped outside and announced, "We have decided to let you stay. But you must hide in the basement, where they will never find you."

We all lived in constant fear of our lives. We had been lucky to find a few French citizens who were brave enough to risk being caught by the Germans. Many of the French, however, openly sympathized with the Germans and there were many, many, informers.

We lived in the cellar by day and slept in the attic at night. "If the Germans come," we were told, "go straight into the orchard. They wouldn't dream of looking for you there because the plants are thick and the trees are close together."

We were treated like part of the family. Many of their relatives visited us, and we would talk with them in the cellar.

About three days later, at four o'clock in the morning, the place was shaking with machine gun fire. Heavy guns were going off and the machine guns were so close that they seemed to be inside the house.

I peeked out an attic window and saw that the place was surrounded by motorcycles. A German soldier was looking in my direction but wouldn't have been able to see me because of the reflection from the glass.

Hurried footsteps rapped upon the stairs and Monsieur and Madame Reant appeared. "Get out, quick!" they shouted, "The Germans are here!"

"Quick, Bill," I said, "into the orchard!"

"You can't go into the orchard!" exclaimed Monsieur Reant. "It's full of Germans!"

"Well, where are we going to go?!"

"We don't know where you'll go," Madame Reant exclaimed, "but get out of here! If they catch us it's more than our life is worth!"

The front door burst open and we heard the stomping of heavy boots. "It's too late!" somebody exclaimed in a loud whisper. The attic was full of firewood and branches. Jock and I dived into the woodpile and Madame and Monsieur Reant covered us with branches, sawdust, anything they could find.

The Germans stomped right up the stairs and into the attic. A German officer pointed to Monsieur Reant and ordered, "Take him!"

Madame Reant cried hysterically as her husband was dragged down the stairs. The German officer and his remaining troops continued to search the attic.

We held our breath and tried not to move. A jack boot crunched down just two inches from my little finger.

"I know damn well they're here." the German officer muttered. To our relief, they clomped down the stairs and continued searching the rest of the house.

Madame Reant had followed her husband down to where they were holding him. A minute later we heard her call, "Quick, they are coming back again!"

Jock and I threw off our cover and opened the attic window. We were about fifteen feet above the ground. Across a narrow lane there were some nettle bushes. I jumped.

Pinpricks of pain tore into my body as I landed among the thorny nettles. A loud thump and a groan told me that Jock had also jumped. I glanced back at the house and could see German soldiers looking out the attic window. We stayed put. At dawn, a large van drove up to the house. Monsieur Reant, the man who had saved our lives, was dragged out the door with his hands tied behind his back. He was pushed into the back of the van, where some other people were already detained, and the van drove off. We didn't know where the van was going.

I was behind the bushes, watching this, as he was taken away.

We didn't dare move. German traffic was very heavy and they were passing just three or four feet away from us as they searched. Soldiers were combing the bushes all over the place. I guess they didn't search our bushes because they didn't think we would stay so close to the house. They were mainly searching in the nearby woods.

We had been laying there about four or five hours when a little girl about seven or eight years old came crawling across the field. When she reached our bush she said, "Shhh... We know you're here. My father's very frightened. He told me to bring you a compass and some food. He said you'll have to stay here until about ten or eleven o'clock at night. There are guards going across the other fields and the bridge. If you can get across the fields..."

The little girl explained the escape plan. "My father is afraid to do anything. We can't take you into our house but here's a map he drew of this area. See, this is a little bridge here and in the next field there is a bunch of horses. You'll have to get past them before you reach the bridge. Just before the bridge there's a sentry who walks by. But you can see him walk by every half hour and between the half hours you can make your escape out of that area. The village is surrounded."

We didn't dare move until it was getting dusk. On our hands and knees, with some food and the precious compass, we began crawling across the fields. One of my legs had been injured when I'd jumped and the pain made it difficult for me to move. It felt like hours that we were on hands and knees and my back began to ache again. We finally reached the fence which encircled the horses.

We climbed the fence and dropped to the other side. The horses were supposed to be tame, but I don't know. I've never seen such a wild bunch. Every time we started to move, they'd run 'yippitty-yoom' all over the place. I was afraid they might trample me. I was more afraid of those horses than I was of the Germans.

We crept across the field. We saw the little bridge in the moonlight and waited for the guard to go by. Hunched over, we dashed across the bridge and dived to our stomachs. Our journey was only now beginning. We didn't know where to go, where to stay.

Our immediate task was to find someplace to hide during the coming day. To be caught out in the open in daylight would have been suicide. With the coming of morning, we spotted a large haystack and crawled under the hay.

I was startled from an exhausted sleep by a sharp pain in my cheek. As I opened my eyes I felt a scurry of little feet and shuddered at the sight of a field mouse disappearing into the hay. The haystack was just crawling with insects and God knows what. I moved my arm across my face and tried to go back to sleep. We later left the haystack and collapsed in a high clump of wheat, where we slept.

Our trek began again under the cover of darkness. Using our compass, we tried to keep heading in a westerly direction. It was difficult, though, because we had so many obstacles to go around and we had to avoid roads. We couldn't take much more of this hard travel and we were practically starving.

"Lou," Bill finally said to me, "I've had enough of this. I think we should turn ourselves in."

I thought he was crazy, and told him so. "Look," he said, "the worst they'd do is make us prisoners of war."

"No fear," I told him, "I'll never turn myself in. Not with a name like Greenburgh."

There was a little house not far from us, with an elderly man out front. "Look, Bill," I said, "please. Let's try this man."

We left the cover of our field and went over to the old man. Fortunately, he took us in. We sat down at his kitchen table and he gave us some food. We were taking a chance, of course, because we didn't know if he were an informer but we were half starved and didn't know what else to do.

"I've heard about you." the old man said. "Many of the people who've helped you have been executed. You can't stay here very long. Here is some food, God bless you, and go on your journey."

We marched on. Before long, we came to a wood and breathed a sigh of relief. We hadn't eaten for hours and thought that this would be a place where we could hide and relax.

"Uh-oh," I muttered, and pointed to the ground. Right in front of us were some caterpillar tracks. Big caterpillar tracks.

The ominousness of my discovery was not lost on Jock. We considered the matter for a moment, then I motioned for Jock to come along and began to follow the tracks into the woods.

We had not gone far before we came across a converging set of tracks. We soon found out that there were tracks all over the place. I was as apprehensive as a hiker following the tracks of a large bear.

We soon reached a clearing and my worst fears were realized. The woods we had chosen as a hiding place were full of armored vehicles marked with the Iron Cross or the Swastika. From behind some trees we could see tiger tanks and heavy trucks with caterpillar tracks and machine guns. People in German uniforms were running backwards and forwards in front of the tanks, issuing orders in guttural voices.

"We'd better get out of here, but quick!" I said to Jock in a hushed whisper. We quietly backed away, then took off down the trail to where we had first entered the woods.

We got down onto our hands and knees again and crawled back into the wheat field. Physically exhausted and heartbroken that our haven had turned into a death trap, our every movement required a strenuous effort. When we could fight off hunger no longer, we ate the last bit of our meager food supply. Then we carried on.

Hours and hours of crawling. My arms felt like lead weights and my knees were raw. My fatigue was aggravated by a dull headache. Hunger gnawed at my stomach.

We finally came to the edge of the wheat field and stood up. In our view was a small mountain, more like a large hill, covered with forest, with trees. I looked at Bill and between breaths stated, "We'll make for that hill. Then we can rest for a bit."

By the time we reached the hill, we had also reached new levels of exhaustion. I heard Jock yelp and saw him topple to the ground. He sat up and grasped an injured foot with both hands. He told me that he couldn't walk any more.

I thought about my own blistered feet. They were bleeding and I didn't know how long I could carry on.

"Lou," Jock said, "we should give up. Like I said, the worst they'd do is make us prisoners of war. I can't go on any longer."

I took another look at my dog tag. All I could see there was one word: Jew. J-E-W. Jew.

"No fear, Bill," I replied, with new determination, "I'm gonna die first. If you can't walk, get on my shoulders and I'll carry you."

Now he was about six foot two and weighed half again as much as I did. After a great deal of grunting and groaning, we managed to get him up onto my shoulders. I collapsed under him.

"Come on," he said, "let's give up."

"Tell you what," I said, as I caught my breath, "let's get to the other side of this hill. Then, if you can't go on any further, I'll go on my own. I'll die before I'll surrender. You can give yourself up to the Germans. I'm not taking any chances with 'Jew' written on top of my name tag. Better crawl on my shoulders again, maybe. I'll try to carry you."

I tried to carry him, again. It must have looked quite funny, the way I was fumbling and he was pushing with one foot to help me on. We could hardly move a couple of feet this way, and here we were trying to go several miles!

I collapsed again. This time we both lay still for about an hour before thinking about moving.

Dawn was breaking. "Let's carry on," I said.

With the coming of daybreak, we could see a little village in the valley below. "Bill," I said, "let's try and make the village. If there's Germans there, and you're turned over to them, okay. I'll hide. I don't know what's going to happen to me, but you'll be able to carry on. Let's try and make it."

Our bodies rebelled at this abuse. We couldn't go on; and yet, we did. There were times when I encouraged Jock, there were times when I dragged him. "No," he moaned, "I can't take this any longer. I'm going to give myself up to the Germans."

Thank God we were going downhill. It must have been about six o'clock in the morning that we descended into the deep fog which shrouded the little village.

We were at the edge of the village when the door of a homestead opened and out stepped a young girl, about fourteen years old, I guess. She had an empty bucket in each hand and obviously intended to haul some water for her family's morning ablutions. She paused a moment to stare at us as we clomped by.

I don't wonder that she stared at us for we must have been quite a sight. Neither of us had shaved for days. We were dressed in rags. The soles of my shoes were loose. We were an awful mess.

I didn't think a young girl like her would pose much of a danger to us so I called to her, "Do you know who we are?"

She hesitated. "Yes, you are escaped Russian prisoners."

"No, we're not."

I could see the panic creep into her eyes. "Yes, you are!" She made a move towards her house.

"Just wait a minute!" I called, in desperation, "We're not escaped Russian prisoners! We're Allied fliers and we've come to help you. We're friends. We're friends of yours."

She seemed confused, uncertain. "Are you really?"

"Yes."

"No!" She shook her head. "No. You are Gestapo! You're just trying to fish out the French people who are not your friends, who are helping others."

"No," I insisted, "we're Allied fliers! We're not German spies."

"Well, wait a minute." she said, beginning to back away. I could tell she was ready to make a run for the house.

"Just a minute!" I ordered, and grabbed hold of her hand. "You're not going in there! I want to know what your stand is. Are you for the Germans or are you for the Allies?"

She tried to pull away but I had her in an iron grip. Tears began to roll down her cheeks. Between sobs, she stammered, "I... I am not for the Germans."

"Alright," I said, releasing her hand. "Go in."

She ran in the door and we could hear her calling to somebody inside. Her father rubbed the sleep from his eyes as he came to the door. He looked us over once and told us to come in.

The man studied my identification disc, then turned around to face the woman who had come up behind him. "Dangereux," he said, in French. "This man is not only an Allied flier in civilian clothes, he is also a Jew."

The woman listened to her husband with a very serious expression on her face. "No," she said, and my heart sank for a moment, until she continued, "take them in, take them in. We can hide them in the basement."

The woman prepared a delicious meal for us, then we were treated to the luxury of a bath in an old wash tub. It was more like a bucket, since there was no running water, but it felt great to scrub off the layers of dirt I had built up. When we had rid ourselves of all the little 'friends' which had been hiding in our dirt, we were brought clean clothes to wear.

There was a large garden in the back of the house, so we didn't have to worry about food. We were allowed on the main floor of the house, but were told that we would have to go down to the basement if there were a knock at the door.

The 'Fauque' sisters. The girl on the right, when confronted by Lou, told him 'We are not for the Germans!' Their family name might, in fact, have been 'Marolle'.

"You were lucky," they told us, "you got the right little house. Most of the houses in this area are for the Germans."

I told them, "You don't know how many times we've been lucky!"

It wasn't long before we got to feel like part of the family. We passed the time playing cards and checkers together and we met some of their relatives. We couldn't go outside for fear of being spotted by an informer, but through the windows we watched German soldiers walking by and saw German trucks and armored cars driving to and from the village.

The cellar-like basement where we slept reeked of mold and mildew, but to us it was a haven. The family, whose name was 'Fauque', had taken a liking to us and we to them. They contacted a member of the underground and told him that we were welcome to stay with them until the end of the war. He shook his head and told them that it was too dangerous for them to keep us for that long.

It is sad that I never knew very much about that family. It was dangerous to know very much. I couldn't keep any notes for fear of the German's finding them.

Strangely enough, I have the girl's picture. I have her picture and a picture of her twelve year old sister. I wanted to write to them, later, but I didn't know where to send the letters. I'm not even sure which town it was.

The Resistance man briefed us on our next move. "We are taking you right into town where there is a garage man. He is working for the Germans, so they would never suspect him of hiding you."

We were escorted into town and introduced to the man who worked in the garage, Monsieur Balandra. We hid ourselves in a little room adjacent to the workshop area. From where we were, we could see and hear the German vehicles as they came and went. We breathed exhaust fumes as our benefactor tinkered with German engines or hoisted a vehicle up on his lift. The Germans never suspected that we were hiding there, watching them and listening to them.

A soldier gave Balandra a good natured pat on the back and remarked, "You are doing a good job for us." Balandra smiled and accepted the complement. I smiled to myself and wondered what the soldier would say in the near future, when he was miles away from the nearest repair facility and his engine mysteriously developed trouble and broke down.

Although we seemed to be safe for the moment, Balandra was concerned that his work with the Germans was putting us into danger and we, of course, were endangering his work. "This is a hive of German activity," he said, (as if we hadn't noticed!).

Before long, Bill and I once again found ourselves bouncing along in a horse and buggy, seated alongside yet another leader of the Resistance. The village dropped into the background and the scenery became more primeval, with trees and bushes, as we entered a park-like forest. "You can stay with the forest ranger," our guide told us. Through the trees we could see the farm type house where the ranger lived. The forest ranger was a great big jovial fat fella with a very, very skinny wife. Because he was the chief forest ranger, we came to call him 'Chiefie'. After we had gotten acquainted, Chiefie's wife went upstairs to the attic to fix up some beds for us. Meanwhile, Chiefie stayed downstairs with us to discuss the war.

Things were not so pleasant with this chief of the rangers. When our accommodations were ready, Chiefie followed us up to the attic. "Oh," he said, "they have killed so many Allied fliers! They have caught so many Frenchmen!" His face took on the serious expression of an executioner taking aim and he formed a pistol with his fingers. "Bam!" he shouted, "Bam! Bam! Bam!"

Bill looked rather uncomfortable as he sat on the edge of his cot and his face grew longer and longer. I was feeling sick to my stomach and I wished that Chiefie would either shut up or talk about something else, anything else. "You can't even go outside now," Chiefie continued, "because you don't know whose next."

These bedtime visits by Chiefie became a daily ritual and they were driving us crazy. While Chiefie droned on and on about the danger we were all facing and the risk he was taking by hiding us, his wife was downstairs cleaning the house and doing all the work. This tired, slender woman did not seem to be afraid as she went about her work and brought us our food.

The ranger had chicken coops behind his house and German soldiers often dropped by to pick up eggs or chickens. We could see them coming and going. I was used to seeing enemy troops up close and there was a time when it hadn't bothered me much but the constant strain was beginning to affect my nerves and I was growing more and more afraid.

One afternoon, Jock had made his way to the outhouse and was doing his business. The outhouse door, which had no lock, swung open and Jock was staring face to face with a German soldier! This accelerated Jock's bodily functions and he nearly fell into the hole. He wanted to escape but the only place he could have gone was down into the hole.

The German soldier closed the door and excused himself in German. Jock could tell that he was waiting outside and figured that the game was over. "I'm coming," he grimaced as he finished what he had to do and did up his trousers. He stepped outside expecting to be arrested. To his surprise, the German Officer rushed past him and took his place in the outhouse! Jock raced back to the attic and refused to ever use that outhouse again. Alternate arrangements were made for him.

Our situation was becoming increasingly dangerous. The Germans were finding crashed airplanes with no crews and it was obvious that somebody was hiding them. There were two barrels of wheat in the attic for us to hide in if the house were ever searched, but I got little comfort from that. One day Chiefie came upstairs looking even more worried than usual. "You've got to leave here," he said, "They're suspicious. They've already caught one family and two people have been executed. They are searching all of the houses in this area." Other

Frenchmen had given the game away, he explained bitterly, and repeated, "You've got to get out of here."

I was at a loss for words. Where would we go? As if reading my thoughts, Chiefie continued. "You will be hidden in a cave. The underground has spent weeks digging it for you. They had to sprinkle the dirt over a large area so the Germans would not discover a mound of earth and figure out what was going on."

We quickly left our comfortable sanctuary and Chiefie, armed with a shovel, led us across the park to the side of a hill. He moved some branches aside and my heart sank. Our new home was nothing more than a hole in the ground.

I got down on my hands and knees and crawled into the tiny opening. I didn't have room even to sit up and loose soil dropped down the back of my neck as I brushed against the overhanging dirt. I breathed in the musty smell of a freshly dug grave.

Jock and I lay down together with barely an inch between us. Chiefie threw in a roll of toilet paper and said he would be back later with some food. He then began to shovel soil back into the hole. The shovel grated against the dirt until he had sealed up the cave entrance, leaving just a tiny hole to keep us from suffocating. We were like rabbits hiding in a burrow.

Claustrophobia! Oh God, I couldn't stand it in that cave. We were buried alive in complete blackness. I couldn't stretch or find a comfortable position to lie in. Whenever I changed position I would bump Jock or else I would bump the side of the cave and dirt would fall in my face or down my neck. I could hardly breathe.

After a few hours, another problem developed. We couldn't leave the cave for even a few minutes and nature was calling us loudly. We designated a spot in the deepest part of the cave for our latrine and the air was soon as foul as that of an outhouse. We were buried in an outhouse.

I lay there in the dark, thinking. I had nothing else to do, I couldn't move, so I had to think. I thought of my childhood, of my poor mother who had had to scrub floors for a living. I thought to myself, "If I ever get out of this alive, if I ever get back to Winnipeg, I'm going to do everything I possibly can for my mother, who suffered so much in life." That's what I was thinking. I would do so much. I had never had a chance to do anything for her.

I could think then, because I had nothing else to do. I had to do something, do anything, so I thought. I tried not to think about the worms. So I thought about my mother. "My poor mother," I thought, "had to scrub floors and take in boarders. She had no money. We lived in a shack. When I get out of this, I'm going to find a good job and I'm going to support my mother."

Time passed, or rather, it crept. It crept slowly. I kept thinking of my childhood days, of everything that went on. "Well," I thought, "this might be the end. All of my plans will never come to anything."

The branches covering our air hole were brushed away, as they were at feeding times, and I could see Chiefie's face against the opening. "I have some news you might be interested in," he gloated. "There has been an assassination attempt against Hitler!"

Chiefie went on to describe how a bomb had exploded during a meeting attended by Hitler and how a solid table had saved Hitler's life by shielding him from the blast. As he replaced the branches, he added, "I thought it might make you feel better to know that the Germans were killing each other."

It didn't. All I cared about was getting out of that hole.

How much longer could I take this? Time had lost all meaning. Each minute, each hour was the same. It seemed an eternity. By the end of the third day I was despondent. "Well," I thought, "there's no use dreaming about anything because I'll never survive. I'll never get out of here." I was almost ready to give myself up. Anything, anything, would be better than another hour in that hole.

What was that sound? A shovel! Never has the sound of moving earth sounded so good. A little bit of light shone through the opening and a French voice, in broken English, ordered, "Come on out, both of you. I know you're in there. Come on out."

I was a bit worried because I thought we might be arrested, but I didn't care. I breathed fresh air into my tortured lungs as I crawled through the opening and decided that I wasn't going back into that cave, no matter what. I stood up on shaky legs and flexed my cramped muscles.

Facing me was a man in a white sweater. He held a shovel in his hands and three or four men stood behind him. "You stay there," he ordered, pointing his shovel towards me and then indicating a spot on the ground, "and you stay there." he continued, pointing to Bill.

The man in the sweater looked at me and demanded, "Where are you from?"

I started to say, "I'm from England." but he interrupted me.

"You're an Allied flier, aren't you?" he stated rather than asked.

"Yeah," I replied.

"I know you are." he said firmly, "As a matter of fact, I was told you are. Now I want to know something. When were you in London last?"

I told him the date I had last been in London, which was a couple of months before.

"Were you ever downtown in London?"

"Yeah."

"What shows were playing in the theatres then? Can you tell me what shows were on? What plays were on?"

I remembered going to one show and I told him that one was on, then told him a bit more about London. He asked me if I'd read the newspapers, then said, "Tell me some of the headlines that were in the newspapers."

I answered all of his questions. "I believe you," he finally said, and introduced himself as an intelligence man. He looked at my identification and gave a long, low whistle.

"Alright." he said, "Come back with me to the ranger's home."

We followed the intelligence man back to the ranger's house. The intelligence man said that we might be able to stay there for a while longer now because the scene had cleared a bit as far as the German Army was concerned. But such was not to be.

A couple of days later, the house shook from an awful noise which was coming from the sky overhead. Jock was afraid to go outside, but I wanted to know what was going on so I ran out of the house. Way up in the sky and heading towards the coast was an awkward looking thing like a cigar with stubby wings and a flame shooting out the back. I had never seen anything like it.

Chiefie ran out of the house in a panic, obviously shocked to see me standing outside in broad daylight. I told him about the strange aircraft I had just seen.

"Oui, oui," he babbled as he guided me back into the house, "They've opened up a travelling platform for these V1's."

About an hour later, I heard the rumble of loud trucks along the road out front. I peeked through a window and saw trucks and strange vehicles with those weird 'buzz bombs' mounted on them, taking them down the road. Chiefie informed me that there was a launch site just a few miles down the road.

The area was becoming a hive of activity as German troops, technicians and support personnel moved in to service the V1's. That same night, one of the head resistance men came to the house. He was greeted at the door and escorted up to the attic. "You've got to get out of here," he said to us. "It won't take long before the Germans will go through every building with a fine toothed comb, because they're in a bit of trouble. Especially now that the Allies have landed on the beaches at Normandy. The Germans are running backwards and forwards. You will be leaving tomorrow night." He suggested that we should perhaps head for Lyon and from there head to the Spanish border.

At that time, I knew nothing of organized escape routes. It was all top secret. All I ever saw was a few individuals trying their best to cope with the dangerous and difficult problem of hiding, feeding, and moving a very frightened pilot cum fugitive.

A legendary escape network known as the 'Comet Line' had been formed by a young Belgian girl named Andree de Jongh and her father, Frederic[52]. They had been smuggling airmen into Spain and from there to Gibraltar. Andree, who was known as 'Dedee', was the moving force behind the Comet Line. She personally escorted fliers on the rigorous trek over the mountains.

By 1944 the escape network had been severely compromised by NAZI infiltrators. Dedee was arrested by the Germans. In order to protect her followers, she confessed to being the leader of the organization. Her captors did not believe that such a petite young girl could have founded an escape network of such scope and complexity, however, and she was thus imprisoned instead of executed. Frederic was subsequently arrested and shot. Many of their followers were to meet similar fates.

Another problem was that guys like me had been wreaking havoc on the railway lines, which were the main form of transportation used to smuggle evaders through France.

An alternate idea was proposed that we head for Chateaudun, which wasn't far from Lyon, and eventually head for the Forest of Freteval. There was some further discussion, but no firm decision was made.

I could not be told much about the forest at that time because it was shrouded in secrecy. It was some sort of refuge that had been set up to hide airmen until they could be rescued by the advancing Allies.

The visitor came back the following night with a horse and buggy. We still didn't know where we were going to go.

"The Forest of Freteval." announced our guide. So it was to be the forest.

Chiefie walked us to the door and wished us luck. He handed me a walking stick and an eye patch, which I put on. Jock was wearing a pair of coveralls and carried a farm implement. "Now people will know why fit young men like you are not in the army." he said with a rueful smile. We waved goodbye to Chiefie and began the next phase of our journey.

---

[52] *Neave, Airey, Saturday at M.I. 9, op. cit., Chapter 13.*

Chapter 13: The Guides

As we bounced along in the buggy, our guide described the forest to us. It was a secret place, known to very few people, where Allied airmen lived in hiding and relative safety deep inside enemy territory. His words conjured up visions of a modern Sherwood Forest inhabited by Robin Hood style 'merry men'. Our guide explained that he would drive us to a bridge, where a woman would be waiting. She would be wearing a white blouse and a black skirt. "Do not speak to her," he instructed, "or give any indication that you recognize her. She will not speak to you, either, but she will lead you to where you are going. Follow her at a distance, keeping at least half a block behind her at all times." I was to follow the woman and Jock was to walk a quarter of a block behind me. Two men walking together would have attracted too much attention.

We approached the bridge, which spanned a small river. I was uneasy at the sight of German sentries marching back and forth across it. "Don't worry," our guide assured me, "they know me and will let us through. After all," he added with a wry smile, "I am a good friend of Germany."

He handed me a purple robe which I slipped on. With the hood pulled over my head I looked just like a monk. Jock put on a black shirt or jacket of some sort.

I felt a change in the motion of the buggy as we rolled onto the wooden planks of the bridge. Our guide must have been quite influential because the guards did not stop him to ask any questions.

"Heil Hitler!" they chorused as we passed them. The sentries stood at attention with their right hands extended towards us in the classic 'Hitler salute'. In their left hands they held rifles or machine guns.

When the bridge was no longer in sight, I took off my monk disguise and dressed as a cripple once again. The driver stopped the buggy near a field and we stepped off. "There she is." He said and pointed to a figure standing in the distance. She was just a young girl. The driver wished us luck and headed off down the road.

The girl walked along the road for a while, then she stepped through a shallow ditch and headed across the field. We followed behind her as we had been instructed. She led us for about five miles, through fields, bushes, woods, until we finally entered a village.

My heart was in my mouth as we followed the girl into a busy railway station. It was just packed with German troops. I guess they must have had a directive from Berlin or something, because instead of using the normal salute all of the soldiers were saluting their officers with the Hitler salute and screaming "Heil Hitler!"

The girl went over to the ticket counter. She spoke with the ticket agent for a moment and he handed her some slips of paper. She left the ticket counter and went to board the train. I was worried that the ticket agent might try to stop us from boarding, but he conveniently directed his attention away from us. We slipped past his unseeing eyes and boarded the train.

Half of the coach was full of German soldiers and the other half had a few civilian passengers. The girl was sitting just behind the soldiers, near the rear of the coach, and Bill and I found seats just across the aisle from her.

I heard the characteristic hoot of the steam whistle and the train began moving towards Paris.

One jovial looking fellow in a soldier's uniform was laughing a deep, good humored laugh as if he had just told a funny joke. He laughed and laughed. He looked right at me, so I began to laugh, too, and I pretended that I had understood the joke. He slapped me on the shoulder such that I nearly fell out of my seat and we both laughed even more. Other soldiers were also laughing and pointing at me, a helpless cripple. I thought to myself, "The jokes on you. If you only knew who I was!"

The train slowed down and stopped to take on and let off passengers. Then it started again. It stopped and went, stopped and went. I tell you, my heart missed dozens of beats.

As soldiers in transit often will, the group ahead of us began to sing a chorus of army songs. I ignored them at first, but before long a couple of them looked back at us and motioned for us to join in. There I was, singing 'Lilli Marlene' with a bunch of German soldiers!

It took about an hour for the train to reach Paris. We finally arrived at our destination, the Gare du Nord. The girl got out of her seat and disembarked. We followed way behind her. She slipped into a large crowd.

The station was crowded with people, mostly soldiers, and there were many, many officers. They were checking people at the gates for papers, identity papers.

I wished the ground would just swallow me up. I was getting worried to the stage of panic. I wanted to run, to hide. I had no identity papers, I had nothing. All I had was the identity disc with the word JEW marked on it.

So, anyway, I was slowly walking with the crowd. I could see the girl way in the distance. One of the officers pointed at me and beckoned me to go before him. Pretending not to see him, I waved to an imaginary friend and hoped

William 'Jock' Brown

I could get lost in the crowd. Some other travelers were rushing to meet their families so I pretended to be with them.

A couple of French civilians went up to the officer to have their papers inspected. He looked at me again but was distracted by the group of people in front of him and began to inspect their identity papers. I slipped past him with Jock right behind me.

We followed the girl through the streets of Paris. We passed a group of artists busy at their easels and I realized that we were walking down Montmartre, where all the artists are.

We were led down that street, through back alleys, and eventually another woman walked up beside us and told us to follow her. She led us to a grimy stone apartment building at #24 rue de Clichy. We followed her up the stairs to the fourth floor and down the hall to an apartment door. The door opened and a woman called us in. "All right," she said, "welcome home boys."

The woman introduced herself as Mme or Mlle Epishere, or something like that. The apartment was rather austere but we were glad to have a place to stay.

Our hostess made us a meal of bean soup. It was delicious. Jock and I were both very tired so when we had downed the last drop of soup, Mme Epishere led us to a little bedroom with two small beds. Jock and I were soon fast asleep.

The next morning, Mme Epishere decided to take us for a walk. The last thing I wanted to do was leave our comfortable little hideout but I didn't want to offend our hostess. We walked back down the Montmartre section of Paris. I glanced uneasily at the German soldiers all around us as Mme Epishere pointed out the sights. We walked as far as the gleaming white Sacre-Coeur Cathedral. "This is where we will be saying Mass," she told us.

Jock Brown was a Presbyterian and I was a Jew. We were going to risk our necks to attend Mass.

When we got back to the apartment, I looked out the window and saw a figure standing in the window of an apartment across the lane. His hair and beard were bright red and he seemed to be watching me. I was a little apprehensive and wondered what he was doing, why he was watching me.

It seemed that every time I looked out the window I would see that red bearded face looking back. I called to Mme Epishere and motioned for her to come to the window. "We're being watched." I told her. "There is a red headed man over there and I noticed that he has been watching this apartment all morning. I wonder if we are under surveillance by the Gestapo."

Our hostess went up to the window with a concerned look on her face but broke into a smile at the sight of my antagonist. "Oh him!" she exclaimed, "He's an American flier who was shot down. He's been here for about a month. He keeps his head out the window all the time."

That evening we had a 'party'. It was attended by members of the Resistance, and was one of the least entertaining 'parties' I've ever attended. They had come together to discuss certain families who were hiding other airmen or Jewish children. Some of the people who were hiding Jewish children were at the meeting. "We treat them like our own children," one fellow told me. "They go to school with our children and we take them to church. No one would guess that they are Jewish. It's the only way to keep them alive."

Once again, our fate was discussed. "You can stay here if you wish," we were told, "but the best bet would be to either go through Chateaudun, Lyon, and into Spain or else be taken to Freteval Forest."

Whichever destination we finally settled on, it was going to be quite a journey because we would have to go through a lot of German special positions and the Germans were not trusting anybody. Things were a bit shaky now that the Allies had landed.

One morning, Mme Epishere, Jock, and I were on our way to church when I decided that I'd like to see a bit of Paris. We had been mingling with German troops for so long that I was beginning to lose my fear of them and was becoming a little brazen. Mme Epishere was pleased by my interest and said she'd be glad to show me a few sights before church started.

After a rather pleasant walk down Montmartre Street we went to Mass at the Sacre-Coeur. When the service was over, we walked down the many stone steps back to Montmartre Street. I was walking with the lady and Jock was following about twenty feet behind us. We had just reached the street corner. I glanced over my shoulder and what I saw made my heart race.

Jock was being interrogated by two German officers. He was waving his hands in the air and his face was white. His jaws were opening and closing like he was trying to say something but no words would come out. It was pathetic.

"Madame, we'd better run like hell." I said to my companion, "They're catching up to us. They've stopped Jock. There's no way... Let's hurry down an alley and get the hell out of here!"

"No!" she said, "We can't leave him at their mercy." She ran back there as fast as she could and threw herself at the two Germans, knocking one of them down.

"What's the matter with you Germans?!" she scolded, "My brother is deaf and dumb. Can't you understand?! What have you done to him? Look what you Germans have done to our people! Do you have to bully deaf and dumb people?!"

The two Germans looked at her as if she had sprouted horns. The one she had pushed down rubbed his aching neck as he stood up and muttered "*Sie ist verrückt!* (She's crazy.) Let's go."

A very nervous looking Jock came over to us and we walked back to the apartment. Jock refused to go on any more excursions. We couldn't get him out of that apartment at all.

"Vous avez besoin (You have need of) a haircut." Madme Epishere said to me one morning. She said that she could not come with me because people were becoming suspicious of her but she told me where I could go to get one.

Now, after that close call with Jock I was not thrilled about the idea of going out for a haircut. But Mme Epishere insisted, saying that I would attract less attention if I were properly groomed.

"Be very careful," she warned. "Walk at a steady pace. Don't walk as though you are afraid of something. Go straight to the barber shop. There will be somebody there who will know who you are and they will ask the barber to give you a haircut."

"Okay," I nodded and left the apartment. I was soon walking down Montmartre again, trying not to look as apprehensive as I felt.

A German soldier approached me and my heart was in my mouth. He asked me if I knew where he could amuse himself. "*Nicht verstehen* (I don't understand)," I muttered and kept on walking.

After a bit of searching, I found a place which looked like this barber shop. I walked in and saw a barber cutting somebody's hair. A few men were seated along the walls, reading newspapers as they waited for their turn.

A man I had never seen before walked up to me and made some comment about the washroom being at the rear of the building. He led me into a back room, then locked the door behind him. We then walked through a passageway into another room.

A second man was waiting for us. "You didn't come here to get a haircut," he told me, "you're going to get a passport picture. We're going to give you a French-German passport. It might be of some help if you are ever stopped."

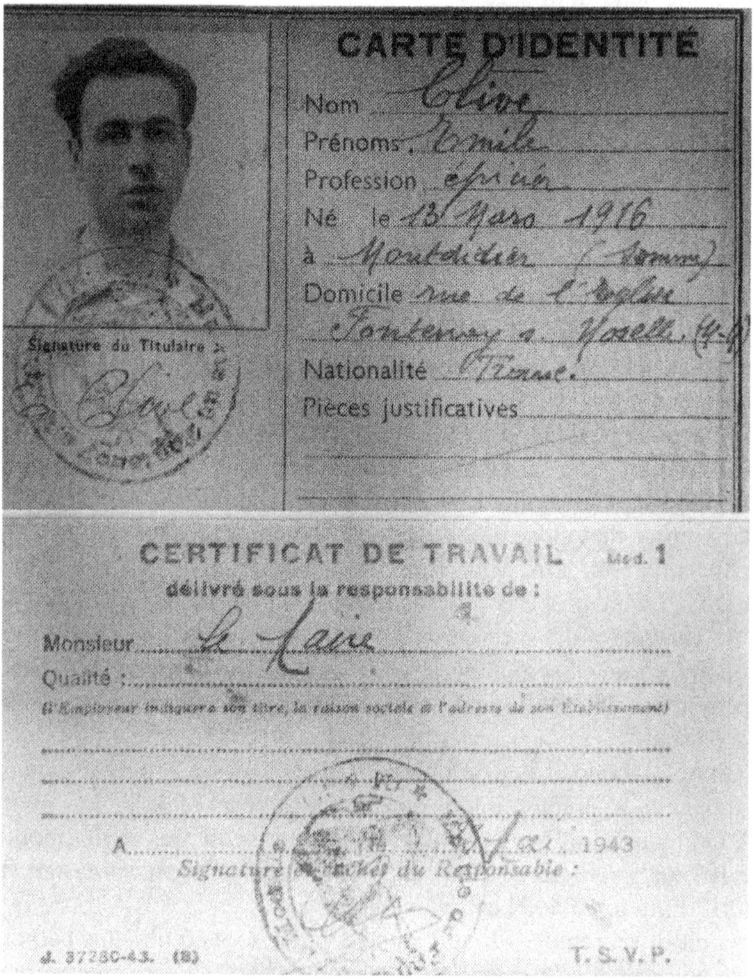
CARTE D'IDENTITÉ

Nom Clive

Prénoms Emile

Profession épicier

Né le 13 Mars 1916

à Montdidier (Somme)

Domicile rue de l'Eglise

Fontenay s. Moselle

Nationalité France.

Pièces justificatives

Signature du Titulaire :

CERTIFICAT DE TRAVAIL Mod. 1

délivré sous la responsabilité de :

Monsieur Le Maire

Qualité :

(L'Employeur indiquera son titre, la raison sociale et l'adresse de son Établissement)

A ... 1943

Signature et cachet du Responsable :

J. 37280-43. (B) T. S. V. P.

False identity card, in the name of 'Emile Clive', issued to Lou by the French Underground.

I was surprised by this development because I had really believed that I was there for a haircut.

Anyway, they took my photograph and stamped out a little paper. I had my fingertips pressed against a pad of black ink and rolled onto the passport paper.

The whole thing took about ten minutes. They developed my photograph and sealed it together with my fingerprints on an official looking passport. At the top of the card were the words "CARTE D'IDENTITE". Upon examining the identity card, I saw that I was now a Frenchman named 'Emile Clive'.

These self-appointed passport officials showed me out the back way and gave me directions back to Mme Epishere's apartment. When I arrived, somebody cut my hair.

The war was intensifying in the Paris area and the Germans were beginning to panic because of General Patton's advances. We had more meetings with the Underground to discuss the new developments.

It was very interesting for me to hear stories of what some of the Resistance people had done, about people they had saved. Once again, a common theme was how they worked against their own compatriots, whom they were more afraid of than the Germans.

An attractive young girl was staying in the apartment with us. Jock would never let me be alone with her for some reason or other.

One day she came over to me with an excited look on her face. "You're going to be rescued pretty soon, Emile." she said, "The Allies have broken through!"

I grimaced a bit and grumbled, "Who the hell wants to be rescued?!"

Just when I was starting to enjoy that God-damned business, the Allies had to break through!

Since the war, there seems to have developed a legend about a powerful 'underground' movement operating with large resources and popular support throughout France. It is my observation that the Underground was composed of frightened individuals doing their best with little support, few resources, and facing an uncertain future.

There was an air of confusion at the last meeting I attended. No one knew what was going to happen; whether there would be a battle for Paris, whether the Germans would retreat, or what have you. Because of this uncertainty, it was decided that Jock and I would have to move once again. We would carry on with our journey to the Forest of Freteval.

Jock and I were going to travel our separate ways. I said my goodbyes and was led through the streets of Paris by another woman to the Paris 'Metro' or

Bomber Command caused considerable damage to the marshalling yards at Trappes. Lou now found that the Germans expected him to help clear it up, little realising that he had already contributed to the mayhem himself.

subway. From there we made our way to the Austerlitz Railway Station. The station was buzzing with the usual crowd of passengers, workers, German soldiers... and slave laborers.

Once again the train went stop and go, stop and go. From what I could see they had all kinds of workers, even Russian prisoners, going here and there to repair the damage caused by Allied bombs.

The train continued on for about forty-five minutes. We pulled into a bombed-out railway center and my jaw dropped at the sight of such devastation. The railway center was so bombed that all of the workshops had been reduced to rubble. I had seen war-torn London, but the damage here was beyond my imagination. The station had only a single remaining track. Through the window I could see the crooked remains of the other tracks, their rails twisted around like threads. Craters were punched right through the middle of the tracks, cutting them like ribbons. Shattered railroad cars lay in heaps with little regard to the location of the tracks.

"My God!" I thought to myself, "How many people must have been killed in this?!" I looked at the massive craters and wondered what sort of weapon the Allies had used to cause so much damage.

The train drew to a stop. It couldn't go any further at present because other trains needed the one track. With all of the trains coming backwards and forwards, the destruction of the tracks had caused a large traffic jam.

Everyone was ordered off the train. As I stepped onto the platform an old sign caught my eye. It said 'Trappes'. I was taken aback; this was the railway station my squadron had bombed just three weeks before. I had been awestruck by my own handiwork.

All over the place were workers clearing rubble and rebuilding. They were being supervised by members of the 'Todt' organization. Everyone, especially the Germans, seemed to be in a panic. No one really knew what was going on but that the Allies had landed and the Germans were in a precarious position.

I was a little bit worried, too, because the Germans were examining everybody. What made me worry even more than usual was the knowledge that this was the Klaus Barbie area. Although his name was not generally known, there were lots of stories about what he was like, what he was doing. If he ever got hold of me...

I looked at the devastation all about me and thought, "Gee-wiz! Is this what I did?!"

The Germans had formed a gate and insisted on seeing everybody's papers. Suddenly, the girl I had been following was gone. I didn't know what to do or where to go.

An official came up to me and demanded to see my papers. I almost panicked, but then I remembered my phony passport. I dug it out of my pocket and showed it to him, being careful not to look him in the eye.

He studied it, looked at the photograph, looked at me, and seemed satisfied. "You!" he ordered, "You go!"

He pointed to a group of about three or four hundred men forming up into a work party. I walked over to them and somebody handed me a yellow arm band with the word "Deutsche Wehrmacht" stenciled onto it. When I had slipped the band around my arm, a burly foreman handed me a shovel and put me to work. I was now part of the German establishment.

I headed for a large bomb crater. Men with picks and shovels were trying to fill it in with bits of rubble. I could tell by their emaciated state that many of the people around me were slave laborers. Some of the others were speaking to each other in a language which was probably Russian, and I guessed that they were P.O.W's from the Eastern front. Still others were French or German citizens who were unfit for military service. I guess I was in that category.

How the hell could I get out of this?! All around us were guards - armed with machine guns - to keep us from escaping. We were directly supervised by foremen from the Todt organization and their supervisors were watching them. German officers hovered about, inspecting the whole works.

I dug the end of my shovel into a pile of broken stones and pitched them into the pit. My aircraft had carried an eight thousand pound bomb on the Trappes raid, and it would have made a crater just like this one. I wondered if I was helping to clean up damage which I had done personally.

The work was hard, and I was getting hungry. I toiled away; scoop up stones - drop them in, scoop up stones – drop them in. I wondered how long we would be kept working, how long before we could eat. The foremen told us to work, work, work.

At last we were allowed to take a break. A large kettle was brought over and I was handed a bowl of slop. I wrinkled my nose at it, for it was nothing but boiled cabbage leaves in water, but I was hungry. I would eat anything.

There were no washroom facilities. We had to relieve ourselves behind some nearby trees. Some people did it right where they were.

Work, work, work. As we worked, an air battle was taking place over our heads. I saw some Lancasters fly past and paused to watch them go by.

"Arbeit! Arbeit!" (Work, work) snarled a foreman.

"My God," I thought to myself as I dug my shovel in once more, "how am I ever going to get out of this place? Now I'm stuck!"

Security was pretty stiff. The Germans weren't taking any chances because they knew that the place was rife with Resistance people. The Resistance people knew it was rife with other Frenchmen; French but informers. There were more informers, apparently, than there were Resistance people. I didn't know who to get close to.

Thank goodness I could speak German! There were so many different dialects mixed up in this place... High German, Low German, Flemish... that nobody questioned my accent.

I couldn't take much more of this back breaking toil. We were fixing roads, bombed out structures, anything which required brute strength. But I knew there were some Resistance people around who knew what was going on and I prayed that they might be able to help me.

It was getting dusk. A man working beside me edged a little closer and, without looking up, began to speak in broken English:

"As soon as it gets darker, a little bit, they're changing shifts. They're going to different places. When they transfer them to different places, there is one spot where there is no officials there. You get into that little bush. Nobody will bother you because a lot of people have to go to the bathroom about there. You sneak in there as soon as we get by and then there is a path. Follow that path as far as you can and we'll have several people that we'll have to save. There's two more guys, Allied people who have escaped from German prisons. You'll probably see them en route, but they were told that they're friends. Don't, the Germans don't know about that place. They've got a big map about that place."

When he had finished his cryptic spiel, my new comrade edged away and concentrated on his work. I longed to ask him questions but we were constantly under the gaze of the Todt officials. I hoped that I had understood and could remember his instructions.

Darkness came and with it came the expected shift change. In the confusion, I headed for what I hoped was the right bush. I entered the woods and looked about for the path. I couldn't find it.

I couldn't find the path. But there was no going back. I stood still in the bush and hoped nobody would see me. A lot of German soldiers, random patrols, went right by me and looked around the bush. I didn't dare move because if anybody saw me in that bush...

Finally, the shifts passed. A night shift arrived to carry on the work. Nobody kept track of who was there. They just commandeered people right and left and put them to work.

When it was dark enough that no one could see me, I crawled away in the opposite direction. The woods I was hiding in were small and I was soon crawling through a field. I kept my eyes open for a path.

My eyes gradually became accustomed to the darkness. I couldn't see a path but there was a thin, little trail, a slight trail, a trail I could hardly see. I stood up and began to walk along that trail.

On my left was a field with lots of horses in it. They were running around and I couldn't cross that field for fear of being trampled.

I kept following the trail along the edge of that field. I must have been walking down that little trail for an hour and a half. I was all alone. I saw no sign of any other people. I was supposed to see other people going down the trail. I saw no sign of them and it was getting even darker.

I was tired and I couldn't walk any more. I had been working for that God-damned Todt organization all day and was still wearing my arm band. I took the arm band off and put it in my pocket. The last thing I needed was to be mistaken for a German and shot by a Resistance man.

I was caught between the two of them. "Well," I thought to myself, "I've got to carry on."

With the coming of daylight, my trek ended. Right in front of me was a stream, cutting off any further travel. I was right near the mouth and it was like a small river. I didn't know how I would ever get across.

I sat down for a rest and lay my head across my arms. "How the hell did I get into this?" I asked myself. "What am I going to do now?"

A drizzle of rain began adding to my misery. I looked up through the mist and saw a formation of aircraft overhead, at about 4,000 feet. I could just make out the distinctive shape of Lancasters. "You buggers!" I thought. It might have been my squadron. Moments later, I heard an echoing thunder and the ground shook as they pounded a nearby target.

The area about me was desolate. I was so tired and depressed that I started to cry. "What did I do to deserve this?" I asked myself, "What did I do? Why did I get into this?"

I listened to the beating of my heart. It felt like it was thumping in my ears. It thumped and thumped and I thought to myself, "I'm sick, I can't stand it any longer."

I eventually composed myself and decided that I had no choice but to cross the stream. I walked upstream for a while, hoping to find a bridge or something to make it a bit easier, but I couldn't see anything like that. I finally took the plunge, so to speak, and stepped into the icy water. The stream was only two or three feet deep so I was able to wade across.

I emerged on the other side, cold and dripping, and began walking across a wood. I reached a country road and heard the 'clip-clop' of a horse's hooves. I looked in the direction of the sound and could see a horse and buggy in the distance. As the buggy drew closer, I could see that an elderly man was driving it. He was going slowly, as if he didn't want to attract any attention.

I didn't know what to do at first, then I realized that I had no choice but to hitch-hike. What did I have to lose?

"Vite, vite!" he urged and beckoned me into the buggy. I hopped in beside him. We then rode cross country, through bushes and everything else. All the while, the old man was encouraging me. He kept saying, "Bon courage, bon courage!"

We came to an isolated village. I could see a row of attached houses which made up a large block. The old man drove around behind those houses and pulled up at the rear entrance to one of them. He swung to the ground, secured his horse's reins to a hitching post, and told me to follow him.

He knocked at the door. It was a special knock: two times, three times, one-two, two-three times.

The door swung open and a man and a woman called me in. The old man left. I don't know if it was through the food I got when I was working for the Todt organization or what have you but I was having stomach trouble and my head was pretty clouded. I swayed a bit on my feet and told them, "I'm finished."

One fellow replied, "Yeah, you look pretty tired. We had our eye on you. You were working for the Germans there."

They made me a bowl of bean soup, or something like that. And then they led me into a tiny vestibule with a cot. It was more like a cupboard than a room. I lay down on the cot with all of my clothes on and sank into a deep sleep.

I was awakened by the crowing of a rooster. I sat up in a daze, unsure of where I was. A woman came up to me and said, "Here, have something to eat."

She made me a bowl of coffee and cooked some potatoes for me. That was all they could spare from their meager food supply. A man, who I assumed to be her husband, urged me to eat quickly. "Vite! Vite!" he said, and added, "Dangereux!"

He told me to get ready, then helped me to shave with an old razor. He told me that I would be taken to a place where I would find some escaped prisoners and some American fliers who had been shot down. He said there would be the odd Russian prisoner there.

"It's a two or three hour walk," he said. "We'll have some people take you there. You'll have to walk through fields and across ditches. You can't take an open road."

My guides were an eleven year old boy and his twelve year old sister. Each one carried a small sack of food. We walked through fields and bushes together for about an hour and a half before stopping for a brief lunch. They could only speak French, but I had picked up some of that language by now and so I could understand a bit of what they were saying. They told me that they had been doing this for the last few months, leading escaped prisoners and downed airmen. They were taking me where they had taken all the others, to one of the district headquarters of the Resistance movement.

As we walked, they told me stories of people who had been caught doing what they were doing and had been executed for it. Even children had been taken away. Many of their playmates were now helping anybody who was fighting the Germans. They were trying to save the lives of Jewish kids and generally worked closely with the adults.

"What would happen to anybody of Jewish faith who was caught?" I asked them and I showed them my identity disc. "Oh," the little boy replied, "all Jews go to the gas chambers. And if you look Jewish, they tell you to drop your pants down, just to make sure."

I think it's strange that these children knew about the gas chambers but, at the end of the war, the leaders of Germany claimed that they didn't know about them. Everybody else knew about them. It's funny how their attitudes changed when their own skins were at stake.

I kept admiring those two little kids. Of course, part of the idea was that we would look like a father with his children.

Anyway, they took me into a town called 'Montbossier', which was slightly larger than the village we had left. They led me to a warehouse which had some houses at the back of it. I went in there and was pleasantly surprised to find a lot of people speaking English. There were about eight or nine of them, having supper. They were all Allied fliers, escaped prisoners, and what have you. One fellow, a flight engineer, had half of his face burned away and a guy whose leg was badly twisted had been given crutches.

A man and his wife and another elderly man were looking after these people. They made me some rabbit stew with potatoes. It was a reasonable meal, (although I disliked the thought of eating rabbit) and I ate with gusto. A short while later I would have to bring it all up.

When I had finished my meal, I was introduced to the other 'guests'. There were quite a few American pilots there, most of whom had been shot down in Flying Fortresses.

I became friends with a Mustang pilot who had been shot down by an FW 190. We were walking around outside when two FW 190's flew by so low that we could see the German crosses. They were 'hedge hopping' to avoid the Allied fighters which were gaining control of the skies.

This Mustang pilot shook his fist at the low flying aircraft and yelled, "Get up there, you bastards, and fight like a man!"

"Those sons of bitches are yellow now," he said with disgust, "they're flying low. You should have seen them a year ago, when they outnumbered us. Boy, they were really brave! Look how they're hedge hopping to keep out of the way of our guys."

I breathed a sigh of relief to be amongst friends once again. It was just like one big family. There was a little notebook there in which a few of us signed our names, as a memento for the people helping us. I signed my real name and wrote down my address in England.

We swapped stories, lots of stories. One fellow told me that he had been rescued by a Frenchman named Philippe d'Albert-Lake and his American wife, Virginia. Philippe was a leader of the Comet Line who was responsible for the

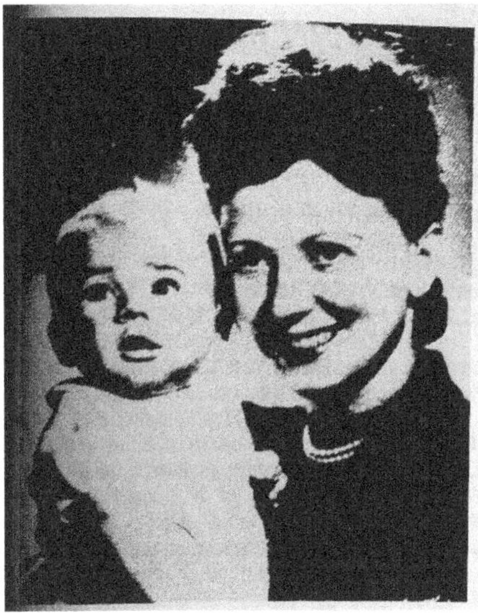

Virginia (left) and Philippe d'Albert-Lake.

reception and dispatch of evaders to the Forest of Freteval.[53] Virginia was leading my companion to the forest when the Germans grabbed her. The man who told me about this could only watch helplessly as Virginia was taken away. Philippe, fortunately, had gone on ahead and was able to evade capture. The following account is quoted, with her permission, from Virginia's unpublished autobiography *An American Woman in Paris*[54]:

'The cart hove into sight around the bend. We mounted our bikes and rode on. A stranger joined us, pedaling in from a side road and we continued this way for about a kilometer, the three of us in single file, the wagon about fifty yards behind. We would soon be coming out into the main highway, I could already see it in the distance, as well as the formidable mass of buildings on the hill beyond, which was Chateaudun.

'A large black car turned abruptly from the highway into our narrow side road. I suddenly felt nervous. What would such a car be doing on such a desolated road? I went off to the side to let it pass, but instead of passing, it stopped. There were three men in it - and they were German police! One of them ordered us to get off our bicycles. They left the car and came over to ask for our

---

53 *Neave, Airey, Saturday at M.I.9., op. cit.*

54 *Mme d'Albert-Lake was kind enough to send the author a copy of her manuscript.*

identity papers. As I write this, I start trembling again. The entire scene comes back in all its frightening vividness. I was the first victim; I handed over my identity card which stated that I was born an American citizen. I had never pretended otherwise, as it would have been impossible considering the strong accent with which I spoke French. The Nazi glanced at my card. "What are you doing in this region when your identity card states that you live in Paris?" he asked gruffly but in perfect French. - "We have been searching the farms for fruit and eggs" I lied. - "Ah," his voice rose with interest, "you have an English accent. I see now that your card states that you were born in the United States." - "Yes, but I am French by marriage". I lied. "I took my husband's nationality when I married. I have the right to circulate."

"Perhaps". Then, he quickly added, glancing back at Al and the stranger: "Are you with these two men?" - "No, we were riding together quite by accident; they joined me from a side road further back." This was my only chance of escape, but all the time I was conscious of Al's coat that was very much in evidence in my basket, and it was a coat which very obviously matched the trousers he was wearing. I wondered if they had noticed it.

'I tried to appear unconcerned and prepared to mount my bicycle, but I was tense and trembling. I knew that this moment was a climax in my life. These few seconds would prove the success or failure of my effort to escape. I hopefully pushed down on the pedal. "Stop," he roared out. "Not so fast."

'Something broke inside me. I knew somehow that there was no more reason to hope. The sun that only a few minutes ago was so bright and warm, now seemed eclipsed by a grey fog. Disappointment and fear clothed me in a hot vapor. Sweat started in my armpits; my scalp tingled; I had no choice but to stand there in the centre of the dusty road, grip my handle bars, and wait.

'Now they questioned the man in black. His papers were in order and it was evident that he was French. He said that we were strangers to him and so they let him leave. Then, it was Al's turn. He looked tense and wretched, but he handed over his identity card with perfect dignity. Then they started questioning him. His card stated that he was French, but he could not speak the language. He tried bluffing at first with a "oui" or a "non", but he did not make sense. The Police Officer pointed at him and said in forceful English: "You are American. Aren't you?" Al declined to answer and from then on, he said nothing.

'During this time I glanced back for the cart. It had stopped beside a farm-house, about 30 yards away, and I saw the boys stealthily climbing out and disappearing into the underbrush at the side of the road. I was so grateful. Once the game was up, I know that I appeared very calm and in perfect command of myself, but, inside, I felt a throbbing excitement and a kind of deep heavy misery, clutching and dragging me down.

'Now that these Feldgendarmes had guessed what we were, they began searching us. They acted very pleased with themselves! The Officer tore open my handbag and, with his gesture, I suddenly recalled something which made terror clutch at my heart. Before leaving Paris I had disposed of every incriminating evidence, but I still had the list of addresses of the Underground at Chateaudun that Philippe had given me only yesterday, prior to my leaving alone to make the necessary contacts. The feeling of guilt which came over me was worse than anything I had yet suffered. All the people I had met the day before: the grocery man and his toddling son; Henri, his wife and baby boy; the farmer and his family - visions of them all rose up before my eyes. I was miserable. The German, in the meantime, was carefully examining everything. He saw the map, food tickets, an envelope with paper money, my fountain pen, compact, nail file, and the piece of note-book paper on which were written the addresses. He hesitated over this and, to my amazement, he put everything back into my bag, addresses and all, and handed it back to me! Then he discovered Al's coat. He made but a simple comment: "It was not right for you to have said that you were not together."

'He went over to Al and left me standing in the middle of the road, with a sergeant to guard me. I had taken off my jacket and was holding it over my arm while my hand clutched the bag hidden underneath. Now was my only chance. Unconcernedly, I slipped my right hand under the jacket, slowly opened the bag and managed to get hold of what I thought and prayed was the right paper. I tore it into tiny bits, found one of the pockets of my jacket and slipped them in. It was impossible to dispose of them in any other way for the moment, as I was too closely guarded. Nothing of interest was found on Al, though, fortunately, he had his "dog tag" to help prove that he was not a spy. After having searched Al, the officer ordered one of his men to wheel our bicycles back to the nearest farmhouse and to leave them there. Now they ordered us into their car.

‘I sat in front between two of the police, and Al was in back with the third. They were very jolly and kept making gay remarks, none of which I understood. After ten minutes, we stopped before the Feldgendarmerie of Chateaudun. We got out and walked through a door and down a narrow hall, turning at last into a big room which proved to be the main office. Before the windows, which looked out on the main street, were two desks and, behind one of them was a German Officer. The man responsible for our arrest went directly over to his superior and began proudly to relate his story.

'There was considerable activity in the big room. Uniformed police were constantly walking in and out. No one appeared to be watching me with any special attention, so I wandered aimlessly around the room, grasping the bits of paper in my hand and, at the first opportunity, popped them into my mouth.

'I had great difficulty in swallowing them. They simply would not be chewed and I had no more saliva. Minutes passed before I was successful. The relief I felt was indescribable. Almost immediately afterward, the German seized my handbag; he emptied the contents onto the desk and I could tell that he was interested in finding the list of addresses. He searched once, turning everything over and over and, then, repeated his search.

'He became nervous and agitated. "Where is that paper?" he exploded at me.

"What paper?"

"You know, the one with the addresses."

"How should I know? I thought you put it back in my bag with the other things. Perhaps you let it drop out on the road."

"No, I didn't. It was there." He began searching again, and looked on the floor, in the hall, even in the car.

In the meantime I was seated in a comfortable arm-chair, but Al had been led away. The German came back again. He had started a more careful search of the room, when suddenly he made a grab for something on the floor. It was one of the tiny bits of paper I had unknowingly let fall. He looked at me with a deep disconcerting stare.

"You ate it." he said finally.

"Yes." I answered simply. Never again did I hear mentioned that list of addresses. He had committed such an unforgiveable fault in giving me back my bag that it was deemed inadvisable to admit it to the Gestapo!'

Virginia refused to reveal the information which had been on that page. She was sent to Ravensbrück concentration camp, where her chances of survival were minimal, but thanks to her coolness and courage the boys and the members of the Underground were saved.

The head of my new household was M. Gaston Duneau, a mechanic. He would fetch the escapers and evaders in little groups of one to five. He equipped us with pitch forks and other implements to make us look like farmers.

I was standing outside one day, talking to a gentleman named M. Foreau. The Mayor of Montbossier, M. Foreau was giving false population statistics to the Germans so that more food rations could be given to the evading airmen.

Gaston Duneau and his family in the company of M.W. Prier, one of the 53 aviators to whom he gave refuge.

Some American P-47 fighter-bombers swooped down on us and we ran for cover as their bombs fell. We were alright, but some civilians were killed in that raid.

I met a little fellow who must have been about ten or eleven years old, I guess, who seemed to like me. He said, "My dad blows up bridges, you know. He helps the Germans build things, then blows them up at night. You wanna meet my dad?"

I said "Sure." The little boy said he lived about twenty kilometers away in a town called Bonnevale.

I said goodbye to all of those fellows I had met and left that quiet little town. I'm not sure how we got to Bonnevale. It might have been by van, by horse, or we might have cycled there. During my travels, I'd had to use bicycles to get from place to place. I wasn't too worried about the Germans at that moment because we had been in a quiet little area without too much activity. That relative tranquility would not last much longer.

Chapter 14: Cloak and Dagger

We arrived at Bonnevale and my new companion brought me to his parents' home. They lived at the inn which his father, M. Pierre Dauphin, owned. He was of medium height and build, with speckles of grey in his dark hair. I met the boy's four year old sister, whose name was Denise, or something like that. Was she ever cute! The boy's parents welcomed me and treated me like one of the family. But I had to enter through the back way because this town was full of German soldiers and some of them regularly visited the inn. The little boy was pleased to have me staying with them. I remember him telling me, "We are having rabbit for dinner!" with such enthusiasm that I didn't have the heart to tell him that the very thought of eating rabbit was enough to make my stomach churn. I wanted to eat a rabbit as much as I wanted to eat a dog or a cat.

While I was choking down the rabbit which had been so thoughtfully prepared in my honor, M. Dauphin filled me in on the details of his work.

There was some pretty serious sabotage taking place and my host was responsible for it. "My people are blowing up German communication centers, blowing up bridges, and harassing German troops on the highways." he told me.

With obvious satisfaction, M. Dauphin informed me that German soldiers were beginning to panic. "There are many deserters from the German army," he said, and told me how German soldiers were stealing horses or whatever they could to get away. They were stealing them from Frenchmen who had helped the Germans. General Patton's army was advancing towards this area.

I was beginning to feel quite happy in my new home. They treated me well and I had plenty of good food to enjoy. I started to lose some of that lingering fear which had constantly gnawed away at my insides.

As I said, I had plenty of good food to enjoy. I put a new twist on an old saying, however; what went down had to come up. After every meal, I would head back to my room and be violently ill, vomiting into the chamber pot which I also used for a toilet. It was too dangerous for me to use the outhouse.

M. Dauphin and his cohorts were deeply involved with the German military commanders. One of the rooms at the inn was suitable for conferences and the Germans were using it as a field headquarters. Every evening at about four or five o'clock, the German officers would arrive. They would sit around a wooden table and map out their strategy. M. Dauphin took part in these discussions, contributing his knowledge of local conditions.

We were having lunch before one of these meetings. M. Dauphin had a thoughtful expression on his face as if he was reaching a decision. "The Germans are planning to cross a nearby bridge." he said, at length. "Once they are across the bridge, they intend to launch a counter attack. But," he added with a rueful smile, "They will never cross that bridge. We are going to blow it up." A shiver went through me as he looked me in the eye and I realized what was coming next.

"We could use a man like you." he continued, "Would you like to join us?"

My young friend was an integral part of this group and knew the score. He seemed thrilled by his father's suggestion. "That would be great!" he said with his usual exuberance, "You could place the explosives!"

Playing with dynamite behind enemy lines was not on the list of things I most wanted to do right at that moment. I was trying to be inconspicuous and it struck me that blowing up a bridge right under German noses was a good way to call attention to myself.

I couldn't let them know how I really felt, so I told them that I would consider their offer.

When our meal was over, I excused myself and headed to my room, as usual. Now it so happened that there was a small transom connecting my room with the room in which the German officers held their meetings. When I heard people entering the adjacent room, I picked up a wooden chair and quietly placed it against the wall beneath the transom. I then stood up on the chair and waited for the show to begin.

The transom was open a couple of inches. I could see everyone in the next room; the German officers with their uniforms and forage caps, one or two of M. Dauphin's men, and M. Dauphin. The meeting began with an exchange of "Heil Hitlers" before they were seated. M. Dauphin seated himself at the table directly opposite from me.

From my understanding of German, I could tell that they were discussing the bridge which M. Dauphin intended to blow up. One of the officers produced some sketches, which were passed around the table to be studied or examined by the others. The tone of this meeting was serious and businesslike and I had to admire M. Dauphin's coolness. One wrong move and he and his family would all be dead. Or worse.

M. Dauphin looked up from the papers he was examining and saw me peeking at him from under the transom. A shocked expression replaced his normal composure and he slapped his hand over his eyes.

"Do you have a headache?" asked one of the German officers, obviously puzzled by my host's unusual gesture.

"Oui," replied M. Dauphin, who looked a few shades whiter, "Yes, I have a headache."

M. Dauphin avoided my eyes for the rest of the meeting. Finally, one of the senior officers said, "Roust!" and they rose to leave. After another round of Hitler salutes, the Germans departed. When his guests had left, M. Dauphin stormed into my room. "Get away from there!" he roared. "God help us if they ever saw you!"

I couldn't sleep that night. I tossed and turned as my head was filled with visions of myself as a German prisoner. I thought of the gas chambers, and imagined the pain of machine gun bullets ripping through my body. I had to bring up, again and again, and I didn't know if it was because of my stomach trouble or because of the terrifying task I was being asked to perform.

The next day, I gave them my decision. "Well," I said, "if I have to, I will; but I can't. I've been through too much, for me to go through this again. But, if you insist, I will be glad to do it."

"No." M. Dauphin shook his head. "I can see you are not well. But you are still very brave."

The resistance men nodded amongst themselves that it was probably best that I not come. Noting that sabotage was not - strictly speaking - R.A.F. business, one of them remarked, "If he were hurt, he could lose his pension!"

M. Dauphin continued, "The best thing we can do is to get you to the forest of Freteval. That is a place set aside. It is a big forest, where many of the Allied escapees, the fliers that were shot down, are hiding."

He went on to say that the Germans were getting wise to it, but they were afraid to go in there because they didn't know what to expect. They thought there was an armed Resistance man behind every tree.

Getting me to the forest was going to be a bit tricky. Up to now, I had been able to sneak across deserted areas like fields and woods, with maybe a sentry or two. That was all in the past. There were heavy troop concentrations all around the forest and it would be necessary to smuggle me through roadblocks. There were about five or six other evaders who would also have to be smuggled.

Things were getting pretty hot because of the assassination attempt and the invasion. German security measures were at their peak.

One night, very soon after the decision to move me had been made, a German government van pulled up behind the inn. M. Dauphin walked me out to it. "This is the van we use to repair all of the German communication lines to the front." He explained. "We then send our Resistance fighters to destroy the work we have done."

The rear doors of the van swung open and I could see that it was full of electrical equipment. "The drivers are electricians." M. Dauphin continued.

About four or five men were already sprawled in the back of the vehicle. We grunted the usual greetings to each other but it was obvious that they were as preoccupied as I was. The thing was a deathtrap. I climbed in.

M. Dauphin wished us luck and slammed the steel door. The driver put her into gear and we began to bounce along the gravel road. The metal floor was uncomfortable and I knew this would be a long trip.

The van slowed down after a while and came to a stop. I could hear the drivers talking to a German sentry and was relieved when he accepted their story that they were on their way to make repairs. After all, they were qualified electricians driving a government repair vehicle and the sentry had probably seen them many times before. We were stopped several times and each time the sentries let us pass. We were getting closer and closer to the front lines.

We had been traveling for a couple of hours when we came to a barricade. German soldiers surrounded our vehicle and a German officer was shouting, "Roust! Roust! Everybody out!"

A metallic clang echoed through the van as the door swung open and I found myself staring down the barrel of a machine gun.

I figured the game was up. I stood up as best I could in the cramped van and leaned on the open door as I prepared to step off the back of the van. One of the soldiers pointed at me and snorted, "I don't like the looks of that one."

The driver gunned the throttle and swerved off the main road. With one foot almost on the ground, I hung onto the swinging rear door as we rattled down a side street. I broke into a cold sweat and wanted to bring up. I swung myself back into the van and secured the door.

We had only gone a short distance before we came to another barricade. They were ready for us this time and there was no chance of escape. The driver didn't know what to do.

Some German NCOs were yelling, "Get out of there, you buggers!" Officers were demanding to see our papers. I resigned myself to arrest and once again prepared to climb out of the van.

"For God's sake!" exclaimed the man beside the driver, "General Patton's forces are almost on top of us. They're breaking through and we had an order to repair a communications system. It's urgent and we don't have time for messing around with papers and stuff like that!"

The senior officer said, "Alright." He turned to one of the NCOs and ordered, "Remove the barricade and let them through. And give them an escort!"

The driver wasted no time in getting out of there. As soon as the road was clear he put his foot down to the metal.

Lou Greenburgh (centre) and Jock Brown photographed with a child during their evasion. The back of the original photograph was inscribed 'Juillet 44 Freteval. Souvenir de la guerre.'

I could hear the buzz of a motorcycle alongside us for several miles. We kept to back lanes and avoided the main roads. You could smell the danger in the air.

We all breathed a sigh of relief. "Boy!" remarked one of the fugitives, "If I ever get back to the 'States again, I'll never leave!"

We neared the forest after about two or three hours. The van left the road and headed across a field because we didn't dare take a road that close to the front. I looked out a window and could see German tanks in the distance. Armored cars sat on a road beside the forest.

The van halted and we climbed out, then made a dash for the trees. A couple of Resistance men, armed with machine guns, stepped out of the bushes and waved us on. We went into the forest. It was a dark forest.

Chapter 15: The Forest of Freteval

By early 1944, the major escape routes being used by Allied evaders had been severely compromised. The Allies were planning to invade Europe so it was decided that rather than create new escape routes back to England, the Allies should establish a holding area in France where Allied airmen could take refuge until they were rescued by the advancing Allied forces. Thanks to co-operation between the British Secret Service, the Royal Air Force, and the French Resistance, this plan resulted in the establishment of camps at various locations including the Forest of Freteval.

The evaders' camp at the Forest of Freteval had been started around the 18th of May, 1944, when Lucien Boussa and Monsieur Jabault, the Resistance Chief, with a small party studied and surveyed the forest[55].

The forest camp was concealed by a ring of trees. Remote from the road was the house of the forester, M. Hallowin, who was in the service of the Marquis of Levis-Mirapoix. It was just the place to become the temporary residence of Colonel Boussa, known mainly by his first name of Lucien, chief of the future camp. Monsieur and Madame Hallowin only occupied part of the dwelling. An adjoining farm would permit the storage of food stuffs and the liaison would be performed by M. Jubault's two young children. A second camp was later established about ten kilometers to the south, not far from the village of Busloup.

It was not long before escorts selected for this purpose brought the first airmen. They were two Canadians, who put up the first tent in what would soon be a curious canvas village. Operation 'Sherwood' had begun.

I arrived at the camp at the end of July, 1944. I was brought before a British officer named F/Lt Berry who had taken command of the camp. Berry was the only evader who was still armed. He asked me for my pistol so I told him how it had been lost with my boots. I'd kept it in my boots so that it wouldn't interfere with my harness but I wouldn't have given it to him anyway. He was only a flight lieutenant and I wondered what business he had bossing everyone else around.

I sat down on a log and began to get acquainted with my new companions. Johnny Sandulak[56], a wiry rear gunner, had bailed out of his turret after his bomber had collided with another aircraft. I told him, and everyone else

---

[55] *Much of the information about the formation of the camp is taken from a pamphlet entitled 'The Extraordinary Adventure of the Forest of Freteval' written by Cecile Jubault in 1967.*

[56] *Much of the information about life in the camp was gained from an interview with Johnny Sandulak in 1990.*

Aerial view of the Forest of Freteval. In the centre, at Bellande, is the forester's house.

who was listening, how I had tried to bring my plane back on my own. I told them it was just barely keeping airborne with everything hanging and sputtering. I cursed the German pilot who'd nailed me. "I told him in every way I could that I was helpless and that all I was trying to do was get home." I complained. "The S.O.B. just pulled back and blew me out of the sky!"

Johnny later said that I looked so mad he was sure I would have throttled that fighter pilot if I could have got a hold of him right there.

I'm glad it was summer time. The little cluster of makeshift shelters would hardly protect one from the elements on a winter night. They were concentrated in a very small area near the center of the woods. I wouldn't really call it a clearing, since there were plenty of trees about, but let's say a clearing in the undergrowth. A few of the guys had proper tents but most of us had only crude shelters. The shelters were constructed of cloth, canvas I think, and there may have been some parachute cloth as well. I seem to recall a few sheets of tin. Pieces of string were stretched between the trees, with wooden branches for support, and the cloth was hung on that. I remember having a wooden pole right beside me when I lay down in mine. We didn't have any flaps to keep out the wind and rain would run right into the shelters. Nobody had a blanket, or even a groundsheet. If this had been a Canadian forest, I probably could have found some pine boughs or something to use as a mattress but these trees were all deciduous. We had to sleep right on the ground, or maybe on a scrap piece of cloth. The only fires we had were small ones we used for cooking and we were worried about the Germans seeing even them.

And yet a camaraderie existed between the fugitives in that forest. There were over a hundred of us in total. We could all be killed at any moment, we all shared the same risks and the same discomforts and that made us close. I would say we were 'like brothers' but I've got brothers I've never been close to. Mind you, there was a bit of friction between the British airmen and their American counterparts.

The forester, M. Halouin, and his wife. They were at the centre of the action, housing Colonel Boussa.

The guys had started a tradition of where each of us would produce a 100 franc note or dollar bill for the others to sign. I signed their franc notes and they signed mine. I wrote 'L. Greenburgh, RAF'.

I met Lucien soon after my arrival. I didn't know much about him except that he was our liaison with the underground. He seemed to know what was going on around the place. I suppose that nowadays some people might say that he was something of a 'secret agent'.

Lucien told me that we were surrounded by enemy formations. He said that the underground had started a rumor, passed on by collaborators or double agents, that the forest was heavily fortified. The Germans knew that something was going on in the forest but they didn't want to send lightly armed troops in there because they were afraid of what they might find. They couldn't launch a major offensive against us at the moment because they were too busy at the front and couldn't spare the necessary troops and equipment. With the invasion front advancing, we were the least of their worries.

The truth was that we were completely defenseless. The only weapon that I knew of in that whole camp was Berry's revolver and I doubt that he even had any bullets for it.

Everything was peaceful one morning and the occupants of the camp were just starting to get mobile when one of the sentries came running in. "The God-dammed Germans are coming!" he yelled.

Within two seconds there wasn't a soul to be seen. Everybody dived for cover just the way he was facing. It was a futile gesture, since the camp was all set up and the Germans were sure to search it.

Fortunately, our Paul Revere was mistaken. What he had seen was just a farmer looking for his cow.

I guess it was about my fourth day in the forest when, far in the distance, we began hearing the sounds of a desperate battle.

Our food was meager. We subsisted mainly on rabbit meat. Boiled, tasteless, rabbit without even a sprinkle of salt or pepper. We used to cook our own. I remember seeing some rabbit meat lying on a little board and feeling sick. We had to eat it with our fingers since we didn't even have knives or forks.

I was lucky once in a while because the children would slip me a little can of stew. I couldn't eat rabbit without getting sick and I could have starved. The farmers provided some of the rabbit meat, delivered by the children, and some of it was caught in the woods. The children would also bring us chunks of bread, usually stale. For a treat they would spread a bit of lard on it. There was no such thing as butter or jam.

We didn't have much water, either. What we did have was brought in buckets or other small containers from a spring at the edge of the forest. Sometimes we had to 'make do' with wine instead.

If there was little water for drinking, there was less for washing. We were filthy and I itched like crazy.

We had communication with members of the Maquis. Some of their supplies were dropped to them from the air, often from a Stirling, but the camp occupants didn't receive anything during my time in the forest. The sort of things dropped were mainly weapons and ammunition, with the occasional spy flown in for good measure. There was nothing for us. We had to fend for ourselves or get along with the help of local French people.

I know of one fellow who was having an affair with the daughter of a farmer who brought us food. The two of them were always sneaking around the fringes of the woods.

He offered to introduce me to his girlfriend and her dad. I went along with him on one of his excursions away from the camp. A little kid appeared at the edge of the woods and said, "It's safe now, you go this way."

The girl's father was quite happy that his daughter was involved with one of the evaders and welcomed me to his home as well. He made me a meal, for which I was very grateful. When we had eaten, he said, "You'd better get back because we don't know what the Germans are going to do." I rushed back into the forest.

One fellow was upset because he missed his girlfriend, whom he had set up with an apartment. I hadn't been there long when he changed his opinion of her. "That bitch!" he exclaimed, "She gave me a dose! I bet she's giving one to somebody else right now. And I'm still paying for her apartment!"

I really felt sorry for the guy because we had no medical supplies to speak of.

Speaking of that, there was one fellow who made me feel less sorry for myself. His name was Sam Dunseith. He was swathed in bandages which covered severe burns to his face and hands. I took one look at Sam and thought to myself, "Gee; I complained?!" Sam was only in camp with us for a couple of days but Johnny had met him at Marchenoir Forest camp before coming to Freteval. He described their first encounter; "I saw this white ghost coming out of the dark. Here was Sam, his whole face all bandaged and both arms and one leg. I saw this thing coming for me and I thought, "Where the hell am I? Did I arrive in Hell already, or what?!"

The guys helped look after Sam. Somehow, the underground had arranged for a nurse to come in once in a while to change the bandages. Poor Sam! As soon as the bandages were taken off and air hit the raw flesh, he would scream in agony.

There wasn't much to do in the camp. Just sit and wait. The monotony was terrible, especially since it gave us time to think. There we were, defenseless, surrounded by Germans and with hardly any food. Our future prospects didn't look very promising.

It was great one day when some Army fellows rode into the forest in a jeep[57]. The leader was Captain Peter Baker, a member of Intelligence School 9 (Western European Area)[58]. His escort had been made up of an officer and five men from the Special Air Service, a British airborne unit which sometimes worked in cooperation with the Military Information departments. They had been fired on by a group of Germans and one man had been slightly wounded. After changing clothes with one of the camp cooks, Baker headed off towards Paris. He intended to write a newspaper story about conditions there.

Baker left the jeep behind. We'd load eight or ten guys onto that jeep and go scouting around the countryside, just for fun.

After I had been in the camp for about two weeks, Johnny and a couple of other guys, Paddy Thin and Ted Rourk, decided to quit waiting and struck off towards the Allied lines on their own.

The Germans were getting worried. There were lots of German troop movements and this time those movements were not towards the advancing Allied lines but away from them. They were retreating, and they were shooting people right and left.

As the days wore on the German traffic around us increased. As best as we could tell, the German bosses had headed for safety in their staff cars and motor vehicles, leaving their own guys behind to run as best they could.

I was hidden out of sight when a couple of German soldiers wandered right up to the edge of the forest. I saw the distinctive outline of their helmets silhouetted

---

[57] *The jeep incident was described in a letter dated December 4, 1991, from Mr. Gordon Hand.*

[58] *Saturday at M.I. 9, op. cit., page 268.*

M. Paul Fougereux at Chenclang, Commune de Gohory. The house was the last stop on the way to the camps.

Mme. Leroy's house on the Sazeray farm near Voves, with one of the aviators rescued by the Comete Line.

M. Rideau and his daughter Micheline, accompanied by M. Jubault, chief of the French Forces of the Interior in that sector. They are in front of the house of the forester oj Richeray. Hidden two hundred metres south was Camp #2.

Two evaders with the canisters from an air drop which took place the previous night.

(Above) A meal in the forest. The man in the centre is Gordon Hand.

(Left) Tents set up in the Forest of Freteval.

Emmett Bone, one of the camp cooks, working in the 'kitchen'.

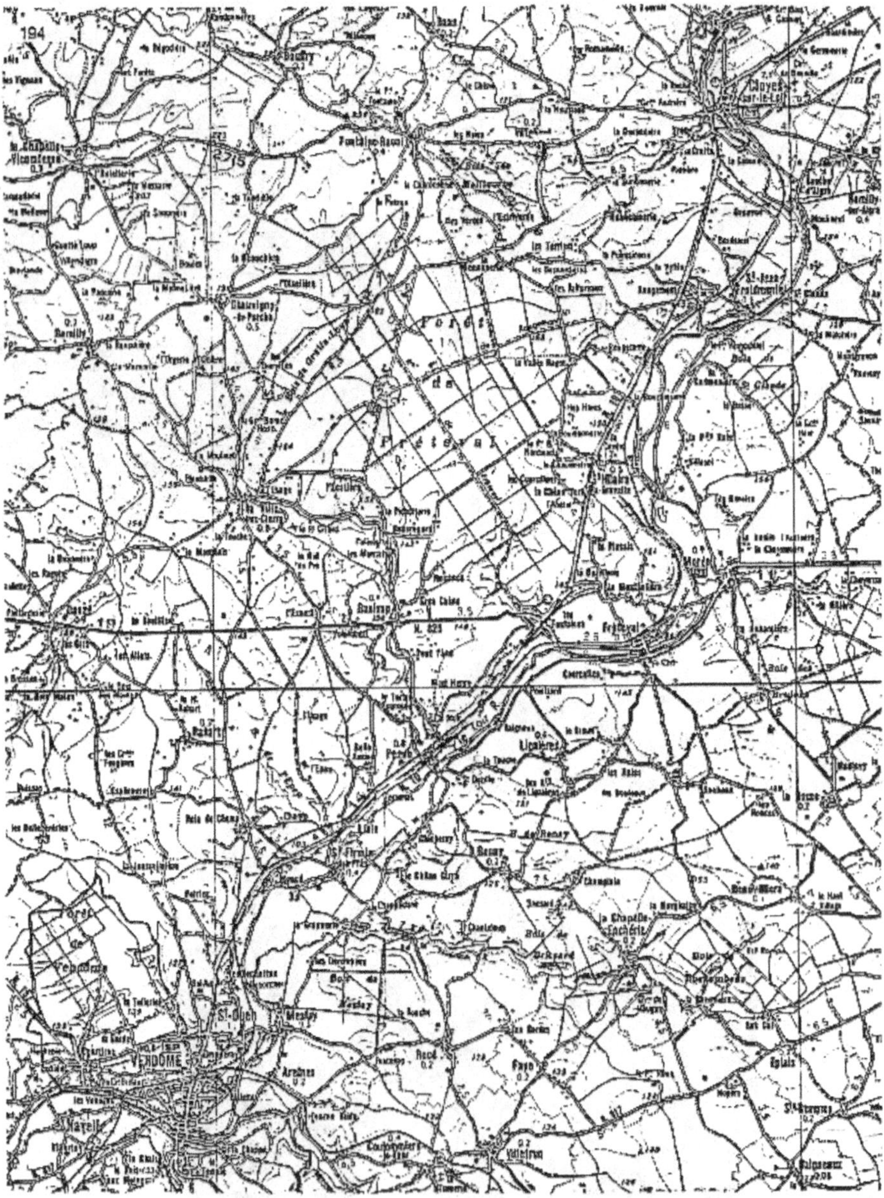

The Forest of Freteval and surrounding area.

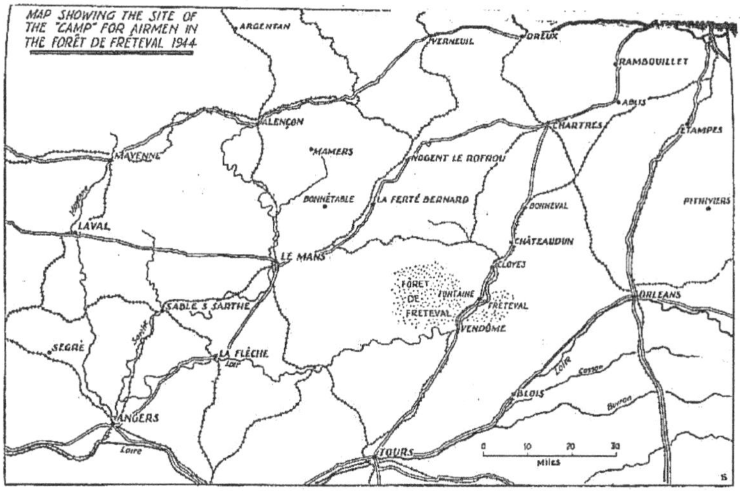

against the moon and was close enough to hear what they were saying. "What are we going to do?" one soldier asked the other. They seemed afraid to come into the forest, maybe because of the rumors which had been spread about an Allied force hidden in the woods.

The troops were panicking. They began stealing transportation from the local farmers, especially the ones who had been collaborating with them. We had to laugh a bit at that and figured it was poetic justice. They were stealing horses and carts, anything they could get their hands on. The squeaking of cartwheels became a constant background noise.

I couldn't sleep at night. The neighing of the horses and the rattling and squeaking of the wagons was a reminder of our peril. I knew that behind all of the fleeing troops there would be heavily armed Panzer divisions fighting a rearguard action. It was only a matter of time before those Panzers might move right through our forest. We began to hear distant explosions. As they came closer, we realized that the Germans were blowing up their own supplies and equipment to keep them from falling into Allied hands. I could see the explosions from camp. We watched the Germans blowing up anything they couldn't take with them. There was a chain of ammunition dumps right outside of our forest. The shockwaves reverberated throughout the forest when they went up. I watched the German's blow them up, one after the other. I was standing behind a tree with the Germans in clear view.

We could soon hear tanks moving in the distance, along with the unmistakable sounds of battle. We were scared to death. "We're finished." we thought, "They're going to make short work of us when they come."

There was nothing to be gained by staying awake. At night, I crawled under my shelter and tried to sleep.

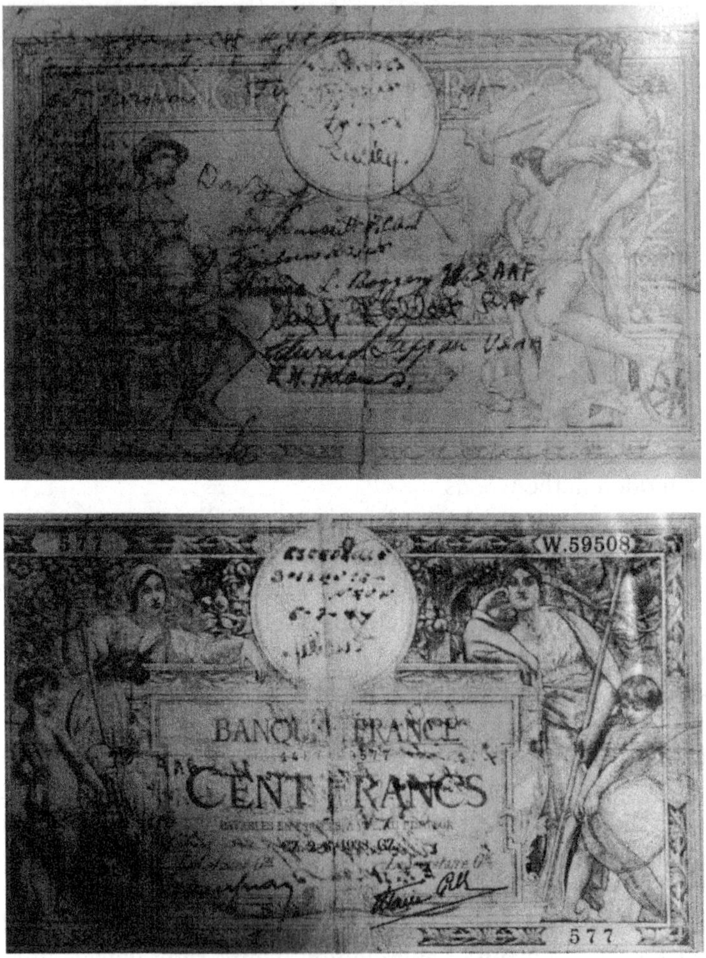

100 Franc note belonging to Johnny Sandulak, of Carman, Manitoba. Notice the signatures on the front (top). Lou Greenburgh's signature is visible in the upper left hand corner, fourth from the top.

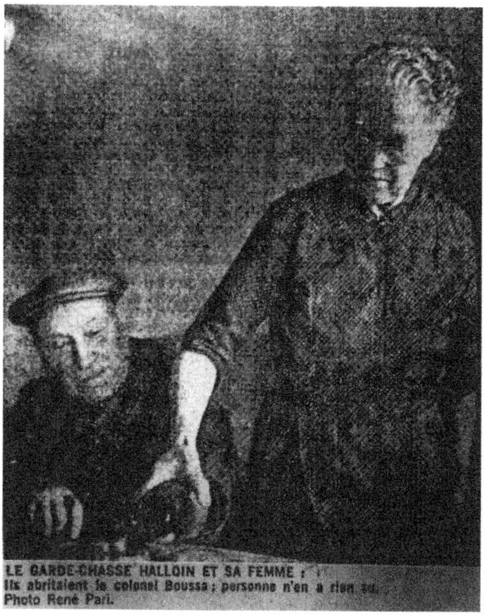

Translation: The gamekeeper Halloin and his wife. They sheltered Colonel Boussa; nobody knew a thing.

Captain Jubault.

The photographs above are from a French newspaper lent to the author by Omer Jubault.

Chapter 16: Liberation

At about five o'clock in the afternoon on August 13, I was awakened from a nap by the rumble of heavy vehicles moving through the bush. To my mind there was only one explanation for those heavy vehicles: the Germans had come.

After all I had been through, after all of the struggles and heart aches I had endured, I was to become a German prisoner and would probably die in a gas chamber.

The motors were coming closer and closer. A large tracked vehicle stopped right in front of my shelter. I could see the steel tracks blocking the opening. I heard orders being given in guttural voices.

Ray Worrall, the fellow sharing the shelter with me, was sitting upright. His face was white. I said to him, "The game is up. We've had it. The Germans are going to make short work of us."

There was no point in hiding because the vehicles were right in front of our shelter. I crawled out and stood up. I saw a soldier standing with his back to me and thought about making a last minute dash. Then I asked myself, "Where am I going to run?"

The soldier turned around and faced me. As he turned, I could see the shape of his helmet and realized that he was an American.

"They're Americans!" I exclaimed, and shouted for the whole world to hear, "Hi fellas!"

They had been talking in English but a lot of the shouted orders, like 'Halt!' sounded the same in German.

Was I ever glad to see them! A young Lieutenant was making a record of who was there. I showed him my phony ID and he recorded the name 'Emile Clive' on his list.

So I was liberated. But I was not yet out of the woods, so to speak, because there was the danger of a German counter-attack. Also, the Americans were rolling on towards the German border.

"Come on, fellas!" called one of the Americans from his jeep, "We're still on our way." I climbed in with him and off we went to Camp #2, where we picked up some more evaders. Most of the others in Camp #1 chose to wait until transportation arrived from the British M.I.9, which eventually picked them up in a commandeered school bus.

We were following the American armored vehicles. We saw abandoned German tanks on the side of the road. I heard machine gun fire and some American soldiers armed with sub machine guns jumped out of the vehicles ahead of us. The next thing I knew, half a dozen German soldiers had surrendered and were being loaded into a truck behind us. I guess they were eventually taken to a makeshift prisoner of war camp.

They were heading towards Germany but I wanted to go the other way. I'd had enough of this business and just wanted to go home. I wasn't prepared to take part in a military offensive. After saying goodbye to my rescuers, I started to walk.

Before long, I was able to hitch a ride. There was a bit of traffic back and forth to the front and I was able to get lifts on trucks, cars, what-have-you as I made my way to the coast. Dozens and dozens of U.S. tanks went by me. There were still pockets of resistance and I had to be careful not to wander into a German ambush.

I saw some horrible sights. Bomb craters from the American Fortresses were everywhere. The fields were full of dead, mutilated cattle, which had been shelled or bombed. There were dead horses. All over the place were little wooden crosses, some of them row upon row. I saw burned out tanks, some of them overturned. I remember one such tank. The Americans thought there was a sniper hiding behind it. I was caught in the middle of all that.

Captured German prisoners became a common sight. There were thousands of them! They had been corralled in cages made from chain linked wire and were guarded by armed sentries. They seemed mighty anxious to make friends with their captors. One German soldier gave me his helmet, and an officer gave me his sword.

I finally reached Le Mans and spent the first night in a German bunker. I could tell that the previous occupants had left in a hurry and I expect that a German soldier had slept in my bed only the night before. There were pictures of Hitler littering the place. (Apparently, every German soldier was supposed to have one.) German slogans were plastered on the walls. One slogan ordered them to fight. Another slogan stated that it was unfair to the wounded if the reader was unhurt.

I ended up sitting with a bunch of other guys on a wooden bench in the back of a great big army truck. One fellow there was an NCO and had taken charge of the others. He issued orders and made sure that everyone 'toed the line'. He tried to boss me around until somebody told him that I was an officer.

The camp flag is displayed in the town of Busloup, August 12th 1944. On the left is William Brayley, of Hudson Heights, Quebec.

"Oh, sorry sir!" he said, and turned over 'command' to me. I was exhausted from my ordeal and the last thing I needed was to be in charge of a group of refugees. "That's okay." I replied, "You're doing just fine."

I was driven past the village of St. Lô. It had been completely destroyed and was nothing but a heap of rubble. I saw other flattened villages.

The truck drove to the American zone of Normandy, where the American troops had landed. I found myself on the beachhead, examining the huge 20 cm guns. They had caused many casualties. Reinforced concrete implements and tank traps were everywhere. I then went on to Caen. It was a real mess.

You know, I got the distinct impression that some of the French people in that area didn't like us very much. It was just a feeling I got from the way they spoke to me and generally reacted to me. I think a lot of them figured they had something good going on with the Germans.

I made my way into the British sector and was slated for a ride back to England in a Dakota, DC 3. Just as I was boarding the aircraft, a French woman came over to wish me well and handed me a bottle of champagne. I thanked her for the gift and stepped into the aircraft, which was soon making its way across the English Channel. As the plane gained altitude, there was a loud bang and I felt wet. The cork had popped out of my champagne bottle and I had been drenched with champagne. On the plane with me was another evader, a Czechoslovakian pilot who had been flying for the R.A.F. He told me that he had earlier deserted from the Russian Air Force, but I don't know what the story is.

I arrived back in Waterbeach on August 20. I was sent straight for interrogation by M.I. 9, the British intelligence agency tasked with rescuing evaders. I thought that the 'Tommy' who conducted the debriefing looked very familiar and then realized that he was the man in the white sweater who had grilled me outside that makeshift cave. I was asked to tell my story over and over again. I guess they figured I might remember more details that way. In the middle of the interrogation I heard a familiar whining sound up above, followed by an abrupt silence. We held our breaths. The building shook from the explosion of the V1 ‘buzz bomb’, then the interrogation continued.

The entire process was exhausting and I was relieved to get to my quarters. My belongings had been gathered up when I went missing and were now returned to me. I was then posted to the Multi Engine Conversion Unit at Longtown, where I would be training students to fly transport Stirlings.

I was walking along the sidewalk of one of Piccadilly Circus' busy streets during a visit to London. It was rush hour, and the streets were crammed with bumper to bumper traffic. I heard the squeal of brakes and saw a large double-decker bus screech to a halt right in the middle of Piccadilly square. A second bus slammed into the rear of the first bus. Yet the driver of the first bus didn't seem to care that his bus had been hit. He jumped down the steps of the bus and ran into the street.

Traffic was piling up like water in a dam because the buses were blocking one of the busiest intersections in the world. Cars were honking and people were shouting and I wondered what was going on.

People were anxious to get a move on because of the V1 buzz bombs. I thought that maybe a dud had landed in front of the bus and that the driver might be running for his life.

The conductor leaned out of the open door with a stunned expression on her face and shouted after him, "Are you crazy?!"

The driver was running towards me. As he got closer, I heard him call, "Canada! Canada!" He was waving at me as he ran. He ran right up to me and grabbed me by the shoulders, shaking me, as if to make sure that I was really

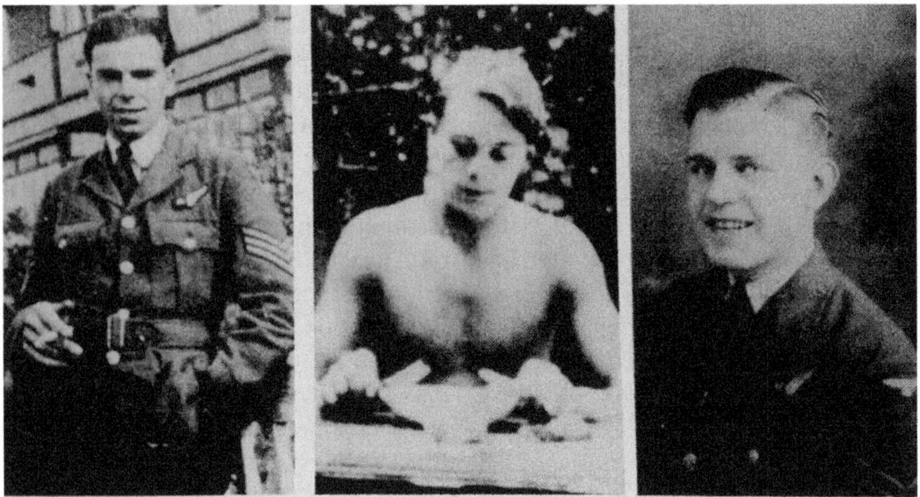

SGT. DENNIS PEPALL FLT.SGT. GORDON HAND SGT. CHARLES WEIR

there. "Canada!" he said again, with a gleam in his eye. I knew him from somewhere.

"Forest of Freteval!" he said, giving my shoulders another shake. "Remember? We met in the Forest of Freteval!"

Then I recognized him. He had occupied the tent next to mine. The excitement welled up in my breast and I nearly danced with joy at the chance to see one of my comrades from that eventful time.

"So how long have you been driving a bus?" I asked him when I finally found my voice.

"I just finished my training." he replied, above the noise of the commotion behind him. Then he told me his full name and suggested that we get together sometime. "I'm in the phone book." he told me, "Look me up in the phone book."

With that, he had to get back to his bus. As he turned away, he called over his shoulder and said to be sure I called him. I told him that I would.

As soon as I could get my hands on a phone book, I turned to the page I thought his name would be on. His name was... What did he say it was? In the excitement of meeting him again, I had forgotten his name.

Les Sutton, the second pilot on my last raid, had evaded capture as had the navigator, Ronald Fox, and Eric Rippingale, the bomb aimer. Fred Carey, the mid upper gunner, Richard Woosnam, the rear gunner, and Frank Collingwood, the flight engineer, all became prisoners of war.

Lou's Back.

In ancient days a favourite phrase,
was "Lulu's back in town."
But now the speachat Waterbeach,
"Lou Greenburgh's back in town."
By wire and phone in bated tone
the news we circulate.
How lucky Lou from out the blue
evaded Bosch and fate.
'Tis said that Lou, in kites he flew,
He're used the exit door.
Holed by barrage in fuselage,
"What else are flak holes for?"
His narrow shave from watery grave
neath Samson's watchful eye.
We thought that sure-completed tour,
a cinch, the lucky guy.
When over France unlucky chance,
Brought Lou and crew to ground.
With nil despair, Lou wandered there
til homeward route was found.
Safe back at last all danger past,
Lou sips a crafty gill,
to dissipate and cogitate,
He's had his share of "mill".
Now he can teach at Waterbeach
to all we other chaps.
What Lou could do-with LACK OF CLUE
We too-can do-Perhaps!

Writer unknown – was on the 514 Sqdn bulletin board & was recently found, 53 years later.

F/O. L. GREENBURGH D.F.C • SPAM.

MISSING: MAISSY - PALAISEAU 7/8 JUNE 1944
ARRIVED WATERBEACH. 20 AUG 194

As stated on the above note, this poem was posted on a noticeboard at RAF Waterbeach after Lou's return in August 1944. The note was recovered 53 years later, and passed to the author. Lou was a legend in his own time.

While he was evading capture, Eric Rippingale had met a young girl named Aissa-Jeanne who helped rescue him. They would be married on June 7, 1947[59]. Les Sutton went on to complete a tour of operations. Ronald Fox became a navigation instructor.

Shortly after my return, I was faced with a gut wrenching situation. I answered the telephone and felt my heart sink when I realized that the young lady on the other end of the line was none other than the girl whom Strommy had wanted to marry. The girl he would have married if I hadn't talked him into making one last trip.

She told me that deep inside she believed Strommy was still alive and that she would see him again someday. "I'm sorry," I told her, "but all I know is what the underground told me." She called me a few times. What could I say to her?

The following information was received from the Commonwealth War Graves Commission:

Gordon Henry Stromberg.
Son of Charles & Mary Stromberg of Watford, Hertfordshire,
Died on June 9, 1944, aged 19.
The exact location of his grave is St. Pierre, Amiens, France.
Plot 7, Row E, Grave 13.

---

[59] *Mrs. Aissa-Jean Rippingale wrote to the author on November 4, 1991. She sadly stated, "Your letter has come at a very distressing time for me as my dear husband died on the 6th June this year, the eve of our 44th wedding anniversary. Eric would have been delighted to correspond with you, as he often talked to me about his war experiences and with great respect about his pilote F/Lt Greenburgh – he was his Air Bomber – F/Sgt Eric G. Rippingale.*

I.S. 9.(W.E.A.)

WARNING AGAINST GIVING INFORMATION ABOUT YOUR ESCAPE OR HOW YOU EVADED CAPTURE

GENERAL STAFF I.S.9 18 AUG 1944 WESTERN EUROPEAN AREA

This applies to Members of all Services and continues even after discharge therefrom.

1. It is the **duty** of all persons to safeguard information which might, either directly or indirectly, be useful to the enemy.

2. The Defence Regulations make it an **offence**, punishable with imprisonment, to **publish or to communicate** to any unauthorised person any information or anything which purports to be information on any matter which would or might be directly or indirectly useful to the enemy.

3. This document is brought to your personal notice so that you may clearly understand information about your escape or how you evaded capture is information **which would be useful to the enemy,** and that therefore to communicate any information about your escape or how you evaded capture **is an offence under the Defence Regulations.**

4. You must not disclose the **names** of those who helped you, the **method or methods** by which you escaped, the **route** you followed or how you reached this country, nor must you even give information of such a general nature as the **names of the countries** through which you travelled. All such information may be of assistance to the enemy and a danger to your friends. **Be specially on your guard with persons who may be newspaper representatives.**

5. **Publishing or communicating information includes :—**

   (a) publication of accounts of your experiences in **books, newspapers or periodicals** (including Regimental Journals), **wireless** broadcasts or lectures :

and (b) giving information to friends and acquaintances either male or female, in private letters, in casual conversations or discussions, even if these friends or acquaintances are in H.M.'s or Allied Forces and however "safe" you may consider them to be.

6. F.O. (557-44) } A.C.I. (1896-43) } A.M.C.O. A89-44 } **prohibit lecturing by escapers or evaders to any unit without prior permission of the Admiralty, War Office, Air Ministry.**

TO BE COMPLETED IN THE PERSON'S OWN HANDWRITING.

I have read this document and understand that if I disclose information about my escape or evasion of capture I am liable to disciplinary action.

Signed L. Greenburgh **Date** 18

Full Name (Block letters) LOUIS GREENBURGH

Rank and Number F/o 49803

Unit 514 SQDN

Witnessed by [signature]

WHAT YOU MAY SAY.

By signing the attached document you have undertaken to maintain a strict secrecy about your experiences. It is realised, however, that your family and friends are certain to ask you questions. *Below you will find suggestions for the best way of answering them :—*

ROYAL NAVY.

(In similar terms to those for Army and R.A.F., altered to suit particular circumstances.)

ARMY (Escapers).

I was captured by the Germans (Italians) and sent to a prison camp in Germany (Italy). I managed to escape and get back to this country, but I cannot tell you how I did that without spoiling the chances of others who are trying to get away. *I am sure you will understand that I cannot tell you anything till after the war, and I have orders not to say more than I have already told you.*

or

ARMY (Evaders).

I managed to evade capture and get back to this country. As many others are trying to do the same, you will understand I cannot tell you anything till after the war. In any case, I have orders not to say more than I have already told you.

R.A.F. (Escapers).

I was shot down by flak during a bombing raid. I baled out, and was captured and sent to Germany. I managed to escape from a prison camp and get back to this country. As many others are trying to do the same, you will understand it is not possible for me to tell you anything till the war is over. In any case, I have orders not to say more than I have already told you.

R.A.F. (Evaders).

I was shot down by flak and baled out. I managed to evade capture and get back to this country. As many others are trying to do the same, you will understand it is not possible for me to tell you anything till after the war. In any case, I have orders not to say more than I have already told you.

Full Name (Block letters) LOUIS GREENBURGH

Rank and Number S/Sgt 49803 Signed L. Greenburgh

Unit 514 Sqdn Date 18

Witnessed by [illegible] Capt.

Official warning notice issued to members of armed forces who escaped or evaded capture. The image quality is that of the original document.

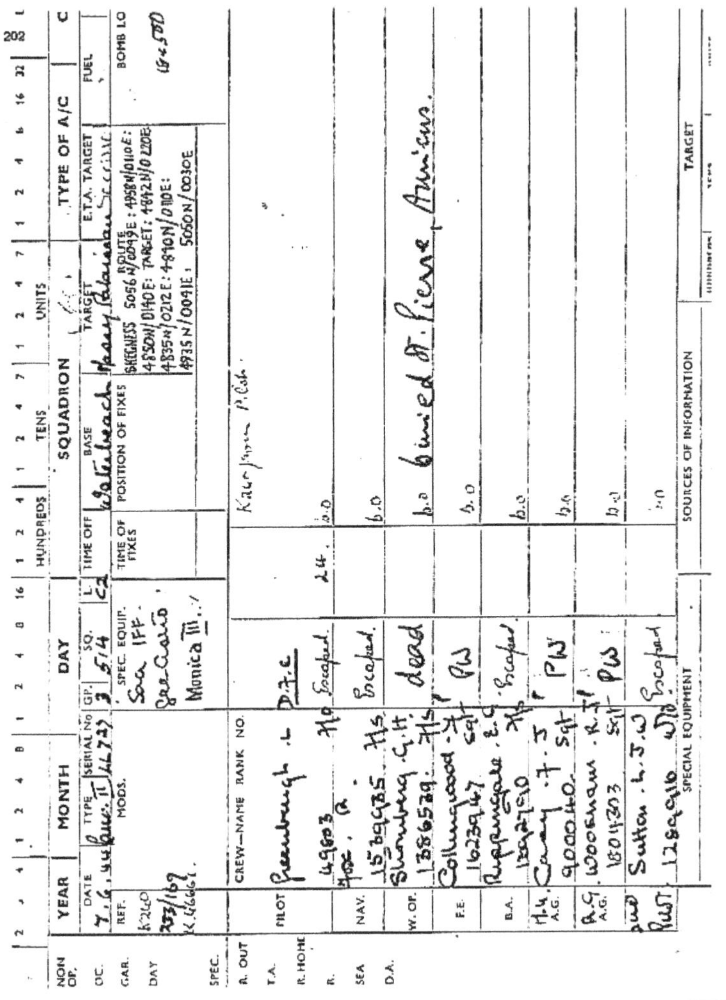

YEAR | MONTH | DAY | HUNDREDS | TENS | UNITS | SQUADRON | TYPE OF A/C

DATE 7.6.44 · TYPE Lanc. II · SERIAL No LL727 · GP. 3 · SQ. 514 · L. C2 · TIME OFF · BASE Waterbeach · TARGET Massy Palaiseau · E.T.A. TARGET · FUEL · BOMB LOAD 18x500

REF. K240 233/169 K.46661 · MODS. · SPEC. EQUIP. Sea IFF. Gee Monica III

TIME OF FIXES · POSITION OF FIXES · ROUTE: SKEGNESS 5056N/0049E: 4958N/0110E: 4830N/0140E: TARGET: 4842N/0220E: 4835N/0212E: 4840N/0110E: 4935N/0041E: 5050N/0030E

	CREW—NAME RANK NO.		
PILOT	Greenburgh L. D.F.C. 49603 F/O	Escaped	b.0
NAV.	Hoe, R. 1589935 F/S	Escaped	b.0
W.OP.	Stromberg G.H. 1386579 F/S	dead	b.0 buried St. Pierre, Amiens
F.E.	Collingwood J. 1623947 Sgt	PW	b.0
B.A.	Rippingale E.C. 1394510 F/S	Escaped	b.0
M.U. A.G.	Carey J.J. 9000140 Sgt	PW	b.0
R.G. A.G.	Woodman R.T. 1801303 Sgt	PW	b.0
2nd Pilot	Sutton L.J.W 128... F/O	Escaped	b.0

SPECIAL EQUIPMENT · SOURCES OF INFORMATION · TARGET

Aircraft Loss Card for Lancaster LL727 A2-C.

Chapter 17: Milk Runs

It had been R.A.F. policy to not send a man back into operations once he had successfully evaded the Germans. It was felt that he might not be so fortunate the second time and the information he possessed might seriously compromise escape routes and endanger the people who had helped him[60]. By the time I arrived back, however, the Allies had advanced far enough that the policy could be relaxed.

I had flown over thirty ops, four of them to Berlin, and had been well into my second tour so I guess the powers-that-be decided that I'd had enough. I admit that I was glad to be taken off of operations.

Shortly after arriving at my new base, I decided to visit the dentist at Crosbie, a nearby air strip. It was quite a hike by road so I decided to cut across a runway.

Rows of C47 Dakotas were lined up on the tarmac. Tractors scurried back and forth, towing trailers full of supplies to be air dropped into some vital area. I walked past a 'gooney bird' that was ready for takeoff. "Hey you!" I heard somebody shout, "Get into that airplane!"

I looked around and saw an officer wearing the rank of wing commander. He gestured towards the transport and repeated his order, "Get in there!" He added, "You're late!"

I tried to tell him that I was going to the dentist. He interrupted me and kept insisting that I get into the Dak.

"What the heck," I thought to myself, "They're just going on a 'milk run'. I can book another appointment with the dentist." I climbed into the C47 and smiled a bit at the obvious case of mistaken identity. After all, it wasn't like there was any danger involved. Some poor slob would be upset when he realized that he'd missed his flight.

The door had hardly closed behind me before we were taxing down the runway. I headed for the co-pilot's seat.

"Hurry up, Griffin!" growled the pilot, "We've been waiting for you."

"My name isn't Griffin," I informed him as I strapped myself in, "It's Greenburgh."

---

60 *Cosgrove, Ed. "The Evaders", 'pocket book edition' published by Simon & Schuster of Canada, Ltd., 330 Steelcase Road, Markham, Ontario, L3R 2M1, 1976, page 3.*

"Look, Griffin...," the pilot started.

"I'm telling you, my name's not Griffin! I came to see the dentist."

The pilot began to realize what had happened and rolled his eyes a bit. I asked him what our mission was.

"I don't know." he told me, "It's secret. We'll be getting directions over the radio."

Milk runs don't normally start out with secret directions, directions too secret to be revealed before takeoff. I figured that I was in trouble. I asked him to take me back, but he couldn't. We were observing radio silence, so he couldn't even notify anybody that I was aboard.

We received instructions to proceed to a supply depot to take on our cargo. It was not until we were ready for takeoff again that were briefed on our mission.

If I had known the plane's ultimate destination, I never would have climbed in. Not in a million years. We were about to make a daylight supply drop to the beleaguered troops in Arnhem.

I soon found myself back over enemy territory in broad daylight. We were in a slow, unarmed airplane which wasn't even maneuverable. All we could do was drone on in a straight line, wing tip to wing tip with other Daks and hope that the onslaught of anti-aircraft fire hit somebody else instead of us.

Planes fell from the sky all around us. It was raining equipment and supplies, as transports were ruptured and their guts spilled out. The Germans were making sure that our troops in Arnhem were bogged down and they made it a priority to shoot down any supplying aircraft. We couldn't even take evasive action.

We released our precious cargo and headed back to base. We weren't returning to the base we had left, however, but to a 'hush-hush' place called 'Blakehill Farm'. Even when we landed, I couldn't leave. This was a secret operation and I was in the middle of it. I had to stick around until the end, flying a total of four dangerous missions as the co-pilot of an airplane I had never been trained to fly. Mind you, a Dak was so easy to fly I could have done it in my sleep.

A funny thing happened to me at Blakehill Farm. I bumped into a cousin of mine who had always looked down on me when I was a kid. He was now a Flying Officer (Engineer). The last time he had seen me, I had been begging for food.

He stared at me as if he had just seen a ghost and blurted out, "I thought you were dead!"

I got back to Longtown and logged my impromptu flying. Shortly afterwards, I misplaced my log book. I eventually found it but by that time I had been to some other stations and have no record of the flying I did there. (I had kept records on separate sheets, which are now missing.) I don't think it was anything very noteworthy.

I know I had to do a lot of training, starting with an academy course on Stirlings. That was an instructors' course. My instructor was F/lt. King. He was teaching us how to handle students, that sort of thing.

I had just come back from a training flight. It was normal for the sergeant in charge of the airplane's maintenance to come up to the pilots, clipboard in hand and pencil at the ready, to record the hours flown. This sergeant looked familiar.

"McIntrick!" I exclaimed, "Good to see you again!"

My old buddy paused a moment, then remarked, "Lou! Boy you've sure come a long way! Whoever would have thought you'd be a pilot? I thought you might be working for me some day!"

McIntrick was one of the fellows I had joined up with in '37.

After the instructors' course, I took a BAN (Beam Assisted Navigation) course, where I learned how to fly 'the beam'. The beam was a radio navigation aide being operated by the U.S.

I remember one British pilot was a bit concerned about relying on a navigation aide of that sort. "But what happens if the beam goes wrong?" he asked one of the Americans. The American snorted at this lack of faith. "The United States Government," he firmly replied, "is making damn sure that the beam doesn't go wrong!"

I was then posted to Nutt's Corner, Ireland, as a Stirling instructor with Transport Command. Nutt's Corner was just outside of Belfast. We used to fly back and forth to Prestwick, Scotland. Our students would go on to fly four engine transports, mostly Yorks or DC 4's, but first they were required to master the Stirling.

I had to 'wash out' a lot of students. As I mentioned before, the Stirling was a difficult airplane to fly; even for experienced pilots. It had that terrible yaw on takeoff. I used to keep my foot on the left rudder peddle and I used it a lot.

One guy must have thought he was still flying a Tiger Moth. We were coming in on our final approach. With about half a mile to go, he cut the engines. The thing dropped right down. I grabbed the controls away from him, put the nose down slightly to gain speed, and we went hedge hopping over fences. We just managed to make the runway.

I failed him. Then he went up with another instructor, and that instructor failed him, too. Then he went up with a third instructor, and that instructor passed him. I still think he was a dangerous man.

One of my students badly wanted to pass. Remembering how hard Myers had worked to get me through, I worked hard on him. I eventually passed him, although I really shouldn't have. He later became an Air Canada pilot. So did another student of mine.

Looking back, I'd say those were my happiest days, those days I spent at Nutt's corner. I loved the Stirling, I had my operational career behind me, I had a stable family life, and my comrades treated with a great deal of respect.

I received a letter from Air Chief Marshall Sir Arthur (Bomber) Harris. He gave me his congratulations and informed me that I was to receive the bar to my DFC. The bar had been awarded on October 31, 1944. I'm not really sure just why I was being given the bar but I think it was probably because of that trip where we lost an engine on takeoff. It's kind of funny that I would get decorated for that, since it really wasn't a big deal, and not get decorated for that incident with my navigator.

Nutt's Corner was not very far from the Short & Harland factory where Stirlings were built. I became very close friends with a test pilot on Stirlings.

Dave Shannon, who had been a flight commander with the Dam Busters, was a buddy of mine.

Belfast was a beautiful city. I kept a room in a boarding house there because I'd often go into town to attend dances at Albert White's or the Floral Hall. I made a lot of friends in Belfast and was quite well known for my aerobatics with a Stirling.

We did a lot of formation flying over the Irish countryside. We had to do a lot of formation flying because we had so many students. I recently acquired a large photograph of three Stirlings in formation and I believe that I'm probably flying the one in the foreground because it has my plane's markings.

It's strange, in a way. There was a war going on, yet we were having a great time as flying instructors, safe from enemy action. I didn't miss the front lines.

We'd fly backwards and forwards to England or Scotland, especially the aerodrome at Prestwick. I knew a lot of people in Prestwick and had many old Air Force buddies there.

After finishing my time as an instructor, I flew a Skymaster to Prestwick, Scotland, as second pilot to Ernie Gann. He later became well known as an author. One of his books was entitled "The High and the Mighty", which was made into a movie. In fact, I was watching that movie in a theatre when I saw his name in the credits. I was pretty surprised, because I hadn't even known that he wrote. He wrote the story for a number of other movies, too.

After I had been at Nutt's Corner for about eight months, the base moved to Riccall in Northern England. At about that time I applied for a transfer to the Canadian Air Force.

My last flight before my anticipated transfer was on April 25, 1945. The entire base was moving to Riccall and I flew one of the aircraft. After we arrived, I saw Wing Commander Edmunds (who had been the Base Commander at Nutt's Corner) in the lounge. He asked me to have a game of pool with him. I wasn't very good at pool, not having played very often, so we sat and shared stories of our flying experiences instead. I told him about the time I tried to visit a dentist at Crosbie, had been ordered into a transport, and wound up dropping supplies to our forces in Arnhem.

"Come on, don't B.S." Edmunds prodded. "You're well known for B.S.ing around the place."

"Look, Sir." I said with an expression of feigned hurt, "You think that was B.S., that some wing commander ordered me, a strange man, into an airplane and sent me on a secret mission?"

"You expect me to believe that?" he snapped.

"Yes, I do!" I stated triumphantly, "Because you were the man who ordered me into that airplane!"

A look of shocked realization came over his face. "Oh my God!" he exclaimed, "I remember that, now. I'll tell you the other side of the story. It was an emergency and we had no time to mess around. The whole transport command was alerted. We had to get every airplane into the air. I ordered all of the engines warmed up, ready for takeoff, and had every available pilot report on the tarmac immediately. But we were left with one surplus pilot and we didn't know why!"

I was posted to a summer resort at Scarborough, pending my acceptance by the RCAF. I was there for a couple of months, with no responsibilities and having a good time at the expense of the government.

In June 1945 I was very sad to receive the following letter and did mail an appropriate reply; assuming that there is such a thing as an 'appropriate' reply to such a letter. I was very grieved to learn that Monsieur Reant had died, especially since his death was the direct result of having saved my life. That was his reward. I carried the guilt with me, and at times I felt ashamed.

From: Flight Officer A.S. Thomson,
AIR MINISTRY, A.I.1(a)P/W
WHITEHALL,
LONDON,S.W.1.

10087/A.I.1(A)P/W

23rd June, 1945.

Dear Flying Officer Greenburgh,

I have received a note from the Awards Bureau in Paris asking me to forward to you the following name and address:

Madame Vueve Reant,
Wavignies, Oise.

It appears that you received help from this lady and that you most highly praised her courage and help but did not know her name.

Unfortunately Monsieur Reant was deported to Buchenwald and died there and we feel certain that Madame Reant would appreciate a letter from you.

Yours sincerely,

A.S. Thomson

Flying Officer L. Greenburgh,
5 Victoria Road,
Bromley. Kent.

After my transfer to the RCAF, I was posted to 426 Transport Squadron at Tempsford.

I was billeted on the base. Pat and the kids moved in with her mother while we waited for a chance to move to Canada. Pat and I had three kids by then; Anna, Joan, and Shirley. I paid her mom a modest rent.

Shortly after my arrival at Tempsford, I walked into the Officers' Mess. A group of guys were listening to one of their number telling stories about somebody. From what I could hear, it sounded like some pilot had been fighting the whole war by himself.

"Every time this fellow went out, he'd come back shot up." the story teller continued, "He'd come back with half an airplane! He was quite a guy."

I asked him who he was talking about. "A fellow called 'Greenburgh'." he replied. "I heard all about him on 514 Squadron. He was flying these Lancaster II's."

I asked if he had ever met this 'Greenburgh' fellow. I then told him, "I happen to know the guy. As a matter of fact, I happen to be the guy."

I rather enjoyed meeting my new squadron leader. It was S/L Don Miller. After the usual introductions and so on he said to me, "I've seen you somewhere."

"Yes, Don." I replied. (It was 'Don' by this time.) "You had me posted."

"Oh!" he exclaimed, "You were the smart-aleck in the pub!"

Miller wasn't sure what he was going to do with me, at first. But it was he who assigned me to the best job I had ever had or would ever have. He made me the captain of a Liberator transport, flying personnel and supplies to the Far East.

On July 18, Miller told me that he was going to Litchfield and asked me to come along for the ride. I climbed into the cockpit of his Liberator and took stock of my surroundings.

I had grown used to flying British aircraft and it was a bit of a culture shock to find myself in an American cockpit. Some of the terminology was different. The undercarriage controls, for example, were labeled 'landing gear'. Everything was electric and I had rows of switches where I used to have knobs and levers. I even had electric controls to adjust my seat. Years later, I had the opportunity to view the cockpit of a new Dash 8. The flying controls were exactly the same as in a Liberator. The bird-dog, the D.R. compass, the needle-ball, and the other flying instruments were exactly the same.

I logged the flight as 2nd pilot time but I hadn't touched the controls. I didn't think I'd be flying Libs.

I received an envelope from Buckingham Palace. There was only one thing it could be. I opened it and found inside a letter written in the King's own hand, commanding me to report to the palace to receive my decorations.

Each member of my family also received an invitation, in the form of a ticket signed by the 'Lord Chamberlain'. They looked something like movie stubs.

The investiture was scheduled for December 11, 1945, at 10:15 a.m. It wasn't long before my family and I were in an antechamber, which reminded me of a large living room with beautiful plush furniture and intricate tapestries. I suppose it was where the Royal Family entertained. Even the adjacent lavatories were richly furnished, with toilet seats made of polished wood. It was really posh.

An Admiral entered the room accompanied by all of these 'Admiralships'. There must have been about twelve of us altogether, all getting different decorations. There were members of the Army, the Navy, and (of course) the Air Force.

A turbaned gentleman, who I presume was from India, was prominent in his bejeweled costume. My daughter, Anna, later said that she thought he was the king because of his gaudy dress.

A young sailor was there in his simple blue uniform. "Holy smokes!" he exclaimed after a while, "We'll be here all day." The King was carrying on conversations with all of the people there and it seemed like the ceremony would never begin. This young sailor was just an 'Ordinary Seaman' not even an NCO and he seemed to feel uncomfortable with all of these high ranking officers around him. "My God," he continued, "by the time all of the 'brass' are finished, I'll be here all night."

I guess I kind of wondered why a simple sailor would be invited here amongst those of such high rank and some of the officers I spoke with seemed to think it inappropriate. But when the time came to receive our decorations, they called him first. He was getting the Victoria Cross. That shut us up.

We all waited our turns. There were the single decorations and two or three of us had double decorations. They finally called my name out.

An Admiral said, "Come here, Mr. Greenburgh." And then I was right up beside the King. He was standing on a dais and I stood there with him, on the same level. I didn't know how to act.

I remembered from my briefing that I was supposed to bow. I forgot to back up before I bowed and we nearly knocked heads. "I'm sorry Your Majesty," I blushed.

"Sir." he corrected me. He just wanted to be addressed as 'Sir', not 'Your Majesty'.

I was impressed by his quiet manner. King George VI appeared to be very modest and timid, not overbearing. He asked me questions like 'how was this' and 'how was that'. "How do you like it over here," he asked, and then he asked me where I had earned my decorations, with which squadron.

I was wearing a little hook on my uniform and onto this hook the King now pinned a large silver cross hanging from a blue and silver diagonally striped ribbon. Across the ribbon was a little silver bar, which represented my second decoration. The King said, "I'm glad to have met you," or something like that. I stepped aside and an Admiral came up to me. He took off the decoration, put it in a little case, and then handed it to me. Then I stepped off the dais and rejoined my family. They seemed quite proud of me at the time.

Rank didn't matter there. I was among wing commanders, air commodores, and the other high ranking officers who were getting decorated. I stayed and watched the rest of the investitures. There was quite a contrast between this and the ceremony at Cardiff, where I had been so rudely treated only a few years before. I had gone from Skid Row to Buckingham Palace.

The citation to my D.F.C. had been published in the London Gazette on March 14, 1944. It read:

"This officer was pilot and captain of an aircraft which attacked Berlin on a recent occasion. During the operation the aircraft was hit by anti-aircraft fire and sustained damage. Some petrol was lost, but in spite of this Flying Officer Greenburgh went on to make a successful attack. Before reaching England on the return flight, the petrol supply became exhausted. Flying Officer Greenburgh brought his aircraft safely down to the sea, however, and he and his crew got safely aboard the dinghy, from which they were rescued the following morning. While they were adrift, Flying Officer Greenburgh did everything possible to cheer his crew, all of whom suffered severely through being buffeted by the heavy seas. Since then this officer has made two more attacks on the German capital, pressing home his attacks with his usual thoroughness."

The citation with the bar read, *"This officer has displayed the highest standard of skill, bravery and fortitude in air operations."*

3614
BUCKINGHAM PALACE.

Admit one to witness the
Investiture
(at 10.15 o'clock a.m.)

11 DEC 1945

Lord Chamberlain.

(Above) Invitation to attend the investiture of F/Lt Louis Greenburgh (sent to the author by Anna Greenburgh). Lou's medal was the Distinguished Flying Cross and Bar (below).

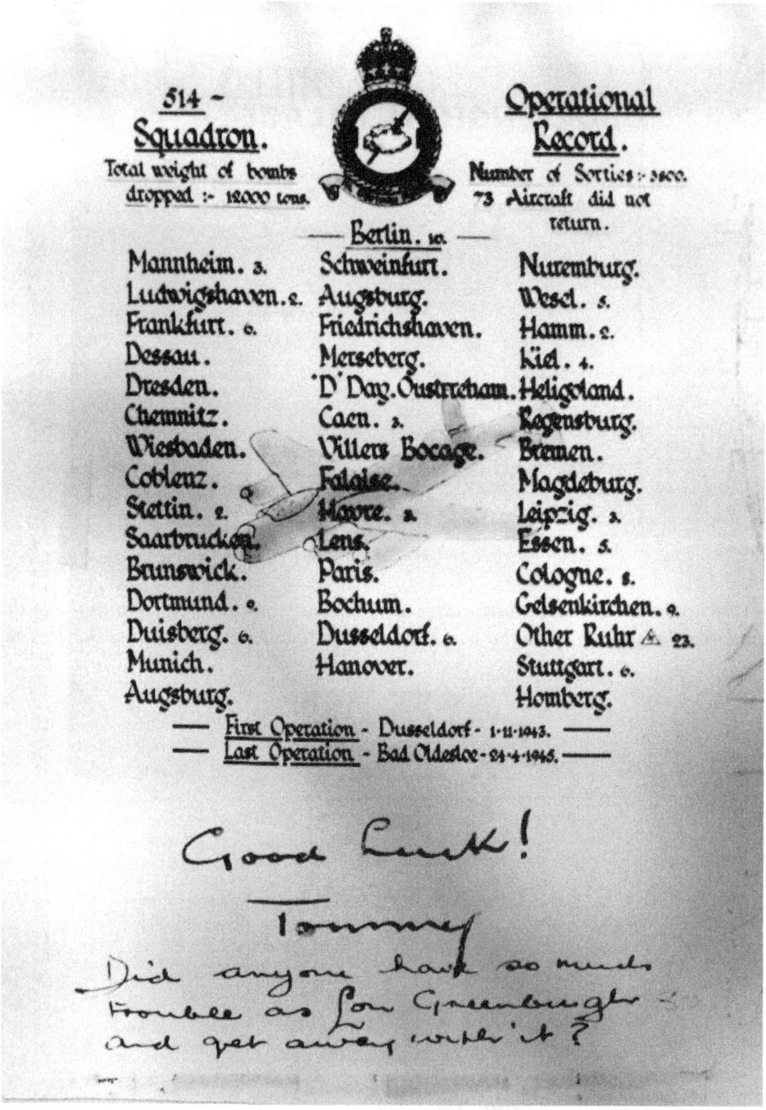

514 - Squadron. Operational Record.

Total weight of bombs dropped :- 12000 tons.

Number of Sorties :- 3600. 73 Aircraft did not return.

— Berlin. 10. —

Mannheim. 3.	Schweinfurt.	Nuremburg.
Ludwigshaven. 2.	Augsburg.	Wesel. 5.
Frankfurt. 6.	Friedrichshaven.	Hamm. 2.
Dessau.	Merseberg.	Kiel. 4.
Dresden.	'D' Day. Oustreham.	Heligoland.
Chemnitz.	Caen. 3.	Regensburg.
Wiesbaden.	Villers Bocage.	Bremen.
Coblenz.	Falaise.	Magdeburg.
Stettin. 2.	Havre. 3.	Leipzig. 3.
Saarbrucken.	Lens.	Essen. 5.
Brunswick.	Paris.	Cologne. 8.
Dortmund. 6.	Bochum.	Gelsenkirchen. 9.
Duisberg. 6.	Dusseldorf. 6.	Other Ruhr △ 23.
Munich.	Hanover.	Stuttgart. 6.
Augsburg.		Homberg.

— First Operation - Dusseldorf - 1-11-1943. —

— Last Operation - Bad Oldesloe - 24-4-1945. —

Good Luck!

Tommy

Did anyone have so much trouble as Lou Greenburgh and get away with it?

514 Squadron operational record sent to Lou Greenburgh by F/O David 'Tommy' Thompson, the squadron intelligence officer. The inscription reads 'Did anyone have so much trouble as Lou Greenburgh and get away with it?'

Chapter 18: The Middle East

On July 1, 1945, my navigator was replaced by a fellow named F/Lt Gordie Ghent. We were to get along very well. As a matter of fact, my whole crew were a pretty good bunch of guys. My copilot's name was F/O Bob Wilson, the radio operator was F/O Jimmy Sime, and the flight engineer was W/O Al Deschutter[61].

I had my first and last training flight in a Liberator on July 26, 1945. My check flight with F/L Longhurts lasted one hour. Then we landed and he certified that I was ready to take charge. I made a few practice flights on August 3rd, 8th, and 10th just to get more familiar with my new aircraft before starting on major journeys to the Middle East.

I was to be freelance, flying wherever in that area I felt there was a need and completely at my own discretion. I was quite proud of myself, mastering a new aircraft so quickly and full of importance at my new role as captain of a transport aircraft flying as far as India.

I was standing near my new command the next day when an attractive young lady gave my aircraft an admiring glance and commented that it must be marvelous to fly such an impressive machine. I decided to play my role to the hilt and invited her to come up for a flight with me.

The girl sat in the copilot's seat and I explained how all of the controls worked. After we had flown a bit I decided to scare her a bit and zoomed down between two buildings. "You've got the wrong pitch setting!" she snorted, and reached over to adjust the propellers. "I've got over four hundred hours on these things." she announced by way of explanation. It turned out that she was a ferry pilot and F/L Longhurts' girlfriend.

"Greenburgh," Don asked me one day, "Do you want to see the places you bombed? Take an airplane and go for a look."

I said to my crew, "Let's take a look at Hamburg, they took quite a pasting."

It was August 13, 1945. We flew low above the rubble and I could see figures on the ground. One fellow shook his fist at us and I could imagine what he must have been shouting. We flew over the area and gloated. It was a great feeling.

---

[61] *The crew members were listed by Gordon Ghent in a letter to the author dated July 15, 1990.*

Lou Greenburgh (left) with his RCAF crew: F/O Jimmy Sime, F/O Bob Wilson, W/O Al Deschutter and F/Lt Gordie Ghent.

We next flew over Bremen, then Karlsruhe. I remembered that before the war I had met two German sailors from the cruiser *Karlsruhe*, and here I was now flying over Karlsruhe itself, which was bombed to hell, you know. Circling, I wondered if their parents lived there, wondered if they'd been killed or what.

It really brought back a lot of memories. Never in my wildest dreams did I ever think I'd be flying my own airplane over their town. I'd been just a kid, having a beer with them. And they were telling me about Germany, inviting me to visit them, and I was begging for sandwiches. I couldn't even pay for the beer.

A fellow named Wyman and his crew came aboard on August 20. I flew them over Holland and then we went 'sightseeing' above Cologne.

I flew to my old stomping grounds at Bassingbourn on September 1, returned to base, and then made another visit there the following day. On September 6th I made a short excursion down to St. Mawgan, on the furthest tip of Cornwall, then carried on to Castle Benito in Tripoli, which had been

Lou Greenburgh's Liberator. Note the Stirling behind it.

Mussolini's personal paradise. I was surprised to find such a Shangri-La in the middle of a war zone. It was fantastic! There were palm trees, gardens, and beautiful fountains. There were beautiful girls all over the place, some of whom had been Mussolini's mistresses. The officers' mess was like a Holiday Inn. I decided that I was going to like my new assignment.

We returned to Tempsford on September 8th. On September 11, I ran into my cousin, Himi, who was an engineering officer. He told me that he was scheduled for a flight to the Middle East and would be leaving the next day. I checked my passenger listing and, sure enough, he was to be one of my passengers. I thought that was great and I looked forward to his company on the trip. I figured I'd let him sit in the co-pilot's seat so we could talk and he would have a really good view.

September 12 came and I readied my aircraft for takeoff. I noticed that my cousin's name was crossed off the passenger list and the station dentist was going instead. I called him up and asked him why he had cancelled his trip. "Well, Lou," he explained, "I have to be careful who I fly with." He had just found out that I was going to be the pilot.

I invited the dentist to sit in the cockpit with me and we had a really great trip.

After a brief stop at St. Mawgan, we headed for Tripoli and landed at Castle Benito. I was growing fond of the place.

We left Castle Benito on September 14 and landed at Lydda airport in Palestine, near the city of Tel Aviv. We spent a day there and left for Shaiba, where we had only a brief stop before heading on to Karachi. That city was in what is now Pakistan but in those days it was still part of India.

Conditions in Karachi were worse than primitive. The washroom facility was just a hole in the ground with a log to sit on. I was about to use the facilities one time when I felt a nudge. I started to tell the person nudging me to get lost when I realized that it was a cow. Cows were considered 'sacred' and wandered the streets at will. The cow did his business right where he was. I walked out.

I wish I'd written a book about Karachi; it was quite interesting. It was also heart breaking. You could see kids with deformed legs. When babies were born the parents often broke their bones so that they could be beggars. It was hard to make a living any other way.

A kid asked me if I wanted to have my shoes polished. I said, "No, they don't need polishing." and walked away.

The kid ran after me and spat on my shoes.

"Why you little...," I started to say. Then I saw the pointy end of his switchblade.

With the kid in pursuit, I ran into a bazaar and hid in a little shop. To my relief, a couple of guys I knew were walking past.

"Hey!" I called to them, "There's a guy wants to kill me!"

They pointed at me and shouted, "We don't know that guy!"

The little boy with the knife had been waiting for me to come out. "O.K." I said, "Polish my shoes. How much do you charge?"

He told me he charged one rupee. So I gave him a rupee and he polished my shoes.

I saw many interesting sights in Karachi. I even saw some real snake charmers.

The air base itself was located in the city of Maripur. It was in the officers' mess at Maripur that our accommodations were located.

I remember one night we spent in Maripur. The aircrew of each aircraft were assigned their own Nissan hut. I lay back under my mosquito netting and watched the insects buzz around. It was so hot! I was just dripping. There was no way I could sleep.

By about three o'clock in the morning, I was getting pretty fed up. "God!" I muttered to myself, "I'll be up all night."

"I can't go to sleep either, Skipper." said my co-pilot from his cot.

(Above) A barber shop in Karachi.

(Right) A landmark in Habbaniya.

Snake charmers in Calcutta.

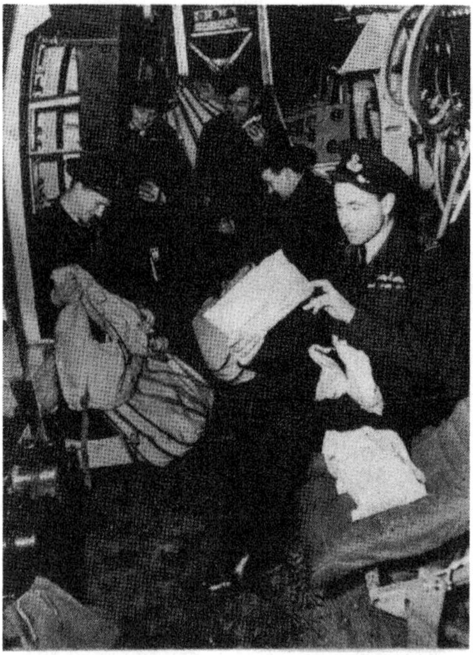

Lunchtime in the Lib. This photograph was taken at Tempsford on November 2nd, 1945, as they were preparing to leave for Malta.

Gordie added, "Me either."

"I can't sleep, either." said the radio operator.

That left only Al Deschutter as a potential sleeper. "I wish to hell I could go to sleep!" he exclaimed. We had all been lying there for hours so as not to wake the others.

We began the return trip on September 18, flying via Habbaniyah, Lydda, Castel Benito, and St. Mawgan. We arrived back at Tempsford on September 21.

Our next journey began on September 29. We flew to St. Mawgan for the night, then carried on to Castel Benito.

Our next stop was to Cairo-West, just west of Cairo. We flew low across the dessert to get a good look at the Pyramids. I flew over them and circled them.

As we circled the Pyramids, I allowed the passengers to come up to my office in front to see what was going on.

One passenger commented, "Why do all of the Jews have to come here? The Arabs will be driven out."

I told him that the Jews needed some place to live, too. I guess he realized that his pilot was Jewish, because he then made some non-committal remark and changed the subject.

We landed at the Cairo-West airport and began some serious tourism. My crew and the dentist stuck together and wandered about Cairo.

We toured the Pyramids and saw the Sphinx,

We left Egypt on October 2 and headed off to Karachi, spent a couple of days in India, then flew to Lydda. From Lydda we flew to Castel Benito and back to base, arriving home on October 7.

On October 10, I spent the day taking planes up for air tests. The planes had just been serviced and it was the practice for whoever was available to take recently serviced aircraft up to check them out. I checked out a total of four

Lou Greenburgh and crew posing with some passengers in front of their Liberator in Malta.

planes. I did another air test on November 10, followed by some night circuit and landings on November 11. The next day we had to decide where we wanted to go. "I've never been to Malta." I said to Gordie, "Let's go there." So Gordie and I worked on the flight plan to Malta, a beautiful island in the middle of the Mediterranean. We flew there on November 12, 1945.

It was raining and after dark when I landed on Malta, which didn't help with my landing. It wasn't a bad landing, really, but it wasn't up to my usual standards.

My senior passenger was a full colonel. As he disembarked, he said to me, "You know, we're all proud of our captain."

"What?" I replied. "Because of that rotten landing I made coming in?"

"No." he explained, "It's quite an honor to have a D.F.C. & Bar piloting us."

Talk about an ego booster. I suppose there weren't as many decorations given out in Transport Command as there were in Bomber or Fighter Command, so a highly decorated transport pilot was something of a rarity. But I wonder what that officer would have thought if he could have seen me a short time later, puking behind the tail plane.

After visiting Malta, we followed what was becoming a regular pattern, touching down at Lydda, Shaiba, Karachi, then back to Shaiba, Lydda, Castle Benito and home, arriving back at base on November 23.

I didn't fly much in December. I took a couple of training flights on December 1 and did an air test on December 18 but it was not until December 20 that we began another trek to the Middle East. We landed at Castel Benito, spent the night, then flew on to Cairo.

Transport crews were classed as transients and we were not made very welcome in some British officers' messes, including the one in Cairo. Besides; Al Deschutter, the flight engineer, was a noncommissioned officer. He wouldn't be allowed in the officers' mess[62].

Anyway, we invited Al to our room in the officers' quarters, brought up a quantity of liquor, and had a Christmas party of our own.

We spent New Year's Eve under the Sphinx talking to some of the Arabs. They sold us oranges and talked about their homeland. I asked them what they thought about the current situation in Palestine.

They were worried about the formation of what is now the state of Israel. "We'll be driven out of our homes." they said. The Arabs were afraid of becoming second class citizens in their own land.

We flew back to Castel Benito on January 1 and arrived back at base on January 2, 1946. February 12 found us in Castel Benito. On February 13 we flew into the middle of the Sahara Desert, to a God forsaken spot named El Adam. I discovered that the C.O. there was a fellow named Bligh. He had been on course with me at Chipping Warden.

We used to go to the pub every night. Some of the girls there would tell us stories about the crews that had been there before us. One of them mentioned a pilot named Murray Peden and told us that he had been with a Stirling outfit which had dropped supplies to the Maquis.

Before we left on one trip, a young lady said to me, "I want to know that you were thinking of me while you were gone. Please bring back a little bag of earth from India to show that you were thinking of me."

We were on our way to a party after our return when Al said, "Hey Skipper, you promised to bring Brenda a little bag of earth from India!"

---

62 *The Christmas party was also described in the above letter.*

"Oh, for God's sake!" I exclaimed. I went back to my quarters and got a little bag. When we arrived at Brenda's, I went into her back yard and filled the bag with sand.

"I never forgot you." I told her when she came to the door. "I brought this from India."

She held up the bag of sand and admired it. "I will treasure this for as long as I live!" she cooed.

It came from her own back yard. I had more to think about than her when we were on those trips.

I'm sad to say that Brenda's story was not happy. She married a very wealthy American, so Gordie tells me, but she developed cancer and wound up taking her own life.

In Jerusalem, we went on a tour of 'the Temple of the Holy Sepulcher'. Our guide announced that no Jew had ever entered the temple. If a Jew ever entered, he continued, it would be a terrible disaster. There would be earthquakes and stuff. Then I bought a piece of the original stone on which Christ had laid his head. It must have been a boulder.

There was no state of Israel in those days and there was constant fighting between the Arabs and the Jews in the area then known as Palestine. Terrorist gangs were killing Arabs right and left.

The Arabs were afraid that they would be kicked out if the Jews ever got control. Some Arabs fled their homes. The Stern Gang blew up houses.

I became good friends with Ruth Buller, the lady in charge of the Red Cross in that area. She was the wife General Buller, who commanded the Middle East peace-keeping forces. They lived in Ramleh and would always invite me over to dinner when I landed there.

I was having dinner with General and Mrs. Buller when a messenger rushed in and handed the general an urgent dispatch. General Buller read it and a look of anguish spread across his face. He put the note down and solemnly announced, "They've done it again!"

An installation had been blown up; I think it was the King David Hotel. Located in downtown Tel Aviv, it was the center of British administration in the Middle East. The Irgun was responsible for that act of terrorism, which damaged a corner of the hotel and killed 97 people. They were mainly Arab and Jewish civil servants[63].

---

[63] *Kirk, George E., "A Short History of the Middle East: From the Rise of Isles to Modern Times, Frederick A. Praeger, Publishers, New York, Washington, 1964.*

General Buller excused himself and rushed off to his headquarters. As we finished our dinner, I asked Ruth, "What's going to happen to all of the Jews that are working for the British Government over here?"

"You don't have to worry, Lou." she replied, "They are British subjects and there'll be nothing different."

On January 15, 1945, we landed in Brussels. We were only supposed to stay long enough for our passengers to embark but Al Deschutter, the flight engineer, was of Belgian descent and wanted to visit his relatives. He set up a small oil leak for the ground crew to repair. That should have just kept us for one night but the repair crew accidentally broke the oil line[64]. Al's little bit of sabotage (which I wasn't supposed to know about, but did) was repaired by the 18th and we took off for Cairo by way of Castel Benito. Most of our passengers had never flown before, and some of them were quite apprehensive.

Shortly after takeoff, I heard a commotion in the passenger compartment and the engineer emerged, looking like he was about to die of laughter. I asked him what was going on.

The entrance to the Church of the Holy Sepulcher.

---

[64] *The information about the oil leak was provided by Gordon Ghent in his letter dated July 15, 1990.*

Between chuckles, he told me that he had noticed something wrong with one of the battery chargers. The generator was powered by a small gasoline motor and it had run out of fuel.

There was a tiny, one pint fuel can at the rear of the passenger compartment. He had called out, "Hey, this things out of fuel. Pass me that gas can."

The passengers nearly threw the gas can to the engineer and their expressions of horror had set off his spasm of laughter. They had thought that a one pint can of gas would keep the plane airborne.

I have to laugh at the thought of those passengers being afraid on that take off, but there was another trip I remember where the passengers weren't afraid but should have been.

We had taken off from England and were flying non-stop to Castel Benito. Once we had cleared the high traffic area and were settled on our course, I engaged the automatic pilot and leaned back in my comfortable leather chair. "I'm really tired, Bob," I said to the co-pilot, "Watch 'Minnie' for me. I'm going to get some sleep." I knew that Minnie, as we called the Minneapolis-Honeywell autopilot, would keep us on course and that Bob would wake me if there were any problems. I closed my eyes and drifted off to sleep.

I was startled from my sleep by a bump as the airplane was buffeted by severe turbulence. I looked out the window at the dark clouds and realized that we had flown right into a storm.

Bob was slumped in his chair, sound asleep. "Gordie," I said to the navigator, "what's going on here?"

I got no reply so I looked over at Gordie and, sure enough, he was also fast asleep. I called to the radio operator and found that he was asleep, too. The remaining crewman, Al Deshutter, was sprawled comfortably across the settee, oblivious to the world. The entire flight crew had been asleep, with the airplane high above the Mediterranean Sea and forty trusting passengers seated in the passenger compartment behind us.

February 20, 1946 found us raising hell in the town of Bordeaux, on the French-Spanish border. We walked into the Cape of Good Hope Restaurant and ordered their best meal. The government paid for it.

On March 19, 1946, we flew from Lydda to Castel Benito for the last time. The next morning, March 20, we flew to Istres Airport near Marseilles for an afternoon on the French Riviera. We then took off for home, landing in Upwood that evening.

Passenger flights were not as common in 1946 as they later became and not many people flew. As one of my passengers was disembarking, he turned to me and said, "I guess this was my last flight."

I smiled a rueful smile and replied, "I'm afraid this was my last flight as well."

Miniature replicas of Lou Greenburgh's medals and decorations. L to R: Distinguished Flying Cross and Bar; 1939-1945 Star; Aircrew Europe Star (France & Germany); Africa Star; Defence Medal; Canadian Volunteer Service Medal; War Medal 1939-1945. Lou also qualified to receive the Bomber Command Clasp to the 1939-1945 Star, issued in 2012.

Chapter 19: The Homecoming

My wife wanted us to move to Canada. After some consideration, I resigned my commission and took her to Winnipeg.

I will never forget the welcome I received from my stepfather. He asked me how much money I had. That was my welcome.

Like a damn fool, I told him how much money I had. It was about two thousand dollars, my Wartime Gratuity. It was my compensation for risking my life on a daily basis and for the guilt of killing other people on a daily basis. It was also a lot of money in those days, equivalent to a year's salary for some people.

He told me to turn it over to him, promising that he would hold it in trust and not let me waste it. I guess I was trying to buy my way into the family, because I did what he said. And to this very day, I have not had the opportunity to waste that money.

I had one cousin who commented, "At least you came back as an officer." I was just glad to have made it back.

You know, I didn't expect them to make a fuss about my being back but it would have been nice if they had done something to celebrate. Other guys came home from the war and their families held parties and invited friends over to welcome them back. My family could have used my return as an opportunity to make up for not letting me have a bar mitzvah. But they didn't.

My stepfather wanted to look big, so he found me a business that I could buy. He then went around telling people that he had bought me a business. In fact, he had found me a broken down business for which I had to borrow $7,000 from the bank. I called it 'Veteran's Jewelers' but it was more of a pawn shop than a jewelry store. It was located on Winnipeg's 'Main Street Strip', next to the sleazy hotels. I didn't even own the building. I had invested in someone else's building, which was little more than an empty space with some shelves.

I had bought a house, the business was not going well, and I was having some real financial problems. I asked my stepfather to give me my money back. He refused. He said that if I needed money I should get it from the bank. I couldn't sleep at night and I wondered how I would ever get out of the financial mess I was in.

My business started to prosper. Mind you, I was learning some 'sharp' business practices. We got in a shipment of watches, for which I only paid about a dollar a piece. I decided to have a sale, so I marked them with, "Regular three dollars, now only two dollars." A friend of mine said, "No, no, no! You say, 'Regular fifteen dollars, now only ten dollars." I did and they sold like hotcakes.

A fellow walked into my shop. He looked a bit self-satisfied, and I guessed that he was a vet who had seen some action. He came up to my counter and commented, "I guess you were in business all the time during the war."

"Yes," I replied (seeing this as an opportunity to have some fun at his expense), "I was in business all during the war."

He smiled rather smugly and said, "I was in the Air Force."

"You were in the Air Force?" I repeated.

"Oh yeah. I was a gunner. I was on one of the roughest squadrons."

"What squadron was that?"

"514 Squadron." he replied. "We were flying Lanc II's, a real powerful airplane."

I sat back in my guise as the 'business man' and pretended to be digesting this information.

I asked him, "Did you ever hear of a fellow called 'Lou Greenburgh' on the squadron?"

An expression of incredulity came over his face and he blurted, "How did you know about that?!"

I asked him, "Have you ever met him?"

The former gunner replied, "Well, I saw him but I never met him personally."

I asked if he would recognize this 'Greenburgh' fellow if he ever saw him. He replied that he would. Of course, he wouldn't have been expecting such an encounter here in my jewelry store.

I said, "Well, you're looking at him. My name is Lou Greenburgh."

We kept in contact after that. He became an electrician, moved to California, and helped build Robert Schuller's 'Crystal Cathedral'.

I called up Jack McGee and we got together to reminisce. He reminded me about the time I had missed that rung. "Boy, Lou," he said, "it's a miracle you're still alive."

"You wouldn't believe it," I laughed, "but I even risked my life during the war."

Jack and I hung around together quite a lot after that. Our travels together on the freight trains must have made a real impression on him because he was working as a CPR train conductor!

CPR used to have what they called the "Moonlight Special" which ran up to Winnipeg Beach. For 50 cents the train would take you to the weekly dance and back again. It seemed like the whole city would go, with Jack as the conductor. He also worked as a conductor on the transcontinental trains.

I was at a dance some place when who should I see but my old chum Kellet Cole. "Kellet!" I exclaimed as I rushed over to see him, "I haven't seen you since we were in jail together!"

"Why'd you have to say that?!" Kellet exploded with a gesture of rage. The young lady who was with him stepped back with a stunned look on her face. "You were in jail?" she gasped.

I realized that I had made a faux pas. "Didn't you tell her about that?" I asked, trying to smooth things over a bit.

"No, I didn't!" He started to explain to the young lady that it was just a political sort of thing which she shouldn't be concerned about but she wasn't being very receptive to his explanation. I mumbled some sort of apology and backed away from the scene.

Just as my business started to go up, my marriage started to go down. I don't want to go into detail, but a lot of the problem was family interference. I don't think my 'parents' could accept the fact that I had married a gentile.

Pat and I separated. She returned to England. I sold my house and my business and applied for a temporary commission back in the Royal Air Force.

I wasn't sure if the R.A.F. would take me back or not. I spoke to a local representative and he agreed that I was a bit older than the candidates the R.A.F. were looking for. "We're looking for young guys." he admitted. He said they didn't usually make exceptions but he would see what he could do.

Since demobilization, many Air Force personnel had been reduced in rank to reflect the smaller size of the service. I would have been willing to take whatever rank they would give me: sergeant, flying officer, whatever. Much to my surprise, I was accepted back with my old substantive rank of flight lieutenant.

About a month before my scheduled return to England, my stepfather said to me, "I've ordered some suitcases for you. They are very handy; they fit one inside the other. They are of solid leather, the finest workmanship. You deserve it."

"I don't need any suitcases." I told him.

"Oh, no, no.," he insisted, "I'm going to give you this present."

"Well," I said, "I don't need them. But thanks anyway."

"No, no, no.," he continued. Then he added, "Oh, by the way... I need a thousand dollars. Just for a week or so. I've had an emergency. Could you lend it to me?"

UNITED KINGDOM AIR LIAISON MISSION

Our Ref: 0/2331

Lisgar Building
OTTAWA

11th July, 1947.

Dear Sir,

It is desired to refer to previous correspondence and to inform you that arrangements can be made for you to proceed to the United Kingdom by the S.S. "Aquitania" sailing from Halifax on the 10th August 1947.

You will be required to report to this Mission by 10:00 hours on 7th August 1947 for documentation and to receive your advance of pay and embarkation instructions.

Arrangements will be made by this Mission for the journey from Ottawa to Halifax.

It would be appreciated if you would acknowledge the receipt of this letter and confirm whether or not you will be able to proceed by the above sailing.

Yours truly,

T.J. Long
Flying Officer.

P.S. Contact your local C.P. Agent in respect of your transportation warrant from your home address to Ottawa.

L. Greenburgh, Esq.,
703 Main Street,
Winnipeg, Man.

'Veterans Jewellery and Novelty Store', which Lou Greenburgh ran for a short time after the war.

So I lent him another thousand dollars. I never heard any more about the thousand dollars or about the suitcases.

I caught the bus down to Winnipeg's Union Station, an impressive structure at the head of Broadway Avenue's wide boulevards. It had been built about the same time as the grand Fort Garry Hotel, located just a few blocks down Broadway and which accommodated CP's elite passengers. Beneath the colossal dome was a hubbub of activity as people greeted friends and relatives or said their goodbyes. Porters wheeled suitcases across the marble floor.

Before I'd left for the station, my stepfather had said to me, "I've got something to give you before you go." It was a little makeup box that held perfumes. It was worth about a dollar fifty. He said, "Here, take this with you, from me. A gift."

I got on the train and gave the box to the first person I saw. I said, "Here, keep this."

Out of my business stock, I kept a suitcase full of jewelry and watches. Those things were pretty expensive in England after the war and I knew I could sell them for a fortune. There was just the formality of getting my suitcase past customs.

There was no problem with customs on the Canadian side, but I was worried about my arrival in England. I worried about it the whole trip. Without saying too much, I had expressed my concerns to a lady sitting next to me in one of the public areas aboard the ship.

"I don't have much trouble with customs," she told me, "They usually just worry about Jews."

At last came the moment I had been dreading. A customs official asked me what I had in my suitcase. I tried to conceal my nervousness and replied, "Just children's toys."

He asked me to let him see them. I wished the ground would swallow me up as he unzipped the bag.

There I was, with dozens of undeclared wristwatches and pieces of jewelry. I have often said, "Honesty is the best policy, if you don't have brains." I wasn't feeling particularly brilliant. The customs inspector wasn't impressed. He called his partner over. I was fair game for a smuggling charge. Smuggling was severely frowned on in post-war England.

The first inspector demanded my passport. I handed him the document and watched him do a double take when he saw my identity. The passport read, "Flt/Lt. Louis Greenburg, DFC & Bar." His attitude softened immediately and he stepped back for a little conference with his partner.

Instead of a heavy fine, or worse, I just had to pay the required duty on my undeclared goods. Mind you, I don't know how much was reported to the R.A.F. I was contacted at a later time to go back and pay the duty, so the Air Force knew something about it. It was not a good start to my resumed career.

Chapter 20: The Berlin Airlift

I was posted to North Luffenham, where I began flying training on Dakotas on April 5, 1948. I was certified on June 18.

Pat gave birth to a son before my arrival back in England. I saw her with a little boy and exclaimed, "Is that Johnny?"

On August 3, I transported some passengers to Netheravon.

Relations between the Allies deteriorated considerably in the years following the war. In the words of Winston Churchill, an "Iron Curtain" descended across Europe and the 'Cold War' began.

Beginning in June, 1948, the Soviets established an undeclared blockade of West Berlin. The citizens of West Berlin and the Allied soldiers stationed there were cut off from the outside world so that the Western Allies would be forced to withdraw. Trains stopped running and roads were closed. The only way to supply the city was by air and that would require so many aircraft at such great expense and with so many logistical nightmares that the Soviets probably thought it was not possible[65].

On August 20, I transported a wing commander to Fausberg so that he could assist in the administration of the air lift. The next day, I made my first flight into Berlin.

Supplies were so badly needed and our supply lines were stretched so thin that the loaders would stuff our little DC 3 until her rivets bulged. We had to fly her in an overloaded condition and in all sorts of weather. In fact, you were only allowed to fly on the Berlin Airlift if you had an instrument rating, the highest of which was known as a 'Green Ticket'. That meant you could fly on instruments at your own discretion and so forth. I didn't have my Green Ticket yet but I had taken most of the training for it and would have it before long.

We were on a holding beam just over Gatow Airport. The weather was right down to the ground. It was one of the most nervous times I'd ever had, this flying around on that holding beam. There were dozens of aircraft flying around all over the place; DC 4's, DC 3's, other types of planes. We knew they were out there but we couldn't see them. We couldn't even communicate with them because we had RT silence. We couldn't talk to anybody because we'd interfere with the controllers. Everything was quiet. We flew around and around, blind.

Out of the blue came a crackle over the radio: "Anybody want a 'Green Ticket'? He can have my f__ker!"

---

[65] *Encyclopaedia Britannica, 1985, Volume 20, page 99.*

My last flight on the Berlin Airlift was on August 29. On August 30, 1948, I flew back to North Luffenham for what were supposed to be routine transport duties. That's not the way things worked out.

Chapter 21: The Crash

On October 8, 1948, I wanted to go to Netheravon to see some friends of mine but I didn't have an aircraft at my disposal. I was checking around for a way to get to that destination when I found out that some troops were slated to return there. "Heck," I thought, "why don't I take them?"

Now that I had an excuse, all I needed was to find an airplane. At first the fellow responsible said that there were no passenger aircraft available. After a bit of coaxing, he admitted that he did have one airplane that wasn't being used at the moment. It was a top-of-the-line, fully equipped, DC 3 which had been outfitted as a flying headquarters and was designated to be used by General Montgomery himself. The fellow at the desk balked at the thought of entrusting this precious airplane to the care of anyone who did not have express authority to fly it. "Come on," I chided, "Don't you think I know how to fly those things?" Besides, I did have some at least semi-official business and I could justify it to anybody to might later raise an objection. As a matter of fact, my last few flights had been in that very same airplane.

"Well, alright," he finally said, "but for God's sake, don't scratch it!"

Things were looking pretty good. The troops thought I was a hero for saving them a long wait at the air station and they were obviously pleased at the thought of flying in a V.I.P. machine. I can picture them goofing around in the office section, pretending to be generals like Montgomery and making jokes at Monty's expense.

Before takeoff, I had sent a message to my girlfriend in Sywell. I told her to meet me at the aerodrome and be ready to take off for Netheravon. Sywell was on the way, and I figured she'd be impressed to see me flying such a fancy machine. She was pretty impressive herself; a medical doctor, she was obviously intelligent and had the looks to match.

As we approached Sywell, the weather started to thicken. I didn't think it was serious enough to cancel my plans to meet my girlfriend and, after all, I had flown in much worse. My better judgement told me that I should contact the tower and get some direction from them but this was going to be an unauthorized landing and I didn't want to attract any more attention than necessary. Sywell was not that busy a place and I figured I could just drop in, pick up my girlfriend, and be off without anyone being the wiser. I started to get worried as we were entering the landing circuit. The fog was thicker than I thought and it went right to the ground, almost zero visibility. It was practically an instrument approach. Then, through the mist, I could vaguely make out the wooden 'T' which marked the wind direction. To my relief, it showed that the wind was correct for my landing approach. All seemed to be in order.

I never had any trouble with short landings, especially in a DC 3. But as my wheels touched down and I lost flying speed I realized that something was wrong. The wind direction indicator had been facing the wrong direction: I had a tail wind. I broke into a cold sweat. Directly ahead of me was a stone wall and the brakes on my undercarriage were useless. I kicked hard left rudder and the plane rotated a quarter turn so that the right wingtip was pointing at the wall. We continued to skip downwind like a leaf caught in a stream. With a stifled curse, I grabbed the undercarriage release mechanism and pulled. As the wingtip speared the wall, the undercarriage collapsed under the weight of the aircraft and the propeller blades beat themselves into swastikas. The belly plating was torn out with a horrible shriek and the plane continued to skid sideways. The wing crumpled like an accordion as we skidded to a stop.

I covered my face in my hands. I was aware of the distant sirens which were coming closer. I was aware of my passengers rushing for the emergency exits. I was aware that the useless metal hulk which had once been an aircraft could burst into flames at any moment, but I made no immediate plans to exit the plane.

"What have I done?" I asked myself, "What have I done?" I sat in the cockpit with my face in my hands and almost wished that the explosion would come. I visualized a board of inquiry, followed by a court-martial. Followed by what? Discharge with disgrace, or some equally unpleasant fate? Dying would have been easier.

I don't want to talk about what happened when I got back to base. I will tell you this; the C.O. was not impressed. I got posted in a hurry. I mean a real hurry. I think somebody did it on purpose so that I wouldn't be court-martialed. The senior officers on the base must have had a meeting to decide what to do with me. Their decision: "Let's get rid of him." I was immediately dispatched to Netheravon on a totally unnecessary temporary duty. I had to inspect a flight or something. While I was there I made three glider towing flights in a Dak. I remember one of the junior pilots was a bit puzzled to find someone of my rank and experience doing a job like that. I let him stay puzzled.

Taking over a flight in the Far East would have entailed a promotion to the rank of Squadron Leader. That would hardly be a realistic expectation after pranging an airplane as thoroughly and as inexcusably as I had done. I thought "To hell with it, que sera." I didn't care anymore. My marriage had ended and I never thought I'd get married again, my business was gone. My flying career was ruined. I'd had enough. I was about thirty years old.

Chapter 22: Stunt Flying

I was posted to a little airstrip near the sleepy village of Watchfield, in the county of Wiltshire, and placed in command of the flying section of the School of Air Traffic Control. My pilots were all Poles who had immigrated to England and joined the R.A.F.

It wasn't a bad job, especially considering that I had been posted there as punishment for crashing an airplane. I was directly responsible for the operation of about twenty Mark XXII Ansons (metal aircraft, not like the old fabric ones) and the station commander would leave me in charge of the station when he was away.

That came in handy from time to time. I was having a lot of fun, flying in the Welsh mountains, when I decided to do a bit of low flying. I spotted an airfield with training machines and dived right down between the hangers. I had a whale of a time.

When I got back to my unit, there was a telephone call. Somebody wanted to speak to the flight commander.

I took the call. "Flight Commander. Flight Lieutenant Greenburgh, here."

The person on the 'phone identified himself as an officer from the field I had buzzed. He said, "One of your pilots was low flying and interfered with a beam approach. We want to report him and we'll take it further."

"You don't have to take it any further." I assured him. "I'll discipline the pilot. Have you got the number of the aircraft?"

Of course, it was my airplane. I said, "You just leave it to me. Put it in my hands." That's the last anyone heard of it. I won't say that I had a reputation as a 'dare-devil,' but some joker changed the wording on a warning sign to read, 'Danger Lou flying'.

I really enjoyed having an airplane at my disposal. It was an Anson, like the rest of them, but mine was painted yellow instead of silver and it didn't have dual control. If I felt like going someplace or just wanted to mess about I would call my mechanic over and ask him to get my airplane ready. My mechanic's name was Tony. I'd say to him, "Tony, I want to take her up this afternoon." He'd say, "Very good, Sir!" and jump to it with enthusiasm. Then away I'd go. I didn't need anyone's permission. I could go wherever I liked and just mark it down as a 'training flight'.

F/Lt Greenburgh and his team posing in front of an Anson at Watchfield.

We had an old Wellington on the base and I would fly it whenever I wanted to go a long distance. One time 'the boys' and I decided to take a trip to Gibraltar. We just hopped into the Wimp and away we went.

We had to make our landing approach from an angle such that the Rock of Gibraltar blocked our view of the landing strip. The mist which floated above the rock didn't help things. I was on my final approach when I finally saw the ground and it looked like we were about to land in the middle of town. I couldn't believe my eyes. There were cars and pedestrians right where I had expected to touch down. I opened the throttles and informed the tower that I was going around for another approach. I asked them to guide me in for a landing.

I was right the first time; we were about to land in the middle of town. At least, we were about to land on a busy street. The main street of Gibraltar ran right across the runway. When we were coming in, the police stopped traffic coming each way and we landed. Traffic was allowed through again as soon as we had passed.

We took a tour of the town and checked in to the Bristol Hotel. We were supposed to stay within the British territory but we were restless so we said 'to

SCHOOL OF AIR TRAFFIC CONTROL, WATCHFIELD

DAY FLYING PROGRAMME FOR 22/9/49

FLIGHT PLANNING	TIME OFF	TIME DOWN	A/c No	PILOT	CREW & STUDENTS	EXERCISE
0900	0930	1200	1	[illegible]	SI.[illegible] FL.[illegible]	To Swinderby & return.
"	"	1630	2		FO.CUSWORTH	To Hendon & return.

Aircraft required:- 2 (1 fitted 117.9)

STAFF PILOTS LINK TRAINER DETAIL

0900-1000 PI.ROBINSON. PII.McCASH. PII.TAYLOR.
1000-1100 PII.TAYLOR. PII.WALENTOWICZ. PII.GIBSON.
1100-1200 PII.WALENTOWICZ. PII.McCASH. PI.GIBSON.

(L.GREENBURGH)
Squadron Leader
O.C. Flying
Royal Air Force
Watchfield

Watchfield Day Flying Programme for 22/9/49

hell with it' and crossed the border into Spain. We didn't give a damn about the politics. The border guards called us back but let us go when they saw who we were.

We went into La Linea, the southernmost city of Spain, and were told that the citizens of that city were all exiles who had been sent there as punishment for fighting against Franco. They were to be imprisoned in La Linea for the rest of their lives.

We entered a night club where a large dance was taking place. Our uniforms were conspicuous amongst the local dress of the citizens. I felt all of their eyes swing in our direction and focus on us. A lady came up to me, pulled me into the shadows where our conversation would not be overheard, and quietly asked, "Sir, could you do me a favor?"

"That depends what it is."

She pointed to a young girl dancing on stage. She couldn't have been more than sixteen years old but she was the prettiest thing you'd ever see.

"You see that little girl there, doing the dance?" she asked with a Spanish accent.

"Yeah."

"She's only sixteen."

I wondered what the woman was leading up to. "She's one of the prettiest girls I've ever seen." I commented.

"Sir," the woman continued, "that's my daughter. I would ask you, and all my life I would never forget you, would you take her with you?"

"Why?" I blurted.

A look of hopeless resignation spread across the woman's face and she spread her hands in a gesture of futility. "What future has she got here?" she asked. "There is nothing here. We are kept down. There is nothing. Please take her, take her with you."

Of course I couldn't. She was the prettiest thing I'd ever seen, and a good dancer.

I enjoyed having airplanes at my disposal and being able to authorize flights whenever and wherever I felt like it. Mind you, there were some limits to what I was supposed to do. I overstepped them regularly. One time, the commanding officer was away from the base. It was a nice day, so I asked the young ladies who did Watchfield's clerical work, the waitresses, and so on, if they would like to take a trip to Tangmere, at the seaside. They were quite enthusiastic about the idea, so I declared a 'holiday' and told them all to pile into my airplane. Ansons were twin engine aircraft which could hold twelve passengers so there was plenty of room.

I was just about to take off when a plane landed with the station commander in there. He took a car and drove up to where we were sitting on the runway, ready for takeoff. There I was, in the cockpit of an airplane loaded with all of his support staff. He swung the door open and saw me surrounded by those young girls. My heroic imaged faded pretty fast and I felt kind of sheepish.

"Lou, what the hell are you doing!?" the C.O. demanded.

"What do you think I'm doing?" I replied. "You weren't around, so I figured I could get away with it."

He looked at all of those disappointed faces and pleading eyes.

"Well," he said, "when you get to Tangmere, don't land near the control tower or I'll be in trouble." He told me where I should land.

The C.O. and I actually got along quite well. I just figured there were some things he was better off not knowing about.

For example, I was friends with one of the air traffic controllers. The guy just loved airplanes and had always wanted to fly one. He knew all of the emergency procedures and stuff because it was part of his job to give directions to pilots flying stricken aircraft. I used to take him up for rides in dual controlled aircraft and let him handle the controls.

One day I took him up and gave him about three hours of really intense instruction. Then I got out of the aircraft and let him take it up by himself. I told him, "Just one quick circuit and landing."

He did just fine, and it was the thrill of a lifetime for him. But I could have been raked over the coals for turning a military aircraft over to somebody who wasn't even a certified pilot.

Some of my amusements were quite legitimate. I was just about to take off for a training flight when I noticed a young woman who I had met at bus stop just a day or two before. She had told me she was babysitting her niece that evening and I had shown up at the address she'd given me. I taxied the airplane over to where she was standing in front of the stores building, rolled down the window, and asked her if she'd like to go up. She was thrilled at the invitation, so she climbed aboard and off we went. I later marked her down as my co-pilot.

Her name was Violet, and she worked as a clerk in the stores. Everyone called her 'Bunty'.

The primary function of the flying section was to go through various maneuvers so that the A.T.C. students could get some experience watching aircraft on radar. We would often simulate accidents and set up difficult situations, such as two disabled aircraft coming in at the same time. Some of the tricks we'd pull looked like the sort evolutions done by aerobatic teams like the 'Snowbirds'. One of my jobs as the Flight Commander was to go up and supervise those maneuvers.

I was leading a flight with two other aircraft. The two aircraft behind me were supposed to roll upwards into a stalled turn and narrowly miss each other at the top of the roll to simulate a collision. I pushed the button on my radio set and ordered, "Okay... Now!"

They rolled upwards. But they didn't narrowly miss each other. They collided. Both aircraft spun in and the pilots were killed.

I was horrified. I radioed the tower and said, "This is not a simulation, this is an accident!"

Bunty was working in an office on the station and she heard about the accident immediately. "Oh my God!" she exclaimed to her boss, Ted Payne, "Lou's been killed!"

Ted was skeptical. "Lou, killed?" he repeated. He led Bunty to the office window and pointed to an aircraft flying very low, circling the smoldering wreckage. "That's Lou," he stated, "I can tell by the way he's flying."

It was such a sad day. The three of us had been chatting together before takeoff, exchanging cigarettes and laughing about going up. Mechanics turned the planes over to us as we left and taxied out. We had taken off together and waved to each other before the maneuver started.

Look how it ended up. Of course a Snowbird got killed the same way recently. Well, that was us.

I decided to take the body of one of the pilots back to his wife in Manchester. He had been a sergeant pilot and his name was Rebotchuck.

He liked me, you know. He was always after me, saying, "Yes, Sir!" outside the office. He was something like little Strommy. He was killed.

I had to take the body back, and I had to take it back by train. There weren't many towns along the way. It was at night.

I was sitting in a compartment by myself with the coffin in the next compartment. A man and a woman were sitting in the compartment behind mine. They didn't know about the coffin.

They were making me sick. They sang a very morbid song which was popular in England at the time. "Stone cold dead in the market," they droned, "Stone cold dead in the mar...ket!"

Oh my God! And there I was, with poor Robotchuck's body. The body was in a box sitting in an aisle between the rows of seats. It was visible but was not distinct as a coffin. "Stone cold dead in the mar...ket!" droned the deep voice of the man, followed by, "In the market, in the market, in market...," in the woman's high pitched whine.

I asked them to please be quiet. They just gave me dirty looks. "What's the matter with 'im?" the man asked his companion. Then they started that horrible singing again.

I finally arrived at my destination. I met Robotchuck's widow and his little girl. Then I left for home.

It had been a miserable trip and I was glad to get back to Watchfield.

The School of Air Traffic control moved to Shawbury. With myself leading the flight, we all took off together, about eighteen of us, and we circled the airfield which had been our home. We gave a bit of an exhibition and came down, the whole lot of us in formation. And right at the end of the airfield, I saw a little girl wearing a familiar blue coat with a belt.

I saw this from the side, at an altitude of about two thousand feet. I waggled my wings to let the others know that something was going on, then I banked towards her. Everybody followed me, eighteen airplanes in line astern formation, and we swooped down on her and flew past. I came within a few feet of her. It was Bunty. I could see her face and it seemed she had tears in her eyes, she looked so sad.

Then we soared back up to the sky. The others thought we were paying a last tribute to our old station but we had, in fact, been saluting my girlfriend.

I was playing a violin in my new quarters when my neighbor from the next room knocked on my door. He said that he'd like to buy my violin and asked me how much I wanted for it.

"I didn't know you played the violin!" I exclaimed.

"I don't." he replied, sarcastically, "But if I buy the bloody thing, you won't be playing it either!"

Shortly after our move, I decided to fly back to Watchfield to visit Bunty. It was close to dusk as I approached the old airstrip so I had to be especially careful as I came in on final. The tower was no longer in operation so I had to make the landing without ATC assistance.

I could barely see the field in the dim light. Just as I lost flying speed and was touching down I saw a bunch of large objects scattered about, looking like dark, shapeless blobs. "What the hell am I landing on?!" I thought to myself as I maneuvered around them.

Unbeknown to me, the field had been converted into a cow pasture. I anchored the plane to a fence and put canvas covers over the engines and the pitot tubes, then walked over to the stone house where Bunty lived with her mother. I hoped the cows would leave the airplane alone. After spending some time with Bunty and her mother, I booked into a hotel for the night. I could hardly sleep. I was up most of the night wondering what those cows were doing to my airplane.

The next morning I uncovered the airplane and made ready for takeoff. Those darned cows were in my way and I had to wait until I had a clear enough path to take off in. At last they ambled out of my way and I gunned the throttles right quick. I had to take off in a cross wind because if I had waited for the cows upwind of me to move I would probably still be sitting in that field. From then on, Bunty would visit me instead.

Lou Greenburgh and the author's mother (left) relaxing in the Mess.

Jet aircraft were just coming into major production in those days and were something of a novelty. Even today, I suppose, some people would get a thrill out of taking a jet fighter up for a spin.

A Vampire jet landed at Shawbury and the pilot let me take it up by myself. That was my first and only opportunity to fly a jet. It was unofficial, of course, so I didn't log it.

One day a movie producer came to Shawbury looking for someone to fly an aircraft for some aerial filming. He was referred to me, and I took his cameraman up in an Anson for some low flying. From what I heard later, I had scared the heck out of him. I forgot the name of the movie they were filming or I would have gone to see it.

One of the most beautiful spots I've ever seen was the area of the Welsh Hills around the village of Shrewsbury. Not far from Shrewsbury was a place called Church Stretton. It was located up on the hillside and had cheerful little streams which babbled their way to the valley below. Bunty and I used to go there for picnics quite often.

We climbed right to the top of a rolling hill and were pleasantly surprised by the sight of a civilian glider squadron soaring off the nearby cliffs. They had a winch or bungee cord which launched them right into the strong updrafts. Away they'd go, soaring off to the sky where they would be free. In the words of John Gillespie Magee Jr., they "slipped the surly bonds of earth and danced the skies on laughter-silvered wings... wheeled, and soared, and swung." It was an aerial ballet.

We gave a flying exhibition at Farnborough, where many air shows were held. Our part involved close formation flying with four other aircraft. You couldn't loop in formation with an Anson but we did steep turns and the like.

After the show, we had to fly back over the Welsh Hills. A sergeant pilot named Zipoznick was flying back with me and he asked me to let him fly the airplane. He didn't have much experience and needed the flying time. I didn't really like the idea, because there was no dual control, but I finally gave in.

We didn't check the weather before takeoff because we had checked it that morning and everything was okay. Although I was uncomfortable sitting in a cockpit with no controls in front of me, I didn't anticipate any problems.

We were above the Welsh Hills when the weather started to close in. I could see a big, dark cloud; it was like a wall in front of us. I pointed to that cloud and said, "We could never fly through that. We'll have to find some place to land. We'd better find a field and land there."

He didn't feel confident enough to land in a field. I could tell that he was worried and I was pretty concerned as well. Why the hell did I let him fly the darned airplane?

Rain began to pour down on us. It started to hail. An engine quit.

I cursed the lack of dual control. Zipoznick was starting to panic. I wanted to trade places with him but we were too low and the turbulence kept me bouncing against my straps. "Listen," I said, "find any field and crash land with your wheels up! Never mind trying to fly on!"

We were getting lower and lower. The tops of the Welsh Hills began to creep above the instrument panel and into full view.

"For Christ's sake!" I insisted, "Find the first open space and crash land!"

"But we'll get into trouble, Sir." he replied.

"Never mind the trouble! It's more than our skin is worth to carry on!"

I felt helpless, completely helpless. I looked along our flight path and my heart nearly burst.

"Watch out for those high tension cables!" I shrieked. "Look, you're going straight towards those high tension cables!"

There was an explosion and the cockpit was flooded with light as we severed the cables. The airplane went down, smack into the forest. The fuselage skidded along the ground at high speed then passed between two solid trees. The wings were sheered right off.

Fortunately, the plane didn't catch fire. It took us a few minutes to clear our heads and realize what had happened. "We'll have to find some place to go." I said, then added, "Where there's a telephone." I did not relish informing the Royal Air Force that they were short another airplane.

It was getting dark. I felt sick about it, but what was done was done. The first thing to do was get out of the rain.

There was a farm house on the hill so we walked up to it and knocked on the door. I hoped the owners would be in a friendly mood and could offer us shelter.

The farmer came to the door. He said hello to us, then blurted, "All of our lights went out!" The lights had gone out in the whole area, in the whole village.

The farmer allowed us in to telephone the base then put us up for the night. A plane arrived the next day to fly us back.

This was the second aircraft I had written off in as many years and I was sure there would be a full investigation. I was wrong. But I'm sure some unpleasant things were being said about me in high places.

I was posted again shortly after the crash. This time it was to No. 1 Air Signals School at Dearham.

I had signed on for a five year commission, and my five years were up. I requested an extension, and it was granted. But only for one year. Some people tried to talk me into applying for a second extension when that one had expired but I decided not to. I was getting old, for a pilot, and I had those two crashes on my record. I thought the R.A.F. might not grant me a second extension and I didn't want my flying career to end that way. Besides, I would soon have been put behind a desk and I didn't want to be in the Air Force if I couldn't fly. When my time was up I simply took my release and moved back to Canada.

I had my last flight on June 20, 1952, and my release medical report was dated June 27, 1952.

Although my substantive rank remained 'Flight Lieutenant', I received a temporary promotion to 'Acting Squadron Leader' about two weeks before my release. That is why some literature describes my rank as 'Squadron Leader'.

The pilots under my direction held a nice going away party for me and presented me with a cedar lined, silver cigarette case. It was engraved:

FLT LT GREENBURGH, DFC
FROM THE PILOTS OF
No.I A.S.S. ROYAL AIR FORCE

It is still one of my most valued possessions.

Chapter 23: A New Beginning

I arrived back in Canada and began making arrangements to bring Bunty over. About this time, my stepfather showed me a beautiful diamond ring which he had brought from his shop. "When your wife comes," he said, "this will be her ring." We never saw the ring again, naturally, but he used it as a ploy to borrow more money from me. I should have learned from those suitcases.

Bunty came over on the Empress of Scotland, a luxurious liner which had originally been taken from Germany as reparations for World War I. She fell in love with Canada's wide open spaces and seemed quite happy to settle in her adopted country. Her first impression of Canada, she said, was a bunch of bananas she saw hanging in a shop in Montreal. You couldn't get bananas in England for love or money in those days. She decided that Canada was a place where, if one was willing to work, one could get just about anything one needed.

I found us some rooms in a rather squalid boarding house on Boyd Avenue. It had mice and we had to share the washroom with another tenant, a crazy woman who used to scream or moan all the time.

While walking around downtown, I stepped into an optometrist's office by mistake and who should I see but Chuck Soloway, who I had delivered papers with as a boy and who had helped me study for my ill-fated bar mitzvah. I invited him over to meet Bunty, which he did, and we have been close friends ever since. It seems that Chuck spent the war in the Air Force, too. He was a navigator with the R.C.A.F., also with Bomber Command.

Chuck had flown on the devastating incendiary raid over Hamburg. He usually stayed in his navigation compartment but on this occasion the pilot called him up to the cockpit. "Look, Charles," his pilot had said, "Hamburg is burning. It's beautiful.[66]"

Bunty and I purchased a modest but comfortable little bungalow on Scotia Street, with a scenic view of the Red River. I had saved enough of my severance pay to use as a down payment but I needed a job badly and decided that the airport was the right place for a man with my background to begin looking.

The first airline counter I noticed belong to a small company called Trans-Northern Airlines. I spoke to the fellow in charge there, named Roy Brown and told him that I was looking for a job. He was very impressed by my Green ticket and experience with Transport Command and offered me a job right on the

---

[66] *As told to the author by Dr. Charles Soloway.*

spot. After completing some conversion training, I would be the captain of a Canso seaplane, a variation of the Catalina Flying Boat. Roy told me that I should come back the next day to sign the paper work and the job would be mine.

After my initial pleasure at being offered employment so readily, I began to wonder if I really wanted to keep on flying. I had flown so much that the glamour had worn a bit thin and I knew that no flying career ahead of me was likely to overshadow my past experiences. I wanted to settle down and have a normal sort of life. I was also worried about job security. I figured that I would be flying from medical examination to medical examination with the possibility of being found unfit to fly before I had the chance to qualify for a pension. I thought that I was young enough, at thirty-five, to start another career but that in a few years it might be too late. I didn't show up for my final processing. My career as a professional pilot was over.

It was not long after this when I received an offer from an unexpected quarter. Israel sent me a letter in which they offered me the rank of Major in their air force. My duties, at least initially, would have been to assist in their pilot training program.

I either turned them down or didn't reply, I forget which. There were several reasons for that. The main reason I turned them down was because I disagreed with Israel's policy towards the Arabs living in the area. I had no desire to help them bomb Arab refugee camps.

Another reason I turned them down was that I was just starting to get settled and I wanted a bit of peace and quiet. Also, I heard that Israel paid their Jewish servicemen less than they paid 'foreign' mercenaries. Besides, you had to be Jewish to become a citizen of Israel. That's the sort of thing I fought against in World War II. And why should I fight for a country which would not accept my wife and children as citizens?

The offer from Israel was soon followed by a telephone call from the Jewish Post. They wanted to know why I had refused Israel's offer.

I thought that such a thing was none of their business. Still, I gave them a reply which was printable. They quoted me as saying "After living out of suitcases all these years, despite the temptations of the offer, and the natural desire of every Jew to help Israel, I'm not ready to make the decision yet. Four thousand flying hours should be enough for any man.[67]"

---

67 *"Four Thousand Flying Hours Under Three Flags Enough; Prefers Quiet Life Here to Israel Airforce Offer," "The Jewish Post•, Thursday, September 25, 1952.*

The above quote (which, by the way, was not exactly what I said) was accompanied by a brief summary of my flying career under the headline "Four Thousand Flying Hours Under Three Flags Enough; Prefers Quiet Life Here to Israel Airforce Offer." I can imagine what they would have written if I'd told them what I really thought.

My wife was having her hair done at a beauty salon and I was waiting for her. I knew the cost was going to be higher than I wanted to pay and I mentioned that to a great big guy who was waiting beside me. He told me that he had been working as a butcher but was going into women's hairdressing himself. With the prices that women paid to have their hair done, he figured it was a surefire way to make a buck.

"What are you doing?" he asked me.

"I'm doing nothing."

He shrugged his shoulders. "Come along with me!"

So we both went down to enroll in hairdressing school. I said to the lady at the reception desk, "Hi. I'm a pilot, this guy's a butcher. We've decided to become hairdressers."

The next thing I knew, I was a hairdresser and I got a job at the Hudson's Bay store downtown. I will never forget my first customer. She was a well-dressed lady with long blond hair.

I accidentally picked up the scissors instead of the thinning shears. Snip! There I was, with a long lock of hair in my hand and a short, stubby spot on the back of the lady's head.

I struggled against the urge to wince. "You know," I said, with as straight a face as I could manage, "I really think you would look better with short hair."

"What have you done?!" she demanded. Her horror turned to anger when she saw the long strands hanging from my fist.

"Please," I pleaded, "This is my first day on the job. I'll get fired if you make a fuss. You don't have to pay for the haircut. It's on the house."

She was pretty upset. She threatened to complain to the manager, threatened this, threatened that. She eventually calmed down and let me finish her haircut.

That lady became one of my best customers and whenever she came in she always asked for me.

I was visiting my mother one day when I happened to see a letter sitting on her dresser. It was addressed to me. The letter had been sent to inform me that my father had taken his own life and went on to say that I was welcome to contribute to the funeral arrangements if I so desired. The letter was dated about six months before.

I showed my mother the letter. "Ma," I asked, "why didn't you show this to me?!"

"I didn't think you would be interested." she replied. She said that she had written back telling the concerned parties that I was not interested in anything to do with my father. She had no right to do that. I would have sent a contribution.

A fellow who sold beauty equipment began taking a real interest in me. At least, he told me that he was interested in me. He asked me why I didn't go into business for myself and said "You'd make a lot of money, with your personality."

He gave me a lot of other 'B.S'. too, and we went for a ride in his car. He took me for a ride, alright. As we reached the Canadian Broadcasting Corporation building on Portage Avenue he pointed at the 'For Rent' sign on a small office building. "You could have a really nice beauty parlor in there, boy," he said, "next to the C.B.C. You could make a lot of money!"

Next scene; I was in business for myself, with lots of money coming in and even more going out. I had to renovate the building myself. It needed a new furnace, I had to put seats in, and all of my investment was going into somebody else's' building because I was only leasing it. And to make things worse, I was trapped into a ten year lease.

There was no way I could get out of it and I was worried. I just couldn't see myself as a hairdresser for the next ten years. After I had paid off my staff, there was nothing left for me. I told Bunty that we might lose our house.

There was a fire in a jewelry store two doors down the street. The owner asked me if he could have some space in my beauty parlor to display his merchandise. I let him have two little counters. So we had a jewelry store in a beauty parlor. The next thing I knew, he wanted to buy me out. So I let him. My wife laughed, "Harry's in the beauty business!" That's how I got off the hook.

I figure that I lost about fifty thousand dollars in that business, not counting the wages I lost by not working. And right after I had washed my hands of the whole thing, my wife told me something. I said, "You're what?! Oh, no!"

The Bay had offered me my old job back, but I could never support a family on what they were going to pay me. I had to get a job at something other than hairdressing. I looked through the paper and saw one job that looked suitable; Stony Mountain Penitentiary was looking for a prison guard.

It was over an hour's drive from where I lived to the Federal Penitentiary in the little town of Stony Mountain. I parked my car and went inside. I saw a whole line up of people waiting to make application for the job. "Get into line, Buddy." somebody grunted in a rough tone of voice.

I was sure the job would be filled long before I got to see anybody. I needed the job badly.

I made the long drive home and got dressed in my R.C.A.F. Reserve uniform. I usually just wore the ribbons for my decorations but this time I put on my gongs. I then drove back to the penitentiary.

Nobody told me to get into line. I went to the door of the office and a receptionist asked, "Can I help you, Sir?"

Louis
the well-known stylist, formerly with the Hudson's Bay Co., takes pleasure in announcing the opening of his new Ultra-Modern
BEAUTY SALON
561 PORTAGE AVE. (near Young St.)
and will be glad to welcome all his patrons and friends.
Louis' BEAUTY SALON
PHONE SUnset 3-3927
As an acquaintance gesture this card is valued at $1.50 on any cold wave and permanent during the month of September.

A coupon advertising Lou's beauty salon (top).

Lou's hairdresser's licence (below).

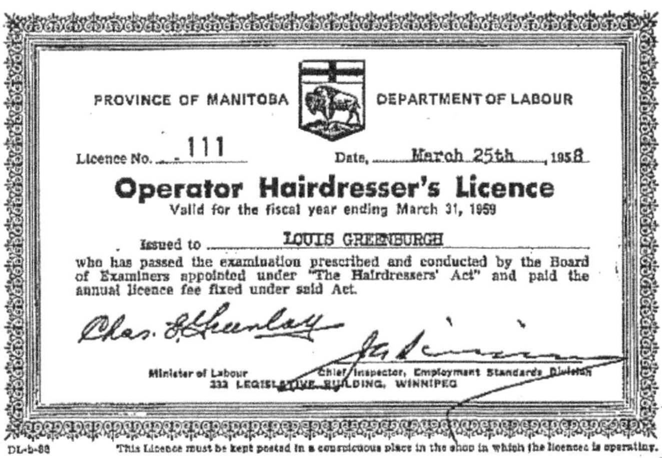

PROVINCE OF MANITOBA — DEPARTMENT OF LABOUR

Licence No. 111 — Date, March 25th, 1958

Operator Hairdresser's Licence

Valid for the fiscal year ending March 31, 1959

Issued to LOUIS GREENBURGH

who has passed the examination prescribed and conducted by the Board of Examiners appointed under "The Hairdressers' Act" and paid the annual licence fee fixed under said Act.

Chas. S. Greenlay — Minister of Labour

Chief Inspector, Employment Standards Division, 333 Legislative Building, Winnipeg

DL-b-88 — This Licence must be kept posted in a conspicuous place in the shop in which the licensee is operating.

"Yes," I replied, with the dignified air of an officer on official business, "I'd like to see the director -the Warden- of this institution."

"Oh, by all means, Sir!" she said and disappeared into the office. I could hear her talking to the Warden's secretary. The secretary called the Warden on her intercom and informed him that there was an Air Force officer to see him. "Oh?" I heard him reply, "Send him in."

I was ushered into the office. The Warden stood up to greet me and extended his hand into a handshake. "How do you do." I said, "My name is Flying Officer Greenburgh."

"Oh, sit down, Sir." he said, indicating a chair in front of his desk. "Can I help you? To what do I owe the pleasure of this visit?"

"Well," I told him, "I'm interested in corrections, especially in the penitentiary aspect." I didn't tell him that I was an out of work hair dresser and desperate for a well-paying job. "I'm in the Reserve now and I'm interested in a new career."

The Warden looked a bit dejected, as if he wanted to help me but couldn't. "I'm sorry, Sir." he told me, "The only position we have available is just a guard."

"Well, it doesn’t really matter," I said to him. "I don't mind starting where-ever you can put me."

So he rang a bell and called the keeper to fetch an application for me to fill out. As I left, he said, "We'll give you a call."

The next day I got a call, made an appointment, and got the job. The funny part of it is, that the day I started work some of those same fellows who had been waiting in line were still there, still waiting.

I didn't like being a prison guard but what the heck, I had to make a living. And I was conscientious! If it looked like it was going to snow, I'd drive out to 'Stony' the night before my shift just to be sure that I wasn't stranded away from work.

I carried a pistol on my belt when I patrolled outside the compound. I was armed with a rifle when I manned the lookout towers.

I had just started my new job when I got a call from my mother. She invited me to a bar mitzvah which was being held for one of my cousins and expected me to take the day off work so that I could attend.

"But Ma," I explained, "I've just started this job and I'm still on probation. I could get fired if I start asking for time off."

Mother snorted in contempt and hung up on me.

I didn't have much to do with my mother's family by this time, although I still wanted to be accepted by them. Occasionally I would bring my children to visit their grandmother and she would sometimes visit them. She would make the odd sponge cake once in a while.

The one member of my family who I have always liked, respected, and got along with was Auntie Meryl. She often had Bunty and I over to her place for dinner and has always been very nice. I have a very high opinion of Auntie Meryl and her immediate family.

My daughter, Linda, had been born and my wife was pregnant with our second child when I received the following letter from the R.A.F. Escaping Society:

R.A.F. ESCAPING SOCIETY

The Secretary,
83 PORTLAND PLACE
LONDON, W.I.

19th June, 1959.

Dear Mr. Greenburgh,

It has recently come to my notice that one of our helpers in France, M. Duneau, A. Montbossier, Par Bonneval, Eure et Loire, now 68 years of age is living alone on a very small income, his son having died in 1946 and his wife, after a long illness, in 1952. The Society is sending him a maximum grant of £25 but I think that even more than the gift of money he would appreciate hearing from some of the "boys" he helped in 1944 in the Montbossier area. I gather that M. Duneau lodged in small groups of one to six men a total of 52 airmen during the period January to August, 1944. Most of them went to the La Gaudiniere camp refuge in the forest. On the arrival of the first Allied troops there were still nine staying at Duneau's house. Among all these men he kept the names of 23, 13 were American and 10 were British. Most of these names were written by the men themselves in a small note-book belonging to Duneau. Your name appears to be among them together with that of three other members of the Society viz Mr. W. R. Pryer, Mr. J. D. Murrie and Dr. I. F. Kennedy.

If you remember M. Duneau I hope that you will try and drop him a line. You can write in English as he has a friend nearby who reads and writes very good English.

Yours sincerely,
Marjorie Craig
Secretary,
R.A.F.E.S.

L. Greenburgh, Esq.,
452 Scotia St.
Winnipeg, 4, Canada.

I believe I did respond to that letter. If I were ever to return to France, I thought, I wanted to look up M. Duneau and pay him a visit.

My son, Edwin, was very small boned which made him quite slender. My stepfather once pointed a gnarled finger at him and rudely inquired, with his heavy Slavic accent, "Why is he so skinny?[68]"

One good thing about being a prison guard; I got to meet some pretty interesting people. Ken Leishman was probably the best known character I ever guarded. Ken had earned notoriety as the 'Flying Bandit'. He used to fly into places, rob banks, and then fly out again. He'd been in a couple of shoot outs with police, but had never actually injured anyone.

Ken and I were pals. I spent hours with him in his cell, talking about flying and teaching him some of the finer points of navigation.

We kept in touch for a while after his release from prison. I once took him up to see a judge who I knew. He looked at my guest and said that he was sure he knew him from somewhere but he couldn't quite place him.

I said, "This is Ken Leishman."

"Ken Leishman!" the judge exclaimed, practically jumping behind his chair, "What is he doing here?!"

I was sorry to hear that Ken was killed in a plane crash. His body was never found and there was some speculation that he may have survived and gone into hiding. I don't think he did. Ken enjoyed publicity and he wasn't likely to hide so long without showing himself.[69]

---

[68] *This was the author's only actual memory of his step-grandfather.*

[69] *Kenneth Leishman (June 20, 1931 – December 14, 1979), also known as the Flying Bandit or the Gentleman Bandit was a Canadian criminal responsible for multiple robberies between 1957 and 1966. Leishman was the mastermind behind the largest gold theft in Canadian history. After being caught and arrested by the Royal Canadian Mounted Police (RCMP), Leishman managed to escape twice, before being caught and serving the remainder of his various sentences. In December 1979, while flying a mercy flight to Thunder Bay, Ken's aircraft crashed about 40 miles north of Thunder Bay. Source - Wikipedia*

P.O. Box 10[illegible]
STONY MOUNTAIN, MANITOBA

Dear Lou — Feb. 16, 1967

Well it took some doing but I finally got you on my correspondence list, so, and to take the [illegible] a hello your way. It was truly a pleasant surprise seeing you at court Lou, isn't it strange the way old acquaintances pop up when least expected. Things are progressing well here, I'm [illegible] with my grade XII Math already and then June and August I'll be writing off some exams. I'm heading for a specialty degree in Engineering - the Lord willing - (and the parole board cooperating) I'll be a cinch to make it. So here you know my plans. It's amazing how short the days can be when you are caught up in studies as I am, and the real part is that I am thoroughly enjoying them. This place has no significance to me as a prison, it is a place to eat, sleep and study so my frame of mind is superb. Of course there are those moments when I could "tear my hanky" - you know how there are frequently "little things" that seem designed and calculated to remind you where you are. And how is your lovely wife and family keeping during this typical Manitoba winter - lawful isn't it! I was a bit surprised and impressed with Magistrate Dwichuk (did I butcher the spelling?), there's a young man with a future. Perhaps some day we can compare notes on flying. Next week is a bit of an event for us, it will be 17 years of marital bliss on the 25th. In spite of the ups and downs we've had some really fine years and of course there are many good years ahead. Did I tell you they have me tailoring in here, how's that for good constructive endeavor? The academic picture has picked up nicely, I'm attending school on a half day basis.

Now that we are well into the [illegible] and you will be pretty well squared away I'll be expecting you to pop in for a hello.

Kindest personal regards
Ken Leishman

Letter sent to Lou by Ken Leishman after their time together in prison; Lou was a guard and Ken an inmate. By the time this letter was written Leishman was one of Canada's most notorious criminals.

Ken Leishman's police 'mugshot'.

One of my talents as a guard was in writing reports. An opportunity came up for me to enter the fledgling probation service and my report writing ability gave me something to offer. When I told my supervisor that I was going to work as a Probation Officer for the Province, he offered me a promotion to Classification Officer. I was pleased by the offer, but I'd had had my fill of the prison and was tired of making such long drives every day.

My new base of operations was in Selkirk, a community just north of Winnipeg. I was responsible for the entire 'Interlake Region' (between Lake Manitoba and Lake Winnipeg) as far north as The Pas. Nobody had ever heard of a 'Probation Officer' in those days and I had to carve out my own operating procedures and policies. I got really involved in the northern communities and there came a time when the Mayor of Grand Rapids wouldn't hold a council meeting unless I was present.

I made the rules in those days. My belief was that all the advice in the world wouldn't take the place of three square meals and a good home. A helping hand is always better than a helping mouth.

I remember one occasion when a judge in Grand Rapids sentenced four boys to two years in the Home for Boys because they had committed a 'break and entry'. I figured that they were basically good kids who needed a bit of guidance so I had a talk with the judge and asked him to let me place them in foster homes.

"Just get them out of Grand Rapids!" was his stern reply.

I gathered the kids together and laid it on the line. "I'm sticking my neck out," I told them. "If this doesn't work, I'm in trouble and you're going to the Home for Boys."

The boys piled in my car and we began the long drive to Winnipeg. I hoped to place all of the kids along the way.

It wasn't long before I spotted a general store which looked promising. I pulled up the dusty trail to the front, got out of the car, and told my charges to stay put until I got back.

I glanced about the cluttered shelves then said hello to the tired looking shop keeper. Before I left, the shop keeper had a new assistant and I had one less boy to place.

One down and three to go. I placed another two boys with farmers. That left me with only one more boy to place.

We were getting close to Winnipeg. I pulled into a farm just outside of Stonewall and went looking for the farmer with the remaining boy in tow. I soon found him working in his barn.

"Hi there!" I said, then introduced myself. I complemented him on having such a beautiful farm and commented that he must have a pretty large staff to run it.

"Oh no," he replied, and told me that he had to do most everything by himself or with just a couple of others. He said he'd like to have more farm hands but couldn't afford to pay them. I told him that I could help him out. I explained that if he would be willing to provide a foster home for the boy I had with me, the government would provide a modest compensation for his upkeep and he would have an extra farm hand to help with the chores.

The farmer seemed to think that would be a good arrangement and we just about had the deal settled. I told him that he would be responsible to provide a good home and to make sure that his new foster son attended school.

"Wait a minute," the boy exclaimed, "I ain't going to no school!"

"Just a minute." I said to the farmer, and led the boy out of earshot. I turned to him and said, "You've got a choice. You can either stay here and go to school, or go to jail. What's it going to be?"

He decided to stay with the farmer. In years to come, I often reflected that that boy was my only failure. He became a Probation Officer.

This beautiful photograph of Lou Greenburgh as a child was found beside the coal chute in the basement of his mother's home.

I was very proud of my foster home program. I used to find foster homes just by knocking on doors. I would take a young kid with me and check out every house in the neighborhood until I found somebody who would take him or her in. I had the largest foster home program in Manitoba.

There were times when I would find myself at the end of a day with a young kid on my hands and no foster home set up. When that happened I usually took the kid home with me.

One boy actually escaped from my house. I walked into the living room, where I had left him, and he was gone. He had climbed out the living room window. The funny thing was, that window had been stuck for years and I don't know how he ever got it open! I was glad to see that he had fixed it for me. He didn't get far, of course, before the police picked him up.

I think that was the same boy who once pulled a knife on me. I was driving along the gravel road on my way from one of the northern communities when my passenger, who was sitting in the front seat beside me, pulled out a jack knife and threatened me with it. With my left hand still on the steering wheel, I just reached over with my right, grabbed the wrist of the hand which held the knife, and twisted it until he let go. It wasn't a very big knife, anyway.

It wasn't the fact that I disarmed the kid that mattered. He was crying and panicking over his future so I said to him, "I'm going to find you a foster home and you're going to be my son. You're going to be alright, so don't worry."

Later, I got a letter from that boy's wife. She said that I was the only father that her husband had ever known.

One girl, named Francis, stayed with us for a couple of weeks. She gave us a few problems and I really wanted to find someplace else for her to stay. I could have sent her to the Home for Girls, but that wasn't something I ever did if I could help it. In fact, it's something I never did.

I remember one time I had to laugh to myself. She was talking to my little daughter, Cindy (my fourth child with Bunty, who was born after my daughter, Heather). "If you don't behave," she told her, "I'll turn you over to the Jews."

Francis wrote a letter to Steven Juba, the Mayor. Shortly after, I received a letter from him. He demanded to know why I was holding Francis 'hostage' and he wanted a reply immediately.

She was driving me nuts. I spoke to a prison guard I knew, and I told him that she was just wonderful. "We were really lucky to get her!" I bragged.

The guard, whose name was Sam, agreed that I was fortunate and seemed to be in deep thought. After a moment, he said to me, "Do you think I could have a foster girl?"

I told him that I couldn't see why not. I played hard to get for a while, but then relented and stated that, since he was a friend, I would even be willing to let him have Francis. He was very appreciative. I sent Francis over before he had a chance to change his mind.

It was a short honeymoon, so to speak. Soon afterwards, I got a call from Sam. "Take her back!" he begged.

My probation career was briefly interrupted by a call from the past. The war was over, yet I couldn't escape from its influence and Europe was calling me back...

Chapter 24: Reunion at Freteval

COMITE POUR LE MEMORIAL
aux Aviateurs Allies
recuellis par la Resistance
Foret de Freteval

Le January 12th, 1967

Siege Social:
HOTEL DE VILLE DE CHATEAUDUN - 28
C. C. P. 3.286-12 PARIS

Dear Sir,

Probably you do not know that we are erecting a memorial to the allied airmen and the Resistance in the Forest of Freteval on Sunday June 11th 1967.

We saw your name on the list of Mr. Gaston Duneau, an old man of the Resistance who died in 1961.

Generally the airmen who stayed in Gaston Duneau's went 15 miles about from there to Mr. Fougereux and then to the camp of the Forest. But we did not see your name on those lists. We should be pleased to hear you evading those days. Did you reach Spain thanks to the Comite line?

For the celebration on June 11th we want to gather as many ex allied airmen and people of the Resistance as possible and to make this day a day of Souvenir and friendship.

We can offer accommodation for 4 days in French families to those who will come to the ceremony.

We have many friends in WESTERHAM (Kent). Among them is Mr. Steven Medhurst Trotts Lane, tel WESTERHAM 2133.

Every year there is a football match between Bonneval and WESTERHAM and some English friends will come in February. They can tell you that our welcome is simple but hearty.

Yours sincerely,

Mme J. GRANGE
9, rue St Martin
BONNEVAL
Eure et lois
28

The above letter had been sent to my old address in Kent but was forwarded to me. I was very pleased at the thought of attending a Forest of Freteval reunion and quickly applied for a leave of absence from work.

COMITE POUR LE MEMORIAL
aux Aviateurs Allies
recuellis par la Resistance
Foret de Freteval

Bonneval 3 - 2 - 67

Siege Social:
HOTEL DE VILLE DE CHATEAUDUN - 28
C. C. P. 3.286-12 PARIS

Dear Mr. Greenburgh,

We were pleased to hear from you. We have not yet told Mr. Feugereux about your letter but he will be very happy. Poor old one he was weeping at the idea to meet again some of allied airmen he helped. These poor and brave people have to bear only, most of time, the jealousy of their neighbours who were too cowards to help. When the people of the French resistance were not denounced they were lucky. Near the wood where you were camping there was a small farm who gave food to the camp. Wife and husband were sent to Germany in deportation. They did not say a word about the camp. Fortunately for all of you. After the war, when the man came back, he found again his farm and his children but his wife died in the deportation camp. Two others were deported and came back with a poor health.

Many people are surprised. Why a memorial after 23 years? Yes, it seems strange at first. Everybody has the idea to write something, to do something but everybody was busy. One after the other the actors of this period are passing away with the same dream. Now it is on the way to be realized. Colonel Remy on the French side is writing a book. Mr Airey Neave members of the Parliament will publish his book in September. He was the leader of the Comete Reseau in England. Jean de Blommaert and Colonel Boussa in France (they were with you in the camp) "le Baron Jean" et "Cousine Lucienne" - they will attend the ceremony. This has not been done before because nobody has neither time nor money. We have got now 30.000 F, but we need 70.000 F. Tradesmen say they will wait and give us time to find money.

We must not count too much on governmental aid. America will send a military band and troop. So will the British, French and Belgian.

The Royal Escaping Society has opened a subscription among his members. Mrs. Russel Tickner in Texas will try to do something on the American side in her newspaper. Mr. Sam Taylor has sent a beautiful contribution of 100 dollars.

But the main thing is to meet one another and have this stone erected in the border of the wood to make people remember and think and do their best to avoid war. I can't tell you now how grand the ceremony will be but I'm sure it will be moving.

When our English footballers come, the old Bernard Johnson from the British Legion of Westerham bring a wreath of red poppies. All of us English and French are marching in an impressive silence from Gaston Duneau's house to the churchyard. There Bernard Johnson says an English poem repeated by the English party. The children of the school sing " la Marseillaise". I have never seen a more moving and sincere ceremony.

Before coming to Gaston Duneau's you had probably spent some days in Vaves in Mrs. Leroy's farm and you were led by her son Valentis. 112 airmen were accommodated in Mr. and Mrs. Leroy's farm. She is 77 now and would be happy to recognize some of you.

We should be very grateful if you could try to contact Canadian airmen - 152 is a lot to come into contact especially with old addresses. Can you call Grimsey in Winnipeg? I only write to Sam Taylor in Canada.

We can't expect many people from over the ocean but am sure the people of our district will appreciate a word from them.

Bye the way, my husband wants to write about the comforting letters we received so can you send 2 photographs and some lines about yourself? We shall inform our people through the local paper.

Did I tell you we have a committee about 23 or 26 members (all Resistance people) except my husband who is a sort of organizer and myself who has to write letters. We enjoy the job but we lack time but we are rewarded by the joy we see in many hearts.

Hoping to hear you soon.

Sincerely yours,

Jacqueline Grange.

P.S. My husband is sending the local papers to you.

COMITE POUR LE MEMORIAL
aux Aviateurs Allies
recuellis par la Resistance
Foret de Freteval

Le April 1
Bonneval

Siege Social:
HOTEL DE VILLE DE CHATEAUDUN - 28
C. C. P. 3.286-12 PARIS

Dear Mr. Greenburgh,

Thank you very much for your contribution to the memorial that all the members of our committee will appreciate on our next meeting on April 9th.

It is so kind of you to help us to let the generations know what you, allied soldiers have done and what our people of the Resistance have accomplished, too.

I did not reply very soon to your letter of March 2d because I am terribly busy by the reception of our English party from Westerham. Mr. Jack Steven and his brother T. Steven, brothers of Harry Steven are coming with 44 others. They arrive on Sat. April 8th. The match will be won by our local football team, we hope, on Sunday. Monday is a free day on the market. Tuesday we are going to the chateaux de la loire. They are leaving on Wed morning.

Colonel Boussa, you must have known under the name of Cousine Lucienne, died in Cloyes near Freteval after a meeting of the committee. His wife, who is in very poor health since she has been in deportation camp, was not able to come from Belgium. His sisters came and they were quite moved by all the sympathy of the population. We were very sad and also very sorry, another member missing and we are so few. I made enquiry about your stay in Bonneval. Probably you have been staying in a stable in a wood and after in the Marolle family where there were 2 daughters and then with an old lady called Mrs. Chauvis. When you come you will meet old these people. We have the pleasure to see the meeting of this American Virginia who saved all the camp with some of her companions. Sam Taylor is trying to arrange a group trip. Can you get in contact with him as soon as possible.

Sam Taylor - general manager - The SHERATON DRAKE HOTEL - 11th Ave. Rose Street REGINA SASKATCHEWAN. Phone 522-7627.

Thank you for the photographs promised. I receive some from Sam Taylor this morning. We shall write an article in the papers.

I am sending you by ordinary mail some articles about the Memorial.

Mr. Sam Taylor is coming with his wife. 3 Toronto boys will be attending with their wives.

Can you get contact with

G.A. MUSGROVE
287 Marckland Dr Apt 810
Etobicoke Ontario

Jonathon Pearson from Schenechady is coming with wife and daughters. Mr. Russel Tickne and wife maybe children come from Texas. Joseph Peloquin - Biddeford Maine. I have not other recent confirmation of some others in U.S.A.

Please tell us more about where you were shot down.

It is time for the mail. I must hurry. Thank you so much for our committee. Please send photos, details, and confirmation of your coming.

Sincerely yours

J. Grange

I said good-bye to my wife and four children at the Winnipeg International Airport at 3:40 P.M. on June 5, 1967. My seven year old son, Edwin, warned me not to get involved in any more wars. Sam Taylor was there and we talked a bit before entering the DC 9 bound for Paris. Minutes later, the plane was at thirty-two thousand feet and I could see the forest fires at Lac Seul. They reminded me of the depression years when I worked at a forest camp in that area. A few more minutes went by and I recognized Port Arthur, where the Salvation Army put me up for a few nights (on the condition that I went along with their prayers).

Some two hours later I was in Montreal. I decided to change my immediate destination to London. Unfortunately, my luggage was accidentally placed on another Paris-bound aircraft. The luggage supervisor's face turned a bit red when the mistake was discovered and he asked me if I was angry with him.

R.A.F. ESCAPING SOCIETY

(Registered under the War Charities Act, 1940)

Kindly address all communications to:

The Secretary,
83 PORTLAND PLACE
LONDON, W.1.
Tel.: LANgham 8161 (Ext. 3)

19th June, 1959.

Dear Mr. Greenburgh

It has recently come to my notice that one of our helpers in France, M. Duneau, A. Montbossier, Par Bonneval, Eure et Loire, now 68 years of age is living alone on a very small income, his son having died in 1946 and his wife, after a long illness, in 1952. The Society is sending him a maximum grant of £25 but I think that even more than the gift of money he would appreciate hearing from some of the "boys" he helped in 1944 in the Montbossier area. I gather that M. Duneau lodged in small groups of one to six men a total of 52 airmen during the period January to August, 1944. Most of them went to the La Gaudiniere camp refuge in the forest. On the arrival of the first Allied troops there were still nine staying at Duneau's house. Among all these men he kept the names of 23, 13 were American and 10 were British. Most of these names were written by the men themselves in a small note-book belonging to Duneau. Your name appears to be among them together with that of three other members of the Society viz Mr. W. R. Pryer, Mr. J. D. Murrie and Dr. I. F. Kennedy.

If you remember M. Duneau I hope that you will try and drop him a line. You can write in English as he has a friend nearby who reads and writes very good English.

Yours Sincerely
Marjorie Craig
Secretary,
R.A.F.E.S.

L. Greenburgh, Esq.,
~~307 Boyd Avenue,~~ 952 SCOTIA ST.
Winnipeg, 17, Canada.

I was very tired the next morning when we arrived in London. The place had changed a lot from the days when I knew it. There were new sky-scrapers on the horizon, St. Paul's Cathedral was being white-washed for the first time in three hundred years, and traffic was really heavy. Cars were all over the place and I thought each one was trying to hit me.

With no reservations, I had a heck of a time finding a hotel room. I had no intention of sleeping in the kind of flop house I had inhabited in my youth. After trying about a dozen of London's famous hotels, I managed to get a place in South Kensington.

I saw many old friends and acquaintances. One of the families I visited had lost a flying member during the war. I took them out to dinner and they afterwards told me that it was one of their most enjoyable days since the war.

Another family I visited was my own.

I arrived at the Paris Orly Airport and was irritated to find that the baggage room would be closed until the next morning. I therefore booked a room at the Hilton Orly.

I entered Austerlitz station and was drawn back to the day when I had entered that same station twenty-three years before. I had been a fugitive surrounded by German soldiers and that young girl had led me into hiding. I boarded a train for the village of Bonneval.

Upon arrival, I booked a room at the Gare Hotel and took a taxi to the residence of Mme. Grange.

Finding her house locked, I wandered around for about three hours. I flagged down a television repair truck and explained my predicament to the driver. He gave me a ride to his office and managed to get Mme. Grange on the telephone. I told her where I was staying and she and her husband met me there. They seemed thrilled to see me and insisted that I visit them at their house that evening.

I really enjoyed sitting in their living room, telling them stories about my adventures twenty-three years before. "Would you like to take a look at the Estaminet?" they asked.

I thought that was a great idea. It was already dark, but my hosts led me through the shadows until I recognized the aging home of M. Dauphin. I was anxious to see my old friend but I didn't want to disturb him at that hour. Mellow with nostalgia but exited by the reunion tomorrow would bring, I headed back to my lodgings.

The next morning, I walked up to my old place of refuge. This time, I went to the front. I knocked on the door and was thrilled to see the weathered face of M. Dauphin. "Sacre-ble!" he exclaimed, "I am seeing a ghost!"

I laughed, shook his hand, and assured him that I was very much alive. He called his wife and family and gestured me inside.

"How can it be?" he asked. "We heard that your party was captured and executed."

I explained how we had divided into two parties, just in case one party got caught, and that it was the other party which had been captured.

We spent several hours reminiscing. I started to excuse myself as it drew near to dinner time but Mme. Dauphin wouldn't hear of it and insisted that I stay for dinner. I sat at the table with M. Dauphin seated right beside me.

When the whole family had been seated, I noticed a little eight year old girl. "My goodness!" I thought, "That's the little girl who led me into the back entrance of the Estaminet."

I pointed to the little girl and remarked that she hadn't changed at all. Her mother smiled at me and I realized that it was she who had been the little girl, but her daughter was the exact image. "Monsieur," she purred, "you forget that today you are twenty-three years younger."

We were served a delicious eight course meal. I was careful not to eat too much, as usual, but most of the food was light and I really enjoyed it. No rabbit this time. There were plenty of drinks and we had a lot to talk about.

After dinner, M. Dauphin showed me his many decorations. He was especially proud to have received France's Croix de Guerre and a special scroll from the President of the United States. It was signed by General Eisenhower and cited the work M. Dauphin had done to save sixty-five airmen, many of whom M. Dauphin had transported to Paris.

We laughed about the time he had entertained German officers while I watched over the top of the door.

That evening, the telephone rang at the house of Mme Grange. It was a Miss Figgis, Secretary of the Escapers' Society, 'phoning from London. She informed us that the British Government had laid on a special transport aircraft for nine members and that they would be landing at Chateaudun Military Airport at eight P.M.

The Granges and I met the party at the Officers' Mess. Some grand acquaintances were renewed. I saw several chaps who had been with me in the Freteval Forest and plenty of stories and lines were swapped over the drinks.

Next day, the Granges told me about Gaston Duneau, who I had been hoping to see. It was in his house that they had found my name and temporary English address. This wonderful patriot had sheltered something like fifty-three evaders in his home. My heart was greatly saddened when they took me to his grave.

I had the good fortune to see M. Foreau, who had been the Mayor of Montbossier during my stay there but was now an old man. He told me that he was overjoyed that I had been able to make the trip. He took me to a house that was all too familiar and led me to the attic where I had been hidden. He shook his head and there was a tear in his eye when he said, "There are many who are not with us." I recalled to him that day when we had run for shelter from those P 47's which had dropped their loads and killed some civilians.

That evening I met Marius Velledien, the little butcher boy who had supplied us with rabbit meat from a nearby farm. I didn't recognize him at first because he had become a family man with three children, but he knew me immediately. "I remember that you are the airman who had a swinging chain in your hand and you never did like rabbit meat." We laughed a bit as we discussed the past. Marius had also received a scroll from General Eisenhower as well as many French decorations.

We visited another French family, where I met Allan Spears, a New Zealand pilot who had been in the woods with me. I just remembered him vaguely but he knew me and he showed me an old ten franc note with my faded signature. He had kept it after all those years. We discussed Colonel Lucien Boussa, the Belgium R.A.F. officer who had worked for British Intelligence and helped organize escape routes. He was the most enthusiastic supporter and organizer of this Memorial Ceremony. I had been really looking forward to seeing him. Unfortunately, as Mme. Grange had mentioned in one of her letters, he had died of a coronary a few weeks before the unveiling.

I went to Cloyes the next day, where I met three Canadian ex-escapers and their wives. There was Sam Taylor of Vancouver, whom I had previously met at the airport in Winnipeg; Stan Lawrence, an engineer who lived in Toronto; and Jerry Musgrave, also of Toronto. I recognized him as the tall, skinny boy who used to run around in the woods with supplies of dried beans.

A bus took our party to Blois. We were given a tour of one of France's largest castles, which had once been the home of King Henry IV. We were shown the room where his wife, Catherine, used to poison her enemies. The French Government tries to maintain the castle in its original state.

We all got reacquainted at the bar before lunch. There was Ted Horrigan from Australia. He had worried about making a living twenty-three years ago. Now he was a Captain with Quantas Airlines, flying 707's. There was Ray Worrall, who had shared a tent with me in the forest and who I had met again when I was a flying instructor at Nutt's Corner, Ireland. We had a lot to talk about. He told me that he was now a Barrister in Leeds, England. I also met an

American officer who had used the name 'Stuart' when we were in the camp together. He was now retired and living in Philadelphia.

A banquet was held in the Marianne Cafe that night. I sat beside Marius and Ted Horrigan. Across from me sat the other three Canadians and their wives. Many people spoke, including the Mayor of Cloyes, but I was most touched by the speech given by Lucien Boussa's sister. She had done time at Ravensbruck Concentration Camp, simply because she was Lucien's sister.

A lady whispered in my ear, "This business was organized by brave ordinary people, but I'll bet at this ceremony it will be the big brass and top politicians who will grab the limelight."

The next morning was Saturday, June 11, 1967. There, gathered at the square in Cloyes, I saw more brass, braid and politicians than I had seen for years. There was a French air chief just covered in gold braid, with a cigarette dangling from his mouth. He was talking with a much decorated British Cabinet Minister. Ambassadors and Staff Officers of air rank represented Canada, New Zealand, Australia and Great Britain. The United States was represented by a highly decorated top ranking Air Force Officer. Flags and banners were carried by dozens of bemedalled people. The Mayor appeared a little tired of shaking hands. I had left my decorations and medals back in Canada, but all of us who had been evaders or escapers wore a red flower in our lapels.

"Charles De Gaulle would have been here," someone told me, "but that would have caused complications as the heads of the other concerned countries would also have had to be present."

There was full television, radio and newspaper coverage, in spite of the big news of the Arab-Israeli war. A large parade was formed. We all marched to the cemetery, where wreaths were laid on several graves.

After the wreaths had been laid, we all climbed into a luxurious coach. It took us to Montagne Chateaux, one of the most beautiful castles in the Loire Valley and the home of the Duke and Duchess of Grillon. They were the first family of France, next to the De Gaulles. The Duke and Duchess opened their private home to us and supplied us with everything to drink from whiskey to the best vintage of champagne.

Church dignitaries with their cloaks, politicians, and military brass stood on the terrace overlooking the Loire Valley and sipped their drinks. I noticed that a very attractive lady wearing many decorations was smiling in my direction. I walked over to talk to her. It was Virginia D' Albert Lake, the American lady who had been dragged away. She was now one of France's great heroines.

The chateau at which the Forest of Freteval reunion was held in 1967.

I mentioned the tragedy which had befallen her twenty-three years before. She was not the least bit embittered and I was intrigued by her natural charm, radiance and sincere friendliness.

As we talked about the past, I heard some sirens from the valley below. "Hee haw! Hee haw! Hee haw!" I looked into the distance and saw the spiraling ribbon formed by a train of limousines and their police motorcycle escort. They twisted up the steep Loire river bank road. When they arrived, they took up the entire courtyard. Charles De Gaulle's representative, the French Defense Minister, stepped out with his entourage and joined our party at the bar.

An eight course luncheon was served in the annex. More speeches were made from the head table.

After lunch, I decided to take a walk outside the castle. I joined Jerry Musgrave and his wife. A young lady was kind enough to offer us a ride to the Freteval Forest, some twenty-five kilometers away.

This trip to the forest was far less eventful than my last one had been. I walked up to the monument, which stood guard at the entrance where we were in

Lou Greenburgh beside the Forest of Freteval Memorial.

hiding in 1944. At various times a total of one hundred fifty-two Allied airmen had been hiding on this spot right under the noses of the German Army.

The actual ceremony took place Sunday morning. We all went out to the site of the monument. There it was, as it had been the day before, but now the obelisk was flanked from behind by flags of the allied nations. I was one of several people who laid wreaths at its base.

I was the master of ceremonies and guest speaker at the banquet that evening. Truth is, I can't remember what I spoke about. I expect that I thanked my hosts for their part in rescuing allied airmen and praised them for their heroism.

Next day was an opportunity for me to wander about Paris. I was looking for the residence of one of the Resistance people I had met during the war. I stopped a man in the street to ask him for directions.

Imagine my surprise when I discovered that the man I had stopped was a cousin of mine who I hadn't seen since before the war.

As most tourists in France probably do, I rode to the top of the Eiffel Tower. Most of the people up there were from Canada.

Souvenir of Freteval: a commemorative envelope.

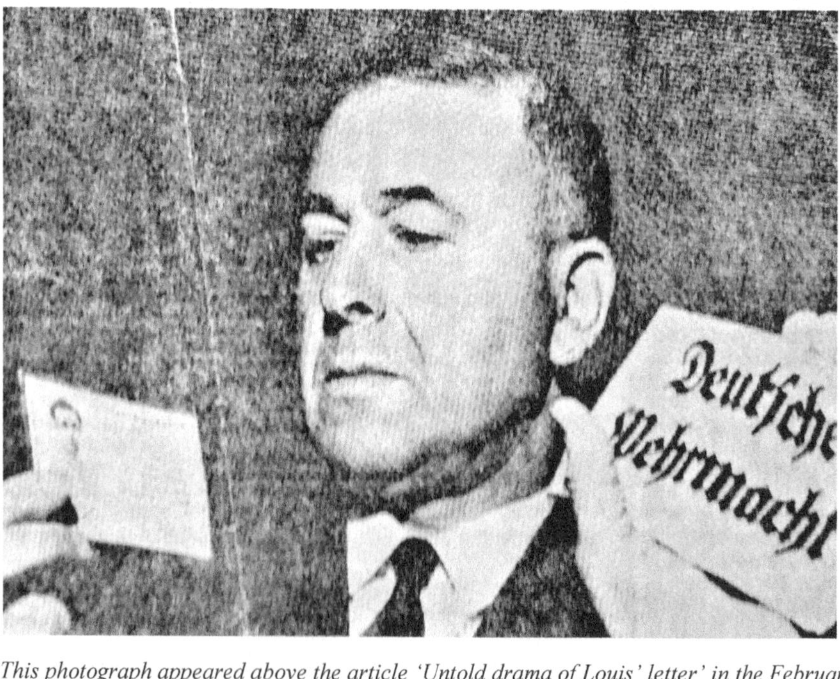

This photograph appeared above the article 'Untold drama of Louis' letter' in the February 11th 1967 edition of the Winnipeg Tribune. The newspaper article is reproduced overleaf.

268

Untold drama of Louis' letter

by
BERT BRUSER

Among his war mementos, Louis Greenburg, of Winnipeg, has a letter from the Air Ministry in London, England.

The letter informs him that a certain M. Reant from the village of Wavignies, died in a Nazi concentration camp at Buchenwald.

Behind that letter lies a fascinating, untold story. M. Reant, was a member of the Maquis — the French resistance fighters — who sarificed their lives to save Allied airmen downed in Nazi-occupied France.

On June 11, the surviving members of the Maquis will unveil a plaque to the pilots they rescued. One of the few Canadians invited to the ceremony at Chateaudun is Mr. Greenburg, a former RAF pilot who was awarded the Distinguished Flying Cross and bar by King George VI in Buckingham Palace.

Now a probation officer working with Indians in the Inter-Lake region Mr. Greenburg is a shy, modest man, reluctant to talk about the heroism which earned him the medals.

He's proud of the fact that as a Jew he fought the Nazis, but he's far more inclined to extol the courage of the Maquis.

At his home on Scotia St., recently, he rummaged through his souvenirs, and the memories started to come back . . .

Flying on D-Day

It was on D-Day, while he was flying his Lancaster on a bombing raid in northern France, that he ran into trouble.

His right wing caught fire and he ordered his crew to bail out.

But, being Jewish, he had no desire to jump down behind the Nazi lines, and he attempted to fly the plane back to England by himself.

An enemy fighter caught up with him, though, and he bailed out of the escape hatch just before the plane blew up.

It was the middle of the night. He landed in a field 50 yards from a German truck convoy.

After lying in the bush for two days, he walked for about 20 miles until he came to a small French village.

At the outskirts he met an old man, who led him to two others sitting in a shack.

"You're lucky you came to us," the men told him. "Anywhere else you'd have been turned over to the Nazis."

For the next four months Louis was led from village to village through the intricate web of the Maquis organization, always keeping one step ahead of the Nazis.

He was given a false German identity card and disguise, sometimes as a priest, sometimes as an old lady or as a bum.

Many of the people who helped him were captured and killed by the enemy.

Once he was handed over to two German soldiers who took him to a large building surrounded by other German soldiers. There he was turned over to the French police, who worked with the Nazis.

Many close calls

But it turned out that the head of the police in that town was also a member of the Maquis, and Louis was saved.

There were many other close calls:

One morning, in the village of Wavignies, Oise, at the house of M. Reant Louis was wakened by the sound of machine gun fire. The town was full of Germans, making house to house checks for allied airmen.

Louis was hidden in the attic of the house and covered with logs.

"Then I heard jack boots coming up the stairs. Soon I saw a boot only a foot away from me," Louis recalled.

The soldiers left the house, but soon Mme. Reant rushed up the stairs, shouting at Louis to leave immediately.

Louis jumped out a window and landed in a mass of nettles. From these he watched German soldiers leading a group of men — among them M. Reant — into a van.

He wandered through the countryside again. At one farm he was told that many of the people who had helped him had been shot.

"I had almost given up when I walked into a farm and a nine-year-old girl kissed me. Her mother told me to stay until the end of the war. But the invasion of Europe was on, and the Germans were panicking and searching the French countryside.

It was decided that Louis should be taken to Paris. He was dressed as a priest and taken to the railway station. He was ordered to follow, but not speak to, a 19-year-old girl.

After taking the train to Paris, he was led to Montmartres, 24 Rue D'esponites, where he and another Allied airman were looked after by a Mlle. Epechere.

One morning she took them to church. On the way back, two German SS officers stopped the other airman. Unable to speak French or German, he could merely gesticulate with his hands.

Sound of gunfire

Louis wanted to run away, but the little woman ran at the officers and punched them each on the back. She told them to leave her deaf and dumb brother alone. The officers went on their way, laughing.

"She deserved the Victoria Cross for that," says Louis.

After a month he was taken out of Paris. A few miles away, he was put on a French communications truck, apparently employed by the Germans.

The Germans were recruiting everybody and Louis was given an arm band signifying that he was in the German army.

The truck passed a number of German sentries and entered the Foret de Freval. There, in the woods, Louis found about 50 other allied airmen.

The Germans had the forest surrounded, and the men expected they would move in at any time.

One morning they woke up to the sound of gun fire and "a thousand motors," and thought the game was up.

But the Americans had arrived, and the airmen were rescued.

Now, 22 years later, the Maquis are holding a ceremony to commemorate the deeds of the past.

Louis, as possibly the only Jewish pilot invited, would like to go.

"With all this business about Von Thadden and neo-nazism, maybe if I went people would remember better what happened," Louis says.

Chapter 25: The Probation Service

My mother passed away shortly after my return from France. I was with her in the hospital just before she died. She told me that I was no longer in the Will, that she had signed everything over to my stepfather and his sons.

"But Ma!" I gasped, "What about the money I lent you? I don't want anything else, but that was my money!"

"Money?" she replied, "I could die and all you can think about is money?"

I left the room. I never saw my mother alive again, did not attend her funeral, and have never visited her grave.

452 Scotia Street,
WINNIPEG,
Manitoba.

22nd January, 1968.

Dear Sir:

As I received no reply to my registered letter to you, once again I repeat my letter as follows:

Before my mother died she told me that you influenced her into pledging her revenue property to one of your sons.

I wish you luck and bear no malice. However, in 1952 and in 1953 I worked in your store for ten months. Sometimes eleven hours a day without remuneration. Promises that I would get paid with interest were never kept.

I loaned you a considerable amount of money and was always told that the money was put into the house, and I would greatly benefit by the Will. Some months ago my mother recalled that at eight years of age I was tied with ropes, brutally beaten and thrown into a disused jail cell where I lay bound for hours. She mentioned how you forced me to leave home at the age of sixteen, but said it would soon be made up with interest.

In 1946, because I was an R.A.F. Officer with fairly high decorations, you welcomed me and borrowed a substantial amount of my war service gratuity. Then the welcome mat wore out. Though it cost me a fortune, I still could not buy my way into my mother's family.

You will recall, (in my wife's presence) one of your sons stated that if anything happened to me you would be stuck with my family. I can assure you your fears are groundless, my children hardly know who you are, and they want nothing from you.

I have constantly asked you to pay for the loans and the work I did for you, but always "when business is better" or "it's in the Will". I do recall on one occasion you gave me $500.00 or $1,000.00, I cannot remember which, but this would only cover about three or four month's work in your store.

I now realize how you and my mother duped me on the strength of the Will. She was very weak and always tried to appease you at my expense, otherwise I would have taken earlier action.

I try to understand your special feelings for your own sons, but I too have a family and feel that the least you can do is to pay me for past labour and the unaccountable sums of money you glibly took.

You recall that before Christmas 1966 my mother stated in your presence your $1500.00 promissory note in my favour would be paid. After years of reminding you, this note has not yet been honored. It was omitted in my previous letter you did give me $100.00 in October 1965, which I am prepared to deduct from the note. I expect payment of $1400.00 forthwith.

Yours truly,

Louis Greenburg.

LG*ej.

The response I received from the above letter was a telephone call from one of my half-brothers. He told me that the family was holding a meeting to discuss the letter and that I was expected to attend. I did.

There was no mention of the fact that my stepfather had swindled me or that I was entitled to any sort of compensation. One brother announced that he had shown a copy of the letter to a psychiatrist who felt that I should be "put away" on the basis of it. My wealthy brothers, who had had all of the advantages which I had been denied, stated that they would fight me in court and were prepared to spend a fortune in legal fees. Not one of them was prepared to contribute a penny towards making good his father's debts.

I tried to take my stepfather to court, but the statute of limitations had run out on most of the debt and, besides, very little of it was documented. I had just handed it over and he had taken it.

When my own son was about eleven, my wife and I took on a foster son named Wallace Spooner, who was thirteen. Wally was to stay with us for several years, and we would have adopted him if he had not declined our offer. It made for quite a large family, what with my own four kids. We also had a dog, a cat, and a guinea pig.

Wally was mechanically inclined and was always taking things apart. It's cliché, but after reassembling my lawn mower he had some parts left over. We had an outboard motor boat in those days and Wally loved to tinker with the engine.

All was not smooth sailing with Wally. He used to play my wife and I against each other and was the source of many heated arguments.

I was greatly relieved when Wally turned seventeen and enlisted in the army. With his mechanical aptitude, he was well suited for a career as a mechanic and he was soon employed as the driver of a staff car. He used to drive the generals around.

He could have done very well if he had stayed in the Armed Forces but such was not to be. He took his discharge after just a couple of years then asked me to help him find a job.

What could I do? I spoke to a friend of mine who had a bit of pull and got Wally a job at the aerodrome near Island Lake, a community in Northern Manitoba. If he'd played his cards right he could have worked his way up to assistant manager. He came to work drunk one day and smashed all of the windows in the control tower.

I was terribly embarrassed, because a friend of mine had given Wally the job. Even then, they didn't fire him. I begged him not to do anything crazy like that again. Shortly after the windows had been fixed, he came back and smashed them all again. This time, the government let him go.

He couldn't understand why he had been fired. "I didn't break them while I was on duty," he complained, "I was off duty at the time."

There was nothing more I could do for him, other than slip him some money now and them. I gradually watched him deteriorate, until one day the damn fool mixed the wrong type of drugs and ended his life. He was twenty years old.

I had a direct line to the Home for Boys. If a judge sentenced a boy to two years in the Home for Boys, the Director of the Home would get a hold of me to find the kid a foster home. If the kid wasn't dangerous, why keep him in jail?

My boss found out about this and told me that such communication should be done through him. The judges, however, didn't want to create another bureaucracy and ensured that my direct liaison with the Home's director was carried on. The judge from Grand Rapids wrote a letter to the Director of the Home for Boys, instructing him to release kids into my custody. He wanted me to look after the kids who were in the Home for Boys.

I was very, very, busy. In addition to my own work, the Social Services were asking me to find foster homes for them, too. You'd think that they could find their own foster homes. People often told me that I was a resource to be used. I once retorted, "You're not going to 'use' me!"

As proud as I was of my foster home program, it wasn't the main thrust of my job. In fact, I did most of that stuff on my own time. My official function was to monitor probation cases and to write presentence reports.

I always prided myself on writing reports which were objective and clear. I've never had a report rejected by a judge and many judges have specifically requested me to prepare their reports.

The probation service grew, with increasing numbers of Social Workers and Probation Officers. The bureaucracy increased right along with it. All of these people were given cars, secretaries, and what have you. I was promoted to the position of 'Senior Probation Officer,' which would now be called a 'Director of Probation,' and had a staff of Probation Officers working under me.

That's when my troubles began. I won't go into detail, but there was a lot of politics and back stabbing. Some of my staff objected to the fact that I didn't have a Master of Social Work Degree, although I don't know what that has to do with probation. Did they think I didn't know about child abuse?

Another thing which didn't help my popularity was the fact that when I felt a meeting was necessary, I would hold it in my office. Other Probation Officers and Social Workers liked to hold meetings at places like Gull Harbour Resort. That way they could discuss the 'poor people' and ways to cut crime in comfort, all at the tax payers' expense.

Mind you, I didn't boycott conferences organized by other people. I attended a conference in Vancouver, for example. I brought along my whole family, including the dog, Princy. We drove along the highway I had helped to build and spent the nights in camp spots. It was a bit of a nostalgic time for me, especially when I spotted the Spiral Tunnels. I stopped the car and let the family out for a look at them. They were on the other side of the gorge, far below us, and they looked like the plaster carvings of a model train set.

I also attended a conference down in Los Angeles. I was there on a 'fact finding committee' for Legal Aid. I brought two of my daughters, Heather and Cindy to that one. We saw Disneyland and Universal Studios and Tijuana, Mexico, so the government's money was well spent. I don't see how it helped fight crime or poverty, though.

I was at a conference where a colleague admitted having some trouble with one of his own kids. All of the ‘experts’ offered their professional advice. After listening to a bunch of psychological theories, I made my contribution. “Tell me,” I asked, “have you tried giving him a good kick in the ass?” Some of the older ladies told me that my comment was the only sensible one they had heard during the whole meeting.

One of my accomplishments in Selkirk was the establishment of the Selkirk Friendship Centre of which I was a founding member. I was also a member of the Selkirk Rotary Club. I worked with several people who later rose to prominence. I shared my office with Howard Pauly, who later became Premier of Manitoba, and we worked together on the Friendship Centre. I knew Ed Schreyer quite well. In fact, my daughter Linda once played the piano in his house and his wife, Lilly, once knocked on my door at home and invited me out for a sandwich. When Ed became the Premier of Manitoba, he held several garden parties and I attended some of them. I rather lost touch with him, though, when he was appointed Governor General of Canada. I also knew Garry Doer, the future Premier of Manitoba, back when he was a Probation Officer.

After several years working out of Selkirk, I was transferred to Winnipeg. There was a pleasant little farewell gathering for me on October 27, 1976, and I said my goodbyes. There were about seventy guests at the testimonial dinner and Tommy Hillhouse, a Member of Parliament, presented me with an engraved silver tray on behalf of the lawyers of Selkirk. I also received a plastic model of a Stirling and a gold digital wrist watch. I then headed for my new assignment at the Law Courts building in Winnipeg.

When I arrived in Winnipeg, I found that there had been a mistake. I had no office and no one was expecting me. I called up my old friend Howard Pauly, who was Attorney General at the time, and he said he would look into it for me.

To make a long story short, I spoke to Judge Harold Gyles and told him my situation. He said, "Don't worry, Lou, I'll take care of things for you." He found me an office and set me up as the Court Liaison Officer.

Not long after I had begun working in Winnipeg, I had a very difficult report to write. It was about a professional killer known as 'The Ox'.

I discussed the case with a psychiatrist who had been assigned to it. "I'm not going to diagnose him." the doctor informed me, "He'd kill me!" The doctor

Tribute To Lou Greenburgh

On Wednesday, October 27th, 1976, friends and colleagues of Mr. Lou Greenburgh gathered at the Pernation Restaurant to honour Lou on the occasion of his promotion to the Law Courts in Winnipeg. Mr. Lou Greenburgh has been the Senior Probation Officer for the Town of Selkirk since 1962. Lou is one of the pioneer members of the Manitoba Probation Service, and he previously worked in Winnipeg and Portage la Prairie.

Lou has been an active member of our community as one of the founding members of the Selkirk Friendship Centre and a former member of the Selkirk Rotary.

Mr. Greenburgh is married with four children. Deeply committed to his work, he and his wife, Vi, took a foster son into their home on a temporary basis and he remained for four and one-half years. Having first-hand knowledge of the problems and joys of being a foster parent, Lou was able to be a valuable resource for social workers and probation officers in setting up other foster home placements. Mr. Greenburgh will be missed by the many children he has helped over the years.

Lou's life has been interesting and varied. He flew with the Royal Air Force from 1938-1952 and rose to the rank of Acting Squadron Leader. He still holds the rank of Flight Lieutenant in the Canadian Air Reserve. Mr. Greenburgh was a war hero, having twice been personally decorated with the Distinguished Flying Cross and Bar by King George VI. Mr. Greenburgh saw extensive action over Europe as a bomber pilot, and was shot down three times. This contributed to his receiving both the Order of the Goldfish and Order of the Groundhog. After the war he was involved in transporting troops from the Far East and he also flew on the Berlin Airlift. Prior to joining the Probation Service, he managed his own hairdressing shop on Portage Avenue, where he was known as "Monsieur Louis". He later became a guard at Stony Mountain Penitentiary.

Gary Hindle, who will be Lou's successor in Selkirk, acted as master of ceremonies at the dinner that turned into a bit of a "roast". Marvin Benson gave the toast to Mr. Greenburgh and a few anecdotes, along with a few related experiences he'd had with Lou during the years they'd worked together.

Tommy Hillhouse then made a presentation on behalf of the barristers of the Town of Selkirk, with whom Lou had worked throughout his career in Selkirk, and obviously he was well respected by them, as both Mr. Hillhouse and later Mr. Jack Walker praised his work. The barristers presented the Greenburghs with a silver pitcher and goblet set.

Gary Hindle then gave a resume of the work that Mr. Greenburgh had accomplished during his work with the department, and again the affair turned into a bit of a "roast". Mr. Hindle then presented Lou with a scale plastic model of the plane he flew during the war, and then more seriously, a gold digital wrist watch.

It was then Mr. Greenburgh's turn to speak, and without any Schmetzkiepetzking around, as he often put it, he very nicely got even, then closed on a serious sincere note, saying "I'm deeply touched, and my family and I are really blessed with having so many friends."

Mr. Greenburgh has had a long and distinguished career and we wish him well in his new position in Winnipeg.

Lou Greenburgh posed briefly after the formal part of the evening, as he mingled with the 70 or more guests at the Pernation. Above [left to right], Maurice April, Probation Officer for Stonewall; Vic Siran, Probation Officer for Ashern; Shelly Watson, one of the testimonial dinner organizers and a co-worker of Mr. Greenburgh's; Lou Greenburgh; Gary Hindle, Probation Officer for Selkirk and Gimli, and Mr. T. P. Hillhouse.

Photo by Ron Scherza

strongly advised me not to prepare the presentence report. He said," 'The Ox' would kill you if you wrote an unfavorable report."

I decided to interview 'The Ox' and entered an interview room at Stony Mountain. On the opposite side of a glass barrier sat one of the biggest men I had ever seen. Beneath his short, sandy colored hair was a man with the physique and facial features of 'Jaws', a giant villain featured in 'James Bond' movies.

His face was impassive. He leaned forward and pointed a finger at me. "I want you to write me a good report." He growled.

I set my jaw. "Don't worry," I replied, "I'll write you a good report."

I knew that an accurate report would be my death warrant if 'The Ox' ever got free. After outlining the pertinent facts, however, I concluded with the following recommendation: "In my opinion, there is no hope of rehabilitation for this man and he should be locked away for the public safety."

I told my son, Edwin, about this case and informed him that my life might hang on the Judge's decision. He agreed that I had done the right thing in recommending a long jail term and told me that he wanted to attend the trial.

'The Ox' had pleaded guilty to attempted murder and so the trial did not require a jury. The defense attorney was almost comical, asking for clemency. He informed the judge that his client had been in Junior Achievement as a youth and had never relied on the state for his support.

The trial did not take long and the judge soon gave the order to rise for sentencing. I felt my pulse rate increase and hoped for a good, stiff sentence. I glanced over to the prisoner, who seemed to dwarf even the large plain clothes policemen who were his guards. His hands were secured behind his back.

"Mr.--," the Judge began, "you are a dangerous man. According to Mr. Greenburgh's report, there is no hope of rehabilitation. I am therefore sentencing you to the maximum sentence available for your offence, ten years in a high security prison, without parole."

I exhaled with relief. I would be seventy years old before 'The Ox' was released. With a sullen expression on his face, he was led out of the courtroom.

I had some good news about six months later. 'The Ox' had been killed in a fight with another prisoner.

As I used to say, "Crime does pay. I've got a job."

It was in the early 1970's that a good friend of mine, Les Allison, began to trace the personal histories of Canadians such as myself who had gone over to England and served with the Royal Air Force. He felt that it was a part of Canadian history which was being overlooked by historians and he wanted to make sure it was recorded. He spent a fortune of his own money travelling across the country interviewing people, studying documents, and trying to get some sort of government support. He even went over to England at his own expense.

Government support was not forthcoming. Those were the days of military 'unification' and 'constitutional patriation', when the Canadian Government was trying (with considerable success) to break all ties with England and British tradition. Perhaps they thought that a book about Canadians fighting together with the British in R.A.F. units harkened back to the days of colonialism. I don't know. But I do know that Les received no financial support from the government and many bureaucratic roadblocks were put in his way.

In spite of his frustrations, Les produced a remarkable book which he entitled Canadians in the Royal Air Force and published himself in 1978. I was surprised and a bit flattered at the coverage Les gave me. Mine was the first story in the book and it was also the longest story. He concluded it by saying, "This story on Lou is very short and many events and details have had to be left out or only briefly touched on. It would take a full book to do justice to his career of adventure and life!"[70]

Edwin was showing considerable interest in aviation, although his poor uncorrected vision made a career as a pilot out of the question. I took him to air shows at every opportunity and he listened avidly as I recounted my own adventures.

When Edwin was fifteen years old, and therefore old enough to begin training for a glider pilot's license, I drove him out to the Winnipeg Gliding Club. The club operated from a small field near the town of Pigeon Lake on Manitoba's 'White Horse Plains'. He sat in the front seat of a Schweitzer 222 high wing glider and beamed from ear to ear as the tow plane took up the slack and pulled the glider into the air.

A few years later, when Edwin was certified for passengers, he would twice take me up for a ride in one of those flimsy fabric scooters.

Before our first flight together Jeff Tinkler, the 'Duty Instructor,' took me aside. "Remember," Jeff said in his quiet, gentle manner, "Ed is the pilot, not you. Let him do the flying."

Edwin sat in the front seat of the Schweitzer 233 with me in the seat behind him. I was never comfortable as a passenger in a light aircraft but things seemed to be going well until it was time to land.

I had watched many gliders in a landing circuit and had a pretty good idea of what to expect. Edwin had apparently misjudged our altitude. I could see that we were much too high and I had the urge to demand that he lose some

---

[70] *Allison, Les, 'Canadians in the Royal Air Force', op. cit., page 5.*

altitude. I remembered what Jeff had told me about letting Edwin fly the airplane, though, so I restrained myself. I was biting my tongue but I didn't know how long I could keep silent.

I reached my breaking point and was about to order Edwin to get lower when he looked over his shoulder and calmly stated "Okay, now. We've got three planes landing ahead of us so I'm going to come in high and look around a bit before we go in."

I realized that Edwin knew what he was doing and calmed down. I found out later that things were less calm on the ground. Bunty was watching the flight and heard someone say, "There's going to be a crash! There's too many planes coming in at once. Here comes Ed and his dad!"

Two gliders had landed beside each other and the third plane had landed in front of the one on the left. Ed flew low over the plane on the right and gently landed in front of it, onto the one remaining spot on the field in which there was room to land.

I had often told Edwin he was wasting his money on gliding and that I couldn't see the sense in his paying to do something that I had been paid to do. He never listened to me, kept on gliding, and was crazy enough to go parachuting a couple of times. He kept encouraging me to get into gliding, saying that I'd enjoy being in a cockpit again, but I told him that to me flying an airplane was like driving a car.

I often accompanied Edwin out to the gliding club. He was certified for cross country flying in the spring of 1979 and was anxious to make his first cross country flight. Actually, Edwin had made one cross country flight already but it happened by accident. He was struggling for altitude in a thermal (the rising air currents that keep gliders aloft over the prairies) and was blown downwind so far that he lost sight of the field. A 'cloud street' (a row of cumulous clouds) had formed between his position and the field so Edwin was able to maintain altitude while finding his way back by flying directly against the wind.

I agreed to act as Edwin's recovery crew, which meant that I would use my car to tow the trailer needed to retrieve a glider that had 'landed out'. We drove to the field every weekend but the gliding conditions weren't very good. Edwin would ready CF-KPP, the Schweitzer 126 low wing single seater, but would leave in disappointment when the thermals didn't materialize. It was July 21 before Edwin was able to catch a decent thermal. Even then, the conditions weren't great with a cloud ceiling only 4,200 feet above ground. There was a cloud bank just within gliding range, however, so Edwin keyed the microphone of his radio and said "Pidgeon Lake Ground this is KPP. I'm going."

The glider made it to the cloud bank. Unfortunately, the plane was down to only 1,000 feet above ground, the point of no return at which the club rules required that a glider pilot begin his landing procedure. Edwin had some 'zero sink', which meant there was enough thermal activity to maintain altitude but not enough to climb. He worked the zero sink for a few minutes but then it was gone and the glider began to sink.

The recommended protocol was to find a fallow field, which would be solid black in color. Edwin couldn't see a solid black field but he did see one that was black with little green speckles. He chose that for his landing site. Unlike powered aircraft, the landing circuit for a glider didn't include a crosswind leg. Edwin therefore entered his downwind leg and went through a brief landing checklist. The last item on the checklist was to pull out the handle that engaged the 'spoilers', an air brake system in the form of flaps that popped up on the upper side of each wing and disrupted airflow to hasten the glider's descent.

Edwin made a 90 degree turn to the right onto his base leg and then another right turn onto his final approach. His altitude would have been about 300 feet above ground.

Just as he turned onto final, Edwin looked down his flight path and saw a fence across the field. The fence wasn't crawling up or down the canopy but was keeping a steady bearing. My son knew what that meant.

There was no time to think so my son acted on instinct. He slammed the spoilers shut, pushed the stick forward and to the right and kicked hard right rudder. The plane whipped into a 360 degree turn and dropped about 200 feet. On a final approach!

Edwin steadied up on his original track at an altitude of about a hundred feet. He was no longer in danger of hitting the fence but now there was a telephone line stretching across his glide path!

The tendency in a situation like that would be to pull back on the stick to extend your glide path and increase your chances of clearing the obstacle. Doing that so close to the ground would be inviting the aircraft to stall and crash. Edwin forced himself to keep the stick forward to maintain his airspeed. Pilots had been known to survive crashing into telephone lines (his own father had survived such a crash) but to stall at that altitude would be fatal.

The telephone lines slid under the glider at a distance of maybe ten or twenty feet. CF-KPP came to rest and Edwin found himself knee deep in sunflowers. The radio wouldn't reach the gliding club without any altitude so Edwin borrowed the farmer's telephone and gave us directions.

The horizontal stabilizer of a light aircraft can be an effective tool for decapitating sunflowers. The farmer wasn't very impressed so Edwin gave him $50 to cover the crop damage. My son then began disassembling the aircraft.

Meanwhile, I was driving all over Hell's half acre trying to find the landing site. I eventually saw some people on the side of the gravel road and pulled over to ask directions. They took one look at the trailer marked 'Winnipeg Gliding Club' and said "We know who you're looking for".

Every autumn the Winnipeg Gliding Club held an awards banquet. Edwin returned from the 1979 awards banquet with a glass beer mug that bore the club's logo. Much to his surprise, it was awarded to him for what the Master of Ceremonies called "The most courageous cross country".

I officially retired from the Manitoba Probation Service on Friday, March 13, 1981. A marvelous banquet was held for me that evening at the International Inn. I was honored to find that some prominent people were slated to be guest speakers; the Chief Judge, Harold Gyles, was one of the speakers, and so was the head of the Law Society. Tommy Hillhouse, the old legislative guy, was there. Garry Doer was there. Many of the Provincial Judges were there. I tell you, I had so many people there that it really made me feel good. In all, about two hundred people showed up.

After we had been served our dinner, the roast began. Many jokes were told at my expense (most of them hitting a little too close to the truth!) but some nice things were also said. I was presented with a pair of moccasins which the Mayor of The Pas had sent down for the occasion.

Bill Norie, the Mayor of Winnipeg, stepped onto the dais and announced that he had a special award for me. It was the City of Winnipeg Award for Outstanding Citizenry. It was a great big thing, a framed document with a gold seal. I came up and he presented it to me. You know, in some ways that award means more to me than my D.F.C.s. It was recognizing years of work, not just a few moments of stress, and it makes me feel like I did make some sort of contribution to society.

As the evening drew to a close, Harold Gyles made the closing remarks. His speech, which was punctuated by waves of laughter from the audience, went as follows:[71]

'We are here to honor Lou Greenburgh after 20 years as a probation officer. He was hired by Ivor Halliday, who a few of you will remember, in 1961 (I believe). This was two years before I was appointed to the Bench and had the

[71] *Speech presented by His Honour Harold Gyles, Chief Judge, Provincial Court of Manitoba, March 13, 1981. Transcribed from a written copy of the actual speech.*

privilege of meeting Lou. ... A Master of Social Work was not a prime requisite. Lou always thought that M.S.W. stood for Main Street Wasp.

'Actually, for a semi-illiterate with a Grade VI education, Lou has functioned quite well. His lack of formal education has been enhanced by a wealth of life experiences. He served in the Air Force during the War. Unfortunately, he was on our side!

'After the war he did a number of things before joining the Probation Service. He worked as a correctional officer at the Penitentiary. Doesn't that boggle your mind - leaky Lou the Screw! The Saskatchewan Rough Riders had better guards. It's like putting Dracula in charge of the blood bank.

'He also variously owned three beauty salons. With a face like his for advertising, no wonder they all went bankrupt. The incredible thing, Lou, is how could someone of your ethnic persuasion lose money on a bankruptcy?

'What is even stranger is that he became a probation officer. I wasn't surprised to hear that a Jew had been made a cardinal in the Catholic Church in France, but what kind of a racket is probation? He even sucked in Norm Swartzman and Phil Simon.

'Lou's pre-sentence reports, unencumbered by polysyllabic words, have become an art form. I seriously considered sending one of them down to Parker Bros in New York to see if they could make a game out of it - something to replace Monopoly. ...

'Lou's success as a probation officer was enriched by his being tri-lingual -- English, Hebrew and Profane. It was once rumored that he personally developed the "Interpersonal Maturity Level Classification System." As I recall, Lou referred to the "I level" somewhat differently, anatomically speaking.

'There are many fond Greenburgian memories. The informal foster home system. He would start from Grand Rapids and drop off a carload of waifs along the way. Unfortunately, he could never remember where he left the kids, which played havoc with those responsible for keeping records of such trivial matters.

'The John Howard Society never knew what to vote for unless Greenburgh the Director opposed it.

'I would be remiss if I failed to comment on the sartorial splendor which our guest of honor invariably displays. It would be flattering to suggest that he obtains his wardrobe from rejected CARE packages. It must take him hours to amass a complete set of raiment so that nothing matches except the color of both eyes. His favorite sports jacket was made out of old pipe cleaners and leaves you with an irresistible urge to strum a banjo.

'Finally, Lou, I will miss the jokes. Fortunately.'

Chapter 26: Memories

I settled down into a less than peaceful retirement. Things always seemed to be in a turmoil. I had my cats to look after and I was doing volunteer probation work. Things have always been pretty hectic for me with one crisis after another and it looks like things are going to stay that way.

Edwin had to miss my retirement dinner because he had been attending Canadian Forces Officer Candidate School out in Chilliwack British Columbia. Bunty and I flew out to watch him graduate as a second lieutenant in the Navy.

He came home on leave shortly afterwards. I invited 'Second Lieutenant' Greenburgh to accompany me to a meeting of the Wartime Pilots and Observers Association at the Officers' Mess at Canadian Forces Base Winnipeg. Of course he wore his uniform.

I stopped the car when we reached the entrance to the base. The commissionaire at the gate came to attention and saluted smartly. I was puzzled by that because he had never saluted me before. I then saw my son returning the salute and felt some parental pride.

I introduced my son to the other members of the Wartime Pilots. Amongst them was Murray Peden, the fellow Stirling pilot who wrote A Thousand Shall Fall.

Edwin pulled a fast one on me. I had driven him to the airport and was having a coffee with him as he waited to board an aircraft for the flight back to the Navy base at Esquimalt BC. His flight was called and he rose to leave. Just as we were saying our goodbyes, he reached into his pocket and pulled out a folded document, which he handed to me. "Here, Dad." he said, "I bought you a year's membership in the Winnipeg Gliding Club. Well, I've got to go. I'll see you!"

What could I do? I didn't want to waste the money my son had spent on my gliding club membership. I went out to the gliding club's little aerodrome (which was only a grass strip with a few gliders, a couple of small tow planes, and a hanger) and told them what had happened. They all knew what my son had planned and had a good laugh at his little joke.

The gliding season had just begun and there were a few young girls there who were just learning how to fly. I saw them talking amongst themselves and knew they were amused at the sight of an old guy like me starting out as a student.

I climbed into the front seat of a Schweitzer 233, a high winged tail dragger which the club used for training and possibly the same plane that I had ridden in with my son. Somebody had to hold the nose down while I climbed in. Otherwise, my weight would have caused the nose to drop abruptly. It made my old Stearman look like a 747. There were only four instruments on the whole instrument panel. Oh yes, and a piece of yarn taped to the outside of the canopy to serve as a crude turn and bank indicator. Fritz Stevens, my instructor, helped me with my straps then climbed into the back seat.

Following the instructor's directions, a club member tested the release mechanism and then hooked up the tow line which ran from the tow plane ahead of us. He then ran over to the wing tip which rested on the ground and picked it up. A glider only has one main wheel, so a 'wing runner' has to balance the aircraft to keep it level during the early stages of takeoff.

Fritz gave a 'thumbs up' signal and the tow plane began to take up the slack. When the line was taught, the wing runner waved an arm in a circle and the tow pilot gunned his engine. We were pulled into the air like a water skier is pulled to the surface of a lake.

We must have forgotten something, I thought, as the glider began to climb. There must be more to do than this. When you're taking off in a powered airplane you watch the revs and the constant speed and you adjust the mixture control, everything. Here we were sitting back with the pilot just holding the stick, just holding it!

When we reached the release height of 2,000 feet above ground, the instructor told me to pull the red knob in the middle of my instrument panel. There was a loud 'pop,' like a small gun being fired, as the tow line released under tension. I watched the end drop away below as the tow plane dived to the left and the glider banked to the right.

After some brief directions, the Fritz turned the stick over to me and asked me to try some coordinated turns. "Wow!" he exclaimed after I had performed some perfect maneuvers, "I can see you've flown before."

When we had landed, Fritz said, "You know, if something had happened to me up there, I bet you could have landed the plane yourself." I thought about the last time I had landed a glider, a large glider with four dead engines. He encouraged me to sign some club documents which would be required before I could go solo. I saw no rush, so I put off signing them for a couple of weeks. When I did sign them, the instructor told me, "Now you can go solo. You could have soloed after your second flight."

I must admit, I had some fun in gliders. Norm Taylor, another instructor, was in the seat behind me. He said, "You take it, Lou."

I pushed down the stick to gain speed, then pulled back before applying right pressure to the ailerons and kicked right rudder. The glider popped into a sharp stalled turn.

"Where did you learn that?!" Norm exclaimed. I was later given permission to do full aerobatics.

There weren't many people at the club who were allowed to do full aerobatics. One of the few, so to speak, was my old friend and C.O. in the Air Force Reserve, Archie Gittle. I used to enjoy seeing Arch out at the field. I am very sorry to say that Arch suffered a great personal tragedy. One of his sons was killed in a flying accident, and it hurt him deeply. Why must flying so often involve death?

I heard on the news recently that Jeff Tinkler was killed in a gliding accident. No one was able to explain how it could have happened, but somehow his glider collided with one under tow at an altitude of about a thousand feet. The second glider released and landed safely but Jeff dived in and crashed. His canopy was shattered and it may have been that he was knocked unconscious by the collision. The incident shocked his fellow club members, for Jeff was an excellent pilot with over twenty years of experience. It was the club's first fatal accident but, sadly, it would not be the last.

Jeff's wife, Hellen, used to come out to the field with Jeff. They would camp out in a little trailer together. Jeff had either retired from his job as an engineering professor or was nearing retirement. My deepest sympathy is for Hellen, who, I fear, will be facing a lonely retirement.

I told my son about the accident. He was very sorry, of course, for he had known Jeff quite well and had flown with him several times. He later told me that he had sent Hellen a bouquet of flowers. The reality of Jeff's death came home to Edwin a few days later when Hellen called him on the telephone to thank him for the flowers. "They were a great comfort to me." she quietly stated.

On October 14, 1990, while watching the evening news, I was shocked to hear that Arch Gittle had joined his son. According to the news broadcast, Archie's glider had dived to the earth immediately after releasing from the tow plane. This upset me, for Arch had been a good friend as well as a fellow pilot. He was probably the most seasoned pilot of the whole bunch.

My son contacted the gliding club to find out what had happened. The scenario went something like this: it had been "a takeoff gone bad". Archie's plane had been too far to the right of the tow plane. The tow pilot figured it was placing them in a dangerous situation so he released his end of the tow rope at an altitude of between sixty and a hundred and twenty feet.

The prescribed procedure in a case like that would have been for the glider pilot to simply dip his nose and land straight ahead in the cultivated field across the highway that defined the north end of the airfield. I don't know why Archie didn't do that. Maybe he was so used to his aircraft that he felt he could get away with something a little more exotic. I don't know. But I'm told that instead of landing straight ahead, Arch tried to make a one hundred and eighty degree turn to land back at the flight line.

Arch wasn't flying a stubby winged Schweitzer 126, he was flying a sailplane with a 56 foot wingspan. One of his wingtips touched the ground and his plane cartwheeled.

Remarkably, Archie's physical injuries were not that severe. He broke his ankle and had a few cuts and bruises. That's all. The club members made him as comfortable as possible while they waited for an ambulance. It took about half an hour because of their distance from the city. Archie arrived at the Health Sciences Centre, was treated for his injuries, and placed in a hospital bed. Two hours after the accident, while talking with his friends and family, Archie died of a heart attack. He was fifty-seven years old.[72]

I don't understand it. How can one person survive an operation over Berlin, flying home in an airplane riddled with bullet holes, while another person gets killed joy riding in a God-damned glider?

On a more cheerful note, I think my favorite gliding experience came as I was preparing to take a flight in the club's Schweitzer 126, a single seater. I had only been flying for a few weeks, so I guess it attracted some attention when I slipped on a parachute and strapped myself in. One of the young ladies who had started the same time as me wandered over and asked me what I was doing in the single seater.

I told her I was going up. She raced back to the group of friends who had laughed when they first saw me. She was pointing at me and their mouths were moving and I could see they were astounded by the thought that an old guy like me could solo before they did.

Contrary to a popular misconception, a glider does not depend on the 'wind' to stay aloft. However, a glider does require rising air currents and the secret to staying aloft is to find those rising air currents and stay in them.

The most common form of 'lift' in the Prairies is from thermals, rising masses of air which have been heated from warm patches on the ground. When a glider pilot has located a thermal, he or she will normally fly in a series of concentric circles intended to work the glider as close as possible to the thermal's core. There are several ways to locate a thermal.

I'll tell you about one of them. I was flying along in my glider, thinking that maybe I should do something about the rate of sink showing on my variometer (a sensitive vertical speed indicator). Floating majestically ahead of me was a bird of prey, a hawk or an eagle, golden brown in color. Around and around it went, behaving for all the world like a soaring glider.

I pointed my glider's nose in the direction of the spiraling bird. As I drew closer, the wings began to tremble as if with anticipation and the variometer needle moved from the 'sink' zone to the 'climb' zone. My altitude began to increase and I banked over to starboard to work the thermal I had just found. Or, I should say, the thermal my fellow soarer had just led me to.

Around we went, together. I looked past the starboard wingtip and there was the bird, flying in formation with me. It was a remarkable thing, man and bird coexisting peacefully in the bird's domain. Seeing that eagle in flight reminded me

---

[72] *Author's note: When I began this narrative, I knew I would tell about my father's lost comrades. I never expected to find myself describing the deaths of my own friends.*

of another eagle I had seen, years before, in man's domain. This was how eagles should be, soaring in the sky.

I flew for that summer but I didn't renew my membership. The club members kept in contact with me for a while, inviting me to club functions and encouraging me to write articles about flying, but I never did. I did, however, receive a memento from the club. They presented me with a glass beer mug identical to the one my son had received the year before. It was for being the oldest member to fly solo.

There was one further 'gliding incident' which I'd like to mention. On July 23, 1983, an Air Canada Boeing 767 ran out of fuel and made a forced landing at the abandoned airstrip at Gimli Manitoba[73]. I later had coffee with Bob Pearson, the pilot of the 'Gimli Glider' as the plane became known.

Bob and I discussed the similarities and differences of our respective forced landings. He complemented me on my exploit I the North Sea, which he had read about in Canadians in the Royal Air Force. "I was in broad daylight," he said, "and I was being controlled by the controller. What you did... I don't know how you did it."

I enjoyed gliding, but I think there are a lot more important things than personal pleasure. And I think the simple pleasures are the best. I guess the thing I get the most pleasure from is helping stray cats.

You know, Winnipeg winters can be brutal to a shelter-less animal. I remember one winter was just awful. Every day, a black cat would sit outside my house and cry. I felt sorry for him and used to leave food out. The cat was frightened of people, though, and he would never let me go near him. People used to tell me that he probably had a cozy burrow some place. I later found out that he had spent the winter living in a tire in a neighbor's back yard.

I became rather fond of 'Blackie', as I came to calling him, and I looked forward to the sight of him gobbling the food I would leave near my door. He actually came into the house once, as I held the door open, but he dashed out again as soon as he saw me.

Maybe I'm so sensitive about homeless animals because I've been there myself. I know what it's like, not having a home and having no one to turn to. It bothers me to see people who have beautiful homes and lots of money, but who wouldn't lift a finger to help a less fortunate creature.

I will never forget the day Blackie came to the house with a large strip of skin hanging from one of his hind legs. He must have been in a fight, or something, and his leg had been ripped right to the bone. I scooped him up and rushed him off

---

[73] *Hoffer, W. and M., "Free Fall, Readers' Digest condensed version, June 1989 issue Readers' Digest Magazine, page 145.*

Cockpit views from a Schweizer2-33 under aerotow. The photo above shows the author's 'best side'. Below is a good view of the Pigeon Lake field then used by the Winnipeg Gliding Club. The Assiniboine River is clearly visible to the south of the field; telephone wires and a highway stretched across the north. You can see the trees on either side of the runway. One of the most obstructed fields in the area, it was an interesting place to land. The photos were taken in 1978.

Schweizer 1-26 CF-KPP, the Winnipeg Gliding Club's single seater, sitting in the sunflower field where the author landed her on July 21st, 1979.

to the nearest veterinarian. I told the vet, "I don't care what it costs, just do whatever you have to do to make him better."

I think of all the things I've done, taking Blackie to the vet is the thing I'm the most proud of. His leg was bandaged up and he allowed me to nurse him back to health. He was never homeless again, and we became very good friends. He died a few years later, which hurt me bitterly, and I still miss him.

Although I couldn't replace Blackie, I could at least help some more stray cats. I presently have three, which is the limit allowed by a city bylaw, and I still leave food out for others. I know that one or two more have moved into my garage. I'd rather have them there than freezing to death outside. It breaks my heart to think of all the homeless animals who are suffering and dying. Where is God?

I had just turned seventy when I was diagnosed as having cancer of the prostate. I guess that means Ronald Reagan and I have something in common. I had the full gamut of radiation and chemicals and it was just awful.

I was lying on an examination table, stark naked and with my private parts under close examination. At least, I told myself, nobody here knows me. At least I have that much dignity left. "Oh, hello Mr. Greenburgh!" exclaimed a cheerful nurse.

It was Barbara Wedlake, a little girl who had grown up on my street.

The treatments were successful and the cancer went into remission but I am still examined regularly. My son once commented on the importance of my regular checkups. I told him that it didn't really matter, since I would rather die than go through those treatments again.

It was during my recovery that I received a letter from my daughter Anna, in England. She had written to inform me that my first wife had passed away. I also received a letter from a young lady named Adeline who, it turned out, was the daughter of my elder son. I had been a grandfather for almost twenty years without even knowing it.

Edwin was very interested in the letter from Adeline. She had been curious about her grandfather and so Edwin wrote her a long reply which included the information that I was recovering from cancer. This led to a visit from Anna and Joan in 1986 and a visit by Adeline the following year. I was excited to see my daughters and my granddaughter, but I must admit that my stamina was not what it had been and I found the visits very tiring. I am pleased that my little grandson, James Louis (who was born to Edwin and his wife, Heather, in 1988), will have some ties with his cousins in England.

In 1970, the first Commonwealth Aircrew Reunion was held in Winnipeg. I wrote the following 'Letter to the Editor,' which was published in the Winnipeg Free Press:

Air-crew reunion

I would like to mention a tradition that should make every Canadian feel ten feet tall.

On September 18, Winnipeg will host the last and greatest Commonwealth Wartime Aircrew Reunion. It is worldwide and represents the greatest gathering of wartime flyers ever assembled. The reunion will include some of the most famous names in military aviation history.

The years of painstaking preparation is unique in its magnitude, and is a tribute to Chairman Jack Johnstone C.M., and his committee. The reunion is a reflection of thousands of heroic stories, especially of Canadian airmen of two world wars. I recall that during the depression thousands of Canadian youngsters rode the rods, travelled at their own expense, and worked on cattle boats to travel to England to join the Royal Air Force. Many arrived in the U.K. with no money, and until they could be processed into the service had to work at menial jobs, such as laundries, warehouses and restaurants. Some of them, including myself, had to live in the odd flop house.
These Canadian boys made history and I believe no country could be more proud of their achievements.

The accomplishments of this small group were many times greater than any other similar company. They suffered 50 per cent casualties and earned over 600 decorations. Certainly the Battle of Britain might have been lost without their help. The 126 Canadians who flew Hurricanes and Spitfires in Fighter Command during this four month critical battle may well have turned a possible defeat into victory.

In Canada, can we not forget our petty disputes and remember the thousands who died in battle? Perhaps this may be one facet of what the reunion represents.

LOU GREENBURG

Winnipeg

The first reunion was followed by a second reunion in 1975 and a third reunion in 1989. As far as I was concerned, the war had been over for years and had passed into history, soon to be forgotten. These reunions helped stir past events into the present and I got much satisfaction from meeting some of my old comrades and discussing the war with people who understood.

I think it was the second or third reunion where Sarah Churchill spoke. She reminded us of her father's devotion to England and of his negotiations with the United States. "I'm not asking anything for myself," Winston Churchill had said

Lou Greenburgh with Sir Douglas Bader (right).

during a speech, "I'm asking for a million tons of steel! That's what I'm asking for!" He got it, too.

It was also on the second reunion that a bunch of us were interviewed on television. I told a bit about my navigator losing his parachute and about my ride in that communications repair truck enroute to Freteval. After the broadcast, people kept asking me what happened to the navigator.

Nothing, however, could match my experiences at the first reunion. I had the rare opportunity of having a photograph taken with both Douglas Bader and Germany's top fighter ace, Adolph Galland. I had another photograph taken, and to my delight discovered that James Doolittle, of the famous 'Doolittle Raid' had been in the background.

I sat down to a coffee with Adolph Galland. I told him about the night when Pat lost his parachute, how there was the heaviest concentration of enemy fighters I had ever seen and how you could see like broad daylight because there were so many flares. He said he could remember that night and that his score had been quite high. He described one bomber going down out of control, the whole airplane on fire. I told him that it could have been me.

Galland gave a speech in which he stated, "The war ended in the only proper manner. The fact that I can get up here and talk to you guys shows that it happened for the best."

I liked Adolph Galland.

It was also at the first reunion when I met somebody who reminded me about Strommy, about how he had followed me around like a little puppy. The years had dulled my memory of Strommy and I felt the guilt once again.

It was in the early 1980's that Canada instituted a Gallantry Gratuities and Annuities Order to provide a monetary reward for Canadian servicemen who had been decorated in battle. I thought that I might be entitled to something because of my two D.F.C.s and sent in the appropriate application. The pension being offered amounted to about a hundred dollars a month per decoration. To my disappointment, I received the following reply:

Government of Canada Gouvernement du Canada
Pension Commission Commission des pensions

Ottawa, Canada
K1A 0P4

FILE 1987189

22 March 1984

Mr. Louis Greenburgh,
452 Scotia Street,
Winnipeg, Manitoba,
R2V1X7.

Dear Mr. Greenburgh:

An inquiry has been received on your behalf from the District Director (Pensions) in Winnipeg, concerning the payment of an annuity with respect to your Distinguished Flying Cross award.

The Gallantry Gratuities and Annuities Order provides for the payment of monetary benefits in respect to awards for gallantry earned while serving in the Canadian Armed Forces.

A review of your file indicates that you were granted the Distinguished Flying Cross while serving with the Royal Air Force. Accordingly, as you do not meet the service requirements, the Canadian Pension Commission is unable to consider your case. I suggest, therefore, that you contact the British Government, which is responsible for considering claims for gallantry awards with respect to service in the British Forces. The address is: Department of Health and Social Security, War Pensions Branch, Norcross, Blackpool, England, FY5 3TA.

It is regretted that the Commission cannot be of assistance to you in this particular matter.

Yours sincerely,
W.H. Eckley,

Director, Communications Division.

The planes of glory: Lancaster bomber leads the flight, followed by three Spitfires and, bottom, a Hurricane.

Wartime aircrew reunion shows strength of unity

Editor, The Tribune:

On Sept. 18, Winnipeg will host the last and greatest Commonwealth Wartime Air Crew Reunion. It is world-wide and represents the greatest gathering of wartime flyers ever assembled, including some of the most famous names in military aviation history.

The years of painstaking preparation are unique in their magnitude, and a tribute to chairman Jack Johnstone C. M., and his committee. But the reunion is a reflection of thousands and thousands of heroic stories, especially of Canadian airmen who shone in two world wars. I recall, as a teenager during the Depression, thousands of Canadian youngsters rode the rods, travelled at their own expense, worked on cattle boats to travel to England and join the Royal Air Force.

Many arrived in the U.K. with no money, and until they could be processed into the service, had to work at menial jobs, including places like laundries, warehouses, and restaurants. Some of them, including myself, had to live in the odd flop house. These Canadian boys made history, and I believe no country could be prouder of their achievements.

Les Allison of Roland, Manitoba, spent years of research and most of his life savings to write a book about Canadians in the RAF. His book contains the biographies of some 2,000 Canadians who joined the RAF mainly before the Second World War. It also contains 33 short stories of those from the air force who were involved in flying and combat which may be described as heroic, tragic, bizarre and controversial. Numerous statistics are included.

The accomplishments of this small group were many times greater than any other similar company. They suffered 50 per cent casualties, but earned over 600 decorations. Their contribution to the cause in the first year of the war, when trained men were so scarce, has never before been assessed. Certainly the Battle of Britain could have been lost without their help. The 128 Canadians who flew Hurricanes and Spitfires in fighter command during this four-month critical battle may well have turned possible defeat into our British victory.

Those many hundreds of Canadians who flew with Bomber and Coastal Command were in constant action against enemy targets in this same period. They suffered even higher casualties, mainly because they had to raid enemy air fields, invasion barges and military targets, plus even Berlin, quite often in daylight. They had no fighter protection because every fighter was desperately needed in Britain.

I recall in early 1940, I was transferred from 242 All-Canadian Squadron to an operational training unit at Bassingborne. I was a flight mechanic and detailed to work on twin engine Wellington bombers. At Bassingborne, I met another Canadian flight mechanic, Billy Young, and a Canadian pilot, Flying Officer Freddie Lanhart. Freddie and I became close friends and I spent extra time making sure that his engines and air frame on the Wellington were in top shape.

On the night of Aug. 18, 1940, I had just serviced the Wellington bomber and before take-off Freddie said that he had something important to tell me and we would get together when he came back from this flight. It was very dark and I watched him take off. The bomber had already left the ground when it collided with another Wellington and exploded. Billy Young and I watched in horror as the flames appeared to reach the sky.

Billy said he was grateful that he could not be accepted for air crew. We shared the same dormitory. Several days later in the middle of the night, when we were fast asleep, a lone German Ju-88 bomber dropped several bombs on our quarters. One bomb exploded in our dormitory and my bed and I were lifted bodily by the blast. Apart from a few scratches, I came out all right, but Billy Young was killed.

Here in Canada, can we not forget our petty disputes, and remember the thousands and thousands of Freddie Lanharts and Billy Youngs? Perhaps this may be one facet of what the reunion represents. Although Freddie Lanhart will be unable to attend, he is one of the millions of Canadians who made this country great. I believe it is the greatest country.

The British Commonwealth Air Training Plan was mainly based in Canada, and was the biggest air crew training force in the world. It was mostly Canadian staffed, and from 1940 to 1945, graduated over 131,000 air crew from 100 training schools.

And speaking of this great country, I found it very refreshing to watch on television our governor-general getting out of the stuffy rooms of Rideau Hall, coming to Selkirk, and playing baseball with the Selkirk boys for a charity benefit. To me, he is another good Canadian of Austro-German background.

Match this in any other country, if you can.

LOU GREENBURG

Winnipeg

I suppose I shouldn't have been surprised to receive the above reply since the Canadian Government has been trying, with success, to distance itself from England. To my disgust, in fact, Canada no longer recognizes such famous awards as the Victoria Cross, the Distinguished Service Order, and the Distinguished Flying Cross. They have been replaced by various levels of the Order of Canada. But during the war, Canadians (even in the R.C.A.F.) were

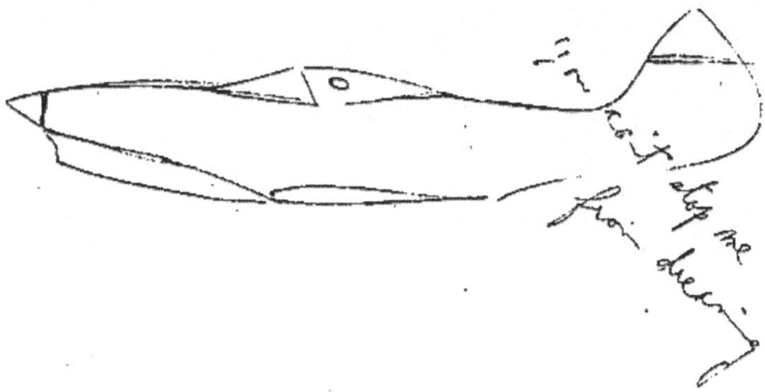

Sketch by Lou Greenburgh, found on the back of his 'Tails Up' magazine which he had saved from his pilot training days.

ultimately serving under British command. There were 'Canadian Air Force' guys flying in my squadron. In fact, my dear friend Tommy Penkuri was in the R.C.A.F. The only distinction was that Canadians had 'Canada' embroidered on their uniforms and were paid more money. Even R.C.A.F. guys who were decorated received their decorations from the British Government.

Actually, some aspects of this forgetfulness require a sense of humor. I was out for a walk in Kildonan Park, a well treed area near my house on the bank of the Red, when I met a young couple and we began to chat. I mentioned that the park reminded me of a forest deep in France, where I had been surrounded by German soldiers until my rescue by the Americans. I had to laugh as they walked away; the guy turned to his girl and remarked, "What a B.S.er!"

My son's naval career did not work out and he had moved back to Winnipeg in 1984. I gave him as much support as I could, which included lending/giving him a large portion of the down payment for a house and driving him to and from work while he was on evening shifts. I guess I enjoyed his company on those brief excursions but he kept pestering me to tell him more and more about my adventures and experiences. He had the silly notion that he was going to write a book about me but I told him to keep his mind on more important things.

Whenever I saw him, Edwin would pump me for more information. At times he even brought out a tape recorder and taped brief passages, which he said he would transcribe later. I warned him that he was putting in a lot of work for nothing, since nobody would be interested in reading my story.

He had a real paranoia for accuracy, too. I told him that the details didn't matter and that he should dramatize things to make them more interesting. "Dad," he once replied, (with a patronizing look) "how can you dramatize something like landing a Lancaster in the North Sea at night?"

I guess what finally got my cooperation was when he told me that he wanted 'little James' to know about his grandfather.

As it happened, I wound up telling my son intricate details of my life, at least as well as I could remember them. Incidents and people I hadn't thought about in years came swimming back into memory, bringing more details by association. Some of the memories were pleasant, and I enjoyed telling half-forgotten jokes and relating humorous situations. I relived some of my adventures, and pictured myself back in the cockpit. Many of my memories were terrible, and opened old wounds which had never really healed.

Edwin and I had been discussing my story as I drove him home from work one evening. He was telling me that he thought my life was very interesting and we chatted a bit about my early childhood. I pulled up in front of the cozy grey house I had found for him back when he and his wife were house hunting. As he undid his shoulder strap and was about to open the door, I asked him a question which, I guess, had been on my mind for my entire life.

"Tell me, Son." I said, looking down at the steering wheel, "If my real father had known what I was going to do with my life, do you think he would have been proud of me?"

Lou Greenburgh playing baseball at seventy-five years of age.

Lou Greenburgh with the author and James Louis Greenburgh at the Western Canada Aviation Museum on October 2nd, 1993. A DC3 can be seen in the background of the top photo. The sleek-looking aircraft in the bottom photo is a Spitfire.

(Above) 'Marshalling Lancasters against Stuttgart' by Carl Schaefer. (Below) Lou with Colonel Pearl McGonigal, the former Lieutenant Governor of Manitoba.

Lou with his closest friends, Chuck Solway (above) and Fluffy (below).

Appendices

Appendix 1: Brave Manitobans Lost Lives in Skies.

The following article appeared in the Winnipeg Free Press on Sunday, September 23, 1990. It is reproduced here with the kind permission of its author, Mr. Vince Leah.

Brave Manitobans Lost Lives in Skies.

A remarkable book that deserves better recognition and is a must for enthusiasts who dote on Canadian military history is "Canadians in the RAF," written and published by Les Allison of Roland, Manitoba.

It may astound some of you to know that over 2,000 Canadians served in the Royal Air Force, travelling to Britain by cattle boat or paying their own way to join the Royal Air Force before the shooting war started. A total of 169 came from or were natives of Manitoba, 111 from Winnipeg, the others from Gimli, Sperling, Elm Creek, Homewood, Mordent Manitou, Carman, Souris, Brandon, Roblin, McCreary, MacGregor, Virden, Hamiota, Selkirk, Pine Falls, Dauphin, Dugald, Transcona as well as our good neighbors in Keewatin and Kenora. Not all of them came home.

Among the 2,000-odd Canadians, two Victoria Crosses, two George Crosses and 40 Distinguished Service Orders were earned. Half of the 2,000 gave their lives before the war ended. The 2,000 also won 340 Distinguished Flying Crosses, 50 Distinguished Flying Medals, three George Medals, 52 Air Force Crosses, two Military Crosses, six Air Force Medals, 20 Orders of the British Empire and 16 foreign decorations. In the Battle of Britain, which helped discourage Hitler from his invasion plans of Britain, 130 Canadians flew for Fighter Command and 30 were killed in action. In Bomber Command 50 Canadians lost their lives before the Luftwaffe attacked England, and 37 more died during the battle over the channel. Coastal Command lost 14 before the Battle of Britain and 10 during this struggle.

Some of the Manitoba lads I knew before the war erupted and I have met several more in the post-war years. Jim Smith, who destroyed seven enemy aircraft and shared in the destruction of another, was a school chum. Strangely, Lou Greenburgh, who I had not seen for many moons, ran into me twice in two days while shopping. Lou joined the RAF in 1937 as ground crew, remustered for flight training. Shot down twice and to be rescued by the French Underground, Lou won the DFC twice and admits he was an acting squadron leader. His adventures make for thrilling reading. Numerous other Manitobans became newsworthy: Jack Kent from Castle Avenue in East Elmwood, Alf Bocking, Jim

Whitecross to name three. Selby Henderson was a St. Paul's High School Lad. He joined the RAF in 1938, earned the DFC and sadly was lost searching for a missing Hampden bomber off the coast of Holland in July, 1940.
John Benzie loved the military life. He served three years with the Princess Patricia's Canadian Light Infantry, the local garrison troops at Fort Osborne barracks, before he paid his way to England and joined the RAF. As the Allies strove to halt the German drive through the Lowlands and France to England, with the troops getting out Dunkirk, he returned to action in July. He was shot down as swarms of enemy aircraft attacked London and crashed in the Thames River.
What many Manitobans do not know is that the first two fighter "aces" served with RAF. FO Allan Angus, DFC, of McCreary destroyed five enemy aircraft before being killed May 18, 1940. PO Mark Brown of MacGregor, DFC and Bar, shot down 18 and shared another before and during the Battle of Britain. Known as "Hilly," Brown was one pilot in three squadrons attacking an enemy fighter and bomber formation. He was hit, slightly wounded and his aircraft ablaze, but he parachuted into the sea and was rescued. In May, 1941, "Hilly" had been promoted to wing commander. Decorated also by the Czechs, who had many of their sons under his command, "Hilly" continued to show brilliant leadership and tactical skills. With Malta under siege by the Germans and Italians, strong leadership of a fighter wing was seen as a necessity. Jack Kent, also a wing commander now, was slated to go but the orders were changed and "Hilly" went instead. In a fighter sweep over Sicily on Nov.12, 1941, he was shot down and killed by anti-aircraft fire. His photograph and memorial can be seen in MacGregor Collegiate.
Other noted fighter pilots from Manitoba include Wing Cmdr.Ian (Duke) Arthur, Squadron Leader Roland Dibonah, Flying Officer Harry Edwards, Pilot Officer Norris Hart of Dugald, and the aforementioned Jack Kent, who scored 13 and a half victories andreached the rank of group captain. The RAF did not recognize the term "ace," made popular in an earlier war. Hugh Halliday of Souris also has written a fine account of 242 Squadron, the RAF's first all-Canadian unit.
It is wrong to ignore the memory of these fine young men who put it on the line when our freedom was threatened. The tradition of courage and sacrifice set by William Barker of Dauphin, Alan Mcleod of Stonewall, William Clayton of Gladstone, William Stephenson and Rochford Mulock of Winnipeg and J.E. Sharman of Oak Lake in 1941 was maintained by these Manitoba men who set out for the high adventure cheerfully ignoring the tremendous price they would have to pay.

Appendix 2: The Story of Eric and Aissa-Jeanne Rippingale.

The following pages are from a letter to the author which was written by Aissa-Jeanne Rippingale, the wife of Lou Greenburgh's bomb aimer:

I thank you very much for your letter of 13th November, 1991, and also for the enclosed passages of your father's biography which were of great interest to me. Once more I apologize for not replying before, but it is a very painful task for me bringing back many very happy memories but also many very sad ones. I could not find the courage to write to you until now. I wanted to do it but could not settle down to it. I hope you will understand.

My husband, then F/Sgt Eric George Rippingale, completed 23 operations with 196 Squadron Witchford and 514 Squadron, Waterbeach. Eight operations were with F/Sgt Symons; the last one (Berlin, 27th January, 1944) resulted in an early return and a crash on landing. He then flew two operations as a reserve bomb aimer before joining the crew of F/O Greenburgh with whom he flew thirteen operations from 20th April 1944 to 7th June 1944.

When Eric bailed out on the night of June 7th, 1944, it could not have been very far from the target. He fell in a wood and walked all night. He told me that he could hear dogs barking in the distance and thought that the whole German army was after him. He walked all night through these woods and in the morning, as he was hiding behind some bushes, he saw a young boy cycling down the lane. He decided to show himself. The boy, whose name was Claude, looked at him and carried on his way. Suddenly realizing that this stranger was not a German soldier, Claudecame back and asked, "English?". Eric answered affirmatively. Claude told him to wait and disappeared. Eric did not know whether to wait or run. The boy soon reappeared accompanied by Captain R.S. Langdon. Captain Langdon and his wife, Madame Andree Forine de Mayerhoffen (a retired actress), were friends of our family. Captain Langdon walked with difficulty as a result of wounds he had received during the First World War. When the Germans occupied France, Captain Langdon was imprisoned at 'Fresnes'. Andree eventually secured his release, but only on the condition that he remain in their country house at the top of the 'Rocher de Saulx-les-Chatreux'. They were prisoners in their own home. Eric was taken to their home (which they called 'La Tour Prends Garde'), fed and put to bed. In the afternoon, F/Sgt Roland Nurse, of the Australian Air Force, walked in through the back garden. After a few weeks, F/Sgt Nurse went to another house in the district.

I was living with my parents in Puteaux, very near Paris, when I received a telegram from Andree. She was asking for help and, reading between the lines,

I guessed what had happened. We were always short of food. My father used to help a lot with what we called 'revitaillement' but, as I was the only one who was able to get out, I had to walk miles and miles looking for vegetables.

Andree introduced me to wood mushrooms. One evening, the two of us decided to go and see if we could 'find' any vegetables in the surrounding fields. We managed to get one small leek and two tiny potatoes before being caught by the farmer, who accused us of stealing tuns of potatoes. They called the Gendarmes. We did not have any identity cards with us, so the Gendarmes said they would call at our house the following day to check our identity cards. We arrived back home at two o'clock in the morning. Eric and Captain Langdon were frantic; they had not expected to see us again.

We knew the Gendarmes would keep their promise to visit our house, so we dressed Eric up in female clothes and sent him into the woods. It was not a good idea, but everything turned out alright. After the war, the Gendarmes told us they suspected something was going on but did not know what. I am sure they thought we were collaborating with the Germans. Situated at the top of the hill, surrounded by woods and with a wonderful view of the countryside, the Tour Prends Garde was in a good position for spying. (The spot was later used as a radar station.)

One had to be always very careful, as some French people were collaborating with the Germans. I had to make sure that I was not followed and that was a bit difficult. I had to travel by underground, crossing Paris from North to South as far as Anthony Station which was in Seine et Oise. From Anthony it was miles and miles on foot and all the time making sure no one was following me. As both sides of the road were covered by fields of cabbages, carrots, etc., it would have been quite easy to spot anyone.

I had to be especially careful after my brother was killed. I had to go to the room in Paris where he had stayed while working for the Resistance. I went there to collect his personal effects: guns, grenades, etc. My brother had been twenty-one years old at the time he was shot. Serge was Sergeant and chief of Group SPARTICUS. He was shot in the back, in the Paris underground at Station Pasteur. He was followed and shot on the spot. A commemorative plaque is still at the place where he was killed on July 19, 1944.

We were always on full alert at La Tour Prends Garde. Eric used to get up between 3 o'clock and 4 o'clock A.M. He would get dressed, make up his bed, and rest on it until breakfast time. Just before 5 o'clock A.M. on July 22, 1944, - three days after my brother's death - Eric heard a noise outside the house. Looking

La Tour Prends Garde

out of his window, he saw a German staff car with a dozen troops being directed by an officer to surround the house. This was done silently. Eric rushed to his hiding place. It was upstairs, in the 'Moroccan' room (so called because of the Moroccan tapestries which adorned its walls). In front of one tapestry was an armchair and behind it was a door that led to a dressing room. Eric hid behind the clothes in the dressing room's wardrobe.

Hammering down the front door, the Germans forced their way into the house. Of course, we acted surprised and tried to look innocent. Eric could hear the sound of their boots on the parquet floor. His knees were knocking so hard that he thought the Germans would hear them. The Germans did not find anything and left, but we really thought that our last hour had come.

Every day, we sat down to what we called our 'English afternoon tea'. It consisted of a weak first cup of tea and a second cup of weaker tea. We managed to get eight cups of tea out of one teaspoonful of tea leaves. One of us would be seated on the monk bench which concealed the battery radio we used to listen to the BBC.

The Germans paid us a second visit. Six of them entered the back garden as we were having our afternoon tea. We saw their shadows through the stained glass windows. Eric picked up his cup, saucer, and plate then disappeared. The patrol did not ask us anything and left us to drink our tea. We thought they might have lost their way in the woods and come up the garden to the terrace. It took Eric some time before he lost the habit of taking the cup and saucer with him when leaving the table.

I had a job as a secretary with a group of fiscal experts in Paris and I was also a member of the Defense Passive. I had the responsibility of looking after people who took shelter beneath the block of flats that I lived in with my parents. I took care of them during and after air raids. I wore an arm band which enabled me to circulate outside during air raids without being stopped by the Germans. The arm band helped me a lot.

I used to go to La Tour Prends Garde every weekend, taking as much food as I could get with me. I started after work on Fridays and returned home on Sundays. After a three week stay at La Tour Prends Garde, I returned to Paris as the Free French Forces, led by General Leclerk, were coming in through the south. I shall regret this to my dying day because of the humiliation Eric had to go through. This would not have happened had I been with him. Against his better judgment, Andree (who was a rather impulsive lady) talked him into going out to find an Allied officer. He was stopped on his way by some stupid F.F.I. who thought he was a German soldier because he refused to divulge his hideout. They would not believe his story or nationality. Eric was marched a very long way through the village of Longjumeau between two German soldiers. He spotted a friend, Madame Gramont, in the waiting crowd and signaled his plight to her. He was dumped in a cell with two Germans but, with the aid of an interpreter, Madame Gramont had him released.

At the liberation of Paris, Eric and some other evaders were taken to the Hotel Windsor in Paris. From there he was taken to the American Air Force base at Fontainebleau and then by Dakota to Northolt (England). I was without news for three months. Then, before Christmas 1944, a printed card arrived to let me know he was safe. That was as soon as the postal service service between France and England started again.

Eric requested a posting to France and was posted at Rennes, in October 1945. He was then moved to Buc, near Versailles, which was close to my home. I came to England with Eric to meet his family in June of 1946. On June 7, 1947, we were married in the town of Puteaux (Seine). We had three wonderful sons and five delightful grandchildren.

We shared forty-four years of happiness. Eric was a very caring and devoted person who was loved and respected by all who knew him.

Eric Rippingale and his bride, Aissa-Jeanne.

Appendix 3: The Extraordinary Adventure of the Forest of Freteval.

The following article was originally written in French by Mme Cecile Jubault on the occasion of the dedication of the Forest of Freteval memorial in 1967. It is reprinted here with her kind permission and that of her husband M. Omer Jubault.

THE EXTRAORDINARY ADVENTURE OF THE FOREST OF FRETEVAL

By Cecile Jubault, from the personal memories of her husband, Omer Jubault and others of the French Resistance who participated in this mission.

30 May 1967

Printed by S. Lembeye, Vendome, France, 11 June 1967

Translated by Mary Hines Johnson, 1986

FOREWORD

The present booklet has for its purpose to make known to the nation one of the most extraordinary adventures of the last war. The modesty of the numerous members of the Resistance of Loir-et-Cher and of Eur-et-Loir who have participated in it has alone impeded, until the present time, the publication of this military exploit unique in the annals of the war.

Unique it is in many ways. More than one hundred fifty allied aviators--American, English, Canadian, Australian, South- African, New Zealanders and Belgians--lived in camps, perfectly organized and in the middle of occupied France in the forest of Freteval, between Vendome and Cloyes during several months under the nose and the beard of enemy troops.

These aviators, whose planes had been shot down over occupied territory, represented the equivalent of fourteen squadrons of pursuit. They took their places again, after their liberation, in the fighting units. This was without doubt a precious contribution to the final victory.

Unique again, the fact that this operation, which necessitated the cooperation of large numbers of members of the Resistance, remained absolutely secret to the point that the inhabitants of the villages surrounding the forest did not know about, until the last days, the presence of this truly allied army near them.

Unique finally and how comforting for the people in charge to know that in the course of the months which elapsed until the successful ending of the mission, the loss of not a single human life was to be deplored among the ranks of the Resistance as well as among those of the allied aviators.

It is the succinct and factual story of this heroic adventure that we propose to you in the following pages. All the persons who participated are cited under their true names in order that they may witness to it.

THE RETURN TO ENGLAND OF THE DOWNED AVIATORS

During the whole duration of the war, from 1941 when allied raids above occupied territories and over Germany started to intensify, the big worry of the staff was to be able to get back these indispensable specialists, the allied aviators whose equipment was downed in the course of the mission, and who succeeded in escaping

A special service called "M.I.9" (Military Information 9) was created within the "Intelligence Service" and received for its mission to organize in conjunction with the local Resistance of different countries and by the intermediary of agents sent from England, channels for escape and return to the British Isles.

One of these channels, whose members were all French and Belgian and which had the name "Comete" was the most important and it succeeded in leading back to combat hundreds of aviators.

The process of the return of the aviators was the following: They were first welcomed by the inhabitants of the region who took by their actions enormous risks. Thanks to the network of information created by the line "Comete" these persons were soon known. "Comete" took charge then of the package or packages (that was the name used in order to designate the aviators thus found) and led them toward centers such as Liege, Brussels, Lille or Reims.

They were then regrouped in the Parisian region before being conducted to the Spanish border which specialized guides helped them cross. They reached thus Gibraltar or Lisbon. Transport planes of the R.A.F. finished finally the trip.

All these moves, so dangerous, were done almost all by railroad and under the guidance of dedicated French and Belgian escorts, many of whom paid with their liberty and often with their lives for the precious aid that they gave to the aviators.

In January 1944 however, when the date and the place of the debarkation was known by a certain select group, the "M.I.9" had to face numerous problems. It was evident in fact that the attacks which were going to concentrate on means of communication in occupied France would completely disorganize the railroads, stopping thus the transportation of aviators toward the Spanish border. No one knew what the behaviour of the German authorities at the time of the landing would be, but it was feared that there would be an intensified surveillance by the police and even perhaps incarceration of able-bodied men. In addition, the members of the Resistance who in great part formed the nucleus of the escorts would have at that moment other vital tasks to accomplish.

It was thus decided to place the recovered aviators in a place, fairly close to the Norman coast, where the losses in sailing personnel would be heavy. The region determined by a triangle formed by the cities of Vendome, Le Mans, and Chartres must serve as a terminal for different organized escape lines. The nearness of the landing beaches allowed hope that the Liberation would take place in the shortest time thus reducing the risks.

In order to lead this very delicate mission to a successful conclusion, a Belgian officer and aviator, Lucien Boussa alias "Cousine Lucienne", serving in the ranks of the R.A.F. since the beginning of the war, was sounded out by the "M.I.9". This choice had been dictated to the authorities of the "Intelligence Service" by the fact that this French speaking officer was perfectly up to date on matters concerning the R.A.F. and had thus the possibility of revealing doubtful recruits who would be able to infiltrate the escape lines and cause to fail the entire foreseen plan.

After having three months of special instruction, Lucien Boussa, to whom had been given as an assistant a radio operator, Francois Toussaint, left England by an air station near London and after several different episodes arrived in Paris the 13th day of May, 1944. The debarkation was near. There was no longer time to lose.

Upon his arrival in Paris and as his instructions envisioned, the Belgian officer was put in contact with one of the leaders of the line "Comete", the Baron Jean de Blomaert, who entered into secrecy in 1940. Still not caught, he operated under several borrowed names, which earned him on the part of the Germans the nickname of "Renard" (Fox). In April 1944, de Blomaert went to London where he finalized the escape network with the leaders of "M.I.9". Finally he returned to France, having for his mission to assemble the aviators in the areas dominated by the woody, hilly landscape from which the fugitives could be led little by little toward Brittany, from there to England by boat. It is at this moment that Lucien Boussa departed from England, arrived in Paris, the carrier of an urgent counter order from the British secret service: "The invasion is near; no longer evacuate the aviators. Hide them on site."

WHY THE FOREST OF FRETEVAL

By the intermediary of the leaders of the line "Comete", Lucien Boussa entered into contact with the departmental head of the French Forces for the Interior of Eure-et-Loire, "Sinclair" (Maurice Clavel). The latter had just taken command and was not aware of the possibilities offered by the resistance grouping placed under his orders. He asked for the advice of a leader of the office of "Air Operations", Andre Gagnon alias Legrand (elected Mayor of Chartres at the liberation) and of two heads of "Liberation Movement", Pierre Poitevan called "Bichat" and R. Dufour alias "Duvivier". These two men advised "Sinclair" to speak to "Andre" (Omer Jubault), military leader of "Libe Nord" for the region of Chateaudun. This man was going to become known as the head of the organization created of all of the groups as well as a loyal and devoted collaborator. Gendarme at Cloyes for 8 years, on the verge of being arrested for his clandestine actions against the occupying group, he had left his brigade on the 10th of January 1944 with one of his colleagues, Robert Hakspille, called "Raoul". Both had been warned of their upcoming arrest by Jean-Felix Paulsen of Chateaudun, who was able to continue sending them their monthly checks until the Liberation. These military men, hunted for deserting, had succeeded in several months to group together numerous members of the resistance. They knew the region perfectly and the degree of patriotism of all the inhabitants.

Changing each day their hiding place, they were lodged by numerous patriots. Foreseeing the operations that their groups would be asked to perform at the time of the Liberation, they had contacted all of the landowners and the guards of the forest of Freteval, located different sites in the woods, including places with water, hiding places for arms, which would be able to serve to organize the woody, hilly land, and asked the help of farmers, millers, and bakers of the area for the provisions. Also when Jubault was called to the position of command of "Sinclair" at Boisville (Eure-et-Loire) and was informed of what was expected of

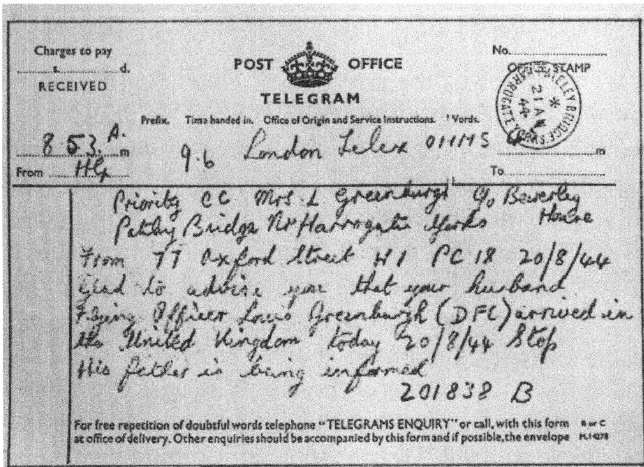
Charges to pay ....s. ....d.
RECEIVED
POST OFFICE
TELEGRAM
No.
OFFICE STAMP
Prefix. Time handed in. Office of Origin and Service Instructions. Words.
8.53 A.m 9.6 London Telex 011115
From HG
To
Priority CC Mrs L Greenburgh c/o Beverley House Pateley Bridge Nr Harrogate Yorks
From 77 Oxford Street W1 PC 18 20/8/44
Glad to advise you that your husband Flying Officer Louis Greenburgh (DFC) arrived in the United Kingdom today 20/8/44 Stop
His father is being informed
201838 B
For free repetition of doubtful words telephone "TELEGRAMS ENQUIRY" or call, with this form at office of delivery. Other enquiries should be accompanied by this form and if possible, the envelope

Cecile JUBAULT

him, he accepted the mission which was entrusted to him in priority, on the actions of harassment planned against the enemy and, the 18th of May 1944, the officer of the R.A.F., Lucien Boussa, his radio operator, Francois Toussaint, accompanied by "Sinclair" and by Sylvia Montfort, took the train with the destination of Chateaudun. At the train station, a group of resistance members waited for them, composed of Omer Jubault, Maurice Serein, Lucien Bezault and Robert Poupard. The wait was long, the train bombed in the course of the trip was three hours late. The four named travellers descended from it.

It was around two p.m., under a sun with a leaden hue, that the little group, furnished with bicycles, left in the direction of the forest of Freteval, twenty kilometers away. A stop had been planned in the woods of Montigny-le-Gannelon, where Joseph Neither, restaurant owner in that area, would bring a lunch. The meal finished, the little group gradually set out again. They arrived without problems at the home of Halloin, gamekeeper of the Marquis de Levis-de-Mirepoix, at the place called "Bellande", township of Villebout (Loir-et-Cher). The lodge of the gamekeeper, hidden behind a little woods, was an ideal place to shelter a secret agent: Lucien Boussa set himself up there. By reason of security, Jubault led the radio operator 10 kilometers from there, to the home of Doctor Chauveau, at Moulineuf, township of Romilly-sur-Aigre.

The liaison was to be assured by Ginette Jubault and her brother Jean, child of the troop at the school of Tulle, that he had abandoned in order to aid his parents; Mme Jubault served as a relay in the clandestine organization of her husband.

THE DIFFICULTIES

In the course of the week which followed the arrival of Colonel Boussa, thirty recovered aviators were entrusted to the new organization. Lodged in Paris, at the home of patriots who could no longer nourish them, it was necessary to evacuate them immediately to the country where, with money, it was possible to procure milk, butter, eggs, meat, flour and vegetables from the farmers. It is difficult to imagine, for those who have not known that period of time, what life was like in France under the German occupation. Everything was rationed in quantities clearly insufficient. To feed oneself, to warm oneself, to dress oneself, to travel, in a word each of the elements of daily life posed at every instant an insoluble problem. One no longer had coffee, nor rice nor chocolate. Wine was distributed only to laborers. No fuel, no gasoline. Imagine thus the difficulties of welcoming an escaped stranger who is unable to speak French, an aviator falling by chance into the hands of an individual isolated without the least notion of the network of the Resistance. From the moment a patriot took in an allied aviator, the first job was to get rid of his military uniform and to dress him in civilian clothes, a fairly complicated job at that time. It was very difficult to get clothing. It was only given with tokens. The Patriot was by this fact obligated to dress his protege himself. The aviator and his rescuer were often of very different sizes; it was not unusual to see a big guy wearing a pair of pants coming to mid-calf and a short jacket of which the sleeves scarcely passed the elbow. The problem of shoes was even more difficult. Some aviators were wearing boots that it was necessary to take off immediately in order to avoid that they be spotted. Others who had walked long distances were wearing shoes very worn out. In order to remedy this inconvenience, Daniel Lance, tanner at Vendome, secretly furnished leather necessary to a shoe maker at d'Amboise. The finished shoes were distributed to the aviators in the shortest possible time.

THE ESCORTING OF THE AVIATORS

In the beginning, the aviators got off at the train station of Chateaudun, escorted the most often by courageous escorts. From a relay set up in a little grocery store owned by M. and Mme Coeuret, it was necessary then to direct them by indirect roads to the area around Cloyes. Daniel Cogneau, of Chateaudun, accepted the responsibility of the escorting. He accomplished this mission, without interruption, for three months with members of his family. He was helped in his job by Maurice Serein, Lucien Bezault, Robert Poupard, Abel Meret, Solange and

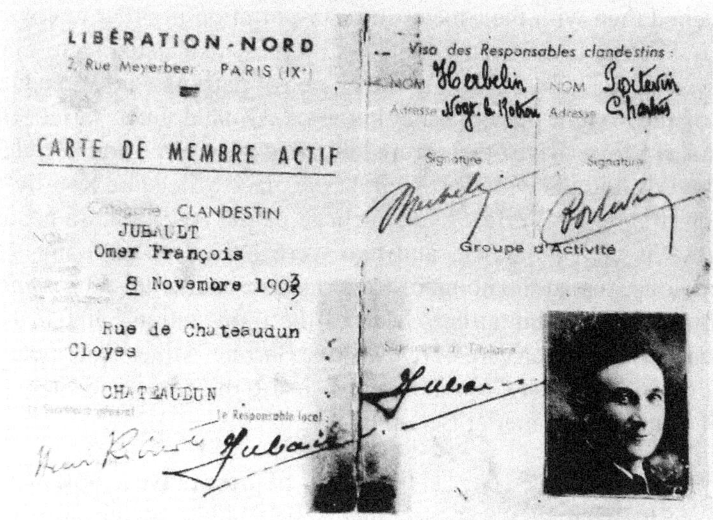
LIBÉRATION-NORD
2, Rue Meyerbeer PARIS (IXe)

CARTE DE MEMBRE ACTIF

Catégorie : CLANDESTIN
JUBAULT
Omer François
8 Novembre 1903
Rue de Chateaudun
Cloyes
CHATEAUDUN

Le Responsable local :

Visa des Responsables clandestins :
NOM Herbelin NOM Poitevin
Adresse Nogt. le Rotrou Adresse Chartres
Signature Signature

Groupe d'Activité

DANIEL COGNEAU

MARIUS VILLEDIEU

Jean Meret, Lucien Thibault, Maurice Gaillard, Jean Gagnebien, Renee Paulsen and Louis Bellier, of Chateaudun; Pierre Dauphin, Marcel Huard, Jacques Gouzy, Paul Roger and Charlette Marolles, of Bonneval; M. Penot of Saint-Martin; the veterinarians, Doctors Dufour, of Chartres, and Renaudon of La Loupe; Joseph Neillier, Andre Saillard and Eugene Legeay, of Montigny-le-Gannelon; Ginette and Jean Jubault, Robert Hakspille and Marius Villedieu, of Cloyes; Pierre Van Bever, of Saint-Hilaire-sur-Yerre; Emile Demouliere and Jules Gallet, ofSaint-Jean-Froidmentel; Gustave Barbier, of Moree; Kleber Olivier, of Danze; Henri Roger of Courtalain and also the inhabitants of Combres and of Chassant where M. and Mme Bacchi assured temporary lodging.

In order to baffle the surveillance of the enemy, it was necessary in fact to change constantly escort, itinerary, and means of locomotion. All means were used, foot the most often, bicycle, automobile, horse drawn carriage, especially after the destruction of the railroad. From that time the aviators were led on foot from Dourdan (Seine-et-Oise). A relay was installed at Montbossier(Eure-et-Loir) at the home of Gaston Duneau, who went to get them at the farm of Leroy at Sazeray, near Voves. He led them by little groups often across the fields, furnished with pitchforks and hoes in order to give the impression that they were farm workers. This patriot evacuated thus a large number of escapees.

From Montboissier, Pierre Dauphin and Marcel Huard led them to a new relay located at Chenelong, near Gohory at the home of Fougereux. The escorts of

Chateaudun intervened then with their means of transportation in order to cover as painlessly as possible the last fifteen kilometers by these exhausted men. The first aviators received were led by Jubault to the homes of patriots who agreed to lodge them. Five of them were placed at the home of Armand Guet, farmer at Audrieres, township of Cloyes, five others were lodged in an isolated house, lived in by Pierre Van Beverly and the widow Tesseir, at the place called "Le Rouilly", township of Saint-Hilaire-sur-Yerre. Doubouchage, bricklayer at Rameau, township of Langey, as well took five, and two were lodged at the home of Chesneau, at Chanteloup, two at the home of Rene Jacques, at the level crossing 103, two at the home of Jean Demouliere, head of the train station Saint-Jean-Froidmentel, while nine were taken care of by Gustave Barbier, Mmes Guerineau, and Martinnez Pedro, living at the Corbonniere, township of Moree and finally, five at the home of Fouchard, farmer at Bellande.

These aviators stayed around fifteen days at the homes of these brave people. The latter knew however to what they exposed themselves since on the 20th of February, 1944, ten patriots of Vendome had been deported for having welcomed to their homes a crew of an allied plane shot down. This fact known in all the region encouraged the Resistance members to act with a very great carefulness and it was certainly an important factor in the success of the undertaking.

CREATION OF CAMP No. 1, AND THE LIFE IN IT

Because of the magnitude taken by the operation, Lucien Boussa, who was obligated to visit daily the aviators scattered in the region in order to assure himself of their conditions of lodging and risk being arrested in the course of his continual trips, appealed to the directors of the network "Comete". Two days later, Jean de Blomaert, accompanied by Philippe d'Albert-Lake, arrived at Bellande in order to assist him.

In agreement with Jubault and the forester Halloin, it was decided to group the "lodgers" in a camp in order to facilitate the surveilance and supplying of food. The interested parties went to a site situated eight hundred meters from the lodge. The location appeared to be perfectly suitable for the creation of a camp. The woods, relatively thick, was going to hide all activity which would take place under its foliage. A spring of pure water gushed up at scarcely one hundred meters. The slight slope leading up to the border of the woods would allow an easy surveillance of the immediate approaches. Moreover, the farm of Bellande, situated near the home of Halloin, cultivated by the Fouchards and their daughters Micheline, Simone and Jacqueline, would be the point of convergence and would serve as a centre for slaughtering animals and a warehouse for the food supplies. Each one set to work. While Lucien Boussa and his two friends, helped by the five aviators of the Fouchard farm furnished the future camp, Jubault visited the farmers to obtain tarpaulins in order to construct tents. For their part, Jean-Felix Paulsen and Doctor Dufour, who had the possibility of traveling by car because of their profession, brought on several occasions material to the camp site, utensils for cooking, provisions and tobacco.

The 10th of June 1944, all the aviators up to this time lodged at the homes of the patriots, had come to the camp. Around fifteen tents were already pitched and life was organized by the inhabitants of this special type of village. Three sentinels posted at the edge of the woods watched the surroundings and warned of the approach of unidentified people by a rudimentary system of warning. Ever increasing, the food supply of the aviator camps had been a true nightmare for the patriots. One will see however that the network set up on foot by Jubault for the underground forces was important. It must function effectively until the Liberation. Some farmers, members of the Resistance, brought living animals, fresh meal, vegetables, butter, eggs to the farm of Bellande, especially Armand Guet, farmer at Audrieres; Maurice Tessiervitarmer at the Durandierre; Cornuau, farmer at Autheuil; Duroc, manager at Convertiere; Laubry, meat merchant at Moree; Andre Barrault, farmer at Saint-Calais; Croissant, farmer at la Flocherie; Robert Guerineau, baker at Romilly-sur-Aigre; Maxime Plateau, farmer at la Touche (in the farm where Emile Zola wrote his novel La Terre), Henry Oudeyer, farmer at Cloyes and Henri Beaujouan at Douy.

Thanks to the flour furnished by the flour dealer EtienneViron, the bread made by Theophile Trecul de Fontaine-Raoul, was brought to the camp by Micheline Fouchard. With her horse cart, this young girl covered each day four kilometers across the forest where she was one time shot at by allied planes. In order to vary the menu, night fishing parties were organised in the Loir, by Andre Saillard and Eugene Legeay, of Montigny-le-Gannelon. Cooks improvised and became very quickly true "chefs". In order to avoid all revealing smoke, the stoves were supplied with charcoal, made in the forest by Henri Lefevre of l'Estriverds and brought to Bellande by his wife.

The different duties inherent to all military life in common were organized and accepted with good humor. These duties included wake up at six o'clock in the morning, starting fires for the first service of breakfast, water duty, cleaning up and putting in order of the tents and their surroundings. If the camp was difficult to detect from the road, it was however visible by planes flying over the region and in this case, allied planes became as dangerous as those of the enemy. It was thus absolutely vital that every morning the tents be re-covered with fresh branches. The tables and seats were made of trunks and branches. The beds were made with trellis work spread out between four posts. The mattresses were made of dry grasses.

Free time was used by each one according to his interests. Some improved the comfort of their tents, others worked on wood sculptures, at sewing, others found a sunny spot in order to dream of their liberation which they believed to be very near. In order to assure a certain comfort to the inhabitants of the camp, Albert Barillet, barber at Cloyes, came each week to exercise his art.

Extraordinary cases of regrouping took place. It is thus that equipment almost complete would be re-divided at the time of arrivals. Such moments were always celebrated joyfully.

CREATION OF A NEW CAMP

Expecting the debarkation and with it the number of aviators arriving at Bellande increased. It soon became evident that the continued growth of the camp which had at this time more than seventy people and twenty-five tents was too big a risk. In order to examine the problem, Lucien Boussa called Etienne Biron and the principal leaders to the home of the forester, Halloin. They decided to create a second centre of lodging. Jubault suggested to set it at Richeray, township of Busloup, on the edge of the forest a spot that he had chosen previously for his underground headquarters He went there accompanied by Jean de Blomaert. Located ten kilometers from Bellande, the location was favorable, so much so that the Germans had made numerous munitions depots in the undergrowth guarded by a small detachment. From the standpoint of conveniences there was a spring and a forester's house.

Commanded by Jean de Blomaert, the "Camp No. 2" was set up on the model of the first one with which it remained in permanent contact. The guard Rideau and his wife, helped by Rene Adrian provided daily the food for the aviators, of which part was furnished by the Derythe couple.

In spite of the close presence of the occupying guards, not a single incident ever took place. It is true that the rules of calm and of silence were particularly severe: not to try to go to England by one's own means; to make the least noise possible. To raise a little bit one's voice risked being fatal. The radio was one of the centres of interest in the life of the camps. Each time that important information was obtained, a bulletin was pinned on a tree, serving as a bulletin board. The best received messages were those which announced parachute drops. Unfortunately, for various reasons, only one was done for the benefit of the aviators during the whole duration of their stay in the forest. That day, several men went into the fields at designated spots several kilometers from the camp, furnished with red flashlights whose rays formed a triangle indicating to the pilot the direction of the wind on the ground. They were thus certain of the perfect reception of medical supplies, cigarettes and French money, things very important for the condition and the morale of the "campers". After the parachute drop, the men went to clean up the fields, straighten the wheat flattened by the containers in order to make all trace of the operation disappear.

THE WOUNDED AND THE SICK

Numerous aviators wounded, most often because of burns, were lodged and cared for by members of the Resistance. M. and Mme Dubouchage, bricklayers of Rameau, gave their aid to one of them during three weeks. Mme Despres, homeowner at Villebout, in her eighties and very alert for her age, could speak perfect English, transformed her home into a hospital and with the help of her lady's companion, had until the liberation an average of five "boarders" in treatment. Doctor Teyssier of Cloyes and his son Louis went each day to visit these sick ones.

In the camps field hospital tents were set up. The sick and wounded were cared for by fellow aviators who had some idea of nursing care. Doctor Teyssier came regularly donating his skills and bringing into the field hospital those that he judged able to be cared for in beds. During a certain time, transporting of these sick ones was done at night time by a young girl of 16 years, Ginette Jubault, accompanied by her brother Jean.

MEASURES OF PROTECTION UPON ARRIVAL AT THE CAMPS

With the exception of the doctors, the barber, very few people were authorized to enter the camps. Very strict rules were applied and when new aviators were found, a welcoming committee presided by a man of big stature, furnished with an enormous club, made them stop in the woods at a distance of a kilometer from their destination. There, he made them submit to a terse interrogation, place of their fall, mission, technical details that an agent of the enemy who had been able to discover the network would not have known how to answer without being confused. Very fortunately, the club in question never was used.

THE INCIDENTS

However the incidents and the accidents were not lacking. One of them would have been able to make the whole undertaking fail without the composure of an escort named "Virginia", American by birth, belonging to the network "Comete" who swallowed a compromising document (plan to go to Bellande).

She had led on foot to Dourdan (Seine-et-Oise) to the farm of Villentiere, township of Civry-Saint-Cloud (Eure-et-Loire), six aviators. One of these escapees, worn-out, stayed at the farm to rest. The five others, placed in a cart driven by Jean Meret, went in the direction of the camp. Robert Poupard stayed on the side of the driver, while Daniel Cogneau and "Virginia" preceded the convoy at some distance one from the other.

Everything went normally to Marboue, where the female escort was questioned by German soldiers who asked her for information. Not knowing the region, she was not able to answer the question and was betrayed by her accent. Arrested, she was stranded at Ravensbruck, where she almost died of hunger. She paid with her liberty for the work that she had done for the aviators.

As soon as they knew of the arrest of "Virginia", the occupants of the cart fled in all directions.

By measure of carefulness, Daniel Cogneau ordered Jean Meret to return rapidly with his cart then go to Villentiere in order to evacuate immediately the aviator who remained there. The farmer's wife did not know him, but as soon as she was informed of what had happened, gave him a horse and vehicle in order to transport the aviator to the camp.

The next day, Daniel returned the horse and vehicle to the brave woman, but the search to locate the five aviators who fled was laborious. Two of them were discovered the same day by Maurice Serein, Lucien Bezault and Robert Poupard, who searched the region. Another, by chance thirty kilometers from there, by M. Prieur, at the market place at Bonneval, who led him and gave him to the Marolles family from the same place. The latter took him to Jules Gouzy, who had his son Jacque take him by bicycle by a circuitous route to Cloyes where Jubault was to have taken him to Bellande. The wife of Jubault was not home so the escort led the aviator to the Meret farm, which was the meeting place.

The two others were taken in by people considered as enemy agents. None dared to go to their home. The good mailman who was on his route suggested that he go. He learned that the supposed collaborators were really patriots watched by the enemy and that they had fed the aviator in a neighboring woods. The aviators were discovered with much difficulty and taken to rejoin their fellow aviators at the home of Abel Meret.

Finally the five escapees were led to Bellande by car by Lucian Thibault of Chateaudun, but the worst luck continued to pursue them. During the trip the springs, overloaded, gave way. The driver had his passengers get out, then returned to his garage where he changed cars. After all these problems, the trip ended without harm.

Some time later, while checking on Camp number 2, de Blomaert and Jubault got lost in the forest and passed by close to a forest house occupied by the Germans. The head of the post who spoke French questioned them during nearly an hour. It was their borrowed clothing which saved them.

July 22, 1944, Maxime Plateau, who furnished a large part of the food destined for the forest camps was arrested following a parachute drop of arms intended for the township of Saint-Hilaire-la-Gravelle

(Loire-et-Cher). Tortured, led to a concentration camp, he revealed nothing.

If the arrest of "Virginia" had brought about worries to the escorts, the alert had also been very strong at Bellande. First, it had been planned to go and free her, but facing all the difficulties, this idea was abandoned. In the camp the sentinels had been reinforced, and the aviators had taken their places in order to flee at the least alert. Madame Halloin remembers that she was in charge of preparing a big fire in the chimney and was to light it if the Germans arrived. The smoke which would come out of the chimney was the signal agreed upon in order to indicate danger. Mme Halloin added "We spent difficult moments, I prayed to the good Lord very often but we truly were lucky."

All the escorted groups didn't meet with the same difficulty, however some merit to be pointed out. It happened that one day, Mme Furet who was the railroad crossing guard between Chateaudun and Cloyes, wanted to keep at her house young Jean Jubault, who was leading a group of aviators, who thought that he was being followed by people who had bad looks [actually, these were the aviators]. In order to reveal nothing, the little boy just insisted on getting back to his bicycle and continuing on his way. Later Robert Poupard, who was taking a group of people between Chateaudun and Douy, noticed after being situated at the top of the hill of Thoreau, that his "packages" were not following him any longer. So he did a little half-turn and noticed that they were in the process of going into the entrance way to a chateau that was occupied by the Germans and he was able to meet them just as they were in front of the grills of the gate before they entered the walkway and they hadn't yet attracted the attention of the occupants.

During July, Doctor Dufour took in his charge at the cafe-restaurant of Crucey (Eure-et-Loir) four aviators, of which one had the face horribly burned. He put them in his little Simca 5 CV [5 horsepower]. Upon arriving at Lugny, he noticed an enemy patrol parked in front of the monument to the dead. Not losing his cool, the driver stopped his car on the edge of a field of wheat and he hid there the aviators and started to put on a wheel and its tire. Several moments later, the Germans passed by without even paying any attention to him.

At Illiers, another new emotion. Some allied planes flew over the city and the occupants ran out and all made signs to Dufour to stop. However he didn't want to stop because he was afraid that maybe his passengers wouldn't be able to be controlled. The rest of the trip took place without any incident, but he had come close to catastrophe. Finally Daniel Cogneau and Lucien Bezault, without intending to do it, led five aviators that they were accompanying on foot, in front of a German musical group that had started to play in opportunity on the square of Saint-Denis-les-Ponts. The parade of the aviators, spread out a hundred meters one from the other, seemed interminable to the escort who kept wondering if the enemy was not going to intervene. They didn't do anything, fortunately. But certainly the heroes of this adventure will remember it again and again.

Touching scenes were produced too. One aviator was lodged for some time at the home of two elderly people who had discovered him in a field eating raw potatoes. They cared for him so well and so much that when Daniel Cogneau came in order to take him to the camp, they asked Daniel where he was taking him and made to him thousands of recommendations. It was finally with regret that they consented to allow this aviator to leave. One would have believed that it was a question of a son of the house. And just when the aviator was about to depart, the elderly gentleman took his package of tobacco (rationed at this period of time) and he divided it equally into two parts and gave one to the aviator.

THE COMMAND POST OF COLONEL BOUSSA AT THE TRAIN STATION OF SAINT-JEAN-FROIDMENTEL

From the first two weeks of July, by measure of supplementary security, because of the traffic that was going to the farm of Bellande for furnishing the food for the camps, Jubault advised Lucien Boussa to put his command post at the train station of Saint-Jean-Froidmentel. It was there that he made up the messages that he transmitted to London by his radio operator. Jeanne Demouliere, who was the acting head of the station, and her husband, who was a wounded veteran from the war of 1914-1918, were definite patriots. They had several times lodged aviators before giving them to the escape line. Besides, the train station of Saint-Jean, located on the Bretigny- Vendome line, was at this time used a great deal by people coming to get food in the surrounding countryside, and this resulted in a continual coming and going which fortunately masked the arrivals and departures caused by the command post of the allied officer. However the danger was great because on one side of the railroad the Germans were occupying the chateau of Rougemont. For his part and for the same reason, the radio operator, Francois Toussaint, changed his place of operation several times. After having spent around a month in the home of Doctor Chaveau at Moulineuf, he went to live with Robert Guerineau, who was a baker at Romilly-sur-Aigre. Roberte, the daughter of the baker, was in charge of carrying messages during this period.

The radio operator next was lodged at the home of M. Houmaire, from where he was able to send his transmissions to the patriots of the region, notably to Gustave Barbier and Jules Gallet and even as far as the farm of Andre Barrault at Saint-Calais (these latter had in their charge during a month three Russian escaped prisoners). Georges Blin, the miller at Vetille and Maxime Fouchet, lodged as well Francios Toussaint and M. Sauvilliers, electrical engineer, who was able to repair the radio of the operator.

A helper of Jubault, Pierre Guillaumin called "Gilbert" was in charge of assuring a permanent liaison between Lucien Boussa and the camps of the forest. He participated in completing the food supply arrangements of these camps. He took charge of this task with intelligence and devotedness. He was furthermore in charge of escorting the recuperating aviators in the region by the movement of the "Francs-Tireurs" and "Partisans-Francais". Those who were responsible in the region for this group, notably:

Armand Lhuillery, Charles Sandre, Guy Fortier and Paul Fenin, dead for France at Cormainville after having been odiously martyrized, Johann called "Kid" and Maxime Fouchet led twenty aviators to the station of Saint-Jean-Froidmentel where they sent them to the commander of the camps. One of these aviators, Stanley Laurence, was shot down above Beauvais, and was headed on foot towards Spain when he was welcomed by Jacques Pikeroen, a school teacher a Mervilliers (Eure-et-Loir) where he stayed fifteen days before being able to join the group at the forest of Freteval.

In a book entitled: "The Fight of the Francs-Tireurs and French Partisans in Eure-et-Loir", edited in 1946, one of the leaders, Roger Blanvillain, tells of one of the rescue missions in which he participated under the assumed names, Roger Chochereau of Cloyes, Louis Lemoues of Chateaudun and Bernard Avisseau of Marboue.

One evening in June 1944, the water was falling in torrents, we were five of us: Jean, Jean-Pierre, Geo, Marcel and I, were seated around a table in our abandoned house of Lorry, our P.C. (Partisan Leader], was discussing the air battle which had taken place in the afternoon above Chateaudun. One of our friends from a neighboring area came suddenly to warn us that two allied aviators had fallen that afternoon and had been seen in a neighboring woods. Soon Jean, the leader of our P.C., gave us our jobs: "Marcel, you are going to Conie, surely you will be able to get information at your friend's home, and if you have a parachutist, lead him immediately" -- "Jean-Pierre, you will come with me, we are going to search in the woods" -- "Roger and Geo, you will stay here, take the Tommy gun and the carbine and keep yourselves on guard, the Germans could be roaming about, don't open to anyone without the agreed upon signal." They left. Geo and I kept ourselves ready. A half-hour after their departure we heard steps outside and two voices. The steps went away and a quarter of an hour later someone knocked at the door according to our code, it was the aunt of Marcel who announced to us that a man had come to her house (her house was next door), and announcing in a mysterious air, said: "I have a package for Marcel, a heavy package! Do you know where Marcel is?" Obviously the answer was no. We were wondering what that meant. She left. Outside it was still raining. A half-hour after that, Jean and Jean-Pierre returned accompanied by two big fellows in gray, two English aviators who had an astonished look, and were perhaps a little worried when they saw us, Geo and me, surrounded by our guns. But their faces brightened up and finally their first words came. "Oh! French Resistance!" Useless to say with what force our hands grasped each other. The poor fellows were drenched from head to foot and our first worry was to dry their clothing, but we understood that they were worried about the fate of their friends who had been on board. Jean explained how he succeeded in finding them: "I was saying: 'French Resistance, comrades!' Do you know that they didn't seem to understand, and I was wondering if we could even get them to come with us, they took such a long time to understand that we were real ones."

The explanation of these famous footsteps that we had heard in the courtyard was given in an instant by a new knocking at the door and by a voice crying: "Roger, Marcel, open in the name of God; you will make me die!" As soon as I got myself up I noticed another friend from a neighboring area all dripping with water. "You are worthless young fellows! Just a little while ago I knocked! I have been next door at the home of Marcel's aunt--impossible to reach you. But you were right to take precautions. I have brought you something difficult to transport. I have a parachutist who has a sprain. I am with my friend Rene; we put him on a bicycle and we have been pushing him. We have just finished six kilometers. The poor fellow asked how long the trip is going to last. He must be hurting. Help us totransport him." We entered and were able to bring him in holding him as well as possible. He found again his two friends, all three from the same plane. We stretched him out on our only bed and Jean-Pierre took care of his ankle. Evidently the discussions were going well with his two companions. At that moment Marcel arrived with another aviator, a young man of twenty years old. With what joy he found again the three others. We understood by their explanations with gestures that they were thanking us for having reunited them. We got them situated so that they were able to sleep. The rest of us went into the hay of the loft. Jean decided to stay downstairs all night. The next day, after having succeeded in talking, thanks to an interpreter we had arranged to have come, we planned how we were going to lead them out. Our four friends, tasting of life on the good side, felt so happy that they, in English, and we in French, altogether we sang "El Rancho Grande". They were so well adjusted that one of them said in very bad French: "Do you have tea? Me like much tea!" To which Jean-Pierre answered him, showing him our little bag of roasted barley: "My old fellow, we aren't in London here." The following night, Jean led the three able-bodied ones to the regroupment camp (twenty-five kilometers, in two stages) he marching in front and they behind, following at a short distance, dressed in civilian clothes, more or less appropriate to their size. The wounded fellow stayed with us a week after that, then he rejoined them, taken during the day in a truck.

If certain aviators had to go long distances before being regrouped in the forest, there was one of them by contrast, who was welcomed very close to the camp by Kleber Oliver, who was at this period of time employed at the Fouchard farm at Bellande, where he was in charge of killing the animals for food for the camps. He led the aviator himself to his comrades.

The last escapee person led to the camp was discovered by the resistance workers operating in Sologne, to which he had been led from the home of M. de la Malene, at Diorieres, the township of Chauvigny-du-Perche. When he finally arrived, the Germans had already left the country so his stay in the forest was of very short duration.

THE LIBERATION OF THE CAMPS

The hardest thing was the waiting. The radio announced continuously the advance of the allied troops, but one waited in vain in the region of Freteval. The impatience was growing. The German troops were in full retreat, sifting through the region. Sometimes shots fired came from the direction of the road toward the forest. The aviators didn't have any arms, in order to avoid any tragic outcomes in case of their arrest. In order to assure security, Lucien Boussa asked the Resistance to furnish little armed groups, charged with patrolling around the camps. This was done, but they never had to intervene.

At the beginning of the month of August, it was no longer a question of Liberation. Having learned by radio that the allies were located in the area around Mans, at seventy kilometers from Freteval, the commander decided to go there in order to hasten the liberation of the camps. Guided by Etienne Viron, in a car, they arrived after a long trip of a hundred kilometers joining the first lines of Americans. Making himself known, Lucien Boussa was led to the staff officers where, by an extraordinary chance he met the head of "M.I. 9", Airey Neave who he had left several months earlier in England. The 10th of August, arrangements were made and it was decided that the 13th, a protective column of British commandos would come to look for these "pensionaires" of the forest.

The extraordinary adventure was going to end. The 12th of August, considering themselves liberated, the aviators went in groups into the villages of Saint-Jean-Froidmentel and Busloup. The inhabitants were astonished to see themselves surrounded by young people speaking English. As soon as the flags were put up in order to celebrate the end of the nightmare, the village people hurried to bring out from their wine cellars fine bottles guarded preciously for the time of the Liberation and in these localities they celebrated late into the night.

The next day the 13th of August, the announced column arrived at "Camp No. 1". It was not without emotion and without regret sometimes, that the aviators cast a last look on this immense forest that had sheltered them during the long months. Several members of the Resistance, notified of this departure, were there to give their adieux. Up until the last moment, luck smiled on the escapees. All were able to resume their service in the air crews. Following this, thirty-eight of them were going to lose their lives in aerial operations above Germany.

The fact of having been able to lead more than a hundred and fifty aviators to the forest of Freteval, to have hidden them and nourished them, constituted a real feat for the Resistance. But how all these men had been able to live from May to August, 1944, in this region open to patrols of the occupying German forces, remains unexplainable.

We would not like to finish this page of history without adding the name of Madame Halloin of La Proutiere, the township of Montigny-le-Gannelon, dead in deportation for having lodged patriots who aided the aviators of the forest, and that of Jean Chauveau of Cloyes, who furnished official papers stolen from the Germans in order to be used by the escorts of "Comete". He was captured the 15th of August and suffered the same fate as the martyrs of Cormainville.

We have endeavored in this booklet to cite all the persons of the region who participated in the escorting service, in the lodging and the supplying of the food for the aviators. Nevertheless perhaps certain ones may have been forgotten. We ask them to please excuse us for it.

Twenty years later, Colonel Boussa wanted to see again this region that had welcomed him under the occupation. He was very happy to find a large number of his friends of the underground activity. He conceived the project of a book retracing the adventure of the "Forest of Freteval", the proceeds of which would serve for the erection of a commemorative monument. This project not having been brought to fruition, a committee composed of twenty-seven members designated below was constituted the 20th of March, 1966, in order to collect necessary funds to erect a monument which would be inaugurated the 11th of June 1967.

Fate did not want Colonel Boussa to see the work that he had so ardently desired. Death surprised him brutally at Cloyes, the 12th of March 1967, in this little section of France where so many memories were dear to him, to which he had come specifically from Belgium in order to assist in an important meeting of the Committee.

A moving funeral service was held for him in the presence of the representatives of the French government, of the army, and of the allied countries.

The sister of M. le Marquis of Levy of Mirepoix, Madame la Vicomtesse of Beaudignies, owner of the woods where "Camp No. 1" was set up made a gift of the land where the memorial has been built. The general advisors of Eure-et-Loir and of Loir-et-Cher, answering the appeal of the Committee, voted each one to subsidise 10,000 francs; the Municipal Advisory of Chartres 5,000 francs, the townships of two departments, of numerous people of the region, and several associations gave important amounts.

The stele, designed by the Dunois artist Divi [citizen of Chateaudun] was entrusted to Baglan of Pontijou (Loir-et-Cher), put in place and engraved by Houdebert of Vendome, the ground prepared by Rendineau of Saint-Hilaire-la-Gravelle, the drainage by Deganwy and the masonry by Rougeaux of Cloyes.

Thanks to the good will, to the understanding and the generosity of all, the inauguration ceremony took place the 11th of June 1967, as had been planned. This celebration had an international character, it was under the patronage of the Ministers of the Interior, of the Armed Forces and of the Combat Veterans and it took place in the presence of the Ambassadors of the allied countries, with the participation of aviators who had stayed in the camps of the forest of Freteval. The Memorial and this modest booklet will permit recalling to future generations the sacrifices that their ancestors made for the cause of peace and of liberty.

At Vendome, the 30th of May 1967

Cecile JUBAULT.

The Committee for the Administration of the Association consisted of the following members: Lucien Boussa, Jean-Felix Paulsen, Omer Jubault, Daniel Cogneau, Pierre Guillaumin, Dr. R. Dufour, Louis Lemoues, Bernard Avisseau, Gilbert Gourmand, Lucien Bezault, Atman Boudet, Leon Chesne, Roger Cochereau, Andre Gagnon, Jean Granger, Jean Grange, Robert Guerineau, Yves

Herve, Yves Jehanno, Yves Jouvelet, Gaston de Levis-de-Mirepoix, Paul Lieugard, Robert Poupard, Maurice Serein, Emile Vivier, Marius Villedieu, Etienne Viron, and Jean Zamponi.

IN MEMORY OF THE INHABITANTS OF THE REGION

Victims of their devotion to the allied aviators

Died in deportation:

Mesdames: Lucienne (Callu) Proux, Marie-Louise (Delbert) Gaspard.

Messieurs: Robert Germond, Rene Roussineau, Raymond Evard, Maurice Pommier.

Survivors of the death camps:

Madame Helene Germond.

Messieurs: Lucien Proux, Paul Taillard, Raymond Cordier.

Virginia in 1989 after receiving France's prestigious Legion d'Honneur.

Virginia and Philippe d'Albert-Lake with the daughter of one of the aviators they had rescued.

Appendix 4: List of Servicemen who took refuge in the Forest of Freteval Camps.

Australia

Andrews, Ken, (R.A.F.); Darwin 5792, Australia.

Eliot, Noel Tardun; West Australia.

Greatz, Edwin (Ted), (R.A.A.F.); Waikerie, South Australia.

Hourigan, Edward; Paxton, New South Wales.

King, W.J.E., (R.A.A.F).

Ibbotson, Dudley T., (R.A.A.F.); Thornlie, West Australia.

Lynch, K.J; Merricksville, New South Wales.

Murray, Ian, (R.A.A.F.); Swan Hill, Victoria 3585, Australia.

Wright, Evans; St. Peterborough, South Australia.

Canada

Agur, Pat, (R.C.A.F.)

Banks, Rod; Flesherton, Ontario.

Barkl...(?), Rod.

Beauchesne (No further details)

Bender, William; Kitchener, Ontario.

Bester, Jack; London, Ontario.

Binnie, Norman; Outremont, Montreal, Quebec.

Bonlacleone, N.

Brayley, William G; Montreal West, Quebec.

Calderbank, James; Hamilton, Ontario.

Campbell, Alex; Humber Bay, Toronto, Ont.

Chapman, Bert; Springhill, Nova Scotia.

Chapman, Jack; Toronto, Ontario.

Dunsieth, Sam, (R.C.A.F.)

Edward(s) - No further details

Fairborn, A.(R.C.A.F.)

Finn, Pat, (466 Squadron)

Forman, C.M; Windsor, Ontario.

Greenburgh, Louis, (R.A.F.); Winnipeg, Manitoba.

Grimsey, Maurice; St. Vital, Winnipeg, Man.

Hortie, Robert; Porcupine, Ontario.
Harvey, Sam A; Vancouver, British Columbia.
Hearty
Hyde, Bruce; DeWinton, Alberta.
Jones, Earl; Calgary, Alberta.
Lawrence, Stanley; Toronto, Ontario.
Mollison, Joseph; Victoria, BC.
Musgrove, Gerry A; Toronto, Ontario.
New(b)ey, H.
Sandulak, John, (R.A.F.); Carman, Manitoba.
Shields, William; Timmins, Ontario.
Struck
Taylor, Sam; Regina, Saskachewan.
Trimsey
Vickerman, William K; Sedgewick, Alberta.
Wingrove, A. W.

England (U.K.)

Berry, Peter; London.
Boness, Lawrence; Leicester.
Clay, Larry; Mapperly, Nottingham.
Dickens, Jack; Rushden, North Hants.
Hand, Gordon; Thirsk, N. Yorkshire.
Gordon, Robert; Stirling, Scotland.
Guild, Harry; Cowdenbeath, Fife, Scotland.
Hallett, Clifford I; Chard, Somerset.
Martin, Charles T; Cardiff, Glam.,Wales.
McCarthy, N; Hastings, Sussex.
Murrie, John D; Kirkintilloch, Scotland.
Pepall, Dennis; West Molesey, Surrey.
Prier, M. W.
Weir, Charles; Cheltenham, Glouster, G150 4NX.
Worrall, Ray; Leeds.
Wright, Eric W; Small Heath, Birmingham.

New Zealand

Speirs, Alan R; Richamond, Christchurch.

Elmhurst-Baxter, J.C., (R.A.F.).

Evans, F.O., (R.A.A.F.).

South Africa (British 8th Army from North Africa. Escaped in France.)

Adams, Everett G., (Army); Cape Town.

Hoover, Rudy, (Army); Escombe, Durban.

United States

Allen, E.G; Robstown, Texas.

Anderson, Eugine; La Crosse, Wisconsin.

Barr, Stuart K; Philadelphia, Pennsylvania.

Bies, Walter C; Detroit, Michigan.

Blair, Clare A; Ravena, Ohio.

Boggan, Thomas L., (U.S.A.A.F.).

Bone, Emmett W; Port Arthur, Texas.

Connables, Joseph M; Memphis,

Tennessee. Clark, Paul F; Chattanooga, Tennessee.

Claytor, Andrew Gordon; Glasgow, Virginia.

Couture, Robert D; Rice Lake, Wisconsin.

Davis, William M; Leesburg, Florida.

Derling, Cliff; Jersey City, New Jersey.

Dillon, William T; Colfax, Indiana.

Eckley, Malcom K; Bellefonte, Pennsylvania.

Gleason, Fred D.- (U.S.A.A.F.).

DiBetta, Geno; Parkersburg, West Virginia.

Goff, Marvin T; Houstan, Texas.

Golden, Guy H. (Jr.); Pine Bluff, Arkansas.

Goan, John F; Chattanooga, Tennessee.

Gorrono, Joseph I; Astoria, Long Island, New York.

Hall, Ralph L; Cleveland, Ohio.

Harrell, Harwood "Max"; Lake Charles, Louisiana

Hewitt, Clyde Edward.- 12251 E. 25th Street, Gary, Indiana.

Hjelm, Rex P; Firth, Idaho.
Hoilman, Donald F; Toledo, Ohio.
Holt, Alfred I; Cardington, Ohio.
Houghton, Kenneth L; San Francisco, California.
Huit, Burl E; Pierce, Colorado.
Johnson, Joseph; West Palm Beach, Florida.
Knight, Marion; Runge, Texas.
Kellerman, William; New York City, New York
Krol, Theodore J; Hammond, Indiana.
Loring, Warren E; Monument Beach, Massachusetts.
Lewis, Donald M; Coalings, California.
Middleton, Charles D; Huntingdon Park, California.
Pearson, Jonothan; Schenectady, New York.
Peloquin, Joseph O; Biddeford, Maine. 04005.
Peterson, Edward I; Wentworth, Wisconsin.
Richards, Lawrence C; Emmaus, Pennsylvania.
Rice, Roy J. (Jr.); Salem, Oregon.
Schilling, Kenneth W; Tacoma, Washington.
Sidders, Robert E; Hastings, Nebraska.
Solomos, George; Detroit, Michegan.
Sounder, David W; Houston, Pennsylvania.
Spiers
Spinks, Hayward C; La Grange, Georgia.
Tappan, Edward; (U.S.A.A.F.).
Tickner, Russell E; Fairfield, Illinois.
Vitkus, Roy D; Chicago, Illinois.
Weseloh, Eldo.C; Los Angeles, California.
Wiseman, Abraham, Lt. (U.S.A.A.F.).
Wright, Norman; Sommerville, Massachusetts.
Yankus, Thomas L; Jamaica, Long Island, New York
Yanzek, William.- 129 North Monmouth Street, Dayton, Ohio.

U.S.S.R.

Killadze

Country Unknown

Meanley, Ralph

Morris (No further details).

The following list of names is from a document dated 28 August 1944 which was provided by the Air Forces Escape and Evasion Society and is a list of American airmen who were "ordered to proceed to points outside the United Kingdom." Included in this list should be most of the remaining names of the Forest of Freteval inmates:

Victor N. Curtis	Albert H. Debacker	Donald W. McLeod
Robert J. Colwell	John L. Collins	Adam P. Tymowicz
Theodore G. Fahrenwald	Harold A. Potter	Philip H. Ewing
James S. Frederick	William S. Matusz	Ragnar E. Gustafson
Walter L. Harvey	Harrison C. Mellor	Franklyn F.Hendrickson
John J. Meade	Richard E. Rader	John L. Milliwen
Edward F. O'Day	Fred L. Shantz	Alfred H. Richter
Robert A. Seaman	John D. Bonnin	Ralph L. Smathers
Harold W. Bolin	John E. Hurley	Donald F. Bridwell
Herman F. Busse	Russell J. Katz	Thomas W. Cannon, Jr.
Robert W. Johnson	Louis W. Lynch	Neil W. Kemper
John C. Larkin	James W. Mc Curley	Peter D. MacVean
Robert H. Magnuson	Joseph P. Murphy	Charles L. Moore, Jr.
Goffred F. Moretto	Wallace A. Richard	Frank W. Ramsey
Jacob L. Rawls	Henry Scheingold	Thomas W. Ruark
Leonard J. Schallehn	Chester R. Tingle	Sam Singer
Theodore R. Stablein	Aubrey D. York	Edward J. Vesely
Zollie P. Webb	Wayne E. Brand	James D. Frink
Camille H. Blais	Ronald W. Reed	Carmine T. Fischetti
Harry G. Pace, Jr.	Cliff G. Latta	Harold C. Brooks, Jr.
Malcom K. Eckley	John R. Rudy	Leo R. Orifici
Edward F. Reedy	Orion H. Shumway	J. Kelly Shaw
Robert M. Shockey	Carle A. Adofson	Leo Williams
Arne G. Ziom	Hulitt O. Kirkhart	Richard J. Burnett
Moses J. Gatewood	Ralph J. Workman	Marion Knight

Appendix 5: Murray Peden's Letter

On Sunday, January 19th, 1992, the Canadian Broadcasting Corporation presented a documentary on Bomber Command which former bomber pilots found offensive. Lou Greenburgh referred to it as "a betrayal and a disgrace." The tragedy was that the documentary was produced with the blessing of the Canadian Government and thus reflects the lack of understanding and appreciation among this country's decision makers.

Murray Peden, who earned the Distinguished Flying Cross as a pilot with Bomber Command, wrote a letter objecting to the manner in which bomber crews had been portrayed. With his permission, I have included that letter in the following pages. I included the letter because it deals with an issue which history may never fully resolve; the morality of strategic bombing during World War II. I believe it is important to remember the reasons that the bombing took place, and its cost.

!8

MURRAY PEDEN, Q.C.
45 ALDERSHOT BOULEVARD
WINNIPEG, MANITOBA
R3P 0C8
(204) 888-5172

MR. PATRICK WATSON
CHAIRMAN C.B.C.
P.O. BOX 8478
OTTAWA ONTARIO
K1G 3J5

Jan. 30th, 1992.

Dear Sir: RE: "THE VALOUR AND THE HORROR"

I write to express my disgust and anger with the C.B.C.'s production "The Valour and the Horror," particularly the instalment on R.A.F. Bomber Command's operations broadcast on Sunday, January 19th.

For the C.B.C. thus to belittle and defame Canada's and Britain's airmen was disgraceful. In my view, that conduct answers the question already mooted as to whether your organization should not be privatized and taken off the backs of Canadian taxpayers. I am sending copies of this letter to some of our legislators and to various media organs in the hope that focusing attention on this despicable example of "Canadian content" will help contribute to that result.

In your six-hour series, any fair interpretation of the C.B.C.'s mandate might have prompted it to remind young viewers that Canada's prominent stature in world councils was largely achieved by the outstanding performance and sacrifice, in two World Wars, of its soldiers, sailors and airmen. Instead, the C.B.C. proffered a consistently negative thesis, with masochistically disproportionate emphasis on setbacks and mistakes, coupled with a tunnel-vision sermon on the killing of civilians which is nothing short of outrageous. That Canada's military efforts contributed substantially to Allied victory in World War II is but one of many facts pointedly ignored.

The series was apparently written by two people in your employ named McKenna. Whatever its origins, it is studded with pustules of the sick viewpoint most Canadians would style peacenik-revisionist. I raise the question of its ancestry because in its total disregard of important facts that do not fit its ludicrous indictments, it bears a suspicious resemblance to the modus operandi of the slime specialists of the National Film Board.

One of the perpetrators of this crude hatchet job solemnly announces at the beginning of each segment -- and with a straight face -- that it is dedicated to the 46,542 Canadians who gave their lives for their country.

The foul episode on Bomber Command might more aptly have been dedicated to Iago, or to Dr. Goebbels, who often peddled a similar pitch. Even Iago was more candid with his audience in disseminating his poison:

"Work on,
My medicine, work! Thus credulous fools are caught;
And many worthy and chaste dames even thus,
All guiltless, meet reproach."

- - -

[Perhaps you could break the news to Terence McKenna and his assistants that there were actually a handful of German civilians not playing violin in the Berlin Philharmonic. And, apropos the relative bombardment accuracy, point out that many were busy developing V-weapons at Peenemunde, buzz-bombs and the V-2 rockets which could only be guaranteed to land somewhere within a 30-mile target circle -- and which the Germans continued to shower on Allied civilians in London and Antwerp even after the war was patently lost. Oh yes, and quite a contingent, until mid-1943, were working on an atomic bomb. Our leaders did not know that they then abandoned its development; the last Allied intelligence was that German (civilian) scientists were considerably ahead of ours in the processing of heavy water, the latter knowledge being a nightmare-generator in our leaders' minds almost until the war in Europe ended.]

Reverting to your Hamburg segment: no doubt your objective C.B.C. researchers will argue it was coincidence, but the fact is that Sir Arthur, the man you portray as a headstrong leader who defied his superiors, in selecting Hamburg for destruction in July, 1943, chose that target complex because it was preeminently the most important in the highest-priority category laid down in the Combined Bomber Offensive directive issued by Churchill and Roosevelt at Casablanca in January, 1943. Published by the Combined Chiefs of Staff for implementation on May 14th, 1943, the six target systems in order of priority were: (1) Submarine construction yards and bases; (2) German aircraft industry; (3) Ball bearings, (4) Oil, (5) Synthetic rubber and tires; (6) Military transport vehicles. [See:THE STRATEGIC AIR OFFENSIVE AGAINST GERMANY, VOL. IV. P273]

This fact, too, somehow goes unreported in the C.B.C. production, nor is there any real mention of the military significance of the results of the raids. The enormous damage did not appear to impress the McKennas; but someone who definitely was shaken was Albert Speer, Hitler's Armaments-Minister. Speer wrote:
" ... Rash as this (Hamburg) operation was, it had catastrophic consequences for us.... The devastation of this series of air raids could be compared only with the effects of a major earthquake.... (On the 1st of August) I informed Hitler that armaments production was collapsing and threw in the further warning that a series of attacks of this sort, extended to six more major cities, would bring Germany's armaments production to a total halt...." [Speer: INSIDE THE THIRD REICH, Avon edition, pp 369, 370.]

Of course, for the C.B.C. to have reminded a younger audience of that assessment, from the most knowledgeable and irrefutable source, would have run the risk of making Sir Arthur look like what in truth he was, a highly capable commander, faithfully discharging the orders of Churchill's War Cabinet and the Chief of Air Staff; hence, there was little reference to the intended -- and achieved-- results of the attacks.

Throughout this disgraceful perambulation through the Crazy-House of military history, the McKennas continued to snipe at Sir Arthur Harris, sometimes openly, more often by innuendo. One of the heroes they chose to spew venom was Freeman Dyson, a young university graduate who clung throughout the war to a safe office job in Bomber Command's research section. Dyson, fresh from school like so many of the Bomber

Command aircrew with whom he mingled, was of precisely the right age and qualifications to enlist and serve in aircrew himself. Some incipient thrust of self-respect nudged him at a late stage into deciding to do so, or so he says in his book "Disturbing the Universe;" but he also says that it took his mother just two minutes to talk him out of that dangerous notion -- by challenging this brilliant scientist's competence to perform aircrew duties. In other words, the C.B.C.'s oft-quoted morals lecturer really suffered, as he makes clear himself, from serious back trouble, his having the color and tensile characteristics of a banana. It is apparent, notwithstanding, that an arrogant sniper like Dyson has far greater appeal as a role model to the C.B.C. than the young men who died for Canada in the aircrew harness he was careful to stay out of.

Dyson, the Ghandi follower and apostle of "Cosmic Unity," was used as the spokesman to make the most outrageously offensive accusation of the whole series: namely, that by our area bombing of the Germans we had given them, particularly their fighter pilots, the high ground, morally speaking, vis a vis the Allies. This is insufferable twaddle, and recognizable as such to anyone beyond the Dick and Jane reading stage. Lost in the C.B.C.'s eulogy of the German fighter pilots, for whom, incidentally, I had considerable professional respect -- they attacked us more than once, and sent me home from a raid on the Ruhr's Nordstern oil plant with my aircraft on fire and two crewmen wounded -- was any recognition of the fact that their fighting tenacity had the obvious result of prolonging the opportunities for some of their countrymen, busily engaged in the hellish work of the Holocaust, to continue murdering droves of innocents in the gas ovens at Dachau, Treblinka and other establishments operating on the same high moral plane. Thus, those sickening operations ran at full speed for a substantially longer period thanks in part to these Sir Galahads in the German fighter force. The death camps, along with the slave labour units, ran until the Allies hammered Germany into the ground, and they would have stayed in operation many months longer but for the Combined Bombing Offensive which the C.B.C. reviles. The C.B.C. disgraced itself, quoting with approval that preposterous affront to Canadian airmen.

Remind your amateur moralists that the Germans' chosen operating plane was not quite so morally elevated as their blinkered presentation would have us believe. This was a fact Germany made clear to all and sundry, incidentally, within ten hours of war being declared, when a U-boat torpedoed the small passenger liner Athenia for the strategic result of drowning 112 civilians.

No rational person could do other than deplore the killing of truly innocent civilians -- on both sides. Unfortunately, war makes that inescapable under some circumstances, as we have seen as recently as the Gulf War. Likewise, the mutual benefits of terminating a war as speedily as possible blur the moral issues almost beyond resolution. As the distinguished historian Denis Richards points out, the ultimate "area bombing" weapon, the atom bomb, quickly ended the war in Japan -- and undoubtedly saved over a million American lives in so doing. Denis Richards, I observe parenthetically, inclines to the view that Sir Arthur Harris was one of the greatest commanders of the Second World War.

In the Bomber Command instalment, it quickly becomes apparent that the C.B.C.'s purpose, through "historians" who are clearly graduates of the Jane Fonda Institute of Military Analysis, is to heap belittlement on Sir Arthur Harris, Air Officer Commanding-in-Chief, R.A.F. Bomber Command, and to denigrate the achievements of his aircrews. Indeed, to say that Sir Arthur is treated with a contemptuous unfairness is to understate the case in the same measure as reporting that the victim of a lynching was treated impolitely. Canadian youngsters, at least those as uninformed as the McKennas appear to be, could easily conclude from this presentation that Sir Arthur had a positive aversion to destroying oil plants or shipyards, and refused to kill anyone other than civilians.

Your scandalous diatribe, which sets out to demean a great commander and dishonour the memories of thousands of Canadian bomber crews, from Andrew Mynarski, V.C. on down, re-confirms the fact that a caricaturist or liar can achieve his object effectively by presenting mainly fragments of the truth, provided he is highly selective in the morsels he focuses on and avoids balancing his vignettes with a reference to the context from which they are drawn. For example, Sir Arthur Harris was in fact optimistic that the war could be won by bombing alone, without our sustaining the infantry casualties of a cross-Channel assault. But Sir Arthur posited a front-line force of 4,000 heavy bombers at a relatively early date, not the 1400 he ultimately achieved at the end of 1944. Neglecting to mention that gross discrepancy between what was envisaged and what was delivered understandably makes him vulnerable to distortionists unburdened with a desire to present the whole truth.

Their account is actually so replete with errors and distortions that to correct them all would run to a score of pages. But let me single out a few examples, illustrative of the abysmally shoddy artistic and journalistic standards permeating it.

One portion, bent on portraying Sir Arthur as an inflexible fool, alleges -- with a deft bit of footwork to cover a five-month jump in chronology -- that he flatly refused to carry out direct orders from the Chief of Air Staff and the Air Ministry to switch temporarily from the strategic targets assigned as his force's primary objectives and concentrate instead on the destruction of objectives essential to the successful launching and furtherance of the D-Day invasion.

For the record, that representation is false. Sir Arthur did have his own views on whether such a detour from the primary mission given him would best serve the Allied cause, and argued that case with vigour; but when his submission was overruled and the contrary decision taken, Sir Arthur carried out his orders with exemplary loyalty and diligence. Here I speak, not as a revisionist, but as a participant who piloted a bomber on several of the missions involved -- under orders from the same Sir Arthur Harris the McKennas say refused to carry out the SHAEF directive. Furthermore, the intractability they portray on his part might best be gauged from his written exchanges at the time. Consider:

When, in September, 1944, Sir Arthur's force was returned to its normal chain of command, this man you pictured as obstreperous in the extreme, wrote immediately to "My dear Ike" to assure Eisenhower that "... our continuing commitment for the support of your forces upon call from you will indeed continue, as before, to be met to the utmost of our skill and the last ounce of our endeavour...... We in Bomber Command proffer ... our utmost service wherever and whenever the need arises. Yours ever, Bert." [Eisenhower, "Crusade in Europe," p 308.]

After the war, Sir Arthur left hanging in his study, amongst dozens of mementos and tributes, letters sent him by General Eisenhower and Field Marshal Montgomery, extolling the unhesitating support lent them by Bomber Command throughout their land battle, from Normandy to Berlin. Were Eisenhower and Montgomery lying? Or are you simply telling the truth the way the N.F.B. told the truth about Air Marshal Bishop, V.C.?

Another protracted segment of your program which strikes anyone familiar with the facts as markedly out of focus, was the coverage of the Hamburg raids carried out by the R.A.F. and the U.S. 8th Air Force at the end of July, 1943. Your coverage centred almost exclusively on the civilian casualties, mainly incurred in the unprecedented firestorm that arose during the R.A.F.'s July 27th/28th strike. It was proper to deal with those casualties, and compassionately; they were, after all, the heaviest of any attack of the European war. But one might have expected at least a passing reference to the strategic factors which prompted the choice of target, and to the military results achieved by the raids.

Likewise, it would have contributed to some semblance of balance to record the fact that the immediately preceding campaign, the Battle of the Ruhr, had been directed for weeks against the most heavily defended and densely concentrated industrial zone in the world. Neither the success of that campaign, nor the remarkable new accuracy in Bomber Command's target-marking achieved from its outset by the use of "Oboe " was mentioned.

As I say, totally absent from your account of the Hamburg raids was the slightest recognition of the fact that Britain was fighting for its life against strangulation by the German U-boat campaign -- and that the biggest submarine builders in Germany were Blohm & Voss, of Hamburg. That prime shipyard, one of a great many in Hamburg, built over 400 U Boats during the war, along with other useful artifacts like the 41,700 ton battleship Bismarck -- you may have heard of it -- the heavy cruiser Admiral Hipper, and scores of lighter naval units. Such mundane trivia do not figure in the McKenna history, nor the fact that, by July of 1943, Blohm & Voss alone were turning out new U-Boats at a rate slightly in excess of one per week. [Middlebrook: THE BATTLE OF HAMBURG, p 61.]

And let <u>me</u> emphasize something, a fact even more studiously ignored by the C.B.C.: these battleships, cruisers, submarines and other naval weapons were not built by uniformed S.S. men, but by German civilians living in Hamburg. Meantime, uniformed Germans, in the U-Boats, E-Boats and other craft fashioned there were busy drowning the civilian sailors of our merchant marine in large numbers, and trying to win the war by starving our civilians in Britain. As Winston Churchill has pointed out, they came frighteningly close to doing so.

On that note, let me conclude by reiterating that your series belittled Sir Arthur Harris and the accomplishments of his crews in a grossly unfair and ignorant manner. The prevailing impression you tried to leave was that beyond killing civilians, their bombing campaign accomplished little. I refer you again to the diametrically opposed appraisal of someone with vastly more knowledge on the subject, Hitler's Minister of Armaments, who said, quite simply, of that campaign:

" ...no one has yet seen that this was the greatest lost battle on the German side." [Albert Speer, SPANDAU, P 375.]

And apropos Sir Arthur's performance, it is material to point out that another historian, one of somewhat more imposing stature than the McKennas, had a view of him directly refuting theirs, and had this to say of him, in a letter urging that high honour be conferred upon the Commander-in-Chief of Bomber Command:

"... No Commander-in-Chief in the Royal Air Force after Lord Dowding bore so heavy a direct burden as (Sir Arthur Harris,) and none contributed more distinguished qualities to the discharge of his duty. As Minister of Defence I had the opportunity and the duty of watching his work very closely and I greatly admired the manner in which he bore the altogether peculiar stresses of planning and approving these repeated, dangerous and costly raids far into the heart of the enemy's country. For nearly four years he bore this most painful responsibility and never lost the confidence or loyalty of Bomber Command, in spite of the fact that it endured losses equalled only, in severity, by those of our submarines in the Mediterranean.

"When we consider also the immense part played by the bombing offensive in shortening the war and thus bringing it to an end before the enemy long-range weapons developed their full potency, nobody can deny its cardinal importance. It was also a grim and invidious task that was laid upon this Air Marshal and which he discharged with unfailing poise and equanimity, although deeply conscious of its grievousness...."

The writer was Winston Churchill. [See Martin Gilbert, NEVER DESPAIR, p 178] With his own patriotism, sense of justice, and deep respect for men who did their duty unflinchingly, Churchill, had he seen the C.B.C. program in question, would probably have closed a letter like this with a reference to W.H. Auden's Epitaph for the Unknown Soldier:

"To save the world you asked this man to die;

Would this man, could he see you now, ask why?"

Yours truly,

Murray Peden

MURRAY PEDEN, D.F.C., Q.C.

Appendix 6: Excerpts from Lou Greenburgh's Logbook

Year 1943 Month	Date	Aircraft Type	Aircraft No.	Pilot, or 1st Pilot	2nd Pilot, Pupil or Passenger	Duty (Including Results and Remarks)	Single-Engine Aircraft Day Dual (1)	Day Pilot (2)	Night Dual (3)	Night Pilot (4)	Dual (5)	1st Pilot (6)
—	—	—	—	—	—	— Totals Brought Forward	92.57	91.36	17.42	11.00	72.55	83.4
October	3	STIRLING	(C)	P/O MALONEY	SELF (CREW)	OPS. (KASSEL)						
"	13	"	(K)	SELF P/O DALE	CREW	WAR LOAD						
"	15	"	(C)	SELF	CREW	ERIC						2.0
"	16	"	(A)	"	"	AIR SEA RESCUE						03.1
"	17	"	(C)	"	"	NIGHT XC						04.[illegible]
"	18	"	(C)	"	"	ERIC						02.[illegible]
"	19	"	(G)	"	"	AIR TEST						0.[illegible]
"	20	"	(A)	"	"	FIGHTER AFFL.						01.0
"	20	"	(G)	"	"	OPS. FRISIAN Is. (MINE LAYING)						
"	22	"	(B)	"	"	FIGHTER AF.						01.0[illegible]
"	24	"	(A)	"	"	" FORMATION.						02.3
"	"	"	(F)	"	"	BOMBING.						01.5
"	25	"	(G)	"	"	AIR TEST						0.4
"	"	"	"	"	"	OPS. MINING - KATTEGAT						01.5
"	27	"	(G)	"	"	AIR TEST.						0.4
"	29	"	"	"	"	" "						
"	31	"	"	"	"	" "						01.2
				Summary for OCTOBER 1943		1. STIRLING						22.0
				Unit 620 'A' FLT. Aircraft		2.						
				Date 31-10-43 Types		3.						
				Signature L. Greenburgh		4.						
				GRAND TOTAL [Cols. (1) to (10)] 512 Hrs. 17 Mins.		Totals Carried Forward	92.54	91.36	17.42	11.00	72.55	105.[illegible]

Excerpt from Lou Greenburgh's Pilot's Log Book.

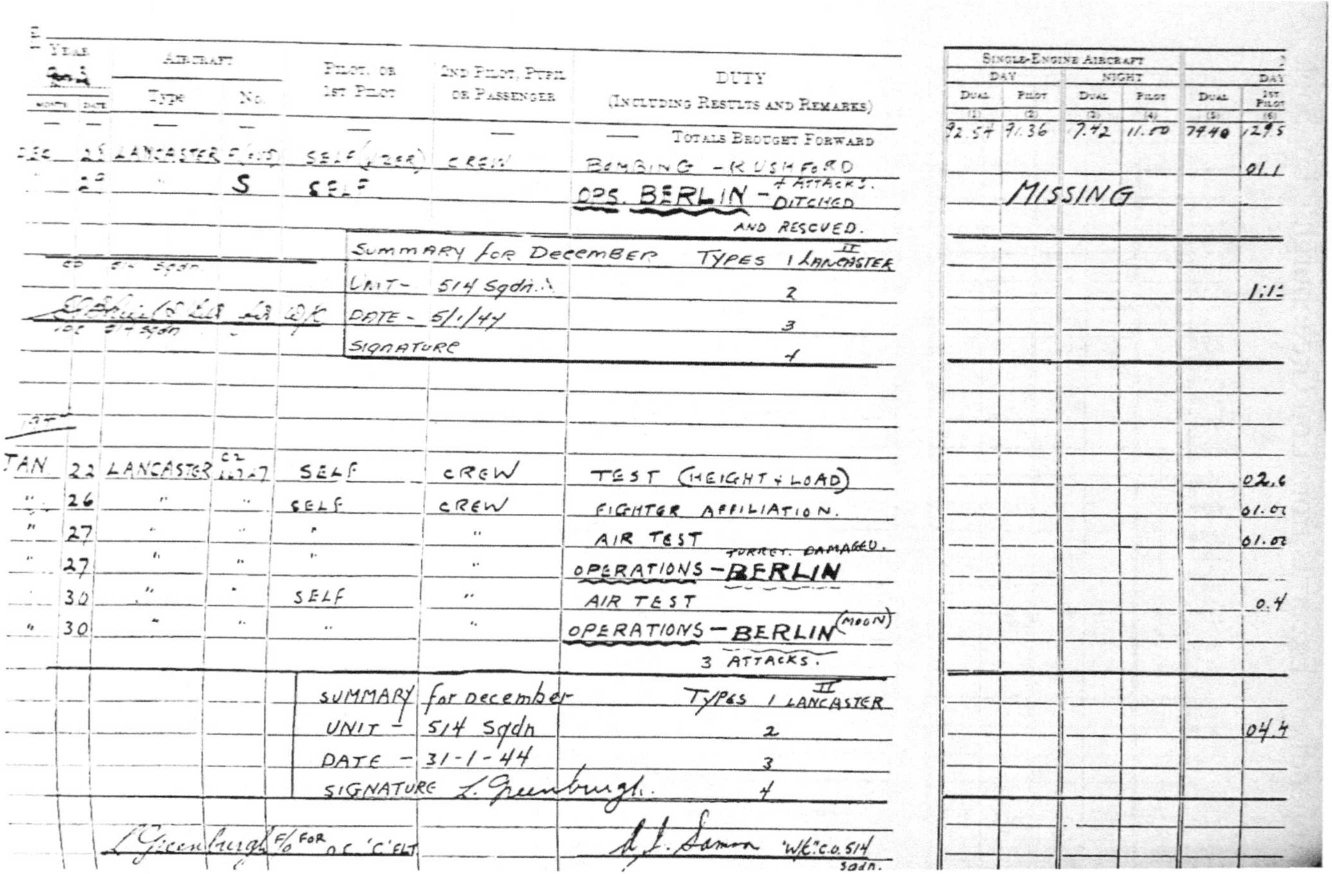

Year / Month	Date	Aircraft Type	No.	Pilot, or 1st Pilot	2nd Pilot, Pupil or Passenger	DUTY (Including Results and Remarks)	Single-Engine Aircraft Day Dual (1)	Day Pilot (2)	Night Dual (3)	Night Pilot (4)	Dual (5)	Day 1st Pilot (6)
—	—	—	—	—	—	— Totals Brought Forward	92.54	91.36	7.42	11.50	7440	129.5
DEC	2[illegible]	LANCASTER	[illegible]	SELF (2ER)	CREW	BOMBING - RUSHFORD						01.1
	2[illegible]	"	S	SELF		OPS. BERLIN - 4 ATTACKS. DITCHED AND RESCUED.		MISSING				
				SUMMARY for DECEMBER		TYPES 1 LANCASTER II						
				UNIT - 514 Sqdn.		2						1:1[illegible]
[illegible]				DATE - 5/1/44		3						
O.C. 514 Sqdn				SIGNATURE		4						
1944												
JAN	22	LANCASTER	LL727 [illegible]	SELF	CREW	TEST (HEIGHT + LOAD)						02.[illegible]
"	26	"	"	SELF	CREW	FIGHTER AFFILIATION.						01.0[illegible]
"	27	"	"	"	"	AIR TEST						01.0[illegible]
"	27	"	"	"	"	OPERATIONS - BERLIN (TURRET. DAMAGED.)						
"	30	"	"	SELF	"	AIR TEST						0.4
"	30	"	"	"	"	OPERATIONS - BERLIN (MOON) 3 ATTACKS.						
				SUMMARY for December		TYPES 1 LANCASTER II						
				UNIT - 514 Sqdn		2						04.4
				DATE - 31-1-44		3						
				SIGNATURE L. Greenburgh.		4						

L. Greenburgh F/O for O.C. 'C' FLT

[illegible] W/C C.O. 514 Sqdn.

Year 1944 Month	Date	Aircraft Type	Aircraft No.	Pilot, or 1st Pilot	2nd Pilot, Pupil or Passenger	Duty (Including Results and Remarks)	Single-Engine Aircraft Day Dual (1)	Day Pilot (2)	Night Dual (3)	Night Pilot (4)	Multi-Engine Day Dual (5)	Day 1st Pilot (6)
—	—	—	—	—	—	Totals Brought Forward	92.54	91.36	17.42	11.00	74.40	135.55
Feb.	2	LANCASTER	C 727	SELF	CREW	AIR TEST						01.10
"	5	"	"	"	"	BOMBING						01.00
"	6	"	"	"	"	ERIC						03.00
"	7	"	L	"SELF" BULBRNGH	"	BOMBING.						01.15
"	8	"	H	SELF	"	H.T. LOAD TEST						02.30
"	10	"	LF727	SELF HARRISON	"	FIGHTER AFF.						01.00
"	11	"	"	SELF	"	BOMBING (CANCELLED)						0.30
"	12	"	"	"	"	MEDENHALL						.40
"	19	"	"	"	"	AIR TEST						.40
"	29	"	"	"	"	AIR TEST						1.00
		SUMMARY FOR FEBRUARY 44				AIRCRAFT TYPES 1. LANCASTER [illegible]						12.45
		UNIT C' FLT. 514 SQDN				2.						
		DATE 1-3-44				3.						
		SIGNATURE [signature]				4.						
		[signature]		O/C 'C' FLT.		[signature] W/CDR O/C 514 SQDN						
MAR.	1	LANCASTER	C LL727	SELF	CREW	OPERATIONS STUTTGART						
"	3	"	"	"	"	BOMBING						01.30
"	7	"	"	"	SG JOHNSON, -S/R CREW.	OPERATIONS LE MANS LOW LEVEL.						
"	10	"	"	"	CREW	AIR TEST						0.45
					GRAND TOTAL [Cols. (1) to (10)] 599 Hrs. 32 Mins.	Totals Carried Forward	92.54	91.36	17.42	11.00	74.40	149.55

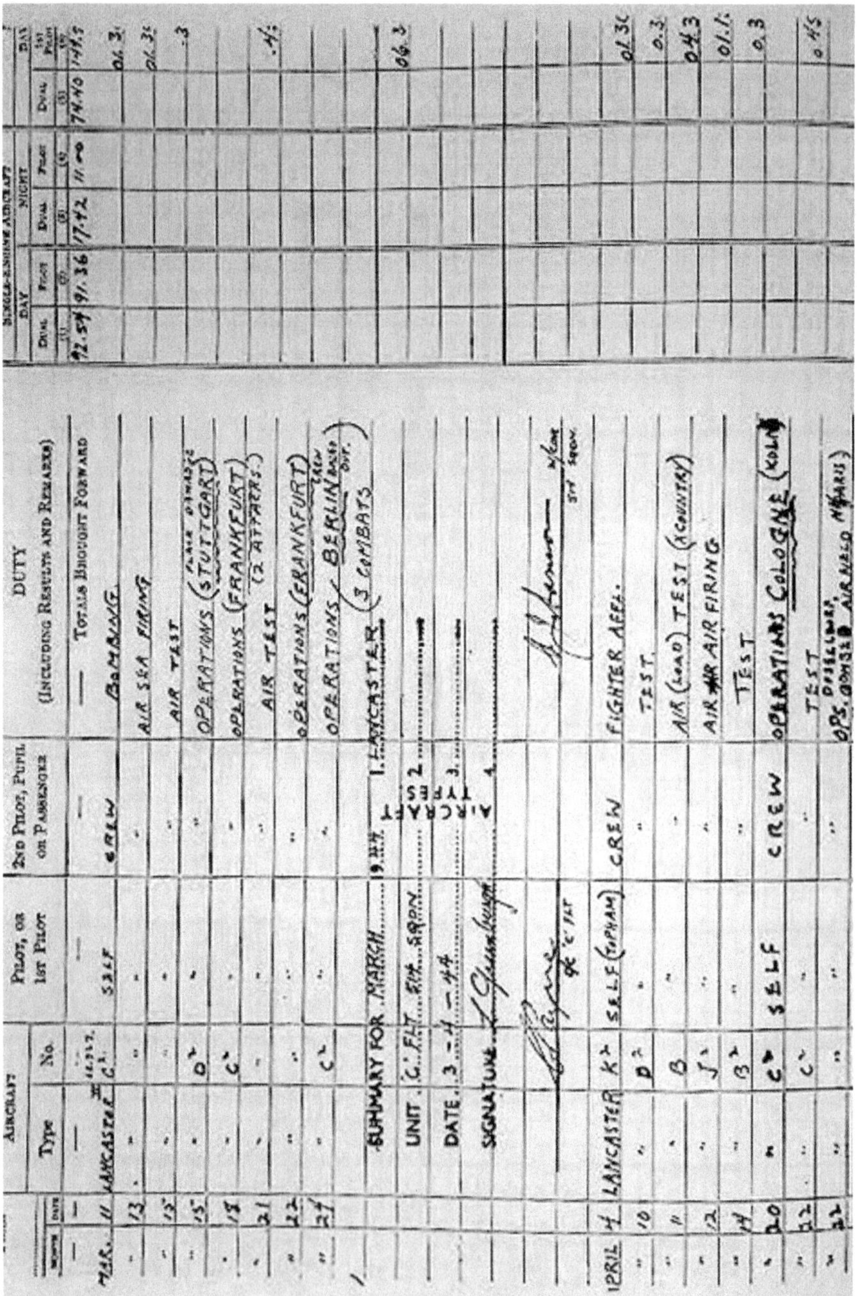

Month	Date	Aircraft Type	No.	Pilot, or 1st Pilot	2nd Pilot, Pupil or Passenger	Duty (Including Results and Remarks)	Single-Engine Aircraft Day Dual (1)	Day Pilot (2)	Night Dual (3)	Night Pilot (4)	Day Dual (5)	Day 1st Pilot (6)
—	—	—	—	—	—	Totals Brought Forward	92.54	91.36	17.42	11.00	74.40	149.5
MAR.	11	LANCASTER III	LL.757. C²	SELF	CREW	BOMBING						01.3
"	13	"	"	"	"	AIR SEA FIRING						01.3
"	15	"	"	"	"	AIR TEST						.3
"	15	"	D²	"	"	OPERATIONS (STUTTGART) FLAK DAMAGE						
"	18	"	C²	"	"	OPERATIONS (FRANKFURT) (2 ATTACKS.)						
"	21	"	"	"	"	AIR TEST						.4
"	22	"	"	"	"	OPERATIONS (FRANKFURT)						
"	24	"	C²	"	"	OPERATIONS, BERLIN CREW BAILED OUT. (3 COMBATS)						

SUMMARY FOR MARCH 19.44. UNIT 'C' FLT 514 SQDN. DATE 3-4-44 SIGNATURE L. Greenburgh

AIRCRAFT TYPES 1. LANCASTER 2. 3. 4. — 06.3

O.C. 'C' FLT — W/CDR 514 SQDN.

Month	Date	Aircraft Type	No.	Pilot, or 1st Pilot	2nd Pilot, Pupil or Passenger	Duty (Including Results and Remarks)	Day 1st Pilot (6)
APRIL	4	LANCASTER	K²	SELF (TOPHAM)	CREW	FIGHTER AFFL.	01.30
"	10	"	D²	"	"	TEST.	0.3
"	11	"	B	"	"	AIR (LOAD) TEST (X COUNTRY)	04.3
"	12	"	J²	"	"	AIR AIR FIRING	01.1
"	14	"	B²	"	"	TEST	0.3
"	20	"	C²	SELF	CREW	OPERATIONS COLOGNE (KOLN)	
"	22	"	C²	"	"	TEST	0.45
"	22	"	"	"	"	OPS. DUSSELDORF, BOMBED AIRFIELD N. PARIS)	

Year 1944 Month	Date	Aircraft Type	Aircraft No.	Pilot, or 1st Pilot	2nd Pilot, Pupil or Passenger	Duty (Including Results and Remarks)	Single-Engine Aircraft Day Dual (1)	Day Pilot (2)	Night Dual (3)	Night Pilot (4)	Dual (5)	Day 1st Pilot (6)
—	—	—	—	—	—	Totals Brought Forward	92.57	91.36	17.42	11.00	74.40	163.05
April	24	LANCASTER	L727 C	SELF	CREW	AIR-TEST.						.30
"	24	"	"	"	"	OPERATIONS. KARLSRUHE. BAD WEATHER.						
"	26	"	"	"	"	AIR TEST						.30
"	27	"	"	"	"	OPERATIONS FRIEDRICHSHAFEN						
"	29	"	"	"	"	AIR TEST PANIC.						01.30
"	30	"	E2	"	"	BOMBING.						.30
		SUMMARY FOR APRIL 1944			AIRCRAFT TYPES 1.	LANCASTER						12.00
		UNIT "C" FLT. 514 SQDN.			2.							
		DATE 3-4-44			3.							
		SIGNATURE L. Greenhough			4.							
		[signature] O.C. 'C' FLT.				[signature] W/Cdr. O.C. 514 Sqdn.						
MAY	1	LANCASTER	LL727	SELF	CREW	A/T.						.30
MAY	1	"	"	"	"	OPERATIONS CHAMBLY (PARIS)						
"	10	"	"	"	"	OPERATIONS COURTRAY						
"	11	"	"	"	F/O NORBURY CREW.	OPERATIONS. LOUVAIN (BELGIUM)						
"	14	"	"	"	CREW	AIR TEST						0.45
"	15	"	"	"	"	F/AFFL.						01.00
"	16	"	"	"	"	FORMATION FLYING						01.45
"	19	"	"	"	F/L. ATTERIDGE CREW	OPERATIONS LE MANS LIGHT FLACK (DENSE)						—
"	21	"	"	"	CREW	AIR-AIR FIRING						01.15
"	22	"	"	"	"	OPERATIONS DUISBURG						
				GRAND TOTAL (Cols. (1) to (10)) 686 Hrs. 59 Mins.		Totals Carried Forward	92.57	91.36	17.42	11.00	74.40	[redacted] 171.26

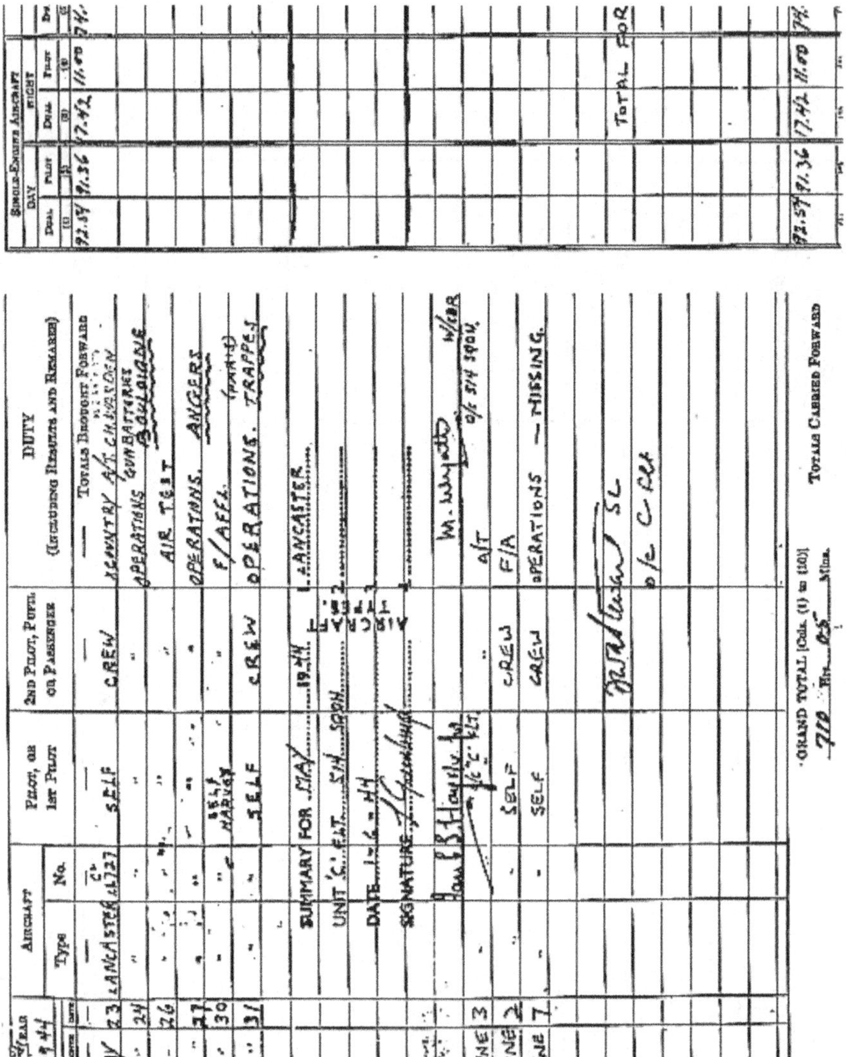

Year 1944 Month	Date	Aircraft Type	Aircraft No.	Pilot, or 1st Pilot	2nd Pilot, Pupil or Passenger	Duty (Including Results and Remarks)
—	—	—	—	—	—	Totals Brought Forward
MAY	23	LANCASTER	C2 LL727	SELF	CREW	X COUNTRY A/T CHILBOLDEN
"	24	"	"	"	"	OPERATIONS GUN BATTERIES BOULOGNE
"	26	"	"	"	"	AIR TEST
"	27	"	"	"	"	OPERATIONS. ANGERS
"	30	"	"	SELF HARVEY	"	F/AFFL.
"	31	"	"	SELF	CREW	OPERATIONS. TRAPPES
JUNE	3	"			"	A/T
JUNE	2	"	"	SELF	CREW	F/A
JUNE	7	"	"	SELF	CREW	OPERATIONS — MISSING.

SUMMARY FOR MAY 1944
UNIT 'C' FLT. 514 SQDN.
DATE 1-6-44
SIGNATURE [illegible]

AIRCRAFT TYPES
1. LANCASTER

[illegible] for O/C 'C' FLT.

M. Wyatt W/CDR
O/C 514 SQDN.

[illegible] SL
O/C C FLT

GRAND TOTAL [Cols. (1) to (10)] 710 Hrs. 05 Mins.

	Single-Engine Aircraft Day Dual (1)	Day Pilot (2)	Night Dual (3)	Night Pilot (4)
Totals Brought Forward	92.54	91.36	17.42	11.00
Totals Carried Forward	92.54	91.36	17.42	11.00

TOTAL FOR

Appendix 7: Combat Reports submitted by Lou Greenburgh

Combat Report 29/30th December 1943:

Aircraft: DS821 - 'S'
Captain: F/O L Greenburgh
Target: BERLIN

1st encounter: Outward bound, flying on a course of 090 degrees at 20,000 feet, IAS 155. At 1815 hours when in the Meppen area Rear Gunner saw exhaust of aircraft on port quarter down at range of about 700 yards, closing in. At 400 yards range on port quarter down this aircraft opened fire on Lancaster and was recognised by Rear Gunner as a JU-88, and Rear Gunner gave order to corkscrew to port and returned E/A's fire with a very long and almost uninterrupted burst of 6 seconds as E/A closed in slowly passing under Lancaster and finally breaking away on the starboard quarter down. MU Gunner did not see E/A but fired some short bursts in the direction of Rear Gunners trace. In the corkscrew Rear Gunner saw what appeared to be a rocket projectile fired at Lancaster from E/A and the Pilot and WOP saw an orange glow or explosion close under Lancaster's port wing. During this attack Lancaster's petrol tank was presumably damaged causing the petrol leak which ultimately resulted in Lancaster's ditching. No S/ L, Flak, or flares were observed.
2nd Encounter: At 2200 hours homeward bound, with bombs dropped, in approximately the same position as during the outward bound encounter, flying on course of 270 Degrees IAS 175 at 21,000 feet, M/ U Gunner reported and identified a JU-88 climbing on the fine starboard quarter level not firing but manoeuvring for attack at a range of 200 yards. MU Gunner immediately gave order to corkscrew to starboard at which moment Rear Gunner also sighted E/A and both Gunners of Lancaster opened fire on E/A simultaneously, MU Gunner with 3 very short bursts and Rear Gunner with a large number of short bursts many of which appeared to be hitting E/A. As E/A broke away to starboard quarter up, Rear Gunner saw it wobble as if out of control and MU Gunner saw a red glow from the centre of the fuselage, and it is claimed as probably destroyed. About half a minute prior to this attack

a bright yellow flare had been observed about half a mile to starboard. There were no S/Ls or flak.
3rd Encounter: At 2215 hours while in the Enkhuizen area homeward bound and shortly after a serious shortage of petrol had been noticed, Lancaster was flying on a course of 270 Degrees IAS 210 at height of 17,000 feet when Rear Gunner reported and identified a JU-88 on the starboard quarter up at a range of 400 yards, closing in and firing on Lancaster. Rear Gunner ordered corkscrew starboard and MU Gunner saw E/A just after the dive had commenced. Both Gunners of Lancaster opened fire simultaneously when E/A was at a range of 300 yards. E/A broke away to port quarter up, repeated a similar attack from there to starboard quarter, and again a similar attack from starboard to port quarter. During each of these attacks MU Gunner was firing a series of short bursts and Rear Gunner a long burst at E/A which was firing at Lancaster. There were no S/L or Flak but 3 orange flares were observed to starboard about a mile away just prior to this encounter.

MU Gunner - Sgt Carey - 500 rounds.
Rear Gunner - F/S Drake - 1240 rounds.

Combat Report 18th March 1944:

Aircraft: LL727 'C2'
Captain: F/O L Greenburgh
Target: FRANKFURT

Outward bound (bombs not dropped), flying at 18,000 feet. At 23.50 hours Rear Gunner reported unidentified twin engined aircraft on starboard quarter up at a range of 800 yards. Enemy persisted in following Lancaster in same position and at same range for considerable time. Mid Upper Gunner and Rear Gunner finally fired 2 or 3 short bursts each at E/A and Rear Gunner gave order to corkscrew to starboard. Enemy aircraft which did not open fire was lost in the corkscrew and not seen again. Visibility was poor. Numerous fighter flares were in evidence but no searchlights or flak directed at Lancaster. No 'Monica' warning.
MU Gunner - Sgt RJ Woosnam - 200 rounds.
Rear Gunner - F/S CA Drake RAAF - 400 rounds.

Combat Report 22nd March 1944:

Aircraft: LL727 'C2'
Captain: F/O L Greenburgh.
Target: FRANKFURT

Homeward bound (bombs dropped), flying at 19,000 feet. At 2220 hours, after 'Monica' warning, Rear Gunner reported a JU-88 on port quarter level at range of 800-900 yards. E/A followed Lancaster in this position and range for 2 to 3 minutes dropping a number of flares and firing 2 bursts at Lancaster, the trace passing close to tailplane. Rear Gunner gave order to corkscrew to port and further trace was observed during this manoeuvre, but not near Lancaster. After 2 or 3 minutes of violent evasive action E/A was lost to view and was not seen again. Neither the Lancaster's Gunners replied to E/As fire as it never approached within effective range.
Visibility was very good. No flak or searchlights directed at Lancaster.

MU Gunner - Sgt FJ Carey. - Nil. Rear
Gunner - F/Sgt CA Drake RAAF - Nil.

Combat Report 24th March 1944:

Aircraft: LL727 'C2'
Captain: F/O L Greenburgh
Target: BERLIN

On the night of 24th March 1944, Lancaster II 'C2' of 514 Squadron was homeward bound, bombs dropped flying 20000 feet on a course 217 deg, IAS 175. At 2235 hours approx. 15 miles south of target Mid Upper Gunner reported a JU-88 on the starboard quarter down 300 yards range closing in to attack. He immediately gave order to corkscrew starboard opening fire with 3 short bursts followed by Rear Gunner with 2 bursts. E/A opened fire almost simultaneously with 2 or 3 bursts and quickly broke away to port up and was soon lost to view. No Claim. Lancaster sustained no damage.
2nd Encounter: - At 2237 hours on the same heading Rear Gunner reported JU-88 on the port quarter up at 400 yards range coming in quickly. He gave E/A a 2 second burst

followed by Mid Upper Gunner with 4 short bursts and ordered corkscrew to port. E/A fired a series of long bursts during encounter but Lancaster suffered no damage. Mid Upper Gunner saw strikes on centre section of E/A. No claims. No flak, searchlights or fighter flares were seen.
3rd Encounter: - At 2245 hours Engineer reported aircraft making an attack from starboard bow down and immediately ordered Pilot to corkscrew to starboard. As Lancaster made first part of manoeuvre by diving to starboard E/A fired a burst putting Lancaster's starboard engine out of action causing aircraft to turn over into a vicious spiral and it became uncontrollable. All the instruments were completely unserviceable and aircraft was losing height rapidly, completely out of control. At 10,000 feet Pilot gave order to abandon aircraft. The Engineer and Bomb Aimer jumped immediately and the Pilot was half way out of his seat but decided to have another attempt to control aircraft when he realised that the Navigator's chute had been thrown out of the Escape Hatch during the spin, and at about 7,000 feet managed to get aircraft on more or less an even keel. At 9,000 feet Lancaster returned to base and Pilot made a safe landing. The Mid Upper Gunner and Wireless Operator were standing by the Rear Hatch almost on the point of jumping when they realised that the aircraft was now by this time under control and returned to their posts. E/A was lost after the Lancaster started spinning and Gunners were unable to get any shots at it. Visual Monica gave warning of approach of E/A on all astern attacks but not from the bow. The Monica caught fire during the spin. No flak was directed at the aircraft, but there were some searchlights and fighter flares in the vicinity. Visibility was very good.

MU Gunner - Sgt PJ Carey - 200 rounds. Rear
Gunner - F/S CA Drake RAAF - 350 rounds

Appendix 8: Transcripts of Official Reports

- Report on Loss of Aircraft on Operations.
- Statement by F/Sgt. Richard Jack WOOSNAM.
- Statement by F/O. L. GREENBURGH, DFC.

SECRET

OPERATIONAL RESEARCH SECTION (B.C.) REPORT NO. K.240
COPY NO. 9

REPORT ON LOSS OF AIRCRAFT ON OPERATIONS

Aircraft: Lancaster II No. LL.727 "C2" of No. 514 Sqdn

Date of Loss: 7/8 June 1944.

Cause of Loss: Attack by fighter & flak causing fire & loss of control.

Position of Loss: Near Froissy (Oise) homewardbound.

Information from: F/O Greenburgh, Captain & Pilot on 24th operation.

Remainder of Crew:

Navigator:	F/Sgt. Fox, R.	Baled out
W/Operator:	F/Sgt. Stromberg, G.H.	Believed P/W
Ft./Engineer:	Sgt. Collingwood, F.	Baled out
Air Bomber:	F/Sgt. Rippingale, E.G.	"
M/U/Gunner:	Sgt. Carey, F.J.	Evading
R/Gunner:	Sgt. Woosnman, R.J.	"
2nd Pilot:	W/O Sutton, L.J.W.	Baled out.

Briefed Route: Base -Sheerness - 5056N.0049E - 4958N.0110E - 4850N.0140E - Target - 4842N.0220E - 4835N.0212E - 4840N.0110E - 4935N.0041E - 5050N.0030E - Gravesend - Base

Narrative.

1. The Lancaster took off from Waterbeach to attack rail facilities at Massy Palaisseau. The moon was full and the sky cloudless so that visibility was exceptionally good. The outward flight was normal and the target area was reached without incident.
2. The Pilot made a good bombing run at 10,000 ft. The Bomb Aimer called out "Bombs about to go", and at the same moment the Mid Upper Gunner called "There is a fighter on our tail, corkscrew to port, go!" The pilot waited 2 or 3 seconds while the bombs were released, although the Gunner continued to urge him to take immediate evasive action. He then began a violent corkscrew, with a dive to port. While still corkscrewing he saw tracer going past

his head, probably fired from the port quarter, level and heard strikes on the fuselage. At the same time a fire started in the starboard wing immediately behind the inner engine. This spread rapidly outwards in both directions and the Pilot could see the bare ribs of the wing. He feared an explosion from the petrol tanks but none occured. When he saw the tracer he dived more steeply but further strikes were sustained in the starboard outer engine which cut. The hydraulic system of the mid upper turret was also damaged in the attack and the turret rendered unserviceable as was the Mid Upper Gunner's intercom. The Lancaster was silhouetted against the moon during this attack.

3. The fire in the wing was still burning when the Pilot pulled out of his dive at 6-7,000 ft. having apparently shaken off the fighter. Flames were licking back just behind the cowling of the inner engine, but the engine itself was not on fire and was functioning satisfactorily. The Pilot began to climb and when a fighter flare was dropped straight ahead, he made a detour round it. He saw some of the crew putting on their parachutes and the 2nd pilot got up from his seat and stood beside him. The Pilot now remarked "I think we shall have to be getting out of this, fellows." He did not intend this remark to be an order to bale out but the crew took it as such and started to leave at once. As the fire appeared to be abating slightly, the Pilot called out "Hold it!", but by this time the Bomb Aimer, Flight Engineer, 2nd Pilot, and Navigator had all left.
4. The Pilot now steered an approximate course avoiding defended areas as well as he could. The aircraft had a slight swing to starboard and it was (necessary to) apply full aileron control in order to maintain course. He was about to feather the starboard outer engine, which he had not been able to do until now, being fully occupied, when the Lancaster was coned in searchlights. The Pilot saw a wall of light flak coming up towards him and heard one of the crew call out "Do we bale out or don't we?". He replied "Hold on!", altered course 45 (degrees)to port and dived straight into the searchlights. Flak appeared to be passing all around, but the Lancaster was not hit. At about 5,000 ft. the searchlights were lost and the Pilot levelled out and then at once started to climb.
5. About 10 seconds later the Lancaster was again coned. The Pilot executed exactly the same manoeuvre as before, pulling out of his dive at 3,000 ft. The flak was again very thick and seemed to come from all directions. This time the Lancaster was less lucky and fragments were heard striking the fuselage which filled with smoke. The Pilot lost rudder control and the Rear Gunner later told him that one of the rudders was shot away.
6. As soon as he was clear of the searchlights the Pilot began to climb again. Even with full rudder, he had very little control and it was still necessary to keep the control column hard over

to port. The Lancaster was vibrating badly, but the fire in the wing seemed to be definitely burning itself out and the Pilot told the remaining members of the crew that he would bring them back to base. He ordered the Wireless Operator to send out an emergency signal that they might have to ditch and asked him to get a fix. He trimmed the Lancaster, feathered the starboard outer engine and steered roughly north east. After the fighter attack he had ordered the Rear Gunner to cooperate as best he could with the Mid Upper Gunner, who was off the intercom. He believes that they had got in touch somehow and arranged a means of keeping a look out in all directions.

7. After a very short interval the Rear Gunner reported that they were being followed by a Ju.88 showing a red navigation light. The Pilot at once dived steeply. He then heard strikes on the fuselage which filled with smoke. The Lancaster started to swing to starboard and the starboard inner engine started to belch smoke.

8. The Wireless Operator, whom informant believes to have been wounded, now came forward and said he thought it was time to get out. The Pilot at first ordered him back, but when he remonstrated gave him permission to bale out which he did at once. In spite of all the Pilot's efforts the Lancaster still kept drifting to starboard and now he had to admit to himself that he could not control it sufficiently to reach base, or even the Channel. He therefore ordered the Gunners to bale out just after the Wireless Operator had gone. They were now flying at 3,000'.

9. The Rear Gunner acknowledged the Captain's order but the Mid Upper did not do so. The Pilot kept yelling to him to get out as he could not hold the aircraft much longer (actually he must have gone by that time). Then the fighter attacked again. The Lancaster went right off to starboard. The Pilot, just saw the blur of the fighter coming in from the port side, and tracer going over his head. He undid his Sutton harness, took off his helmet and dived straight out of the hatch, from about 1200 ft. He was wearing a seat type parachute.

10. P/O Greenburgh pulled the ripcord at once and when the parachute opened he lost his boots and escaper's kit which was loose in his blouse. The descent only occupied a very short time and he landed rather heavily in a field about 10 miles north east of Froissy (Oise). The Lancaster crashed about 100 yards off and exploded. Informant later saw two Gunners on the ground.

2084/5
BC/S.30270/ORS.
3rd September 1944

SECRET
M.I.9/S/P.G./LIB/773.

The information in this report is to be treated as

SECRET

STATEMENT BY
1804303 F/Sgt. WOOSNAM, Richard Jack., 514 Sqn., Bomber Command, R.A.F.
Captured: WAVIGNIER, France, 3 Jul 44
Liberated: LUCKENWALDE, May 45.
Date of Birth: 10 Jun 20.
Peacetime Profession: Mate, Mercantile Marine.
R.A.F. Service: Since Mar 42.
Private Address: 7, Belsize Park Mews, HAMPSTEAD, LONDON, N.W.3.

1. EVASION AND CAPTURE.

I was the rear gunner in a Lancaster which was shot down on an attack on the marshalling yards near PARIS on the night of 3 Jul 44.

After the aircraft was shot down I landed in a wheatfield and hid in a barn till 1630 hrs the next afternoon. I came out of the barn and some young men of the Resistance Movement came to me and gave me clothes and provided me with a guide. They also brought me my Captain, F/O. L. GREENBURGH. The guide led us to a small village near BEAUVAIS. Here I was taken to a hideout which had been built in an old bomb crater within sight of BEAUVAIS aerodrome. There I met my mid upper gunner F/Sgt. F. CAREY.

We stayed in this dug out till 10 Jun and then we were taken to a Chateau near WAVIGNIES where F/Sgt. CAREY and I stayed with the gamekeeper and his wife, who were employed by the owner of the Chateau. We stayed in this place till the morning of 2 Jul 44. While we were there we awaited instructions from the Resistance Movement.

On the morning of 2 Jul we were moved as word had been given that the Germans knew of our whereabouts. We were moved to a little house in the village of WAVIGNIES - belonging to a Hungarian who had a Russian wife.

At about 0500 hrs the next morning, the Germans searched the place and we were found hiding in the rubbish heap.
We were arrested, questioned and were taken via COMPIEGNE, LAON, S. QUINTEN, BRUSSELS to DULAG LUFT.

We were suspected of being British agents, but after being roughly treated we established our identity.

2. CAMPS IN WHICH IMPRISONED.

STALAG LUFT VII	(BANKAU)	Jul 44 - Jan 45
STALAG III A.	(LUCKENWALDE)	Feb 45 - May 45

3. ATTEMPTED ESCAPES.

Nil.

4. LIBERATION

We were liberated by the Russians at LUCKENWALDE in Apr 45.

INTERVIEWED BY: I.S.(9) on 6 Sep 45.

Distribution of this report.
M.I.9/19(G)., I.S.9, I.S.9(A.B).,
I.S.9(W).,A.I.1(a)P/W (2 Copies).,
H.Q., Bomber Command, R.A.F.,
A.L.O., M.I.9.,
Hist. Sect. Air Ministry, (Mr. J.C. NERNEY).,

APPENDIX A.
I.S.9
I.S.9(A.B).
I.S.9(W)(File).

SECRET
I.S.9/WEA/2/149/321.
EVADED CAPTURE IN FRANCE.

The information in this report is to be treated as

SECRET

STATEMENT BY
49803 F/O L. GREENBURGH , D.F.C. 514 Sqn 3 Group, Bomber Command, R.A.F.
Date of Birth: 13 Mar 16. Peacetime Profession: R.A.F.
R.A.F. Service: 7 years.
O.T.U. : No.12 (CHIPPING WARDEN).
Conversion Unit: No.1851 (WATERBEACH).
Private Address: 5 Victoria Road, BROMLEY, Kent.

Other members of the crew:

W/O SUTTON (co-pilot)(Baled out);
F/Sgt. FOX (navigator)(Baled out);
Sgt. RIPPINGALE (bombardier)(Baled out);
F/Sgt. STROMBERG(radio operator)(P/W - Injured);
Sgt. CAREY (top turret gunner)(Evading);
Sgt. CONNINGWOOD (engineer)(Baled out);
Sgt. WOODSHAM (tail gunner)(Evading with Sgt. CAREY).

Type of aircraft, place, date, time of departure.
Lancaster Mk II, WATERBEACH, 7 Jun 44 - early morning.

Where and when did you come down?
North of FROISSY OISE, 7 Jun 44.

How did you dispose of your parachute, harness and mae west?
Hidden.

Were all secret papers and equipment destroyed?
Aircraft destroyed.

7 Jun 44. Bombed target. — I took off on 7 JUN 44 to bomb MASSY - South of PARIS.

Saw JU attacked.

As we dropped our bombs at 10,000 feet the mid upper gunner saw a Ju 88approaching from the rear and shouted CORKSCREW PORT. I waited a second or two to let the last bomb go on to the target and as I made a violent corkscrew the starboard wing burst into flames.

Engine stops.

The starboard outer engine was also put out of action. Tracer was coming over my head and the fuselage was hit.

Dives and puts fire out.

I put the aircraft in a very fast dive hoping to put the fire out, made a wide detour round the fighter plane and was now a visible target.

Crew put on parachutes. Warned crew to get out of it.

Some of the crew put on their parachutes and although I had no intention at that time of leaving the aircraft myself but try to bring it back, I told the crew I thought we should have to get out of it.

Four bale out. Pilot stops remainder.

After four of the crew had baled out and the fire did not seem to be getting any worse I told the remainder to hold on. I increased speed to put the fire out.

Coned in search light. Coned again. Hit by flak. Control difficult.

I avoided fighter planes when I got coned in a Searchlight. I took evasive action out of it but ten seconds later I was coned again; this time being hit by light flak and losing rudder control. The tail control surfaces were damaged. I dived to 3,000 feet out of the searchlight. The fire was dying down although part of the wing was burnt away making the aircraft difficult to control.

Steers course. Tells crew he would get aircraft home.

I got a fix from the wireless operator, steered a course N.N.W. and told the crew I would get them back to ENGLAND if we were not attacked again, but sent an emergency message in case we ditched.

Attacked by another night fighter. Fuselage hit.	I tried to gain height but in five minutes the rear gunner warned me we were being followed by a Ju 88 with navigation lights on, who then flew beneath us. I took what evasive action was possible with the damaged aircraft, and cannon shells hit the fuselage and navigator's compartment, filling it with smoke.
Another engine goes.	The aircraft lunged to starboard and the starboard engine went out of action belching smoke. The fire on the wing had died down but I could not keep the aircraft on a straight course with both starboard engines out.
W/O Bales out.	The wireless operator ran forward and baled out. I tried to gain height but failed to hold the height I had.
Attacked again. Orders crew to bale out.	Another burst from enemy aircraft hit us on the port side, the mid upper turret was out of action, the aircraft spiralling and as it was impossible to fly it much longer I ordered the crew to bale out.
Remains in aircraft being no reply from turret gunner.	I had no reply from the mid upper turret so I remained and shouted to him to get out not knowing he had already left the aircraft. At 1200 feet the aircraft turned on its side and was about to crash and I jumped.
Lands by aircraft on fire.	I landed about 100 yards from the wrecked machine about ten miles North of FROISSY (Sheet 8, N002023)the enemy aircraft overhead dropped three flares and I could see the parachutes of some of my crew in the distance.

Hides gear Starts walking.

My back was slightly wrenched, I had lost both boots, burning pieces of the aircraft were lighting up the area and ammunition was exploding so I wanted to get away quickly. I hid my parachute, harness and mae west in some tall nettles and started to walk South in the direction of the descending parachutes.

On a main road I saw a German lorry, so turned down a lane and in 20 minutes came to a small village. I rested for half an hour then heard French voices and crawled towards an old farmer with a young girl.

Approaches farmer.

I took off my tunic and approached him holding out my hands saying "AMI". He hesitated but finally took me indoors where I put on my tunic to convince his family.

Warns farmer about rest of crew.

They welcomed me, gave me food, shoes and cut off my badges. I told them there were three others in the neighbourhood so the son went to warn other farmers to look out for them and I remained there that night.

8 Jun 44. Wireless operator injured - taken P/W.

I was woken up by Thunderbolts shooting up a convoy and the young woman came in with my parachute which she kept. She said one of my crew (it was the wireless operator) had been caught up in the telegraph wires, was injured and taken P/W.

Meets remainder of crew.

Some farmers brought me civilian clothes, showed me a picture of my mid upper gunner and later one farmer took me to a farm where I met my rear gunner.

Meets another of crew.

The farmer then cycled with me to a village 20 minutes away where he took me to a lady who spoke English, who sent me along to a farm where the rear gunner came out and together we were taken to a bomb crater where my mid upper gunner was waiting. We three lived in a cave dug out of the crater for three days fed by the farmers.

11 Jun 44. Taken to FROISSY.	On 11 Jun 44 three men came and took only me to FROISSY where I was feted. From here my journey was arranged.

INTERROGATOR's NOTE:

This was this officer's 26th operation and the third time his aircraft has been disabled.

Appendix 9: Les Weddle's Story

This account was originally published in 'Lancasters at Waterbeach – Some of the Story of 514 Squadron' by Harry Dison, (Mention the War Ltd., 2015)

After spending October and November 1943 flying Stirlings on 620 Squadron Chedburgh, Bury St Edmunds, we returned to 1678 Conversion Unit, Waterbeach, converting to Lancaster IIs and joined 514 Squadron in December 1943.

Our first operation from Waterbeach was on 29th December 1943. Flying in spare aircraft 'S' Sugar we took off for Berlin. Following one or two fighter attacks we finally reached our target, released our bombs and headed for home. After leaving the target we were twice attacked by JU.88s puncturing at least one of our petrol tanks. After a while I informed the Skipper we were losing quite a lot of petrol and we may not reach England and would probably have to ditch. We flew on as long as possible but as the engines started cutting out the Skipper ordered us to ditching stations. After a successful ditching we eventually got out but had to inflate the dinghy as it was only partly inflated.

We ditched about l0pm, 70 miles east of Yarmouth. We spent an horrendous night - high winds and waves and by daylight we felt pretty desperate – seven very wet bedraggled airmen in a partly inflated dinghy. We were eventually spotted by Wing Commander Sampson of 514 Sqn, who, at daybreak, scrambled a scratch crew as he knew time was very valuable, and one of his crews was somewhere in the North Sea. Shortly after, a Liberator arrived and dropped a spare dinghy which was greatly appreciated as we were rather low in the sea. A high speed launch was then directed to our position and we got picked up about 2pm. Needless to say we were very relieved after spending 16 hours in the North Sea. We spent the night in hospital and after a checkup Wing Commander Sampson flew down to Coltishall and gave us a lift back to Waterbeach. We were then given 16 days leave - one day for every hour spent in the drink. All this entitled us to become members of the 'Goldfish Club' of which I am still a member.

A few more Ops - Stuttgart - Le Mans - Berlin - Frankfurt - Frankfurt, and finally Berlin on 24th March 1944, where, after a rough trip there, the Skipper ordered us to bale out. The bomb aimer left first, followed by myself. The navigator was to follow me, but the 'plane veered violently and he lost his parachute out of the escape hatch. Also the rear gunner was trapped in his turret. So while the two of us were drifting down to earth the skipper decided to try and get the 'plane back to England - which he did, and was awarded the bar to his D.F.C. - won when we ditched. All this I found out when I was released as a P.O.W. Baling out and saving my life by parachute enabled me to become a member of the 'Caterpillar Club'.

I found life on the Squadron very pleasant and satisfying with the occasional exciting episode, like the time we took off on air test only to find the pitot head tube cover still in place. After a few anxious minutes a second aircraft from 514 was flying alongside to give us an indication of our speed and guided us in to a perfect landing.

The highlight of my life was at the 1993 Squadron Reunion where I met Pat Butler (Navigator) and Fred Carey (Mid Upper Gunner). What a re-union after 50 years.

The crew of Lancaster II 'C' Charlie, LL727, 'C' Flight.

Pilot: F / O Louis Greenburgh
Navigator: Sgt Pat Butler
B / Aimer: F/ Sgt Don Bament
W/Op A/G: Sgt Gordon Stromberg
F /E: Sgt Leslie Weddle
M / U Gunner: F / Sgt Fred Carey
R / Gunner: Sgt Colin Drake

Made in the USA
Middletown, DE
06 January 2025

68958231R00225